THE ENGLISH PEASANTRY
AND THE ENCLOSURE OF
COMMON FIELDS

THE ENGLISH PEASANTRY

AND THE ENCLOSURE OF

COMMON FIELDS

BY

GILBERT SLATER

[1907]

REPRINTS OF ECONOMIC CLASSICS

AUGUSTUS M. KELLEY · PUBLISHERS
NEW YORK 1968

First Edition 1907

(London: Archibald Constable & Co. Ltd., 1907)

Reprinted 1968 by

AUGUSTUS M. KELLEY · PUBLISHERS

New York New York 10010

By Arrangement with Constable & Company Ltd.

Library of Congress Catalogue Card Number

68-27295

Printed in the United States of America
by Sentry Press, New York, N. Y. 10019

OPEN FIELDS AT EPWORTH, ISLE OF AXHOLME.

Frontispiece.

THE ENGLISH PEASANTRY AND THE ENCLOSURE OF COMMON FIELDS

BY

GILBERT SLATER, M.A., D.Sc.

WITH AN INTRODUCTION BY THE RIGHT HONOURABLE
THE EARL OF CARRINGTON, K.G., G.C.M.G., Etc.
President of the Board of Agriculture

LONDON
ARCHIBALD CONSTABLE & CO. Ltd.
1907

AUTHOR'S PREFACE.

THE investigations embodied in this book were begun in 1894, on the suggestion of Mr. Graham Wallas, and at the request of Mr. J. A. Spender. They were continued in subsequent years, in conjunction with the London School of Economics, and the results were summarised in a thesis entitled "The Enclosure of Common Fields in England in the Eighteenth and Nineteenth Centuries," which was submitted to the University of London in 1904, and approved as a thesis for the degree of Doctor of Science in Economics. That thesis consisted in the first place of a series of maps, partially reproduced in this volume through the kind assistance of the Royal Geographical Society; and in the second place of manuscript matter which has been revised for publication in the form of this volume and under the present title. The original maps are in the custody of the London School of Economics, and can be seen by those who desire to examine them. They include a series of county maps, on which parishes in which common fields have been enclosed by Act of Parliament are coloured and marked according to the date of enclosure, and maps illustrating the process of Parliamentary enclosure, and the working of the common field system. Those who are interested in the enclosure history of any particular county may also be recommended to consult the Victoria County History.

It is my pleasant duty here to gratefully acknowledge my obligations to the two gentlemen above mentioned for the original impulse to study the process of the destruction and decay of English village communities; to the London School of Economics; and in particular to its first Director, Mr. W. A. S. Hewins, its present Director, Mr. H. J. Mackinder, and Mr. Hubert Hall, for assistance, encouragement, and advice; to many labourers, farmers, clergymen, and other rural residents, for information and personal kindness; to the Royal Geographical Society for defraying the cost of the production of the blocks of the illustrative maps herewith published; and to Earl Carrington, the President of the Board of Agriculture, for reading the book in proof, and recommending it to those who are willing to study rural history because they desire to improve rural conditions of life.

In writing this book I have deemed it a matter of conscience to preserve the attitude of mind of the student of history, pure and simple. I have felt, and feel, that historical investigation can only be rightly carried on when all motives except the simple desire to know the truth are excluded from the investigator's mind. Yet the investigation undertaken having been thus far completed, and its results placed on record, I cannot refrain from attempting to read out of them some lessons for the present and the future.

My conclusions have been in large measure expressed for me by Lord Carrington's Introduction. The policy of the legislature and of the Central Government, expressed in the Enclosure Acts of the eighteenth and nineteenth centuries, though it claimed, and on the whole rightly claimed, that it effected an immediate and great increase in the country's output of agricultural produce, and an improvement in the breeds of sheep and cattle, was nevertheless essentially a policy directed towards the enhancement of agricultural rents, the building up of large and compact landed estates, the establishment of capitalist farming, the uprooting of peasant proprietors and of small holdings together with the communal use of land, and the multiplication of the class of landless agricultural labourers. There is need in the twentieth century for a new agricultural policy. As I read the economic signs of the time, industrial conditions are beginning to favour a great agricultural revival in the British Isles. A wise programme of rural reform is necessary both in order that the possible agricultural prosperity may be secured, and in order that the nation may reap in full its possible fruits of physical and moral well-being for the people.

In all times the fading memories and traditions of the past have contributed to form in men's minds the ideals of a possible better future state of society which are the inspiration of progress. The memories and traditions of the English village community, together with its visible relics in the form of commons, commonable meadows, and (rarely) common fields, have had their influence on the formation of the ideals of the Labour and Democratic movement of our country from the time of Cobbett onwards. Through historical research the past may become more definitely suggestive.

The suggestions borne into my mind for the agricultural policy of the twentieth century may be summed up in the phrase, British agriculture must be democratised. By this I mean that the principle of collective ownership of the soil must be established or re-established; that agricultural co-operation must be revived in new forms suitable to modern conditions; that the ancient right of independent access to the soil for every tiller of it must be restored; that a career of industrial advance in agriculture must be made possible for the competent worker. On one important side of the life of the old English village community I have not touched at all in this book, viz., its social and recreative side. In this respect also the losses of the past will probably be recovered spontaneously if the nation aims in its agricultural policy at the three essentials of wholesome, hopeful, human work, as opposed to dehumanised toil, Freedom, Training and Mutual Aid.

GILBERT SLATER.

January 10th, 1907.

CONTENTS.

ILLUSTRATIONS.

———◆———

INTRODUCTION.

THE ENGLISH PEASANTRY AND THE ENCLOSURE OF COMMON FIELDS.

THE enclosure of common fields, and the passing away of the English Village Community to make room for the agricultural organisation prevailing to-day, is a subject not merely of historical interest, but one which touches very closely some of the most vital national problems of the twentieth century.

During the past five generations mechanical, industrial, and commercial progress, with the consequent creation of great towns and cities, has so occupied the national activities, and has made us to such an extent a nation of town-dwellers, that there has been a tendency to overlook rural life and rural industries. But in recent years social reformers have come to see that the solution of many of the problems of the town is to be found in the country, and increasing attention is being paid to the causes of the rural exodus and the best means by which it can be arrested. No industry can be in a healthy condition which does not provide an opportunity for the small man to improve his position ; and consequently such questions as the provision of allotments and small holdings, agricultural co-operation, the preservation of the independence of spirit of the agricultural labourer, and the securing for him the prospect of a continually advancing career on the land are recognised as matters of urgent national importance.

In this book Dr. Slater shows that the movement for the enclosure of arable open and common fields has been a movement for the sweeping away of small holdings and small properties ; that the "Village Community" which any Enclosure Act of this character abolished was essentially an organisation for agricultural co-operation. He shows that at least in certain parts of the country even in comparatively recent times enclosure has produced rural depopulation, and has converted the villager from "a peasant with a mediæval status to an agricultural labourer entirely dependent on a weekly wage." He further makes us doubt whether these little village revolutions, while they temporarily stimulated agricultural progress by facilitating improved stock-breeding and the economy of labour, did not also to a certain extent destroy the opportunities of future progress by separating farmer from labourer by a gulf difficult to cross, and thus cutting off the supply of new recruits to the farming class.

At the same time, whatever reasons there may be for regretting the enclosure of our Common Fields, and for wishing that the interests of the humbler tillers of the soil had been more sedulously guarded on enclosure, in the main the process was inevitable. Common field Agriculture was a survival of customs and institutions which had grown up when each village lived its life to a great extent in isolation. It was necessary that the villager should almost forget that he was a Little Pedlingtonian to realise that he was an Englishman. Village patriotism had to die down temporarily to make way for national patriotism; and when the spirit died out of the Village Community its form could not be preserved.

Now and in the future there is need that local patriotism, pride in the local community, and willingness to serve it, whether it be village or city, should be kindled again to its old vigour.

With the revival of the spirit will come a revival of some of the old forms of village common life, and a creation of new forms in place of those which will remain among the forgotten facts of the past. The Village Community is a hope of the future as well as a memory of the past, and therefore those who are interested in the movement for reviving British Agriculture on democratic lines and for improving the social and economic conditions of our villages have reason to welcome Dr. Slater's attempt to describe existing and recent survivals of the English Village Community, and to ascertain the circumstances, causes, and consequences of its gradual extinction.

CARRINGTON.

28th November, 1906.

THE ENGLISH PEASANTRY AND THE ENCLOSURE OF COMMON FIELDS.

CHAPTER I.

ENCLOSURE IN GENERAL.

THE internal history of our villages is a more obscure, but not less important a part of English history, than the internal history of our towns. It is, indeed, more fundamental. A town is ordinarily by origin an overgrown village, which never loses the marks of its origin. And it was by agricultural and social changes in the villages that the way was prepared for the great industrial revolution, or more properly, evolution, which is the underlying fact of the history of English towns, especially during the last two centuries.

The central fact in the history of any English village since the Middle Ages, is expressed in the word "enclosure." Primarily "enclosure" means surrounding a piece of land with hedges, ditches, or other barriers to the free passage of men and animals. Agriculturally, enclosure of arable land in the midst of unenclosed arable land is a preliminary step to its conversion into pasture, the hedge is erected to keep animals in; enclosure of land in the midst of open common pasture is a preliminary step to tillage, the hedge keeps animals out. But in

either case the hedge is the mark and sign of exclusive ownership
and occupation in the land which is hedged. Hence by enclosure
collective use, usually accompanied by some degree of community
of ownership, of the piece of land enclosed, is abolished, and
superseded by individual ownership and separate occupation.

The form of enclosure which is familiar to our minds is the
enclosure of land previously uncultivated ; in the legal phrase,
" enclosure of waste of a manor," in the ordinary phrase,
" enclosure of commons." Enclosure in this sense has been,
and is still, a matter of very vital interest to the urban population, a fact which might be brought vividly to our minds by a
recital of the commons within London and its immediate
neighbourhood which have been lost or preserved with difficulty.
It is sufficient to refer to Epping Forest, Hadley Wood, Hampstead Heath, Wimbledon Common, Hayes and Keston Commons,
Bostall Heath and Plumstead Common.

Far more important from a broad national point of view, is
the enclosure of common fields—the enclosure, that is, of land
previously cultivated according to a system which did not involve
the separation of one holding from another by any tangible
barrier. Enclosure of this sort, when suddenly effected, as by
a Private Act of Enclosure, is rightly termed the extinction of a
village community. In the following chapters it will be shown
in detail from existing and recent survivals, what was the nature
of the system of cultivation in open and common fields in different parts of England, up to the time of enclosure ; the question when and how enclosure was brought about in different
counties will be discussed ; and light will be thrown upon the
result of the transition from the medieval to the modern system
of village life upon the material and moral condition of the
villagers, the peasants, farmers or labourers, who underwent the
change. In these chapters facts drawn directly from observations and inquiries in the villages themselves, from the observations of agricultural writers who speak from direct and intimate
knowledge, and from the Enclosure Acts, will be left in the main
to tell their own story. But a generalised statement will perhaps
make that story clearer.

Here is a typical Enclosure Act of the type which encloses common fields, taken at random, and a good example of the 2565 Acts of its class enumerated in the Appendix, by which about 3000 parishes were enclosed. It was passed in 1795 (c. 43) and begins :—" Whereas there are in the parish of Henlow, in the County of Bedford, divers Open and Common Fields, Meadows, Pastures, Waste Lands, and other Commonable Lands and Grounds, containing by estimation, Two Thousand Acres, or thereabouts . . . And whereas the said Open and Common Fields, Lands, Grounds, Meadows and Pastures, lie intermixed, and are inconveniently situated, and are in their present state incapable of Improvement, and the several Proprietors thereof and Persons interested therein are desirous that the same may be divided and enclosed, and specific Shares thereof set out and allotted in Lieu and in Proportion to their several and respective Estates, Rights, and Interests therein ; but such Division and Inclosure cannot be effected without the Aid and Authority of Parliament. May it therefore please your Majesty——."

The total area of the parish of Henlow is 2450 acres, and it has a large park. It appears, therefore, that when the Act was passed practically the whole of the arable, meadow, and pasture land in the parish lay entirely open, and was commonable. The more remote and least cultivable parts of the parish were, no doubt, common pastures; on these the villagers kept flocks and herds according to some recognised rule based on the sizes of their holdings in the arable fields. A drift would lead from the common to the village, passing through the arable fields, and fenced or hedged off from them. Immediately behind the cottages, clustering together to form the village, there would be small closes for gardens or paddocks ; beyond these all round the village would stretch the open, common, arable fields, in area probably considerably more than half the parish. These were probably divided into three or four approximately equal portions, and cultivated according to a three or four year course, imposed rigidly on all occupiers by a mutual agreement sanctioned by custom. The holdings would be of various sizes, from three or four acres of arable land upwards, but all small ; and a holding of, say, twenty acres of arable land would consist of about thirty separate strips of land of from half an acre to an acre each, scattered over all the three or four arable fields, but approximately equally divided between each field, so that each year the occupier would have, for example, about five acres under wheat, five under barley, five under pulse, and five fallow, provided that were the customary course of husbandry. Right through the year the fallow land would be used as common pasture, and the land under crops would become commonable after the crops were carried.

Along the streams flowing into the river Ivel would be the open commonable meadows. These would be divided into a number of plots, half-acres, quarter-acres, or even smaller, marked by pegs driven in the ground, or stones; and a certain number of these plots were assigned to each holding, in proportion to the amount of arable land. During the spring, while the cattle were on the common pasture, the meadow would be let grow for hay; when the time for hay harvest came, each peasant cut his own plots, and the meadow became commonable during the rest of the summer. Some of the peasant occupiers would be small freeholders, some probably copyholders, others legally annual tenants. All would meet together on certain occasions to settle questions of common interest.

We might say, though the expression must not be too rigidly interpreted, that under the common field system the parish, township, or hamlet formed one farm, occupied and cultivated by a group of partners holding varying numbers of shares. It may well be imagined what a village cataclysm took place when an Act for the enclosure of the parish was passed, and commissioners descended upon the village, valued every property and every common right, and carved out the whole parish into rectangles, instituting the modern system of separate exclusive ownership and individual cultivation. We shall see that ordinarily the holdings on enclosure became fewer and larger, that very many of the peasants were in consequence driven from the village, or became landless, pauperised agricultural labourers. We shall see also that the traditions of the common field system where they have perished as distinct memories, have survived in the form of aspirations for agricultural reform. In fact, the great rural question for the twentieth century to determine, is whether there were not beneath the inconvenient and uneconomical methods of the common field system, a vital principle essential to true rural prosperity, which has to be re-discovered and re-established in forms suitable to the present environment.

It is not intended in this book to go into the vexed question of the origin of the common field system, or of the English village community. It will be noticed that the researches upon which this book is based do not as a rule go further back than Leland's Itinerary in 1536 and following years. From such materials only hypotheses can be obtained, which require to be tested by all the evidence from earlier records. A hypothesis, however, has a certain value as a mental thread by which the facts can be connected and more clearly conceived.

Judging entirely from eighteenth and nineteenth century evidence, one is in the first place driven to accept most unhesitatingly the prevailing theory that the English common field system was based on co-aration. But one is tempted to very summarily dismiss the theory of Roman origin. Rather one is inclined to say that as long as a considerable portion of the villagers of the parish were accustomed to yoke their oxen or harness their horses to a common plough, the system was a living one, capable of growth and modification according to the ideas of the people who worked it. It became, as it were, fossilised and dead, incapable of other than decaying change, when each occupier cultivated his own set of strips of land by his own plough or his own spade. One is therefore inclined to suppose that the introduction of each new element in the population of a village—Saxon, Angle, Dane, and in a less degree, Norman—profoundly modified earlier customs, and that in each part of Britain a local type of village community resulted from the blending of different racial traditions.

This hypothesis is directly suggested by the evidence of recent survivals. The most familiar type of village community is characteristic of the Midlands; I have termed it the Mercian

type. It is most easily conceived as a compound of the pure
Keltic system, known in the Highlands and Ireland as Run-rig or
Rundale, and the North German system traditional among the
Angles, in which the two elements in equal strength are very
perfectly blended together. In the South of England we find a
different type, here termed the Wessex type, in which the
influence of Keltic tradition is more strongly seen. The village
community in Norfolk and the adjoining part of Suffolk shows
some remarkable special features, traces of which are found in
adjoining counties, but which appear to be easily accounted for
as the result of the later intrusion of Scandinavian traditions.
Further, throughout the West of England, from Cumberland to
Devon and Cornwall, we find evidence that the primitive type of
village community approximated very closely to the Keltic
Run-rig.

Enclosure of the common fields, meadows and pastures, of
any particular village may have taken place in the following
ways :—

(1) By Act of Parliament, viz., (a) by a private Act, (b) under
the authority of the General Enclosure Acts of 1830 and 1836,
(c) by the Enclosure Commissioners and their successors, the
Board of Agriculture, under the General Enclosure Act of 1845
and its amending Acts.

(2) By common agreement of all the collective owners.

(3) By the purchase on the part of one owner of all conflicting
rights.

(4) By special licence of the Tudor monarchs.

(5) By various forms of force and fraud.

Commonable waste may have been enclosed in any of the
above ways, and also under the Statutes of Merton and Winchester (1235 and 1285), which give Lords of the Manor the right
of enclosing commons provided proof is given that the tenants of
the manor are left sufficient pasture.

Enquiry into the history of Enclosure naturally begins with
an examination of the Enclosure Acts.

The first fact elicited by this examination is that there is a perfect *legal* similarity between Acts for enclosing commonable waste, which may be termed *Acts for extending cultivation*, and Acts such as that for Henlow, for enclosing all the open and common arable and other lands of a parish or parishes, which may be termed *Acts for extinguishing village communities*. About one-third of the Enclosure Acts belong to the former variety, about two-thirds to the latter. As from the economic and social points of view, the two classes of Enclosure Acts are as widely different as they are legally similar, no statistical summaries of the Acts can have much value until the two classes are sorted out. To do this involved a separate examination of all the Acts accessible.

Appendix A contains a statistical summary of the Acts for enclosing commonable waste passed between 1727 and 1845; Appendix B contains a list of Acts for enclosing common arable fields with or without other commonable lands passed between 1727 and 1900.

CHAPTER II.

LAXTON, AN OPEN FIELD PARISH.

PERHAPS the best surviving example of an open field parish is that of Laxton, or Lexington, in Nottinghamshire, about ten miles from Newark and Southwell. It lies remote from railways and high roads, and is only to be reached by bye roads. From whatever quarter one approaches the village, one enters the parish through a gate. The village is in the centre of the parish, and is surrounded by enclosed fields. Other enclosures are to be found on the most remote parts of the parish, in some cases representing, apparently, old woodland which has been converted into tillage or pasture; in other cases portions of the arable fields. But nearly half the area of the parish remains in the form of two great arable fields, and two smaller ones which are treated as two parts of the third field. The different holdings, whether small freeholds or farms rented from the Lord of the Manor, who owns nearly all the parish, consist, in part, of strips of land scattered all over these fields, in a manner which can best be understood by reference to the map. Within these arable fields cultivation is not carried on according to the discretion of the individual farmer, but by strict rules of great antiquity. In each of the fields a three year course is rigidly adhered to.

First year, wheat.

Second year, spring corn (*i.e.* barley, oats, peas, beans, vetches, tares, &c.).

Third year, fallow.

If, therefore, Laxton be visited early in June, the following description of the appearance of the parish will be found correct. The traveller passes through the boundary gate. He finds his road leads him through the " Spring corn " field, which lies

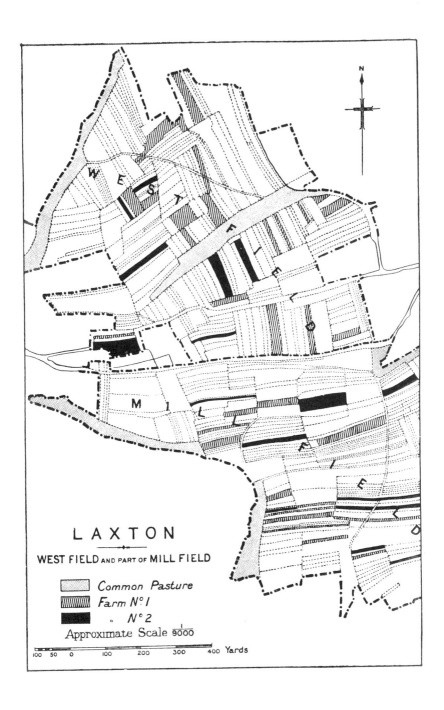

LAXTON

WEST FIELD AND PART OF MILL FIELD

Common Pasture
Farm Nº 1
    „   Nº 2

Approximate Scale $\frac{1}{9000}$

100 50 0   100   200   300   400 Yards

N

open on either side of the road. A phrase which is continually used by old farmers when attempting to describe common fields will probably occur to him in this field : "It is like allotments." But it is like an allotment field with many differences.

All the great field is divided up into oblong patches, each patch growing its own crop, but with no more division or boundary between one crop and the next than a mere furrow.

If, then, the traveller looks again at a strip of land growing, say, beans, he will find that this strip consists of one, two, or more ridges, locally termed "lands." A "land" in Laxton has a pretty uniform width of $5\frac{1}{2}$ yards, and a normal length of one furlong ; but by the necessity of the case the length varies considerably. Owing to this variation in length the various strips of land which make up the different holdings in the common fields, when their area is expressed in acres, roods, or poles, seem to have no common measure.

Because the soil of Laxton is a heavy clay it is customary to plough each "land" every year in the same manner, beginning at the edges, and turning the sod towards the centre of the "land." Hence each "land" forms a long narrow ridge, heaped up in the middle, and the lie of the "lands" or ridges was at some unknown date so well contrived for the proper drainage of the land, that it is probable that if the whole of a field were let to a single farmer, he would still plough so as to maintain the old ridges.

The same ridges are to be found on the other two fields, one of which is a stretch of waving wheat ; while the third, or fallow field, is being leisurely ploughed, a number of sheep getting a difficult living from the thistles and other weeds in the still unploughed portions, and on the "sicks," i.e. certain grassy parts of the field which are defined by boundary marks, and are never allowed to be ploughed. In one extreme corner of the parish is Laxton Heath, a somewhat swampy common covered with coarse grass. Here, too, sheep are grazed in common, according to a "stint" somewhat recently determined upon. Before the stint was agreed to, every commoner had the right of turning out as many sheep as he could feed in winter, the result being that the common was overstocked, and the sheep nearly starved. The stint regulates the number of sheep each commoner may graze upon the common according to the number he can feed on his other land in the parish. It was not adopted without opposition on the part of those whose privileges it restricted.

This brings us to the question, Who are the commoners? There are two sorts of claim by which a man may be entitled to common rights, and to a voice in such deliberations as those by which a stint is agreed to. One is by a holding in the common open fields, the other is by the occupation of a "toft-head." A "toft" is not very easy to define. One may say that it either is, or represents, an ancient house or cottage in the village; but that immediately suggests the question, How ancient? It is well known in the village which cottages are "tofts" and which are not. Those which are, command a rent about £2 a year higher in consequence. It is to be noted that if the house or cottage which is the visible sign of "toft-head" be pulled down, and a new one erected on the same spot, the new house has the same rights attached to it. One is naturally led to the hypothesis that up to a certain date[1] all cottages erected

---

[1] The following extract from a sixteenth century writer throws some light upon this point :

> "Another disorder of oppression
> aduerte this wone wiche is muche odyous,
> A lord geauyn to private affection
> lettinge the pooareman an olde rotten howse,
> which hathe (to the same) profyttes commodious
> its Cloase, and Common, with Lande in the feelde
> but noate well heere howe the pooareman is peelde.

> "The howse shall hee haue and A gardeyne plott,
> but stonde he must to the reperation :
> Close, Comon or Londe fallithe none to his lott;
> that beste might helpe to his sustentation.
> the whoale Rente payethe hee for his habitation,
> as though hee dyd thappertenauncis possesse
> Such soare oppression neadethe speadye redresse."
>
> "The Pleasaunt Poesye of Princelie Practise" (1548)
> WILLIAM FORREST, Chapter III., 21 & 22
> E.E.T.S. Extra Series, XXXII.

We have here the practice of divorcing the cottage from its common right described as a novelty. The Act of 31 Elizabeth, c. 7, by prohibiting the letting

in Laxton carried common rights, but that after that date no
new common rights could be created. There are, therefore, two
classes of commoners : the farmers who hold land in the common
fields, and the labourers who occupy the privileged cottages. A
farmer may possess a number of common rights in respect of
(1) his farmhouse, if it be a " toft," (2) his arable holding, and
(3) any toft cottages he may own or rent and sub-let to labourers,
retaining their common rights. The labourer has but one
common right. Each common right entitles the holder to one
vote, and to one share in the division of the money revenues
drawn from the commonable lands, besides the right of feeding
an indefinite number of sheep on the fallow field, and the
regulated number on the common. The money revenue that
comes from the commonable fields is obtained as follows : The
grass lands (" sicks ") in the two common fields which are under
crops cannot be grazed upon conveniently, because any animals
would be liable to stray into the crops. They are, therefore,
mown for hay, and the right to mow them is sold by auction to
one of the commoners, and the price realised is divided.
Recently this has worked out at about 14s. per common right.
Each commoner also has the right of pasturing animals upon the
two fields that are under crops, directly the harvest has been
carried.

The exercise of this right, which appears to be most keenly
valued, as it is found to persist in many parishes after all other
traces of the common field system have died away, obviously
opens the door to quarrels. It is not to be expected that all
farmers should finish carrying their crops on the same day ; and
the position of the man who is behind all his neighbours, and so
is standing between the commoners and their right of pasture, is
not an enviable one. But a constitutional system of government
exists for the purpose of dealing with these and other difficulties.
A " Foreman of the Fields " and a " Field Jury " are elected :

of cottages without 4 acres of land, in effect prohibited the letting of a cottage
without a common right, as the 4 acres *would* not be the highly valued Close,
and *could* not, unless the rights of other villagers were infringed, be waste or
common pasture. Four acres in the common arable field was implied, and this
of course carried a right of common.

the field jury settles all disputes between individuals, while the duties of the foreman include that of issuing notices to declare when the fields are open for pasturing ; on which day all the gates, by which, as I have previously mentioned, the parish is entered, must be closed, while all the gates of the farmyards are thrown open, and a varied crowd of animals winds along the drifts and spreads over the fields.

It will be noticed that the commonable lands of Laxton include only arable fields and common pasture. The commonable meadows which the parish once had, have been partitioned and enclosed at a date beyond the recollection of the oldest inhabitant. The neighbouring parish of Eakring still has commonable meadows. In this respect Eakring is a more perfect example of the open field parish than Laxton, though its common arable fields have been much more encroached upon ; and have, in fact, been reduced to scattered fragments, so that the rector was unable to tell me whether there were five, six, or more of them. The villagers, however, say simply " Three : the wheat field, the bean field, and the fallow field." The commonable meadows are, like the common fields, held in scattered strips intermingled ; and are commonable after hay harvest. The rule in Eakring is that if one man only has any hay left on the meadows, the other commoners can turn in their cattle and relieve him of it ; but if he can get a neighbour to leave but one haycock also, he is protected.

The constitution of Eakring differs somewhat from that of Laxton. There are regularly four toft meetings every year, presided over by the steward of the lord of the manor, at which all questions relating to the commonable lands are settled. Further, all toft holders have an equal right to feed an indefinite number of sheep on the fallow field, and the other fields when available, but the exercise of the right is regulated by a species of auction. The number of sheep that can be pastured with advantage is agreed upon, and since the total number of sheep which the assembled toft holders desire to put on is sure to exceed that number, a price to be charged per sheep is by degrees fixed by mutual bargaining, till the numbers of sheep for which their owners are willing to pay is reduced to the number that the pasture can bear. The cottager and toft holder, therefore, who though not holding an acre of land in the parish, has yet enterprise enough to bid for the right of keeping a flock of sixty sheep on the common fields, is therefore heartily welcomed by that section of the toft holders who have no desire to bid against him, because he forces up the value of their rights.

A Recent Enclosure—Castor and Ailesworth.

Up till 1898 an even better example of an open-field parish could be seen in Northamptonshire. In that year was completed the enclosure of Castor and Ailesworth, two hamlets forming part of the parish of Castor, situated three miles from Peterborough on the road to Northampton. In 1892, when application was made to the Board of Agriculture, which now represents the Enclosure Commissioners of the General Enclosure Act of 1845, there were in the two hamlets, out of a total area of 4976 acres, 2,425 acres of common arable fields, 815 acres of common pastures and meadows, and 370 acres of commonable waste, and only about 1300 acres enclosed. In Laxton the commonable land is less than half the area of the parish. The greater amount of old enclosure in Laxton has had its effect on the distribution of the population. There are some, though very few, outlying farmhouses. In Castor and Ailesworth all the habitations and buildings, except a watermill and a railway station, are clustered together in the two hamlets, which form one continuous village. At present very nearly all the land of Laxton and Eakring is in the ownership of the respective lords of the two manors ; in Castor and Ailesworth the Ecclesiastical Commissioners are the largest landowners ; but nearly as much land is the property of Earl Fitzwilliam, and there are besides a number of small landowners. Before enclosure all these properties were intermixed all over the area of the two hamlets, the two chief properties coming very frequently in alternate strips.

Though the area of commonable land in Castor was so much greater than in Laxton, those customs of village communal life which we have described had retained much less vigour; and to the decay of the power of harmonious self-government the recent enclosure was mainly attributable. The customary method of cultivation in Castor and Ailesworth was a three-field system, but a different three-field system to that described above. The succession of crops was:—First year, wheat; second year, barley; third year, a "fallow crop," or as locally pronounced, "follow crop." Each year in the spring the farmers and toft-holders of Castor, and similarly of Ailesworth, would meet to decide the crop to be sown on the fallow field. One farmer, who held the position—though not the title—of "Foreman of the Fields," kept a "stint book," a list of all the villagers owning common rights, and the number of rights belonging to each. The number of votes that could be cast by each villager depended upon the number of his common rights. The fallow crop might be pulse or turnips or other roots or anything else that seemed advisable; but it was essential to the *farmers'* interests that they should agree upon some crop. For a tradition existed in the village that unless the farmers were agreed as to the crop to be sown on the fallow field, that field could be treated as though it really were fallow. It could be pastured on all the year by all the toft-holders, and any crop which any farmer might sow would be at the mercy of his neighbours' cattle and sheep. I could not find that this had ever happened. On the other hand, the farmers being agreed about the crop, they could also determine the date when the fallow field should become commonable.[1] The wheat-field and barley-field became commonable after harvest; the meadows and pastures were commonable between August 12th and February 14th.

The reason why the medieval three-field system was retained in Laxton, but was altered in Castor to an improved three-field system, is to be found in the nature of the soil. That of Laxton

---

[1] This is good law. By 43 Geo. III. c. 81 these agreements could be made by "a three-fourths majority in number and value." *See* Chapter IX.

is a heavy clay, growing wheat of noted quality; that of the Northamptonshire parish is lighter, in parts very shallow and stony. Another result of the difference of soil was a different system of ploughing. The Castor method was that technically known as " Gathering and Splitting," viz., alternately to plough each strip from the margin inwards, turning the sod inwards, and the reverse way, turning the sod outwards, so that the general level of the field was not broken into a series of ridges. In Castor, as in Laxton, no grassy " balk " divided one man's "land " from his neighbour's, the furrow only had to serve as boundary, and sometimes the boundary was bitterly disputed. Before the enclosure there was one spot in the common fields where two neighbours kept a plough each continually, and as fast as one ploughed certain furrows into his land, the other ploughed them back into his.

Another difficulty occasionally arose when high winds prevailed at harvest time. The great extent of the open fields, and the slightness of any opposition to the sweep of the wind, at such times allowed the corn to be blown from one man's land, and scattered over his neighbours'. Indeed it recently happened that one year when peas had been chosen as the fallow crop, that a storm carried the whole crop to the hedge bordering the field, and so mixed together in inextricable confusion the produce belonging to thirty or forty different farmers.

Another source of dispute was one that has been a prolific cause of trouble in common fields for centuries. Where the extremities of a series of adjoining "lands " abut on a land belonging to another series at a right angle, the land so abutted on is termed a " head-land," and the occupiers of the lands that abut on it have the right of turning their ploughs on the headland, and taking the plough from one strip to another along it. The occupier of the headland therefore has to defer ploughing it till all his neighbours have finished, and often chafes at the delay. Recently a farmer in the unenclosed parish of Elmstone Hardwick, near Cheltenham, in Gloucestershire, attempted to find a remedy for this inconvenience. He ploughed his headland at the time that suited his convenience, and then sued his neighbours for trespass when they turned their ploughs in his land. Needless to say he lost more by his action than by the trespass.

In Castor quarrelsome farmers were wise enough to avoid the law courts. Instead, they wrote appealing against their neighbours to their respective landlords, but the landowners were unable to restore harmony. The death of a farmer who had won the highest respect of his neighbours, and who had continually used his great influence to allay ill-feeling and promote harmony, brought on a state of tension that gradually became unbearable; and the appointment by the Ecclesiastical Commissioners of a new agent, who could not understand and had no patience with the peculiarities of common-field farming, led to steps being taken for enclosure.

The first step necessary was to obtain the agreement of the great majority of the people interested. The agent in question, assisted energetically by the leading farmer in Ailesworth, succeeded in doing this without much difficulty. In 1892, application was made for an order to the Board of Agriculture, whose inspector reported warmly commending the project. The simple statement of the farmers with regard to their farms, *e.g.*, "I hold 175 acres in 192 separate parcels," would convince him that a change was necessary. The figures for holdings are not given by the enclosure award, but a summary of the facts with regard to some of the smaller properties gives the following :—

The glebe consisted of—

					A.	R.	P.
16 scattered strips of land in	Wood Field,	area	10	1	16
5	,,	,,	,,	Nether Field,	,,	3	1	12
7	,,	,,	,,	Normangate Field,	,,	4	0	2
33	,,	,,	,,	Mill Field,	,,	20	2	28
34	,,	,,	,,	Thorn Field,	,,	24	2	29
50	,,	,,	,,	Milton Field,	,,	37	0	37
18	,,	,,	,,	four meadows,	,,	10	1	20
2 Lammas closes,					,,	7	2	24

making a total of 165 outlying parcels of land, scattered far and wide over a parish of five thousand acres in extent, and yet

amounting, with some small closes near the village, only to
118 acres in area. Further—

			A.	R.	P.			
Proprietor	A	owned	17	3	19 in	32	parcels
,,	B	,,	3	0	16 ,,	6	,,
,,	C	,,	80	1	5 ,,	164	,,
,,	D	,,	9	0	18 ,,	8	,,
,,	E	,,	2	0	2 ,,	5	,,
,,	F	,,	2	3	14 ,,	6	,,
,,	G	,,	1	2	10 ,,	5	,,
,,	H	,,	2	2	3 ,,	9	,,
,,	J	,,	2	1	18 ,,	7	,,
,,	K	,,	166	2	24 ,,	217	,,
,,	L	,,	13	3	37 ,,	30	,,

Parliamentary enclosure, however, is not to be obtained
without conditions. That reckless disregard of the wider public
interests both of the locality and of the nation at large in the
land to be enclosed of which the administration of the General
Enclosure Act from 1845 to 1874 has been accused, has been
dispelled by the vigorous and ably-conducted agitation to which
we owe the preservation of Epping Forest, Hampstead Heath,
and many other priceless commons. In the enclosure of Castor
and Ailesworth, in the first place, Ailesworth Heath, which
occupies the highest and most remote corner of the parish,
was excluded from the operation of the Enclosure Act. It is
a wild little common which, beyond feeding a few sheep and
furnishing a quarry, seems to be fit for nothing but picnics and
blackberrying. Situated at the distance of about five miles from
Peterborough, which again stands on the margin of the fen
country, it will probably come to be valued by the townsmen
for its unprofitable wildness.

Next, the parish boasts its antiquities, the remains of a part
of the ancient Roman road from London to York, and certain
blocks of stone, locally known as Robin Hood and Little John.
The Enclosure Act provides for the preservation of these.

A bathing place in the River Nen, which bounds the parish

on the south, selected at the most convenient spot, and three recreation grounds of 6 acres each, and one of 14 acres, are handed over to the safe keeping of the parish councils of Castor and Ailesworth, besides four pieces of land, making 42 acres in all, for allotments and field gardens. The farmers mournfully point out that these 76 acres thus reserved for the common use and benefit of the villagers are some of the best land and the most conveniently situated. The recreation grounds in particular they scorn as foolishness. Possibly, however, because the village prides itself on its prowess in the football field, the indignation against this supposed fad of the central government is mild compared with that expressed by some of the thrifty people of Upton St. Leonards, near Gloucester, which was being enclosed at the same time. Here the recreation ground was dubbed by some the "ruination ground," enticing as it did the young lads from digging in their fathers' allotments to cricket and football, and so subverting the very foundation of good morals.

Subject to these deductions, the whole of the open commonable lands and many of the old enclosures, after being surveyed and valued, and after roads, where necessary, had been diverted or newly set out, were redistributed among the old proprietors so as to give each his proportional share, as far as possible in the most convenient manner. This was both a lengthy and a delicate task, but it was finally completed in 1898, six years after the matter first came before the Board of Agriculture. Each several proprietor was then required to fence his allotment in the manner prescribed by the commissioners who make the survey and award. The cost of the survey and allotment usually works out at about £1 per acre; the cost of fencing may be a great deal more. Though the Parliamentary expenses are now trifling, the total cost of abolishing the "system of mingle-mangle," as Carew called it in 1600, in any parish where it still exists, is not to be lightly faced in times of agricultural depression.

CHAPTER III.

Two Dorset Manors—Stratton and Grimstone.

Dorchester is bounded on the south by Fordington Field. The parish of Fordington, up to the year 1875, was unenclosed; it lay almost entirely open, and was divided into about eighty copyholds, intermixed and intercommonable, the manor belonging to the Duchy of Cornwall. But in 1875 the Duchy authorities bought out the copyholders, and the old system disappeared.

About three or four miles from Dorchester, along the road to Maiden Newton and Yeovil, are the two adjoining villages of Stratton and Grimstone, forming together the Prebend of Stratton, belonging till recently to the See of Sarum, which have only been enclosed since 1900. The enclosure was effected without any Parliamentary sanction; it was brought about, I am told by the present lord of the two manors, by the refusal of the copyholders, who held by a tenure of lives, to "re-life." In consequence, all the copyholds, except a few cottages, have fallen into the hands of the lord of the manor; all Grimstone has been let to a single farmer, and Stratton divided into three or four farms.

Besides the very late survival of the common field system in these two manors, there are two other features which make them specially notable. In the first place they are, agriculturally, thoroughly characteristic of the Wessex type of open field village, the type that prevailed over Berkshire, Hampshire, Wiltshire and Dorset. In the second place, the manorial system of village government survived with equal vigour; the proceedings of the manorial courts and the customs of tillage and pasturage forming manifestly only two aspects of one and the same organisation. It is fortunate that the court-rolls for the last two hundred years have been preserved, and that they are in the safe custody of the present lord of the manor.

On the south-west the lands of Stratton and Grimstone are bounded by a stream, the River Frome, flowing towards Dorchester, from which Stratton Mill has the right of taking a defined amount of water. Between the stream and the villages are the commonable meadows ; on the north-east of the villages the arable fields, tapering somewhat, stretch up the hill slope to Stratton and Grimstone Downs. The whole arrangement is shown very clearly in the tithe commutation map, dated 1839. The two manor farms were separate and enclosed, and lay side by side along the boundary between the two manors, in each case comprising about one-third of the cultivated land. The remaining arable land in each manor formed, so far as fences were concerned, one open field, divided into three oblong strips, known respectively in Stratton as the East, Middle, and West Field ; in Grimstone as Brewer's Ash Field, Rick Field, and Langford Field. The rotation of crops was : (1), wheat ; (2), barley ; (3), fallow. The lower part of the fallow field was sown with clover, and was known as the "hatching ground"—a term we find elsewhere in the forms "hitch-land" and "hook-land"—the upper part was a bare fallow. More recently an improved method of cultivation was adopted. The barley crop every third year was maintained, but after it was carried Italian rye grass was sown in the upper part of the barley field (instead of a bare fallow). This was fed off with sheep in the spring, and then put into turnips ; the following year barley was sown again. The lower part, however, continued to be sown with clover in the fallow year, this was fed off with sheep, and wheat followed.

The arable fields consisted of "lands" or "lawns,"[1] each supposed to be 40 "yards" (*i.e.* poles) long, and one, two or four "yards" broad—hence supposed to be quarter acres, half acres, or acres. Half acres were the more common ; but

[1] Mr. A. N. Palmer notes the terms "loons," "lawnds" and "lownts" in N. Wales and Cheshire ("The Town, Fields and Folk of Wrexham," p. 2).

whatever the area in theory it was somewhat less in actual fact.

The West Field in Stratton was somewhat smaller than the other two in consequence of the extreme portion—that next the down and farthest from the village—being enclosed. These enclosures in shape and arrangement exactly resemble the lands in the open field; they are about one acre each. They are called "The Doles." Further there are a series of small square enclosures taken out of the down, called "The New Closes." All the Doles and New Closes were in grass.

A remarkable fact is that all the "lands" were scrupulously separated from one another by meres or balks of turf, which, however, were not known by these names. Among the people they were, and are, known as "walls," but in the court-rolls one finds the term "lanchetts," which one connects with "lynches," and "land-shares," which seems to explain the term "launchers" which I have found in Devonshire. In the level parts of the fields the "walls" were mere strips of turf about a foot wide; but in the sloping parts they formed steep banks, sometimes several feet high, and the successive "lands" formed terraces one above the other.

All the cultivators, except the tenants of the two manor farms, were copyholders, holding for a tenancy of three lives, the widow of the holder having the right to continue the holding during the period of her widowhood. By the custom of the manor the lessee of the manor had at any time (even though his lease had but a day to run) the right to grant a copyholder two lives, i.e., to accept a fine and substitute two new names for those of dead or dying persons on the "copy."

The copyholds, when not "cotes" or simply cottages with common rights, were either "half-livings," "livings," or, in one or two cases, other fractions of a living. A half-living consisted of four or five nominal acres in each of the common fields, and common rights upon the meadow, common fields and common down, in Stratton, for one horse, two cows, and forty sheep. A whole living consisted of a share about twice as large in the field and meadow, and a common right for two horses, four cows, and eighty sheep. But each copyhold, whether a whole or half-living, included one dole and one new close. There were three whole livings and twelve half-livings in Stratton, and five " cotes," *i.e.*, cottages with one or two strips of land in the arable fields attached to them. In Grimstone there were four whole livings, six half-livings, one three-quarters living, and one whole and a-quarter living. In either manor, therefore, if we reckon two half-livings as equal to one whole, there were nine whole livings in all; those of Stratton being normally held by fifteen copyholders, those of Grimstone by twelve, though the number might happen in practice to be less. Thus at the time of the tithe commutation (1838) there was in each manor one copyholder who had two half-livings. In all formal documents a " living " is termed a " place," and a half-living a " half-place." The common rights attached to a living in Grimstone were slightly different from those in Stratton. They are further explained below.

Once a year, at about Christmas, the tenants of each manor met, the steward presiding; the elected officials submitted their accounts, and resigned their offices, and their successors were re-elected. The most important of these were two " viewers of the fields and tellers of the cattle," commonly known simply as the " viewers." There was also a " hayward," and two " chimney peepers " (described in the Court-rolls as " inspectors of chimnies "). The inspectors of chimneys do not appear in the rolls of the eighteenth century; instead are the more important officials the " constabul " (*sic*) and " tythingman," who ceased to be appointed presumably after the establishment of the county police and the commutation of the tithes.

The duty of the " chimney peepers " was, as their name implies, to see that chimneys were kept properly swept so as not to endanger a neighbour's thatched roof. The hayward was in charge of the pound; he was entitled to charge 4*d*. a head for all stray beasts impounded if they belonged to the manor, and 8*d*. a head for outsiders.

The " viewers " had more varied duties. In the first place they had to appoint one villager as " Lacy's Bridge man."

"Lacy's Bridge" is a structure of loose stones at a place where the stream, which for the most part bounds Stratton meadow, crosses it; and the duty of the bridge man is to keep it in sufficient repair to enable sheep to cross. The viewers used to appoint the cottagers in turn, going down one side of the road to the end of the village and up the other side.

Next the viewers provided the manor bull. They bought the bull, they charged a fee for his services, and made all necessary regulations. The breed favoured varied from year to year, and the viewers were never known to please everybody with their choice.

Then the viewers appointed the common shepherd, in whose charge were the sheep of the whole manor almost all through the year. And in general they had to enforce all the decisions of the court with regard to the times when sheep or cows should be allowed in the meadow, when the sheep should come into the "hatching ground," how and where horses should be tethered, and particularly to see that each tenant sowed his clover properly. And when the hay in the meadow was ripe, they marked out to each tenant the plots which fell to his share that year. It was usual to re-elect one of the viewers, so that though there was an annual election, each viewer held office for two years, being for the first year the junior viewer, for the second the senior.

There is much that is interesting in the management of the sheep flock. From April 6th to September 18th the sheep fed by day on the down, and were folded by night on the fallow field. The fold began at the top of the field, and gradually worked downwards, covering about half-an-acre every night, and so manuring the whole. There being no other water supply on the downs, all the tenants had to take turns to carry up water to fill the water-troughs, and the viewers saw that they did so. On September 18th the sheep came into the "hatching ground," on which, as we have seen, clover had been sown; and it is noticeable that this crop, sown individually by each copyholder on his own lands, was fed off by the common flock under the supervision of the common shepherd. In winter the sheep belonging to each tenant had to be folded separately; and the doles and new closes were used for wintering the sheep. Some made it a practice to sell off their flock when feed became scanty, and to buy again the next spring; but the traditional custom was to keep the sheep till they were four or five years old, at which age they became fat, perhaps by superior cunning; meanwhile, of course, they had been yielding wool and manure. In later years, though every half living was entitled to forty sheep, by a common agreement the number was limited to twenty-five in spring, and later in the year to thirty-five, when the lambs reached the age at which they were counted as sheep in the calculation of common rights.

Perhaps the most curious feature in the local system of agriculture was the management of the common meadow. Sheep were allowed in it from March 1st to April 6th (it would only bear ten or eleven), then they had to come out and join the common flock, and the grass was let grow to hay. At hay time the viewers went out and by the help of some almost imperceptible ridges in the soil, and certain pegs driven into the river banks, they marked out to each tenant the plots on which he was allowed to cut and gather the hay. There were forty-seven of these little plots; twenty-seven of them were definite parts of particular copyholds, but nineteen were "changeable allotments," each of which belonged one year to one holding, the next year to another, according to certain rules; while the remaining allotment, a little three-cornered plot in the middle called "100 Acres," amounting perhaps to five perches in area, was divided among the holders of the adjacent "Long lands." On July 6th, the hay having been carried, the cows came in, and grazed in the meadow till November 23rd, and then the meadow was watered.

I have before me the map of the meadow, now somewhat tattered, being drawn upon a half sheet of thin foolscap, and a little notebook recording particulars of the different plots in the meadow, and in the case of the changeable allotments, who were entitled to them each year from 1882 to about 1905, which the

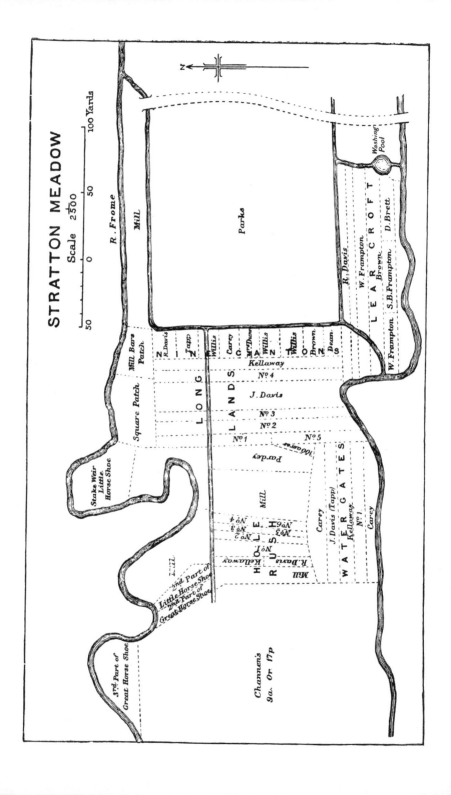

viewers used in partitioning the meadow. The map I reproduce. The notebook reads [1] :—

STRATTON COMMON MEADOW.

Lear Croft Changeable Allotment next the Yard but one to Sparks.[2]

    1882. Ozzard.
    1883. Brett.
    1884. Ozzard.
    1885. Green.

Water Gates Changeable Allotment No. 1.

    1883. M. Dean (Newberry).
    1884. R. Davis.
    1885. Dean.
    1886. Davis.

Hole Rush—Changeable No. 1.

    1883. Mr. R. Davis.
    1884. Mr. Dean (Newberry).
    1885. Mr. Davis.
    1886. Mr. Dean.

Hole Rush No. 2.

    1882. Ozzard.
    1883. Brett.
    1884. Ozzard.
    1885. Green.

Hole Rush No. 3, or All Rush.

    1883. R. Davis.
    1884. Dean (Newberry's).
    1885. Davis.
    1886. Dean.

Hole Rush near the Parish, No. 5.

    1883. Mr. Dean (Newberry).
    1884. R. Davis.
    1885. Dean.
    1886. Davis.

---

[1] I give only four years, or a complete cycle, which is usually one of two years, but sometimes of four, and in two cases of eight years.

[2] " Parks " in map.

Hole Rush No. 4.

1883. Mr. Kellaway.
1884. Brown.
1885. Kellaway.
1886. Brown.

Hole Rush No 6, near the Parish.
1883. Brown.
1884. Kellaway.
1885. Brown.
1886. Kellaway.

Long Lands No. 2.
1883. Mr. Dean (Dunn).
1884. Brett.
1885. Brett.
1886. Dean.

Long Lands No. 3.
1883. Ozzard.
1884. Mrs. Dunn.
1885. Mr. Dean.
1886. Mrs. Dunn.

Long Lands No. 1.
1883. Mr. Tilley.
1884. Ozzard.
1885. Tilley.
1886. Ozzard.

Long Lands No. 5.
1883. Ozzard.
1884. Tilley.
1885. Ozzard.
1886. Tilley.

Long Lands No. 4.
1883. Mrs. Dunn.
1884. Mr. Dean (Newberry's).
1885. Mrs. Dunn.
1886. Dean.

The first part of the Three Patches in the Great Horse Shoe is the " Mill Bars Patch," containing about 26 perches.

The second part is the narrow strip next to Mr. Channen's—
17 perches.

The third part is the lower patch adjoining Mr. Channen's—
1 rood 10 perches.

Total, 2 roods 13 perches.

CHANGEABLE ALLOTMENTS IN THE GREAT HORSE SHOE.

The Three Patches are one part.

Three Patches.

1883. Ozzard.
1884. Mr. Dean (Dunn).
1885. Mr. Tilley.
1886. Mill.
1887. Tilley.
1888. Mill.
1889. Ozzard.
1890. Brett.

The Square Patch is joining the patch by the Mill Bars, may be
called the fourth part of the "Great Horse Shoe," it contains about
2 roods and 4 perches.

1883. Mr. Tilley.
1884. Mill.
1885. Ozzard.
1886. Brett.
1887. Ozzard.
1888. Green.
1889. Tilley.
1890. Mill.

The Stake Weir is one part of the "Little Horse Shoe," about
1 rood and 9 perches changeable.

1882. Ozzard.
1883. Dean (Newberry's).
1884. Tilley.
1885. Mill.

The "Little Horse Shoe" changeable. The narrow strip and the strip round the corner next to Stake Weir patch is one part.

1883. Mill.
1884. Ozzard.
1885. Dean.
1886. Tilley.

Narrow strip, 16 perches.
Patch round the corner, 1 rood 22 perches.

The small strip of land called "Hundred Acres" is a part of the Long Lands and is divided amongst the half-acres.

The nine Cantons under the Parks Hedge are about 10 perches each.

About the agricultural merits of the whole system of managing common fields, down and meadow, there is naturally a difference of opinion. An old labourer says that before the old customs began to decay "they made the most of everything," that the crops are not so good now, and "you can't get the butter or the cheese" which used to be produced. The butter nowadays goes rancid immediately, and the cheese has no taste. On the other hand, the enterprising young farmer who now holds the manor farm at Stratton, who has himself been a "viewer," says: "They always had two crops," *i.e.*, the corn crops had to struggle with couch grass, which partly for want of sufficient ploughing, and partly because it had a secure foothold in the "walls," was never properly got rid of.

That the life of the old system was gradually dying out before it was ended by the extinction of the copyholds appears from two circumstances: the old habit of mutual help in ploughing, one tenant lending his horse to another, had died out; and the viewers had difficulty in getting their expenses refunded. The wonder is that its vitality was so persistent.

The history of the manors can be pretty fully traced by means of the Court rolls, from 1649, when a Parliamentary survey was held, to the present day. In 1649 Stratton had one copyhold tenant holding a place and a-half, four holding one place each, and ten holding half a place each, making 10½ "places" or

" livings " altogether.   There were, besides, 12 copyholders who
each held a " customary cottage with thappurtenances." During
the next two hundred years (from 1649 to 1838) the number
of " livings " diminished from 10½ to 9 ; the actual number of
holders of livings or half-livings diminished only from 15 to 14 ;
but the twelve " customary cottages with thappurtenances,"
which included one or two acres of arable land and corresponding
common rights, diminished to five " cotes." The other
cottagers, however, retained the right of cutting as much furze
on certain " sleights " on the down, at any one time, as they
could carry home on their head and shoulders ; and the total
number of cottagers was just two less in 1838 than in 1649.

The Court rolls contain, besides declarations of rights of the
manor to water from the stream, and to the allegiance of certain
residents outside, and a record of the changes in the tenantry,
the names of the officers elected, and regulations agreed upon
for the management of the land.   Thus, there is usually some
regulation as to the length of the rope by which a horse may
be tethered in the common fields ; mares are continually being
prohibited from being kept in common or common field ; pigs
must not be allowed to stray ; cow dung must not be removed
from the meadow, nor certain thorny bushes in the meadow be
cut, nor may ducks or geese be fed in it.   The penalty for each
of these offences is a fine of 5s. or 10s.   The neglect to carry
water up to the down for the sheep is another punishable offence.
In 1748 it was found that the sheep pond needed to be mended ;
the viewers accordingly had to see to its repair, and penalties
were agreed upon for refusing to pay the proper share of the
cost.

Previous to 1765 the dates for, e.g., turning cows into the
meadow or sheep into the " hatching ground " varied from year
to year ; but the settlement then arrived at was maintained
for a succession of years.   The jury

" PRESENT that the Common Meadow be broke with horses
on November 22nd,[1] that it be laid up on January 5th and

---

[1] At this time the Court met in October.

continue unfed till February 5th, then be broke and fed with sheep.

" That the Hatching Ground be laid up on January 5th, and not be fed again till September 19th.

" That the Cow leaze must not be fed with sheep in time of sheep shearing, nor with horses or mares at winnowing time."

The year 1789 was a comparatively important date in the agricultural history of Stratton during the eighteenth century. At the Court held on October 9th, it was agreed that " the tenants shall meet in the West Field on the 14th inst. between 9 and 10 in the morning, to bound out the several lands, and afterwards each shall leave a lanchett of a furrow between his and the adjoining land under penalty of a fine of 20s. And no tenant shall turn his plough on his neighbour's land after the 21st of November." It would appear that the scrupulous observance of the " walls " dividing one man's land from another, which was such an exceptional feature of Stratton and Grimstone Common Fields, dates from this meeting.

Fordington parish, until the extinction of the copyholds, had many features which compare curiously with those of Stratton and Grimstone. It is very much larger; for whereas Stratton and Grimstone together have an area of only about 1200 acres, the area of Fordington is 2749 acres, of which, up to 1876, nearly 1800 acres was common field and common meadow, and 618 acres commons adjoining the common field. Fordington is also peculiarly divided into three portions : the arable field and common pastures lying immediately south of Dorchester, the meadows forming a detached area by the side of the River Frome, and the village itself a third detached area.

The copyholds in Fordington were known, some as "whole-places," "half-places," as in Stratton and Grimstone, but others as "farthing holds." One cannot help asking what were the original meanings of these terms, and how they are related to the " virgates " of Domesday, and to the " yardlands " of the Midlands, and the " broad " and " narrow oxgangs " of Yorkshire and Lincolnshire. Concerning these terms it appears to be established that a " yardland " or " virgate " was originally one quarter of a " carucate," or ploughland, *i.e.*, the amount of arable land (about 120 acres in average soil) which a plough team of eight oxen could plough in a year, together with its due share of meadow and common pasture. A broad oxgang was about 24 acres of arable land, and therefore apparently the northern representative of a yardland or virgate ; and a narrow oxgang was about 12 acres of arable, or half a broad oxgang.

In Stratton, as we have seen, every " whole place " or " whole living " had common rights for two horses, four cows, and eighty sheep ; every half-place common rights for one horse, two cows, and forty sheep. The areas of land attached to the three whole places were respectively 18 a. 3 r. 35 p., 19 a. 2 r. 3 p., 22 a. 0 r. 11 p., averaging just 20 acres ; the half-places varied from 9 a. 0 r. 19 p. to 13 a. 2 r. 25 p., the smaller half-places having an advantage in quality of soil, and the average being almost exactly 11 acres.

In Grimstone the common rights as well as the area of land belonging to particular whole or half-places varied somewhat. The half-places consisted respectively of—

				Area.			Common Rights.		
				A.	R.	P.	Horses.	Cows.	Sheep.
A	...	...	...	11	0	28	1	2	56
B	...	...	...	12	0	7	1	3	48
C	...	...	...	16	3	7	1	3	60
D	...	...	...	12	3	1	1	2	44
E (two half-places)			...	19	2	27	2	5	96
			(average 12 acres)						
The Whole Places.									
A	...	...	...	21	1	25	2	5	104
B	...	...	...	21	1	38	2	5	96
C	...	...	...	21	0	19	2	4	96
D	...	...	...	20	2	32	2	5	96

The " whole and a-quarter place " had 26 a. 0 r. 13 p. of land and rights for three horses, five cows, and 120 sheep, and the "three-quarter place " 16 a. 1 r. 2 p., with rights for

one horse, five cows, and eighty sheep. If these be added
together and divided by two we arrive at two whole places of
21 a. 0 r. 27 p., with the common rights for two horses,
five cows, and 100 sheep. This may be taken as the typical
whole place, and the half-place is just a little more than the
mathematical half of a whole place. The fact that the common
rights attached to a given unit were more extensive in Grimstone
than in Stratton is the natural consequence of the fact that
Grimstone had 244 acres of down and 35 acres of cow-common,
Stratton only 190 acres of down and 26 acres of cow-common.

But when we compare these with the whole places, half-
places, and farthing holds of Fordington, we find rather a
puzzling discrepancy. In the latter parish the fourteen whole
places each had, in 1841, the date of the Tithe Commutation,
rights for four horses, three cows, and 120 sheep, except
one, which had no common rights at all, but, apparently by
compensation, had 66 acres of arable land, eleven more than
any of the others. The smallest of the others had 42 a. 3 r.,
the largest 55 a. 0 r. 22 p., the average being about 48 acres ;
in other words, in Fordington a whole place had more than
twice as much arable land as in Stratton or Grimstone, and
carried a common right for four horses instead of for two.

Each of the twenty-one half - places in Fordington had
common rights for three horses, two cows, and sixty-six sheep
—which more closely approximates to three-quarters than to a
half of the rights of a whole place. The area of land attached
to a half-place is, however, on the average somewhat less
than half that attached to a whole place, the largest having
25 a. 1 r. 6 p., the smallest 15 a. 1 r. 36 p., the average being
just under 21 acres. It happens curiously that the largest
" farthing holds " had more land than the smallest half-places,
as their areas range from 11 a. 1 r. 7 p. to 17 a. 3 r. 35 p. There
were nineteen of them, and their average area was 14½ acres.
Each had a common right for two horses, two cows, and forty
sheep.

The following tentative hypothesis may be suggested as an
explanation. It is based on the presumption that the *names*

represent a more ancient set of circumstances than the actual facts recorded in the tithe apportionment.

I think it, on the whole, more probable that these units of holdings are based upon ploughing by horses than upon ploughing by oxen. In other words, I think that the system of co-aration persisted unimpaired in these particular villages after horses had superseded oxen for ploughing purposes, which might have happened at a very early date. This seems plainly indicated by the fact that during the 190 years from 1649 to 1839 the majority of the copyholders in Stratton and Grimstone had only one horse apiece, therefore they must have combined to work even a two-horse plough ; and, as I have said above, the practice of helping one another with horses for ploughing only died out in very recent years.

I think further, that in all three manors, a " whole place " or " whole living " meant the land cultivated by one plough, but that in Stratton and Grimstone the plough was a light and shallow one drawn by two horses only, and in Fordington a heavier plough drawn by four horses. The soil in Stratton and Grimstone is very thin and stony, and would not bear deep ploughing ; that of Fordington is much deeper and heavier. Further, Stratton and Grimstone fields lie on the steep slopes descending from the downs ; Fordington field is gently undulating. Therefore, a four-horse plough in Fordington would plough more than twice as much land as a two-horse plough in the other villages. A whole place then in Fordington naturally would have common rights for four horses ; in Stratton and Grimstone for two horses only.

A half-place in Stratton and Grimstone was, therefore, the holding allotted to the tenant who had one horse, and it carried a common right for one horse. Though a half-place in Fordington carried in 1841 a common right for three horses, I am inclined to believe that it originally was the holding of a tenant who had two horses, i.e., half a plough team, and originally had a common right for two horses only ; and, similarly, though a farthing hold in 1841 had a common right for two horses, I am inclined to think it originally was the share of the man who had one horse only, and only carried a common right for one horse. That is to say, I think the *names* here a better guide than the nineteenth century common rights. If one were to adopt the opposite view on this point, one would infer that a "half-place" was a misnomer for a "three-quarter place," and was the allotment of the man who had three horses, and that a "farthing hold" should properly be called a half-place. But on this assumption it would be hard to explain the fact that the arable land attached to a half-place is, on the average, a little less than half that attached to a whole place, and that attached to a farthing hold only a little more than one quarter.

It seems quite probable that when in the course of the gradual improvement of horses and ploughs in Fordington, the stage was reached at which three horses were sufficient for a plough, the holders of half-places already possessing two horses each endeavoured to emancipate themselves from the necessity of joint-ploughing, by obtaining an additional horse; and that when they had generally succeeded in this they obtained the right of pasturing three horses each on the commons and common-field; and when a two-horse plough had come into general use, the holders of farthing holds would naturally take similar steps, and so acquire common rights for two horses each.

There is one other noteworthy fact with regard to Fordington revealed by the Tithe Apportionment. Certain lands scattered over the fields of a total area of 4 a. 2 r. 20 p. were the property of the parish constable for the time being; the churchwardens similarly held 1 r. 7 p., the parish hayward 1 a. 3 r. 18 p., and the parish reeve 3 a. 0 r. 17 p. These ancient village offices were therefore in Fordington not entirely unremunerated.[1]

In its main features the common-field system of Stratton and Grimstone appears to be typical of that prevailing before

[1] The Boldon Book shows that in the Bishopric of Durham in the twelfth century, the pounder, carpenter and smith generally occupied holdings of about 12 acres in virtue of their callings, to remunerate their services to the manor and to the common ploughs of the manor.

enclosure in the counties of Dorset, Wilts, Hants, Berks, Oxfordshire, and Gloucestershire.

The report of the Select Committee on Commons Enclosure gives a map of a "rotation meadow," in which each strip was held in rotation by different occupiers, in Shilton, Berkshire; and one of a "lot meadow," in which the rotation was not by rule, but by lot, in Bestmoor, Oxfordshire.

CHAPTER IV.

A "RETURN of the Acreage of Waste Lands subject to Rights of Common and of Common Field Lands in each Parish of England and Wales, in which the Tithes have been commuted under the Tithe Commutation Acts, so far as the same can be ascertained from the Maps, Agreements, Awards, and Apportionments relating to the Commutation of Tithes in the custody of the Tithe Commissioners for England and Wales, deducting any lands inclosed under the General Enclosure Acts since the Commutation; also the estimated Total Acreage of such lands in the remaining Parishes of each county," dated 27th November, 1873, ordered by the House of Commons to be printed, April 13th, 1874, gives us the following results :—

County.	Number of Parishes stated to have Common Fields.	Area of such Common Fields.	Estimated Area of other Common Fields in the County.
ENGLAND.			
Bedford	9	7,056	12,925
Berkshire... ...	21	13,227	2,705
Buckingham ...	16	2,315	2,365
Cambridge ...	9	4,798	2,678
Cheshire	16	599	116
Cornwall	16	895	6
Cumberland ...	22	1,177	868
Derby	11	1,119	638
Devon	15	1,125	32
Dorset	29	6,793	810
Durham	6	1,936	171
Essex	48	4,614	295
Gloucester ...	33	4,327	2,986

County.	Number of Parishes stated to have Common Fields.	Area of such Common Fields.	Estimated Area of other Common Fields in the County.
ENGLAND—*contd.*			
Hereford	32	2,309	189
Hertford	39	9,311	1,785
Huntingdon ...	4	1,336	2,336
Kent	21	4,183	126
Lancashire ...	22	2,125	1,173
Leicester	3	42	93
Lincoln	24	6,258	10,823
Middlesex ...	6	697	870
Monmouth ...	2	64	3
Norfolk	52	3,560	394
Northampton ...	3	4,103	13,446
Northumberland ...	1	44	7
Nottingham ...	14	4,282	6,617
Oxford	12	4.120	4,839
Rutland	6	3,930	5,726
Shropshire ...	12	485	40
Somerset	77	7,794	728
Southampton ...	25	5,725	663
Stafford	26	1,138	402
Suffolk	34	2,395	184
Surrey	19	3,732	277
Sussex	22	2,969	122
Warwick	5	1,232	1,208
Westmoreland ...	8	425	359
Wiltshire	44	18,167	4,503
Worcester ...	20	3,092	1,161
York, City and Ainsty	4	187	372
York, East Riding	14	4,046	7,359
York, North Riding	7	547	240
York, West Riding	44	6,488	4,361
WALES.			
Anglesey	2	414	33
Brecon	2	1,549	5
Cardigan	4	372	0
Carmarthen ...	8	489	38
Carnarvon ...	1	100	7
Denbigh	4	278	18

County.	Number of Parishes stated to have Common Fields.	Area of such Common Fields.	Estimated Area of other Common Fields in the County.
WALES—contd.			
Flint	5	297	4
Glamorgan ...	10	783	40
Merioneth ...	2	110	8
Montgomery ...	3	1,885	24
Pembroke ...	8	642	18
Radnor	3	6,167	158

TOTALS.

	Number of Parishes stated to have Common Fields.	Area of such Common Fields.	Estimated Area of other Common Fields.	
England	853	153,867	97,001	250,868
Wales	52	13,086	353	13,439
	905	166,953	97,354	264,307

We have therefore the assurance of the Copyhold, Inclosure and Tithe Commission that in the year 1873 common fields existed in 905 parishes of England and Wales, of a total area of 166,953 acres, and that there was reasonable ground for inferring the existence of 97,354 acres of common field land, scattered presumably over some four or five hundred more parishes ; in other words, that about one parish in every ten in England and Wales presented an example of the medieval system of land holding and cultivation similar, though as a rule on a smaller scale, to the survivals described above.

The statement is amazing, and would be received with incredulity by anyone familiar with the rural districts of any county of England, so far as it relates to that county. The Commission invites our suspicion of its statistics. The main purpose of the return was to give the acreage of surviving commons; these are estimated at 2,368,465 acres. As late as 1871, however, the Commission had declared, on the basis of an estimate made in 1843, that 8,000,000 acres of commons still existed, and 1,000,000 acres of common field or meadow. A little scrutiny of some details confirms one's suspicions.

Thus, to take a single county, Kent has from the early days of the enclosure controversy been famous as a well enclosed county. The author of the " Discourse of the Common weal of this Realm of England " mentions " those countries that be most inclosed, as essex, kent, devenshire " (1549). Skipping two and a-half centuries, we find the reporter of the Board of Agriculture in 1793 declaring that such a thing as a common field did not exist in Kent.[1] We are confirmed in our acceptance of this statement by finding that there have been no enclosures in Kent of common fields by Act of Parliament, either before 1793 or since. Yet the return gives Kent twenty-one parishes having common fields of an ascertained area of about 4183 acres. It therefore is necessary to criticise the methods by which the figures in the return were arrived at.

They are based on the tithe maps, the Commissioners remarking that " the common field lands are generally distinguishable by the particular manner in which they are marked on the Tithe maps, and their area has been estimated from those maps." The Tithe Commission was appointed in 1836 (6 & 7 Will. IV. c. 71), and the tithe maps and apportionments were made mostly before 1850 ; we are told " the total area embraced by the Tithe Documents is 28,195,903 acres. The total area of the remaining parishes is 8,961,270 acres."

In order, therefore, for the Commission to have obtained a correct result, it was necessary—

(a) that the common field lands should have been *rightly* distinguished from other lands ;

---

[1] Boys' " Kent," 2nd edition, 8vo. (1786), p. 53.

(*b*) that their area should have been *rightly* estimated;

(*c*) that due allowance should have been made for enclosures between the date of the tithe apportionment and the date of the return;

(*d*) that the area of common field in the parishes for which there are no tithe maps should have been estimated on correct principles.

Not one of these conditions was satisfied.

(*d*) Taking these in reverse order, it is assumed in calculating the area of common fields in parishes that have no tithe maps, that they have the same ratio of common field to other land as those which have tithe maps. This principle is entirely wrong for two reasons: (1) because Private Enclosure Acts usually arranged for tithe commutation, so that parishes enclosed by such Acts before 1830 are ordinarily among those without tithe maps—and equally among those without common fields; and (2) the existence of unenclosed common fields would be a reason for demanding a commutation of tithe. The importance of this may be shown by taking Bedfordshire as a test case. For sixty-eight Bedfordshire parishes there are no tithe maps, and the Commission estimates that these sixty-eight parishes have 12,925 acres of common fields. But sixty-six out of these sixty-eight parishes were enclosed by Private Acts, leaving two parishes only, of a combined area of 3578 acres, in which a survival of common field might reasonably be deemed possible, though even in these extremely improbable. Instead of 12,925 acres of common field for this part of the county, the only reasonable estimate would be 0.

Similar statements might be made with regard to any other county which was mainly enclosed by Act of Parliament, as Northampton, to which 13,446 acres of common field are attributed to the non-tithe map parishes; Lincoln, to which 10,823 acres are similarly attributed: Berkshire, with 2705 acres; Buckingham, with 2365 acres; Cambridge with 2678 acres; Huntingdon, with 2336 acres; Nottingham, with 6617 acres; Oxford, with 4839 acres; Rutland, with 5726 acres, and the East Riding of Yorkshire, with 7359 acres. For this cause alone by far the greater part of the 97,354 acres added on to the total estimated from tithe maps must be rejected, and of course any error of over-statement that we find with regard to parishes which have tithe maps will still further reduce the remainder.

(c) Due allowance has not been made for enclosure between the date of the tithe apportionment and the date of the return. It is of course very difficult to say how this could have been done without an elaborate and expensive local enquiry, so far as relates to enclosure without Parliamentary authority.   As a matter of fact, no allowance at all has been made for this sort of enclosure.   This is justifiable ; but at least a general statement should have been made to the effect that a very large deduction had to be made on this account in order to obtain a correct idea of the position.   Further, great carelessness was shown even in allowing for Parliamentary enclosures subsequent to the tithe apportionment.   Thus, to take one glaring instance, 1500 acres of common field are credited to Beddington and Wallington, near Croydon, in Surrey.   These common fields were enclosed by an Act dated 1850, and the award, dated 1853, was at the time of the return deposited with the Copyhold, Inclosure, and Tithe Commission.

(a) and (b) But it is in distinguishing the common fields and in estimating their area from the tithe maps that the worst mistakes have been made.   The Commission says that "the common fields are generally distinguishable by the particular manner in which they are marked on the tithe maps."   From a comparison of a good many tithe maps with the figures given in the return, I infer that those to whom the duty of distinguishing the common fields was entrusted, were told that areas divided into sub-divisions on the maps by means of dotted lines were common fields.   These dotted lines indicate a division of owner-ship marked by some slight boundary and not by a hedge.   They might indicate allotments, for example, or a number of other local circumstances, besides common fields.   The statements that 4183 acres of common field were to be found in Kent, and 13,439 acres in Wales, being specially in direct contradiction of all other evidence that I had collected, I tested these by two

instances. In Kent 1400 acres were assigned to the parish of
Northbourne. By a close examination of the tithe map I could
find nothing indicating any common field at all ; the only excuse
for the statement was a few dotted lines, which by a reference
to the Award were proved to indicate only that some fields were
inadequately hedged. For Wales, I got out the map and award
for Llanerlyl, in Montgomery, credited with 1675 acres of common
field. Here there was something to be found on the map looking
exactly like common field, but the Award showed that these
dotted strips of land were " turbaries."

We have seen that the open field parish in its perfection, as
Castor and Ailesworth before enclosure, possessed common
arable fields, common meadows, common pasture, and frequently commonable waste, like Ailesworth Heath. Where the
parish as a whole becomes enclosed without an Act of Parliament, particularly if the enclosure is gradual, the waste
frequently remains common. Thus we have the numerous
commons of Kent, Surrey, and other counties. Less frequently,
but still in a considerable number of cases, the common meadows
remain open commonable and unenclosed. Port Meadow at
Oxford is a familiar instance. These common meadows are
included in the return under consideration among the common
fields. Thus, for instance, the surprise with which one receives
the information that Tottenham, in 1873, had 300 acres of
common fields, disappears when it is perceived that the marshes
along the River Lea are meant.

It will also be noticed later on that in parishes where the
common field system has disappeared for generations, there are
frequently still remaining in the midst of enclosed fields strips
of land of different ownership from the rest of the field, but let
to the same farmer, and without any visible demarcation. Such
fields in Wales and the north-west of England are called
" quilleted fields." The tithe map records, with its dotted lines,
the area and position of the " quillets." Such fields are included
under " common fields " in this return.

In at least the great majority of cases where the supposed
common fields are small, it is probable that nothing more notable

than quilleted fields existed at the time the tithe map was made; and even this survival would, in most cases, have disappeared since.   Out of the 905 alleged cases of common fields, in 670 cases the areas given are under 100 acres.

In fine, this return of commons and common fields, which gives such a fair promise of numerous surviving common fields, in reality gives little assistance, because there is but the remotest probability in any particular case that those common fields exist.   The probability is sufficient in some cases to encourage one to make local enquiries, but these enquiries nearly always end in disappointment.   The following cases in which common arable fields theoretically survive, are chiefly interesting as illustrating the phenomena of the decay of the common field system in villages where it has not died a sudden death through enclosure.   I omit the case of Hitchin, made famous by Mr. F. Seebohm.

CLOTHALL (HERTS).

Clothall is a parish lying on the north slope of the chalk hills of Hertfordshire, just off the Great North Road, which passes through the adjoining parish of Baldock.   Approaching it from the south, one gradually ascends the long slope from Hertford, and suddenly at the summit has before one a far-stretching view over the flat country of Bedfordshire and adjoining counties. The road descends steeply and passes through the Clothall common fields.   At the time of my visit the harvest (of barley) was being gathered in ; the arrangement of the field was clearly visible.   The long, narrow strips of stubble, never quite straight, and never quite of uniform width, were divided by "balks" of grass, grown tall and gone to seed.   Each balk was reduced to as narrow dimensions as it could be, without endangering its continued existence, for the sake of separating one strip from another.   A view of this field is shown in Mr. Seebohm's "English Village Community."

But there is in Clothall the husk only, and no surviving kernel of the English village community.   The whole of the field, estimated at about 600 acres, is let to a single farmer, who cultivates it on modern principles, but who is bound to preserve the balks. There are but three owners of land in the field. Fifty-six acres are glebe, the remainder belongs in alternate strips to the lord of the manor (the Marquis of Salisbury) and to a gentleman to whom possession passed by marriage, from a family which had been engaged in brewing. The land is famous for barley, and the owner of a local brewery in the early or middle part of the nineteenth century gradually bought up nearly all the land in the common field that did not belong to the lord of the manor. Application was made in 1885 to the Board of Agriculture for enclosure, the manorial authorities and the vicar both desiring it, but the other owner objected.

It is interesting to find that the villagers still hold to the tradition that they have rights of common upon the balks, a tradition which is probably well founded. But they dare not attempt to exercise those rights. An enclosure here, accompanied by the provision of ground for allotments and recreation, would be a boon for the villagers; and it would probably pay the landowners to get rid of those balks, which are as great a nuisance agriculturally as they are interesting from an antiquarian point of view.

The counties of Hertford and Bedford have been, in recent years, particularly rich in survivals of common field, for the enclosure of Totternhoe (p. 65) was only completed in 1891; Yelden had a common field of about 600 acres up till about the year 1881, when the chief proprietor, by buying out or compensating all the other proprietors or owners of common rights, obtained exclusive ownership of the unenclosed land; and at Studham and Renhold similar voluntary enclosures were carried out under the pressure of the chief landowners within the memory of old inhabitants. Fragments of commonable pasture in three different parts of Renhold parish, and a common of about 60 acres in Studham, remain as memorials.

BYGRAVE AND WALLINGTON.

Beneath the long sloping hillside of Clothall lies the little town of Baldock, adjoining Letchworth and the "Garden City";

and on the other side of Baldock is the parish of Bygrave ; which is, like Clothall, still unenclosed, and for the same reason ; the Marquis of Salisbury being here again the lord of the manor, and the other Clothall proprietor the next largest landowner. But in Bygrave the farms, as well as the properties, are very much intermixed. Here and there there are grassy balks between adjacent properties ; and in places the growth of bushes on these has almost made them into hedges, but as a rule there is no boundary between strips belonging to different holdings and different properties. A road through the open fields at one point cuts off the end of a strip of land belonging to Lord Salisbury from the rest of that strip ; it forms a triangular plot too small to repay the trouble of bringing the plough across the road to plough it ; and the men who hold the adjoining land revere the rights of property too much to touch it ; it therefore remains a refuge for all manner of weeds.

As in Clothall, no common rights are exercised over the common fields of Bygrave by the poor of the parish, nor could I hear of any tradition of rights belonging to the poor or to cottagers. But the different occupiers of land in the common fields have, and exercise, the right of shackage, *i.e.*, of grazing cattle after harvest, over one another's holdings. And the lord of the manor has a special right of " sheep-walk " over the whole, for a month, from the first week in May and October. This right is let with one of the farms. It is not actually exercised, because the other occupiers of lands in the open field buy exemption.

The hamlet of Luffenhall, also near Clothall, has " shack lands " held under similar conditions.

The next parish to Clothall on the east, Wallington, is also unenclosed. It has a small common on which cottagers have the right to keep a cow and a calf, but so far as the rest of the parish is concerned, the only surviving feature of the externals of the common field system is the wide, breezy stretch of open land, under wheat, roots and grass; and of the spirit of the " village community " there is nothing. There are but two farms ; the wages paid are only 10s. to 12s. per week. Such wages, so near London, naturally fail to keep the labourers in the village; and the population is now (1903) less than 100, though the church has seats for 260. As the men go, more and more land is laid down in grass, and machinery is more and more used; the absence of hedges of course facilitates the use of certain kinds of agricultural machinery. The unenclosed parish of Wallington, in fact, represents in an extreme degree the triumph of all those tendencies against which the opponents of enclosure waged war—great farms, absolute dependence of the labourer, low wages, rural depopulation.

SUTTON (NORTHAMPTONSHIRE).

The parish of Castor, or Caister, includes, besides the hamlets of Castor and Ailesworth, the enclosure of which has been described, the townships of Sutton and Upton. Sutton had not at the time of the enclosure of Castor and Ailesworth been legally enclosed, and the parish is described from the tithe map as consisting of 450 acres of common field and 150 acres of common, out of a total of 888 acres. The vicar, who had bought nearly all the land in the parish, and also the manorial rights, in 1899 applied for an Act of Enclosure, which he obtained in 1901. There were in Sutton certain lands belonging to the township, intermixed with those in private ownership. The rents of these were paid with the poor rates. Up till 1880 the two farmers who between them occupied nearly the whole of the cultivated land, used to confer every year and agree upon their course of tillage. They were then persuaded by the vicar to disentangle their farms, and cultivate them in the ordinary way. At that time there ceased to be in Sutton any visible sign of any exceptional features in the system of landownership. The lands belonging to the township are recorded in the tithe map, and their measurement in the tithe award, but no balks to mark them are preserved.

I am indebted to the vicar of Sutton for the following illustration of the possible evils of the common field system. It occurred in a parish where he had formerly been resident, which he did not name.

In this parish two adjacent strips of land were occupied respectively by a farmer and a shoemaker. The farmer, who was a careful and diligent cultivator, having well manured and laboured his strip, sowed it with wheat, and as harvest approached saw the prospect of an exceptionally good crop. The shoemaker left his strip entirely untouched. But when the farmer was about to begin to reap, the shoemaker intervened, and claimed that the strip which was cultivated was his, and the untilled strip belonged to the farmer. The field jury was summoned, and the extreme positiveness and assurance of the shoemaker carried the day, and the shoemaker reaped the wheat. The farmer then begged his successful adversary for some compensation for his lost labour and expense, but was told that he might consider himself lucky not to be prosecuted for trespass. The farmer then proceeded to make the best of his bad bargain, and set to work to plough up the weeds and thistles that covered the strip of land awarded him. But as he ploughed he continually turned up pieces of leather, corners wasted in cutting out "uppers," and other refuse of a shoemaker's workshop. These he collected and brought before the field jury. The previous decision was then reversed and the shoemaker was compelled to make restitution to the man he had wronged.

ELMSTONE HARDWICKE (GLOUCESTER).

Elmstone Hardwicke is an extremely interesting example of the common field system in a state of natural decay. Very nearly the whole parish belongs to the Ecclesiastical Commissioners, but the holdings are intermixed and in small parcels, over a large part, perhaps 1000 acres, of the parish, the farms having been granted on leases of three lives. The farmers would be glad to consolidate their holdings and enclose, but the Ecclesiastical Commissioners effectually discourage this, as I was told, by exorbitant demands for increase of rent. On the other hand, I was informed that the Commissioners themselves desired to enclose, but did not care for the expense of proceeding by Act of Parliament, and they were endeavouring to obtain their object by refusing to "re-life," in order that the leases might fall in, and be converted into leases for short terms that might be made to terminate simultaneously. Thus an old farmer who had a lease of 60 acres in 100 different parcels scattered over the common fields, informed me of the negotiations that had been entered into with him. He was by no means disposed to readily part with his lease, as he had two good lives remaining, both being his nephews, one aged 40 and the other 50. "They'll both mak' 'ighty," he said, that being his own age, though he looked a score of years younger.

This one farmer still (in 1899) followed what had been the customary course of cultivation for the parish—a four years course of wheat, beans, wheat, fallow; this being a modification of a still earlier course of wheat, beans, barley, fallow, the soil being more suitable to wheat than to barley. The other farmers followed no fixed rule, each one cultivating his farm as he chose, subject, however, to the right that was still recognised and exercised, that each occupier could turn horses, cattle and sheep on to the common fields after harvest until the first of November. In consequence of the abandonment of the traditional course of cultivation the common use of the fallow-field has been dropped by general consent, for the last forty or fifty years. The institution of the field jury has also disappeared; though the above-mentioned old farmer still posts the notices declaring the fields open or closed, and so may be said to fill the post of " foreman of the fields," he does so by right of inheritance rather than of election, in succession to his father.

Various controversies have arisen recently in Elmstone Hardwicke with regard to the rights of various persons interested. I have referred above to the case of the farmer who, in the spring of 1899, occupying a "headland" in the common fields on which various strips belonging to his neighbours abutted, instead of following the customary practice and waiting to plough till the last, ploughed his headland before the abutting lands were ploughed, and then sued for damages when his neighbours turned their ploughs on his land.

Another farmer who occupied a very small holding in Elmstone

Hardwicke, and a much larger holding in an adjoining parish, made a practice of turning great numbers of sheep on the Elmstone Hardwicke common fields in the open time, which he was able to keep in the close time on his other land. The question arose whether this unfair procedure was lawful. The coming into force of the Parish Councils Act of 1894 also had the effect of suggesting enquiries into the claims of labourers to share in common-right privileges.

The vicar, the Rev. George Bayfield Roberts, accordingly obtained the opinion of Sir Walter Phillimore on the subject. It was as follows:—

"As far as I can gather from the facts laid before me, I think that every freeholder and copyholder has a right to turn cattle upon every part of the common field, and that the right is not confined to the particular field or part of the common field in which he holds land.

"This right passes to the tenant or occupier under each freeholder or copyholder. The tenant, or occupier, has it, not in his own right but merely as claiming under his landlord.

"I know of no rule of law which would give this right to farmers as such, and deny it to cottagers as such, if the latter have holdings on which they can keep their beasts during close time. But the right to turn on to Lammas lands (as this common field is) can only be exercised in respect of beasts used in the cultivation or manuring of the holding in respect of which the claim is made (*Baylis* v. *Tyssen-Amhurst*, Law Reports 6 Ch. D. p. 500).

"As the cottagers are said to be tenants of the farmers, the latter can make it clear in all future lettings that they do not let with the cottages the right to pasture in the common field.

"(2) The tenant of the Barn farm should keep his land unenclosed during open time, and anyone who has a right to turn on cattle can sue him if he obstructs (*Stoneham* v. *London and Brighton Railway Co.*, Law Reports 7 Q. B. p. 1), or can pull down the fencing (*Arlett* v. *Ellis*, 7 B. & C. p. 346).

"(2a). I do not think it would be wise to pull down a whole fence, or sue for the damage caused by the fence, if substantial and easy openings were made during open time. But there is some authority for saying that the whole fence must be removed (*Arlett* v. *Ellis*, cited above).

" (3) The only *locus standi* for the Parish Meeting is, if it has been given by the County Council all the powers of a Parish Council under section 19, sub-section 10, of the Local Government Act, 1894 (56 & 57 Vict. c. 73), to apply to the Board of Agriculture under section 9 of the Commons Act, 1876 (39 & 40 Vict. c. 56).

" This power is given to Parish Councils by section 8, sub-section c, of the Local Government Act, 1894.

" Section 9 of the Commons Act, 1876, enables the Inclosure Commissioners (whose place is now taken by the Board of Agriculture) to give information and direction ' upon application' in order to bring about ' the regulation of Commons '; and for this purpose Lammas lands are included as Commons, as they also came under the Inclosure Acts.

" By section 3 a Provisional Order made by the Board for ' regulation ' may provide for the ' adjustment of rights,' and section 4 shows how much can be done upon such an adjustment."

This opinion was given in March, 1897. The very significant passage which pointed out that since the cottagers held their cottages from the farmers, they could not effectively claim any rights which the farmers did not choose to grant them, threw cold water on the agitation.

Elmstone Hardwicke is apparently another case in which something would be gained and nothing lost by an Act of Enclosure.

EWELME (OXFORDSHIRE).

Rather more than half this parish, near Wallingford, is legally in the condition of open common fields, and there is besides a very extensive " cow-common " on which is a golf course. The neighbouring parishes of Bensington [1] and Berwick

---

[1] The Vicar of Bensington has the custody of a remarkable eighteenth century map of the three intermixed parishes.

Salome had until 1852 common fields which were in part inter-mixed with those of Ewelme, and there were commons common-able to all three parishes. In 1852 an Act was passed which was carried into effect in 1863 for the enclosure of Bensington and Berwick Salome, and the parts of Ewelme which were inter-mixed with these. Ewelme is owned by a number of small proprietors who chiefly farm their own land. These made a voluntary division,[1] but they still enjoy certain rights of common and of shooting over one another's land. No labourers enjoy rights of common.

There are two significant facts about this parish.

In the first place, one particular farm enjoys a special right of pasturing sheep on the cow-common, not shared by other farms. This is significant when taken into consideration with the facts for Cambridgeshire and elsewhere related below.

Secondly, this gives a typical instance of the effect of enclosure of *commonable waste* on the poor. One of the commons enclosed was known as the "Furze Common," and it supplied the poor of the neighbourhood with their fuel, for *every* inhabitant had the right of cutting furze on it. After enclosure the Furze Common was allotted to one man, who allowed no trespass on it, and the *owners* of cottages were awarded allotments of land in considera-tion of rights which the *cottagers* had exercised. The lands so allotted became part of ordinary farms, and the poor simply lost their supply of fuel without any compensation whatever. This was done under the sanction, not of an Enclosure Act rushed through Parliament before 1845, but of the Enclosure Commis-sioners, appointed expressly to prevent any injury to the class least able to guard its own interests, as well as to facilitate enclosure.

---

[1] Exchanges of land in common fields so as to enable proprietors to consolidate their properties are authorised by 4 & 5 Will. IV. c. 30.

CHAPTER V.

To catch the spirit of the common field system, to see that system no mere historical survival, but developing in harmony with modern needs, one must go to the Isle of Axholme. Starting from Doncaster eastwards, through somewhat devious roads, one descends gradually to a wide belt of reclaimed fen. Between this fen on the west, and the river Trent with more fen on the east, is a ridge of low hills, comprising the four large parishes of Haxey, Epworth, Belton and Owston. These constitute the Isle of Axholme—an island, indeed, up to the time of the great drainage operations of Vermuyden in the reign of James I. It was, no doubt, a very ancient home of fishermen and fowlers, who gradually brought the island itself into cultivation, using the plough as a subsidiary means of subsistence. The strenuous opposition offered by the people of Axholme to the work of the Dutch engineer is well known. Even after they were beaten, and the greatest drainage scheme of the seventeenth century was carried through, the four Axholme parishes retained extensive fens, used as common pastures.

When in the eighteenth century the great trade of driving Scotch cattle to the London market, in which Sir Walter Scott's grandfather was a pioneer, sprang up, the route followed diverged from the great north road in Yorkshire, in order to avoid turnpikes, and the cattle, grazing as they slowly plodded southwards, and fattening on the roadsides, came through Selby, Snaith and the Isle of Axholme. To protect their fields the islanders hedged them along the roadsides, leaving only narrow thoroughfares; then, to make these thoroughfares passable for themselves, they laid down for footpath a stone pavement which still exists for twenty miles. But the old hedges have in many places disappeared, so that the fields lie open to the road; and in particular, the gates which then guarded every entrance to the fields are now generally represented by gaps.

At the end of the eighteenth century by far the greater part of the island proper was in the condition of open arable fields, with properties and holdings intermixed, as in the open fields of Laxton; though near each village there were enclosed gardens, and closes of pasture. It would appear that the original system of cultivation was a four-year course of husbandry, so that one-fourth of the arable land was at any time fallow, and used as common pasture, and common rights were exercised on two of the other three-fourths after harvest; one-fourth probably being under turnips. On the margin of the hill there were perhaps commonable meadows, though I cannot trace them. Beyond, the common fens and marshes, used mainly for grazing horned cattle, extended over an area of about 14,000 acres.

Arthur Young visited the island at this time, and thus describes it:

"In respect of property, I know nothing more singular respecting it (the County of Lincoln), than its great division in the Isle of Axholm. In most of the towns there, for it is not quite general, there is much resemblance of some rich parts of France and Flanders. The inhabitants are collected in villages and hamlets; and almost every house you see, except very poor cottages on the borders of commons, is inhabited by a farmer, the proprietor of his farm, of from four or five, and even fewer, to 20, 40, and more acres, scattered about the open fields, and cultivated with all that minutiae of care and anxiety, by the hands of the family, which are found abroad, in the countries mentioned. They are very poor respecting money, but very happy respecting their mode of existence. Contrivance, mutual assistance, by barter and hire, enable them to manage these little farms, though they break all rules of rural proportion. A man will keep a pair of horses that has but 3 or 4 acres by means of vast commons and working for hire.

"The enclosure of these commons will lessen their numbers and vastly increase the quantity of products at market. Their

cultivated land being of uncommon fertility, a farm of 20 acres
supports a family very well, as they have, generally speaking, no
fallows, but an endless succession of corn, potatoes, flax,
beans, etc.   They do nearly all their work themselves, and are
passionately fond of buying a bit of land.   Though I have said
they are happy, yet I should note that it was remarked to me,
that the little proprietors work like Negroes, and do not live so
well as the inhabitants of the poor-house; but all is made
amends for by possessing land." [1]

In 1795 the chief landowners took steps to obtain an Act for
enclosing all four parishes.   There were stronger reasons for
enclosing than in the majority of the East Yorkshire and
Lincolnshire parishes all around, in which Parliamentary
enclosure was being pushed furiously on, for the fens were
capable of enormous improvement.   But in the Isle of Axholme
it was not possible for the chief landowners to overbear the
opposition of the villagers.   One peculiar feature of the locality
was that every cottage had a common right, and there were no
rights attached to land apart from cottages.   This fact, and the
peculiarly wide distribution of property, caused the decision to
rest with the peasantry.   They raised no objection to the
division and drainage of the marshes, perceiving that their
allotments would be far more valuable after drainage than their
common rights before ; so this part of the scheme was generally
agreed to.   But on the question of the enclosure of the arable
fields they were not complacent.   They saw that the expense
of hedging a small allotment would be heavy, and the injury done
by the hedge to a small plot, of say 1 or 2 acres, by shading the land
and sheltering it from the wind would more than counterbalance
the advantage of having that holding in one piece instead of in
two or three, to say nothing of the loss of the space given up to
hedges.   They also probably feared that the arable land, if
enclosed, would largely be laid down to grass, and so the benefit
of an increased demand for labour and higher wages promised
by the enclosure of the marshes would be lost, at least in some

---

[1] " Agricultural Survey of Lincolnshire," p. 17.

degree, through the enclosure of the fields. Accordingly the
necessary consent of a "three-fourths majority in number and
value" of the owners was not obtained, and the proposal to
enclose was defeated. It would appear that all the educated,
intelligent, and influential people did their best to overcome
this "ignorant prejudice." But on the other hand there were
the votes of all those cottagers who did not as yet possess strips
in the common fields, but who hoped to be able to purchase them.
They saw that while thousands of acres of land lay immediately
round the villages in acre, half-acre, and rood strips, there was a
chance of buying one, and so taking the first upward step from
the rank of the landless labourer. On enclosure those strips
would give place to closes of at least several acres each, and the
closes would be quite out of their reach. Blind, obstinate,
wilful, and prejudiced as the villagers seemed to their betters,
the event shows that they were entirely accurate in their view of
the situation.

Arthur Young's account of these proceedings is as follows :
"In the Isle of Axholm there is an immense inclosure on the
point of beginning, the Act and survey having been passed of no
less than 12,000 acres of commons in the four parishes of Haxey,
Hepworth, Belton, and Owston. I passed these commons in
various quarters, and rode purposely to view some parts ; they
are in a wretched and unprofitable state, but valued, if inclosed,
in the ideas of the islanders at 10s. or 11s. an acre.

In Haxey there are 305 claims on account of 3810 acres.

,, Hepworth	,,	236	,,	,,	2285 acres.
,, Belton	,,	251	,,	,,	3664 acres.
,, Owston	,,	229	,,	,,	4446 acres.

"*Cottage rights are claims, but lands without a cottage have
none.* It was a barbarous omission that when the Act was
procured they resisted a clause to divide the open arable fields
subject to rights of common. But they have here, by a custom,
a right of inclosure which is singular ; every man that pleases
may enclose his own open field land notwithstanding the rights
of common upon it while open ; and accordingly many do it

when, by purchase, they get five or six acres together, of which I saw many examples." ("Agricultural Survey of Lincolnshire," p. 79.)

Somewhat later a second attempt was made in the parish of Owston to obtain an enclosure with partial success. Three of the four fields were divided and enclosed : but the same motives which prevented the enclosure of the four parishes at the previous attempt were strong enough to secure that one field should remain open. It was in 1811, I was locally informed, that the Owston Enclosure took place. I can find no record of the Act.

As we saw above, the old system (probably a four-field course) of cultivation had dropped into disuse even before the beginning of the nineteenth century, but still, up to about the year 1850, the custom remained that on one of the four fields, that under wheat, after the crops had been carried, the "Pindar" gave notice that "the fields are to be broken," and over that field common rights of pasture were exercised for about a month, from some day in October to Martinmas (November 23rd). Then the Pindar kept watch over the grazing animals night and day, and by night built up enormous bonfires, with all the boys of the village clustering round and roasting potatoes.

But about 1850 even this custom disappeared, and now every holder of lands in the open fields cultivates them as he chooses, but they must be under some form of tillage as long as they remain open. But the tendency, observed by Arthur Young, for the larger owners of lands in the common fields to buy, sell and exchange strips with other owners with the object of getting some half-dozen acres in one continuous piece and then enclosing them, has continued up to the present day. Such enclosures are laid down in grass, and in this way the area of the open fields has gradually been reduced.

The strips of land in the open fields are known as "selions," the auctioneers' notices of a sale reading, "All that selion piece of land," etc. They are also known as "acres," "half-acres," "roods," etc., but these terms must not be taken as exactly defining their area. A nominal acre varies in area from a minimum of about half an acre to a maximum of an acre and a

half. As the half-acres and roods similarly vary, it follows that
the largest "half-acres" are bigger than the smallest "acres."

The general aspect of the fields is well shown in the photo-
graph taken for me by Mr. Newbit, of Epworth. I asked in a
bar-parlour in Haxey, "Are these allotments both sides of the
road?" A labourer answered, "Yes, but there are seven miles
of these allotments." But the publican corrected him. "Well,
it's not allotments exactly, it's *a very old system*, that's what it
is." Further conversation with one man and another gave me
a strong impression that the people of Axholme are proud of
their "very old system." That they have some reason to be
proud of it Mr. Rider Haggard bears witness:

"The Isle of Axholme is one of the few places I have visited
in England which may be called, at any rate in my opinion,
truly prosperous in an agricultural sense, the low price of
produce notwithstanding, chiefly because of its assiduous
cultivation of the potato."[1]

Axholme may be described as a district of allotments, cultivated, and in great part owned, by a working peasantry. The
"assiduous cultivation of the potato" is rather an indication of
the real strength of Axholme agriculture, than a true explanation
of it. At the time of Arthur Young's visit, the isle was noted
for the cultivation of flax and hemp; and this continued to be a
feature of the local agriculture till about thirty or forty years
ago, when the "assiduous cultivation of the potato" succeeded
it. Now, as Mr. Rider Haggard notices, experiments are carried
on with celery. The small holders, I was assured on all sides,
cultivate the land much more thoroughly than large farmers do
their farms, and the very look of the crops confirmed this
eloquently, even to my unskilled observation. Mr. Rider
Haggard quotes a local expert, Mr. William Standring, as
saying, "Wheat crops in the isle *averaged seven quarters* (56
bushels) an acre, the oats nine or ten quarters, the clover hay,
which grew luxuriantly, two or three tons an acre, and the roots
were splendid." He continues, "That Mr. William Standring

[1] "Rural England," Vol. II., p. 186.

did not exaggerate the capacities of the isle, I can testify, as the crops I saw there were wonderfully fine throughout, particularly the potatoes, which are perhaps its mainstay." [1]

The secret of the agricultural success of Axholme is clearly *la carrière ouverte aux talens,* which is secured to agricultural labourers by the open fields. The spirited and successful cultivation of varying crops follows naturally.

How the upward ladder is used, was well explained by a Mr. John Standring, himself a holder of ten acres, before the Select Committee of the House of Commons on Small Holdings in 1889.

It is first to be noticed, however, that the general level of wage is exceptionally high for a purely agricultural district at a considerable distance from any considerable town. The customary wage, I was informed in 1903, was 3s. per day. Mr. Rider Haggard, in 1901, found it "2s. 9d. a day for day men, 18s. a week for horsemen, and 16s. a week, with cottage, for garth-men. Men living in the house with foremen and owners receive about £24 per annum and food, and horsemen £30 per annum and food."

But when the labourer who has been living in marries and takes a cottage, he also takes up a holding in the fields. He begins with one "land," then takes a second, a third, and so on. The following table, showing the way in which land is held in the parish of Epworth, was submitted to the Select Committee [2] by Mr. J. Standring :—

Of holdings over 200 acres there are 2 occupiers.

,,	,,	100	,,	and under 200, there are 12 occupiers.
,,	,,	50	,,	,, 100 ,, 14 ,,
,,	,,	20	,,	,, 50 ,, 31 ,,
,,	,,	10	,,	,, 20 ,, 40 ,,
,,	,,	2	,,	,, 10 ,, 115 ,,
,,	,,	½	,,	,, 2 ,, 80 ,,

The eighty holders occupying from half an acre to two acres would all be men in regular employment, as a rule, agricultural

---

[1] " Rural England," Vol. II., p. 194.   [2] Report, p. 189.

labourers. A body of these sent their deposition to the Select Committee in the following form:—

" We, the undersigned, being agricultural labourers at Epworth, are in occupation of allotments or small holdings, varying from 2 roods to 3 acres, willingly testify to the great benefit we find from our holdings. Where we have sufficient quantity of land to grow 2 roods each of wheat, barley and potatoes, we have bread, bacon, and potatoes for a great part of the year, enabling us to face a long winter without the dread of hunger or pauperism staring us in the face."

But the more enterprising of these labourers do not rest content with so small a holding, and these pass into the next class, those who hold up to 10 acres. "Many such," says Mr. J. Standring, "keep a horse and a cow and a few pigs. And on some of the stronger land two or three of these will yoke their horses together and work their own land, and also land belonging to other men similarly situated who do not keep horses. As a rule they have done very well—I scarcely know a failure." The payment for horse-hire is usually made in labour.

The most successful of these again recruit the ranks of the larger farmers. " I do not believe there is one in ten in my parish, and in the adjoining parish, among those who are renting from 50 to 100 acres, but what, in my time, has been an agricultural labourer or an agricultural servant before he was married ; and each of them, to my own knowledge, has commenced with two or three acres, and in some cases not more than one acre . . . . one man who is now occupying 200 acres was a labourer in his early days."

These bigger farmers sometimes move elsewhere, and take larger farms, or bring up their sons in other occupations than farming, so that the farm of 150 to 200 acres becomes again available for division into small holdings. Thus, in spite of the continual growth of the holding occupied by individual men at different stages in their career, the average size of holdings does not show any tendency to increase. This is well shown by the figures given for Epworth, respectively, by Arthur Young and Mr. J. Standring, at about an interval of a hundred years.

There were only 236 claimants of allotments in the Epworth commons at the end of the eighteenth century; in 1889 there were 291 occupiers of the 5741 acres in the parish, occupying therefore, on an average, less than 20 acres each.

The same eagerness to own land which Arthur Young noticed has also continued to prevail. Land is bought on the building society principle, money for the purpose being borrowed usually at 5 per cent. per annum, very frequently through the lawyer who conducts the sale. In the days of agricultural prosperity land in the open fields of Haxey, Epworth, and Belton was sold at £130 per acre; land in the one remaining open field of Owston as high as £140 per acre. Even now, in spite of the tremendous fall in price of agricultural produce, the ordinary price is about £70 to £75 per acre; which is about twenty-five years' purchase of the rent.

It is obvious that a man who borrows money at 5 per cent. to buy land which can only be let at 4 per cent. on the purchase price embarks on a speculation which from the purely commercial point of view, can only be profitable provided the land is appreciating in value. There were naturally cases of men who, at the time when prices were falling most rapidly, were unable to keep up their payments of interest and instalments of principal, and who had in consequence, after a severe struggle, to forfeit their partially won property. At this time the Isle of Axholme won the evil repute of being "the paradise of lawyers." But it would, I believe, be fair to say that the peasantry on the whole stood the strain of agricultural depression exceptionally well, and that their prosperity, with steadier prices, revived exceptionally quickly.

The Isle of Axholme has been singularly successful in preserving the spirit of the common field system—social equality, mutual helpfulness, and an industrial aim directed rather towards the maximum gross produce of food than towards the maximum net profit; while at the same time it has discarded those features of the system which would have been obstacles to agricultural progress. The "barbarous omission" to enclose the open arable fields has been abundantly justified.

Soham.

The parish of Soham, in Cambridgeshire, is another example of a great development of small holdings in connection with the persistence of open arable fields. This parish, unlike most Cambridgeshire parishes, has never been enclosed by Act of Parliament, and the tithe map indicates the survival of about 1100 acres of common field and 456 acres of common in a total of 12,706 acres. Since the tithe commutation the area of common has shrunk to about 236 acres, but from the Ordnance map it appears that there is still a very large area of open field land in four large fields, known as North Field, Clipsatt Field, No Ditch Field, and Down Field ; and a smaller one, Bancroft Field. Mr. Charles Bidwell gave the Special Committee on Small Holdings (1889) the following account of holdings in this parish :—

Under 1 acre	...	...	...	...	195	holdings.
Over 1 and under 5 acres		...		...	77	,,
,, 5 ,, 10 ,,		...		...	34	,,
,, 10 ,, 20 ,,		...		...	43	,,
,, 20 ,, 50 ,,		...		...	57	,,
,, 50 ,, 100 ,,		...		...	32	,,
,, 100 ,, 200 ,,		...		...	6	,,
,, 200 ,, 500 ,,		...		...	8	,,
,, 500 ,, — ,,		...		...	5	,,

(Appendix, p. 501.)

Thus the total area of the parish is held by 457 occupiers, who therefore hold, on an average, 28 acres each. In this case it is stated that the occupiers of the smallest holdings derive considerable benefit from the common. A German enquirer who visited Soham as an example of an unenclosed parish, found it less poverty stricken than the other parishes in the neighbourhood, on account, he was told, of the existence of the common pastures. (W. Hasbach, Die englischen Landarbeiter, 1894.)

Weston Zoyland.

The idea occurs to one, whether it would not have been possible to secure by an Act of Enclosure for a common field,

the abolition of common rights which hindered each farmer
or peasant from cultivating his holding to the best of his
ability, and the laying together of the scattered strips which
formed each holding, without ruining the small proprietors and
small farmers, or encouraging the laying down of tilled land
under pasture.

We find *one* example of such an attempt. The parish of
Weston Zoyland, in Somerset, in 1797 enclosed 644 acres of
commonable pasture, and at that time and in that neighbourhood
the enclosure of Sedgemoor was being rapidly pushed on, as
rapidly, in fact, as the local farmers could be induced to take up
the land. Perhaps in consequence of this quenching of the land
hunger of the farmers with capital, when in 1830 it was resolved
to deal with the common fields, the Act took the form of one for
dividing and allotting, but not enclosing, Weston Field. The
consequence is that this great field of 500 acres still remains open
and unenclosed ; the land is specially fertile, there are an exceptionally large number of small properties in it, and it is all kept
under tillage. I am informed that one of the first acts of the
Weston Zoyland Parish Council, when, on coming into existence,
it took over the custody of the parish maps and documents, was
to re-define the roads that passed through the field, in accordance with the Commissioners' map and award.

CHAPTER VI.

UPTON ST. LEONARDS (NEAR GLOUCESTER).

THIS enclosure took place at the same time as that of Castor and Ailesworth, and was completed in 1899. The common fields consisted of 1120 strips of arable land, total area 520 acres, and the "balks" or "meres" separating the strips were estimated at 14 acres. There were more than eighty owners.

No recognised course of husbandry had been followed for about sixty years previously. It is believed that before that time a four-year course obtained, but when mangel wurzels were introduced to the neighbourhood the recurring fallow was discontinued. The right of common after harvest was, however, still maintained. If any cultivator chose he might grow turnips, but he did so at his own risk, and had to keep a boy to guard them from the opening of the fields to the time they could be pulled. Old mere stones are found in the meadows of this parish, and various local traditions remain belonging, apparently, to a period when the village customs resembled those described for Stratton and Grimstone.

TOTTERNHOE (BEDFORDSHIRE).

The Enclosure Act was passed in 1886, and the award is dated 1891. Before enclosure Totternhoe was a typical open-field parish ; there were only 370 acres of old enclosure, to 1797 acres of common field arable, and 193 acres of common. The situation of Totternhoe is like that of Clothall, on the steep northern slope of the Hertfordshire chalk hills, which here have an almost mountainous appearance. The greater part of the parish was in the ownership of the lord of the manor, but there were forty

owners of land altogether, the others being chiefly yeomen. The
movement for enclosure came from these yeomen. They took this
step in order to protect themselves against the tenants of the
lord of the manor, who, whether from ignorance or otherwise,
endeavoured to prevent the exercise of well-known rights of
common over land in their occupation. The hill top was saved
as an open space, and is a favourite picnic resort for the people
of Dunstable. Recreation grounds and land for allotments were
also set out, as has been the rule since the passing of the
Commons Act of 1876. I asked one of the yeomen, who had
taken a leading part in bringing about the enclosure, whether it
had benefited the parish. He said undoubtedly it had done so,
but "the parish has not recovered from it yet." Questioned as
to how this could be, he gave me to understand that the actual
increase to the cultivators in annual value was not equal to the
interest on the capital expended on carrying out the enclosure;
that the assessment had gone up, and the burden of rates and
taxes was consequently increased. The land allotted to the
lord of the manor still, in the summer of 1900, was mainly unenclosed, and one could get something of the impression of
the "champion" country, an impression of great open fields
sweeping up to bare downs.

North and South Luffenham and Barrowden (Rutland).

The first steps towards the enclosure of these three parishes
were made immediately after the passing of the 1876 Act; the
Enclosure Act was passed in 1878, and the awards were made
in 1881 and 1882. Out of 5480 acres in the three parishes,
4800 were common-field arable, a heath claimed by both Barrowden and South Luffenham occupied 390 acres, and much of the
remainder was commonable meadow and pasture. Two systems
of cultivation obtained. Part of the land being heavy clay was
on a three years' course of wheat, beans, etc., and fallow, as at
Laxton and Eakring; the lighter land was under a six years'
course. The report of the Enclosure Commissioners says of
Barrowden that the 1240 acres of arable land "is divided in

2790 strips, some not more than 12 feet wide, each divided from
its neighbour by a green balk, which is a nursery of weeds."
Old farmers, however, assured me that the balks were mostly
gone before enclosure. Field reeves were elected, and they
settled any dispute that arose in consequence of the absence of
balks, and individual farmers quickly detected, by pacing across
their strips, if a furrow had been appropriated by a neighbour.

Here, again, I asked whether the enclosure had been a benefit,
and I was told that the labourers had benefited by the allotments and recreation grounds ; that the lord of the manor of
South Luffenham had benefited, because he got the disputed
moor, but that farmers, as farmers, had gained nothing, and as
common-right owners they had lost through the enclosure of
the moor.

Enclosure in this case originated in what may be called the
normal way, *i.e.*, on the initiative of the lords of the manors. It
was the doubtful ownership of the Barrowden and Luffenham
moor which had until 1876 prevented enclosure ; then the
respective lords agreed to combine to obtain an enclosure of all
three parishes, and let the Commissioners determine to which
parish the moor belonged. It was awarded to Luffenham, but
the Luffenham freeholders lost it just as much as those of
Barrowden ; it is now the private property of the lord of the
manor.

Ham Field.

A curious case of enclosure by Act of Parliament uncon-
nected with the General Enclosure Acts is that of Ham Field
by the "Richmond, Petersham and Ham Open Spaces Act,
1902" (2 Edward VII., c. ccliii.). It is entitled, "An Act
to confirm agreements for vesting common and other land
in the local authorities of the districts of Richmond and Ham,
and the Surrey County Council as public open spaces, and for
other purposes." But while it does incidentally confirm these
agreements, the "other purposes" comprise the main object of
the bill, which is to allow the owners of Ham Common, of whom

the Earl of Dysart is the principal, to enclose Ham Common Field, and convert it into building land.

The preamble is similarly misleading. The first sentence runs, " Whereas the prospect from Richmond Hill over the valley of the Thames is of great natural beauty, and agreements have been entered into with a view to preventing building on certain lands hereinafter mentioned "—a sentence admirably framed to disguise the fact that the effect of the Act is to extinguish the common rights over Ham Field which had previously prevented building, and so to convert the middle distance of the famous view from Richmond Hill into an expanse of roofs, perhaps of villa-residences, and perhaps—— !

The agreements recited in the Act represent the consideration for which the public authorities mentioned bartered away the beauty of the view. Kingston Corporation gets nine acres for a cricket field ; Richmond Corporation is confirmed in the ownership of Petersham Meadows, which was formerly a subject of dispute, and acquires a strip of land along the river ; and the Surrey County Council acquires 45 acres of riverside land. The meadows and riverside land in each case are to be maintained as open spaces by the authorities. Ham itself merely gets the freehold of Ham Common, which means, in effect, that what slight danger there might have been of the enclosure of this part of the open and commonable land of the parish is removed.

The Earl of Dysart, at the cost of a sacrifice that is probably apparent rather than real, obtains by this Act the right to convert some 200 acres of arable common field into a valuable building estate ; the smaller owners acquire a similar right without any compensating sacrifice at all ; and the only losers by this profitable transaction are the people of London, who were not consulted in the matter.

MERROW.

The parish of Merrow, adjoining Guildford on the east, is stated in the return of 1873 to have had 350 acres of common field. The land in question covers the lower slopes of the chalk hill, the higher portion of which is Merrow Down ; beneath it is Clandon Park, the seat of Lord Onslow. Up to about the year 1873 this common field did exist; the properties of Lord Onslow, the chief proprietor, were very much intermixed with those of smaller proprietors ; the farm holdings were similarly intermixed with one another, and with a number of strips of land occupied by labourers and cultivated as allotments. But no common rights were exercised over these lands, either by the occupiers over one another's lands, or by the villagers, within living memory ; nor, except that the whole of the field was in tillage, was there any common rule for its cultivation. The existence of a great extent of common is in itself a sufficient explanation of the disappearance of common rights over the tilled land.

In 1870 the present Lord Onslow came into the property, and when a year or two later he attained his majority, he proceeded to consolidate his property in Merrow Field, by buying out the other proprietors, or giving them land elsewhere in exchange. The field is still bare of hedges, and under tillage ; but enclosure, in the technical sense, has been completely carried without an Act of Parliament.

Since the enclosure the allotments, which had been numerous, have generally been given up ; but the labourers do not attribute this to the enclosure, but to the industrial evolution. " There are no farmers nowadays, only land spoilers. They've turned market gardeners, and they sell *milk* " (with intense scorn). " The land ought to grow beef, and barley to make good beer, that's what Englishmen want,—yes, and wheat to make bread. But now they all grow garden stuff, what's the good of an allotment to a man ? If you have anything to sell, you can't sell it. It's no good growing any more than you can eat."

It may be added that along the river Wey, from Guildford down to Byfleet, there are some very extensive lammas meadows, known by such names as Broad Mead and Hook Mead. The holdings in these are intermixed, individual pieces sometimes not exceeding an acre.

Steventon and the Berkshire Downs.

That part of Berkshire which lies between the valley of the
Kennet and the Thames would appear, from the return of 1873,
to be specially rich in surviving open fields.   The Blue Book
assigns to

Brightwell	1000	acres of common field.	
West Hagbourne... ...	550	,,	,,
East Hendred	2794	,,	,,
West Hendred	1900	,,	,,
East Ilsley	1400	,,	,,
Wallingford St. Leonard...	570	,,	,,
Yattenden	252	,,	,,

As Brightwell was enclosed in 1811, and East Hendred in
1801, the statement with regard to these two parishes plainly is
incredible ; but in view of the undeniable fact that Steventon,
which lies almost in the centre of this district, was not enclosed
till 1883, there seemed so much possibility of survivals in the
other parishes that in July, 1904, I traversed the whole district
in search of such survivals.   But the search was entirely
unsuccessful ; it was plain that Steventon was at the time of its
enclosure the last remaining example of the old system in this
part.

Here, as in the Hertfordshire district described above, and in
the Wiltshire district dealt with in Chapter X., "Enclosure and
Depopulation," enclosure is one aspect of a change of which the
most vital aspects are the engrossing of farms and the consolidation of properties.   In each parish this movement proceeds
along the line of least resistance ; in one parish all impediments
in the way of the most profitable management of estates are
swept away by the drastic remedy of an Enclosure Act ; in others
they are removed gradually.

The latter method I was enabled, by the help of Mr. Bridges,
to trace in detail in the case of Yattenden.   The Board of
Agriculture return, as we have seen, assigns 252 acres of
common field to Yattenden.   The tithe map, dated 1845, on

which this is based, shows in one corner of "Yattenden Great Field" about 20 acres of intermixed ownership and occupation, forming part of one "furlong," remaining in the characteristic common-field arrangement ; the rest of the so-called "Yattenden Great Field" and "Everington Field" were in part divided into hedged fields, and in part into compact stretches of about 20 acres each, still unhedged, with here and there single acres detached in the midst of them ; many of these single acres being glebe.

An older manorial map, dated 1773, showed that at that date nearly half the parish was open ; the eastern part was already divided into closes, except for a small stretch of lammas meadow, divided into small intermixed holdings, by the river Pang ; but the western part, Yattenden and Everington fields, were almost entirely open, and divided in furlongs, and the furlongs in acre and half-acre strips. These strips on the map are all marked with the letters of the alphabet, to indicate whether they are held by the lord of the manor, by his tenants, or by other owners.

In other words, the process of gradual enclosure, which began before 1773, was continued afterwards, and was nearly complete in 1845. The end came about the year 1858, when Frilsham Common, in an adjoining parish, was enclosed. About half of the intermixed strips in Yattenden Great Field belonged to a yeoman, who was, his brother told me, "a great man for defining his boundaries." The enclosure of Frilsham Common gave the slight stimulus to the mind of Yattenden necessary to evercome its mental inertia, and make change possible, so the yeoman in question was able to effect the exchanges he desired, and others following his example, the lay properties were all separated. But still the glebe consists in part of an acre here and an acre there in the midst of lands belonging to laymen. These are let with the lands in which they lie ; they have no mark to distinguish them, nor boundaries to limit them ; the tithe map and award preserve the record of them, and the vicar receives their rent.

This circumstance of the glebe lying in part in separate

unfenced strips scattered over the parish, let with the lands in
which they lie, and so not influencing the agriculture of the
parish, though testifying to the past system, is by no means
uncommon in the parishes not enclosed by Act of Parliament.[1]

In general the results of the two different methods of enclosure in this district are practically identical. Superficially the
characteristic features of the " champaign " or " champion "
country remain. The population is concentrated in the villages ;
the sites of which appear to have been originally selected for convenience of water supply ; outside the villages are the long sweeps
of open fields of barley, wheat or beans, lying generally open to the
roads, and to one another, and to the open down, though one notices
a tendency to an increased use of wire fencing. The monotony is
broken by the beautiful curves of the hill slopes, and by clumps
of trees ; here and there, on steeper inclines, lynches are clearly
visible, and occasionally what looks like an inconsequent hedge,
beginning and ending in the middle of the field—an old " mere "
or " balk " on which bushes happened to grow.

On the other hand, the farms run generally from 200 to over
1000 acres each ; machinery is extensively used ; the supply of
labour, though not so superabundant as a generation or two ago,
is still sufficient, the customary wage being 2s. per day. The
men themselves struck me as being of finer physique than the
agricultural labourers I have seen in any other part of the South
or Midlands of England ; but they appear to be as completely
shut out from any rights over the land, from any enterprise of
their own upon the land, or from any opportunities for rising
into the farmers' class as can well be conceived. Only one man
whom I met could remember a different condition. He, a
labourer of seventy-three, said that in North Moreton before
the enclosure (completed in 1849) every villager who could get
a cow could keep it in the open fields, and all the villagers also
had rights of cutting fuel. Under the Enclosure Act some

---

[1] Mr. A. N. Palmer, in "Ancient Tenures of Land in the Marches of North
Wales," gives a list of parishes in one Hundred containing, or known to have
contained, "quilleted fields," *i.e.* fields containing strips of land belonging to a
different owner from the rest of the field, these strips being usually glebe.

moneys were set aside to provide the poor with fuel in compensation for these rights, but latterly the amount provided had much diminished.

Steventon, which lies in the centre of this district, is to some extent exceptional. The manor has always been in ecclesiastical hands, from the first time when the village was founded as a settlement from the Abbey of Bec in Normandy to the present day, when it is held by the Ecclesiastical Commissioners. In the intervening period it belonged to Westminster Abbey.

No doubt it was in consequence of this that through the greater part of the nineteenth century, while all the other parishes passed into their present condition of large farms, the farms and properties in Steventon remained small. Up to about 1874 there were some eighteen yeomen farmers in the parish, which comprises 2,382 acres, fully three-quarters at that time being arable. In addition, the lands belonging to the Ecclesiastical Commissioners were divided into small holdings, and all these were intermixed. The system of cultivation was very simple. The arable land was divided into two fields, one known as the " white corn field," growing wheat or barley, the other as the " black corn field," growing pulse or some other crop.

In the severe agricultural depression that followed 1874, culminating in 1879, the yeomen were obliged to borrow in order to continue farming, and they mortgaged their lands to certain gentlemen in the neighbourhood who had money to invest. As one bad season followed another, loan had to be added to loan, till the security was exhausted, and the land passed into the possession of the mortgagee. In this way the number of landowners was reduced to five. Then enclosure, which had been proposed and rejected in the forties, was resolved upon. The Act was obtained in 1880, and the award was made in 1883.

There was considerable disappointment among those who carried out the enclosure at the results. They were surprised and disgusted at the amount of land reserved for allotments and recreation ground ; they were also surprised at the expense, which amounted, I was told, to nearly £10,000. Some were unable to meet the calls upon them, and went bankrupt. But a large portion of the cost was for road-making, and when this had been paid for, the chief advantage which had been gained by the whole proceeding, economy in horse labour, was realised. Where previously it had taken three horses to get a load of manure to a given spot in the open fields, along the tracks assigned for that purpose, one horse could draw the same load to the nearest point on the metalled roadway, and a second horse hitched in front would enable it to reach its destination.

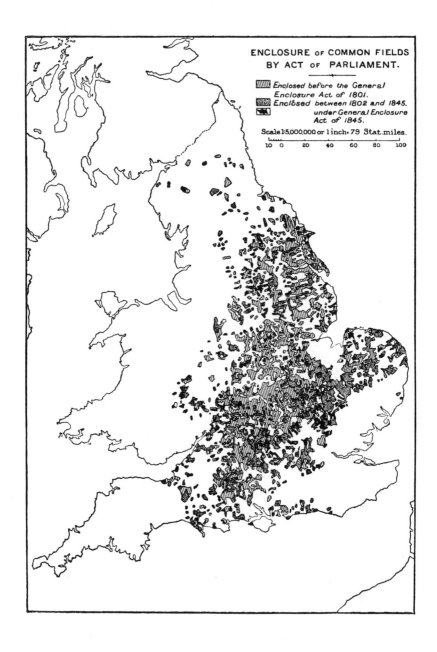

ENCLOSURE of COMMON FIELDS
BY ACT of PARLIAMENT.

Enclosed before the General
Enclosure Act of 1801.
Enclosed between 1802 and 1845.
under General Enclosure
Act of 1845.

Scale 1:5,000,000 or 1 inch - 79 Stat.miles.

10 0   20   40   60   80   100

CHAPTER VII.

A GLANCE at the accompanying Enclosure Map of England
will indicate the importance of common fields in the social life
of rural England at certain dates. It was prepared in the
following manner: On the Ordnance County diagrams each
parish which had an Enclosure Act by which common field
arable was enclosed was coloured; if the Act was passed
between 1700 and 1801 it was coloured yellow; if passed after
the general Enclosure Act of 1801 and before that of 1845, it
was coloured green; if after 1845, purple. A map of England
was drawn summarising the results of the county maps. On
this *at least* all purple patches showed parishes which possessed
open field arable in 1845; *at least* all the green and purple area
combined indicated parishes which had open field arable in
1802; *at least* all the coloured area had open field arable in
1700. In the printed map these colours are represented by
three forms of shading. Of the unshaded area one can simply
say that the Enclosure Acts throw no light upon its agricultural history so far as the land under tillage is concerned. To
a very great extent it was undoubtedly being enclosed otherwise
than by Act of Parliament simultaneously with the progress of
Parliamentary enclosure, but to a still greater extent it either
never passed through the common field system or was enclosed
before 1700. This statement raises questions which are dealt
with below. For the present I have to deal with the general
history of those parishes which did pass through the common
field system.

The original Board of Agriculture, which was an association
on similar lines to those of the Royal Agricultural Society, but

enjoying a grant from the Treasury, was founded in 1793, with Arthur Young as secretary and Sir John Sinclair as president. It immediately took in hand the work of making an agricultural survey of Great Britain, county by county. Some counties were surveyed several times, but the original survey of England was completed in the years 1793 and 1794. William Marshall, the ablest agricultural writer of the time, single-handed accomplished an agricultural survey of England, ignoring county divisions and dividing the country according to natural divisions marked by similarity of soil, crops and agricultural methods. The two surveys together give us ample information on the different methods of cultivating open or common fields at the end of the eighteenth century.

On the whole, the most general system, particularly in the midland counties where common fields remained most numerous, was the following form of the three-field system :—

"One part" (or one of the three fields) "is annually fallowed, a moiety of which is folded with sheep and sown with wheat; another moiety is dunged and sown with barley in the succeeding spring. The part which produces wheat is broken up and sown with oats, and the part which produces barley is at the same time generally sown with peas or beans, and then it comes in routine to be again fallowed the third year."[1] This gives us the following rotation of crops: (1), wheat; (2), oats; (3), fallow; (4), barley; (5), peas or beans; (6), fallow. This was the system prevailing in Huntingdon.

The same system prevailed in the heavy clay lands of Bedfordshire, but in the lighter lands sometimes a four-field course was adopted, sometimes the half of the nominally fallow field that had the previous year given crops of wheat and oats was sown with turnips, and clover was sown with barley the succeeding year.[2]

The commonest four-field course is that described for Isleham, Cambridgeshire : (1), wheat; (2), barley ; (3), pulse or oats ; (4), fallow; the fallow field being dunged or folded with sheep.

---

[1] Maxwell, " Huntingdon," p. 9.   [2] T. Stone, " Bedfordshire," p. 8.

At Castle Camps, also in Cambridge, a two-field course of alternate crop and fallow obtained.[1] Coming further south for Hertfordshire, we are told that the " common fields are mostly by agreement among the owners and occupiers cultivated nearly in the same way as in the enclosed state."[2] In Buckinghamshire the regular three-fields course was followed in some parts, but in Upton, Eton, Dorney, Datchett, Maysbury and Horton, "the occupiers have exploded entirely the old usage of two crops and a fallow, and now have a crop every year."

Two Buckinghamshire parishes underwent experiences which have been wrongly cited as typical of the inconveniences of common fields, whereas they are rather instances of the lawless conduct of village bullies. Steeple Claydon had 2500 acres of common field, on which the customary course was one crop and a fallow. " About fourteen years ago " (*i.e.*, about 1779) " the proprietors came to an agreement to have two crops and a fallow, but before the expiration of ten years one of the farmers broke through the agreement, and turned in his cattle upon the crops of beans, oats and barley, in which plan he was soon followed by the rest."[3] The agreement, if that of a three-fourths majority (see below), was legally binding on all owners and occupiers, and the first farmer was liable to the same pains and penalties as if he had turned his cattle into crops standing on enclosed fields belonging to another farm. Possibly, however, the crops were a failure, and feeding them off with cattle was as good a way of dealing with them as another.

A still more difficult case to understand is that of Wendon (3000 acres common field). It is reported as follows :—" About fourteen years ago the parishioners came to an agreement and obtained an Act to lay the small pieces of land together. . . . . When the division took place, the balks were of necessity ploughed up, by which a great portion of the sheep pasture was

---

[1] Vancouver, " Cambridgeshire," p. 33.
[2] D. Walker, " Hertfordshire," p. 49.
[3] William James and Jacob Malcolm, " Buckingham," p. 30.

destroyed.[1] It then became expedient, and it was agreed upon at public vestry, to sow clover and turnips as a succedaneum for the balks. Two years since, one of the farmers, occupying 16 acres of these common fields, procured in the month of May a large flock of lean sheep, which he turned on the clover crops; being then nearly in bloom, the greater part of which they devoured."

Of Oxfordshire we are told " the present course of husbandry is so various, particularly in the open fields, that to treat of all the different ways of management would render this report too voluminous. It may suffice generally to remark that some fields are in the course of one crop and fallow, others of two, and a few of three crops and a fallow. In divers unenclosed parishes the same rotation prevails over the whole of the open fields; but in others, the more homeward or bettermost land is oftener cropped, or sometimes cropped every year." [2] Where one crop and a fallow was the custom the crop might be wheat, barley or oats; and sometimes tares were sown on the fallow field and cut green. The three and four-field systems prevalent were those described above.

In Berkshire a six-year course, evidently evolved from an older three-years course, was found :—(1), wheat; (2), barley; (3), oats, with seeds; (4), clover, mowed, and then grazed upon in common; (5), oats or barley; (6), fallow.

An agreement to withhold turning out stock during the time in which a field was commonable by ancient custom, in order that turnips, vetches, etc., might be grown, was practised, and termed " hitching the fields." [3] We get the same expression for Wiltshire, where a part of a field set aside for vetches, peas, beans, turnips, or potatoes was called a " hookland " or " hitchland " field.[4] In Wiltshire customs similar to these described as surviving recently in Stratton and Grimstone were prevalent;

---

[1] James and Malcolm, "Buckingham," p. 29. I have been unable to find any trace of this Act.

[2] Richard Davis, "Oxfordshire," p. 11.

[3] William Pearce, "Berkshire," p. 29.

[4] Thomas Davis, "Wiltshire," p. 43.

clover was generally substituted for fallow, and was partly mowed for the individual benefit of particular occupiers, and partly fed upon by the village flock. The following systems are reported :—

(a) First, wheat; second, barley with clover ; third, clover part mowed, part fed.

(b) First, wheat; second, barley; third, oats with clover ; fourth, clover part mowed, part fed.

(c) First, wheat; second, barley with clover; third, clover mowed ; fourth, clover fed (one-third or a quarter of this field being " hitchland ").[1]

Turning northwards again from the centre of England, in Rutland the old three-year course of two crops and a fallow was universal in the unenclosed parishes ;[2] in Lincoln two, three and four-field systems were practised ;[3] the two-field course was also prevalent in Yorkshire.[4]

A singular practice was followed in the East Riding Wolds. " The greater part of the Wold townships which lie open have a great quantity of out-field in leyland, i.e., land from which they take a crop every third, fourth, fifth, or sixth year, according to the custom of the township." [5]

In constrast we may mention the Battersea common fields, which were " sown with one uniform round of grain without intermission and consequently without fallowing." [6]

[1] Thomas Davis, " Wiltshire," p. 43.
[2] John Crutchley, " Rutland," p. 8.
[3] Thomas Stone, " Lincoln," p. 26.
[4] Isaac Leatham, " East Riding," p. 40.
[5] Isaac Leatham, " East Riding," p. 42.
[6] James and Malcolm, " Surrey," p. 48.

CHAPTER VIII.

WHEN we come to Norfolk we find hints at so many special features that Norfolk agriculture demands separate treatment. The preamble of a Norfolk Enclosure Act is remarkably different from those for the rest of the country. A typical one is 1795, c. 67 :

"Whereas there are in the parish of Sedgeford in the county of Norfolk divers lands and grounds, called whole-year lands, brecks, common fields, half-year or shack lands, commons and waste grounds . . . . . . And whereas there are certain rights of sheep-walk, shackage and common, over the said brecks, half-year or shack land, commons and waste grounds. And great part of the said whole-year lands, as well as the brecks, common fields, and half-year or shack lands, are inconveniently situated," etc.

Or again 1804, c. 24 :

"Whereas there are in the parish of Waborne in the county of Norfolk divers lands and grounds called whole-year lands, common fields, doles, half-year or shack lands, commons and waste grounds."

"Whereas the said common fields, doles, half-year lands, shack lands, commons and waste grounds, are subject to certain rights of sheep-walk, shackage and common, and great part of the said whole-year lands, common fields, and half-year or shack lands are inconveniently situated for the various owners and proprietors thereof. . . . . . ."

Other Norfolk acts mention doles, ings, carrs, and bus-callys. Buscallys we may take to mean woods in which rights of common for fuel were practised. Dr. Murray's Dictionary gives us bushaile or buscayle, from Old French *boschaille*, Low Latin *boscalia*, shrubberies, thickets, etc. "Dole," is connected etymologically both with "deal" and with the word "run-dale," concerning which see below. The word is frequently found elsewhere, as in the "dolemeads" at Bristol and Bath, and usually means meadows, the ownership of which is intermixed in small parcels, which are commonable after hay harvest, but sometimes the word is used of arable land (see below). The Act for Earsham, Ditchingham and Hedenham (Norfolk, 1812, c. 17) has the sentence, "The said dole meadow lands lie intermixed and dispersed." The "ings" and "carrs" are best understood by the help of the old Ordnance Survey map for Norfolk. The carrs are the lowest, swampiest part of the common pastures which reach down to the rivers ; the ings, while also low-lying, are separated from the rivers by the carrs, and intervene between the carrs and the tilled lands.

There remain the expressions whole-year lands, half-year or shack lands, and brecks, to interpret.

Half-year lands obviously means lands commonable for half the year, i.e., after the crop has been carried. They are also "shack" lands, or lands on which right of "shackage" exists. "Shack" is connected with "shake," and right of shackage appears to be the right to carry off the gleanings after the crop has been carried and the fields are thrown open. It is, however, to be noticed that half-year or shack lands are mentioned as something distinct from common fields. The distinction is said to be that common rights on shack lands can be exercised only by the owners or occupiers of those lands. Shack lands may be termed common fields, but the term common field may be reserved for those fields over which cottagers or toft holders or others also possess rights of common.

"Brecks" are asserted by William Marshall ("Rural Economy of Norfolk," Vol. I., p. 376) to be "large new-made enclosures," but as is seen from the wording of the Acts quoted, they are enclosures still "subject to certain rights of shackage, sheepwalk, and common." [1] Lastly, what are "whole-year lands"?

---

[1] 1820, c. 29 (Blakeney, Wiverton and Glanford) mentions " whole-year lands, whole-year brecks, whole-year marshes." In this case, apparently, brecks are not commonable.

Since half-year lands are lands which for half the year are common, and for half the year are in individual ownership and use, one would argue that whole-year lands must be lands which are in individual ownership and use the whole year; for if they were common the whole year they would be termed simply "commons." We get further light by comparing the preambles of other Norfolk Acts. Some instead of whole-year lands mention every-year lands, others speak of "whole-year or every-year lands," while finally Icklingham in Suffolk (1813, c. 29) gives us "every year lands or Infields."

Now "infields" is a familiar expression in Scottish agriculture. Even in the Lothians, up to the middle of the eighteenth century the cultivated land was divided into infield and outfield. The outfield, like the outfield on the Yorkshire Wolds, only bore occasional crops, and was never manured, all the manure being reserved for the infield, which was made to bear a crop every year. In Haddington the customary course was: (1) pease; (2) wheat; (3) barley; (4) oats; and then the land was dunged and planted with pease again; and leases stipulated for "the preservation and regular dunging of the mucked land shotts."[1] Such lands might obviously be described as every-year lands, and since this method of cultivation implies that immediately one crop is carried preparation must be made for the next, and therefore is not easily consistent with common rights, so these lands are also "whole-year lands." It may be noted that the Norfolk preambles (as in the Sedgeford example, quoted above), while stating that the "whole-year lands," as well as the brecks, common fields and half-year lands are inconveniently situated, *i.e.*, are intermixed, by implication give us to understand that they are not subject to rights of shackage, sheep-walk, and common.

It is the more curious to find that Norfolk and the adjoining part of Suffolk followed a traditional method of cultivation in this respect similar to that of the East of Scotland, because there

[1] George Buchan Hepburn, "Agriculture of East Lothian," 1794, p. 49.

are so few traces of anything similar in the intervening counties. I find infields mentioned twice in Northumberland, once in Lincoln, whole-year lands once in Huntingdon. There is also mention of half-year lands in Yorkshire and Cambridgeshire. The Wessex custom of "hitching the fields," or "cropping the homeward or bettermost part of the common fields every year" is not the same thing, because there, as we saw in the case of Stratton and Grimstone, the extra crop was raised for common, not for individual, benefit. Battersea common fields were worked as every-year lands, and so are the Axholme fields to-day; but in these cases the custom was locally derived from some other form of cultivation; whereas in Norfolk and Suffolk the peculiar customs must have been indigenous and ancient.

One is also tempted to ask whether it is a coincidence that Norfolk farmers in the latter half of the eighteenth century, and Lothian farmers in the nineteenth, enjoyed and deserved an extremely high reputation for scientific, enterprising, and skilful agriculture. The ancient custom of raising crops every year from the same land must have necessitated the gradual accumulation of knowledge on the best ways of preventing exhaustion of the soil, by marling, manuring, deep ploughing, and various rotations of crops. When turnip culture was introduced into England, it was to Norfolk that the new idea was brought. There was no obstacle to growing turnips on the Norfolk whole-year lands, such as would have arisen if toft holders had the right to turn horses, cattle and sheep on to the lands at Lammas; and the intervention of a new crop which gave an opportunity for getting the land clean of weeds, and increased its fertility for grain crops, was a far more obvious boon there than on lands subject to a periodic fallow.

But to return to the typical Norfolk Enclosure Act preamble. We have only half explained the problem suggested by the four different names, each evidently with a distinct meaning, but all meaning arable land in which ownership is intermixed as in an ordinary common field, viz., whole-year lands, half-year lands or shack lands, brecks and common fields. The rest of the explanation is, I think, to be looked for in the direction suggested by the prominence given to the statement, " They are subject to rights of sheep-walk." Elsewhere one finds a close connection between sheep and common fields. Thus we have seen that at Eakring certain common right owners make a speciality of pasturing sheep on the common fields. The Swedish traveller Kaln, whose account of his visit to England has recently been translated into English, observed the same thing on the open field parishes of Hertfordshire and Bedfordshire in the year 1748 (p. 302). But in 1793 where there were open chalky downs in open field parishes the right of pasturing sheep on the downs and of having the combined flock of the village folded over the arable in the common field was valued too highly by every occupier to be ceded to an individual speculator (Davies, "Wiltshire," pp. 8, 15, 61, 80). In these cases right of common for sheep has been democratically shared.

But this is not universal. The Enclosure Commissioners, in their thirty-eighth report (1883), record the application for an Enclosure Act for Hildersham, Cambridgeshire. In this parish the two *manor farms* had the right of turning their sheep every sixth year on to the stubbles of the other farms. Similarly, I am told by Major Barnard, of Cheltenham, that in the Cambridgeshire parish of Bartlow, where he was born, which was enclosed with Shudy Camps and Castle Camps in 1863, that the right of feeding sheep on the common fields belonged to the lord of the manor only. These Cambridgeshire parishes are close to the borders of Norfolk and Suffolk, and the following passage from Tusser's " Champion and Several " (date 1573) suggests the same rule as applying to Norfolk and the " champion " (*i.e.*, open field) part of Suffolk :—

> *In Norfolk behold the despair*
> Of tillage, too much to be born,
> By drovers, from fair to fair,
> And others, destroying the corn,
> By custom, and covetous pates
> By gaps and by opening of gates.

What speak I of commoners by
　With drawing all after a line ;
So noying the corn as it lie,
　With cattle, with conies and swine,
When thou hast bestowed thy cost
Look half of the same to be lost.

The flocks of the lords of the soil
　Do yearly the winter corn wrong,
The same in a maner they spoil
　With feeding so low and so long,
And therefore that champion field
Doth seldom good winter corn yield.

If it be urged that the two italicised lines are not necessarily
to be read together, in view of the other topics touched on in
the intermediate lines, the argument is not much affected, for
Tusser shows no knowledge of any " champion " counties other
than Leicestershire, Cambridgeshire, and Norfolk, and elsewhere
in the poem he deals with the special evils afflicting the two
former counties.

I may also refer to the Act, 25 Henry VIII. c. 13, to limit
the number of sheep which may be possessed by a single owner,
in which occurs the passage :—

X. Be it also further enacted by the authority aforesaid,
That no manner of Person or Persons, of what Degree soever
he or they be, being Lord or Lords, Owner or Owners, Farmer
or Farmers, of or in any Liberty of Fold Courses within any
Town, Tything, Village or Hamlet within any of the Counties
of Norfolk or Suffolk, from and after the Feast of the Nativity
of our Lord God next coming, shall take in farm, for term of
years or otherwise, any Quillets of Lands or Pastures, that is
to say, any number of Acres of Land or Pasture appertaining to
any other Person or Persons, lying and being within the limit
Extent or Precinct of the said Liberty of the said Fold Courses ;
but that they shall permit and suffer the said Persons, having
or being, for the time, Owner or Owners, Lessee or Lessees of
the said Quillets, to manure and pasture the said Quillets ; and

also to suffer sheep of the said Owner or Owners, Farmer or Farmers of the said Quillets, after the Rate of the said Quillets, to go with the Flock of the Owner, Farmer or Occupier of the said Liberty or Liberties of the said Fold Courses, paying the customary charge for the same, after the Rate and Use of the Country, there commonly used, without any interruption therein to be made by the said Owner or Owners, Farmer or Farmers, or Occupiers of the said Liberties, upon pain of forfeiture for 3s. 4d. for each offence.

"XI. Provided . . . it shall not . . . be available to any tenant Owner or Occupier of any such Quillet or Quillets to claim, have or use hereafter any such pasture, or Feeding of his sheep, in or with any such Fold Courses, but only where the tenants, Owners and Occupiers of any such Quillets have had, or might have had heretofore of Right and Duty, or used to have Pasture and Feeding in the said Fold Courses, by reason of their tenures, and Occupations of the said Quillet and Quillets, and none otherwise ; and where they have not used, nor ought to have any Sheep fed or kept within such Fold Courses, by reason of the said tenures, that the Owners or Occupiers of such Fold Courses may take such Quillets, lying within their Fold Courses, in Farm, agreeing with the Owners or Occupiers of the said Quillets for the same."

It would appear from these clauses that there had been in still earlier times generally throughout Norfolk and Suffolk a right pertaining to the Lord of the Manor of feeding flocks of sheep over the whole manor, that this right, in the reign of Henry VIII. was frequently sold or leased under the denomination "A Liberty of Fold Courses" ; secondly that the exercise of this right was apt to interfere with the cultivation of peasants' holdings in the common fields ; thirdly that it was customary for the sheep belonging to the peasants to be pastured and folded with the flock of the Lord of the Manor for a fixed customary fee.

There is yet another respect in which Norfolk agriculture shows a difference, but of degree, not kind, from other common-field agriculture. Complete enclosure of common-field arable involves three processes—

(1) The laying together of scattered properties, and consequent abolition of intermixture of properties and holdings ;

(2) The abolition of common rights ;

(3) The hedging and ditching of the separate properties. This third process is the actual "enclosing" which gives its name to a series of processes which it completes.

But sometimes the hedging and ditching takes place independently of the other two processes, and strips of an acre, two or more acres, and even half-an-acre are enclosed in the middle of the common-fields, and, what is more remarkable, the little enclosed strips are sometimes the property of several individuals. In the collection of maps of open field parishes belonging to certain Oxford Colleges, published by Mr. J. L. G. Mowat, several such instances may be noticed.

Such enclosures were at first commonable ; but common rights were of course exercised over them with greater difficulty than over the open parts of the enclosed fields, a fact on which the above quoted opinion on the Barn farm at Elmstone Hardwicke incidentally throws some light. The maintenance of these common rights is a sort of test of the democratic vigour of the village, and it may be noticed that old enclosures subject to common rights were particularly numerous in Yorkshire.

Norfolk was remarkable for the extent to which actual hedging and ditching preceded legal enclosure. The Board of Agriculture reporter says, " for notwithstanding common rights for great cattle exist in all of them,[1] and even sheep-walk privileges in many, yet the natural industry of the people is such, that wherever a person can get four or five acres together, he plants a white-thorn hedge round it, and sets an oak at every rod distance, which is consented to by a kind of general courtesy from one neighbour to another."[2]

Two Acts incidentally show to what an extent such hedges

---

[1] *I.e.*, of the enclosures he is going to describe.
[2] Nathaniel Kent, " Norfolk," p. 22.

enclosed lands belonging to two or more proprietors. One Norfolk Act has the provision, " All enclosures where two or more proprietors are connected and where the property is not separated by a hedge or ditch shall be deemed to be Common Field." The same clause differently expressed occurs in the Act for Ormesby and Scratby (1842, c. 9): " All old enclosures within the said parishes in which there are lands belonging to different proprietors, shall be deemed to be open Fields."

A brief account of a surviving Norfolk open field parish is given in Appendix E., p. 331.

CHAPTER IX.

13 GEO. III. C. 81.

ONE of the most striking and interesting features of the open field village life is the existence of a self-governing constitution for the settlement of disputes, and the most profitable use of the village lands—the annual meetings of farmers and common-right owners; the institution of field reeves and field juries; the division among commoners of the profits of the common property. One cannot but look upon this as the survival of an ancient village communal life, which must have been much stronger and more vigorous in earlier days, when each village was more of a self-contained and isolated economic unit; and particularly while the co-operative ploughing persisted, from which the intermixture of lands in common field arable is admitted to have originated. Even in its degenerate state, when co-operative ploughing has been extinct for generations, the open field parish involves a certain partnership among the cultivators, necessitating some recognised rules, mutual consultation, and organised combination: how much more binding the necessity must have been in the Middle Ages? Hence from the very necessity of the case, there must have been a bond between the village workers, such as is conveyed by the words "village community," which probably preceded, and underlay as a foundation, the better known manorial and parochial institutions, the manorial organisation arising from the contact between the village community and the Central Government, or outside enemies, the parochial from its contact with the Church.

But while these features of common-field management in general are survivals of "the village community," it is possible *in any particular village* that such institutions and customs were the creation of the legislature since the latter part of the

eighteenth century. For in the year 1773 a noteworthy Act was
passed for the better regulation of the culture of common arable
fields. It enacts that "where there are open or common field
lands, all the Tillage or Arable lands lying in the said open or
Common Fields, shall be ordered, fenced, cultivated or improved,
in such manner as three-fourths in number and value of the
occupiers shall agree, with consent of the owner and tithe-
owner."

Such agreements were to be binding for six years, or two
rounds, "according to the ancient and established course of
each parish or place"; *i.e.*, presumably, in a parish where the
ancient customary course had been one crop and a fallow, the
agreement was binding for four years; where it had been three
crops and a fallow, for eight years. Further, every year between
the 21st and 24th of May a field reeve or field reeves were
to be elected. These field reeves, acting under the instructions
of a three-fourths majority in number and value, might delay
the opening of the common fields, might give permission for
any balks, slades or meers (those words are synonyms) to
be ploughed up, an equivalent piece of land being laid down
in common, and boundary stones being put down instead. Since
this Act was designed in the interest of better cultivation, and
for the advantage of the proprietors and large occupiers, special
provision is made that if the cottagers owning common rights
feel themselves prejudiced, they may claim to have a separate
piece of land set out as a common for them.

The effect of the Act was to enable the common-field system
to be adjusted to the new agriculture of the eighteenth century,
which was marked by the introduction of turnips, artificial
grasses, and the abandonment of frequent fallowing. A precise
account of the adoption of a scheme under the Act is given us
by the prime mover.

In the township of Hunmanby, in the East Riding of Yorkshire, the cultivators had fallen into one of the besetting
temptations to which "champion" farmers were liable. They
had gradually extended the arable fields at the expense of the
common pasture, till the manure produced by the latter was

insufficient for the needs of the former, and the land was losing its fertility. Isaac Leatham got his brother farmers to agree to abandon the old (three-year) course of husbandry, and to substitute the following six-year course : —

1. Turnips, hoed, and fed off with sheep.
2. Barley with grass seed.
3. Grass.
4. Grass.
5. Wheat.
6. Oats or peas.

The grass seed sown with the barley was bought in common, and paid for proportionately. From the time the barley was carried until it was time to plough for the wheat crop, one gathers that the grass, which had been sown with the barley, was being fed with sheep ; therefore, at any particular time after the course was established, half the common field area was feeding sheep, or growing turnips for sheep, and half was growing grain or pulse. The sheep flock was managed in common ; each occupier was allowed to contribute sheep to it in proportion to his holding ; the whole was under the care of two shepherds, who folded the sheep nightly upon different strips of land in succession, so that all occupiers received equal benefit. Field reeves were appointed.

"Thus," says Isaac Leatham, "an open field is enjoyed in as beneficial a manner as if it were enclosed . . . two persons are fully sufficient to attend the sheep-stock, instead of many . . . the precarious rearing of fences is avoided, and the immense expense of continually repairing them saved." [1]

I take it that Isaac Leatham, who, by the way, was a strong advocate of enclosure in general, meant that the open field was, *on the whole*, enjoyed in as beneficial a manner as if it were enclosed, because there still remained the great disadvantage that each occupier had his lands in widely scattered strips, and had to waste much time and labour in cultivating them ; cross-ploughing, which might, or might not have been desirable, was

---

[1] Isaac Leatham, " East Riding," p. 46.

any way impossible ; the village lands had to be treated as one whole, so no enterprising and original man was able to experiment with new ideas, nor could any further improvement be adopted without the consent of a three-fourths majority ; and, perhaps, the keeping of sheep in a common flock put obstacles in the way of improving the breed.

I may add that an Act for the enclosure of Hunmanby was passed in the year 1800, so that Isaac Leatham's course was abandoned just seven years after he wrote about it so triumphantly.

The Act of 1773, therefore, was, perhaps, not a brilliant success in Hunmanby ; perhaps, on the other hand, improved agriculture excited an appetite for further improvement, and one novelty having been accepted, the stiff conservatism which might have postponed enclosure, was broken down. But, as a glance at the map for the East Riding will show, the whole countryside was subject to a rage for enclosure, and the famine prices for grain of 1796, doomed to recur again in 1800–1, in 1812, and 1817, were acting as a powerful solvent to all old agricultural customs.

It is quite obvious that the Act of 1773 was an endeavour to select out of the customs and traditions prevailing in different villages those which were most in harmony with advanced agriculture, to further amend these, and to make them universal.

So far as I know, Hunmanby is the only place where it has been recorded as having been put into execution, and it has been doubted whether it was not practically a dead letter. My own impression is that the distribution of the " sicks " at Laxton was consciously arranged in accordance with the provisions of the Act, that originally the method of choosing the fallow crops in Castor and Ailesworth was an application of it, and also the six years' course used for part of the fields of Barrowden and Luffenham, but I can bring no evidence to support this view. If, however, it is correct, the Act may have been of considerable use to many other parishes also by clearly defining methods of procedure which otherwise would be determined by custom only.

CHAPTER X.

THE very word " enclosure " to a historical student suggests "depopulation." The two words are almost treated as synonyms in Acts of Parliament, tracts, and official documents of the sixteenth century. In the seventeenth century we find the proverbs, " Horn and thorn shall make England forlorn," " Inclosures make fat beasts and lean poor people," while the superstition grew up that inclosed land was cursed, and must within three generations pass away from the families of " these madded and irreligious depopulators," these " dispeoplers of towns, ruiners of commonwealths, occasioners of beggary . . . cruell inclosiers."

After the Restoration, the literary attack on enclosure becomes more feeble, the defence more powerful. W. Wales in 1781, the Rev. J. Howlett in 1786, published statistics to show that enclosure had the effect of increasing the population, the latter tract being widely quoted ; there ceased to be any opposition from the Central Government to enclosure, and private Acts were passed in continually increasing numbers ; finally the one practical measure carried through by the Board of Agriculture was the General Enclosure Act of 1801, to simplify and cheapen Parliamentary proceedings. Dr. Cunningham sums up the case as follows : " He (Joseph Massie) was aware that enclosing had meant rural depopulation in the sixteenth century, and he too hastily assumed that the enclosing which had been proceeding in the eighteenth century was attended with similar results ; but the conditions of the time were entirely changed. Despite the reiterated allegation,[1] it is impossible to believe that enclosing in the eighteenth century implied either more pasture

[1] By the opponents of enclosure.

farming or less employment for labour. The prohibition of export kept down the price of wool; the bounty on exportation gave direct encouragement to corn-growing; the improved agriculture gave more employment to labour than the old."[1]

Taken in one sense, I must admit the substantial accuracy of this opinion. On the other hand I am disposed to maintain the general accuracy of the statements with regard to depopulation made by the opponents of enclosure, (*a*) provided these statements are understood in the sense in which they are meant, and (*b*) statements only with regard to the part of the country the writer is familiar with are regarded, and his inferences with regard to other parts are neglected.

For it must be remembered that side by side with the movement for the enclosure of arable fields, there was going on a movement for the enclosure of wastes. From Appendix A. it will be seen that 577 Acts for enclosing wastes and common pastures were passed between 1702 and 1802, and over 800,000 acres were so added to the cultivated area of England and Wales. There were besides enclosures occasionally on a large scale by landed proprietors of wastes on which either common rights were not exercised, or on which they were too feebly maintained to necessitate an Act. The Board of Agriculture report for Notts records that 10,666 acres had recently been so enclosed from Sherwood Forest alone.[2] Lastly there was the continual pushing forward of cultivation by farmers, squatters, etc. It is impossible to do more than form a vague guess as to the quantity of land so enclosed, but reasons will be given later for the belief that it was far greater than the area of commons and waste enclosed by Act of Parliament.

Now the opponents of enclosure of the sixteenth, seventeenth *and* eighteenth centuries almost without exception opposed simply the enclosure of arable common fields; they usually expressly approve the enclosure of waste, as increasing the means of subsistence of the people. The advocates of enclosure on the other hand are equally concerned in advocating both

---

[1] "Growth of English Industry and Commerce," Vol. II., p. 384 (1892).

[2] Robert Lowe, "Nottingham," Appendix.

kinds of enclosure. Hence we have statements to the effect that the enclosure of arable fields in the " champion " districts of England (*i.e.*, the part much shaded on the map) caused rural depopulation, met by statistics and arguments to prove that all kinds of enclosure proceeding over all parts of England and Wales, on the whole, tended to increase population, urban and rural. Through looseness of wording on both sides, the controversialists seem to be contradicting one another ; whereas, in reality, both might equally be right.

At the present day this particular issue is dead, though a similar question, the question whether by means of the modern representative of the open field, viz., the allotment field, and modern representative of the ancient co-operative ploughing, viz., co-operative purchase of machines, manures and seeds, borrowing of capital, sale of produce, and perhaps co-operative stockbreeding, the decay of the agricultural population can be arrested, is a living issue. Nor is there any period of the nineteenth century in which any serious rural depopulation as a result of enclosure, and consequent laying down in pasture, of common fields, could be asserted. Since Free Trade began to seriously affect the prices of British grain—and that was not for a good many years after 1846—the common fields have been too few, and the other forces tending towards rural depopulation too great, for this particular force to be felt. And if it were felt, no one would seriously urge that the hardly pressed farmer should be compelled to cultivate the land in a manner wasteful of labour, in order that more labourers might be employed. In the earlier part of the nineteenth century war, protection and a rapidly growing wealth and population so effectively encouraged tillage that attempted prohibition of conversion of arable to grass would have been superfluous.

Yet much, I think, can be learnt on the historical question from the present aspect of the country, even by anyone who merely travels by express train through the Midlands. Having spent a day in traversing the length and breadth of the great fields of Castor and Ailesworth, yellow with wheat and barley or recently cut stubble, I went straight through the county of

Northamptonshire, seeing on either side scarcely anything but permanent pasture. From Northampton to Leicester was the same thing; again from Leicester to Uppingham. Just beyond Uppingham the cornfields become far more extensive; what were the Rutlandshire common fields till 1881 are still mainly under tillage. All this country of permanent pasture was mainly enclosed during the eighteenth century. Very frequently one can see on heavy land the old ridges piled up in the middle, ending in the middle of one field, crossing hedges, and showing plainly that very little, if any, ploughing has been done since the enclosure was effected.[1] The impression made on my mind by this apparent confirmation of all that the denouncers of " cruell Inclosiers " alleged was a very powerful one.

Before examining the evidence for and against rural depopulation in particular parts of England as the result of the extinction of common fields, it is well to consider the *a priori* arguments put forward by Dr. Cunningham.

It is urged, in the first place, that owing to the relatively high price of corn and low price of wool, there was no motive for laydown arable as pasture. Dr. Cunningham seems to ignore the fact that sheep and cattle produce mutton, beef, milk, butter, cheese, and hides, as well as wool, and it is by the profit to be derived from all of these products together, and not from any one of them, that the question of laying down in pasture will be determined. That laying down arable in pasture was profitable is indicated by the surprise Arthur Young expressed in 1768 that landlords did not enclose, and put the land to grass, on passing through Bedfordshire,[2] and by Adam Smith's reference in " The Wealth of Nations " to the exceptional rent commanded by enclosed pasture.[3] We have, further, the clear statement of the Board of Agriculture : " Whereas the price of corn from 1760 to 1794 was almost stationary, the products of grass land

---

[1] Arthur Young (" Eastern Tour," Vol. I., p. 54) noticed this in 1771 in the great pasture closes of Northamptonshire : " All this fine grass on so excellent a soil lies all in the broad ridge and furrow."

[2] " Northern Tour," 2nd. ed., p. 56.

[3] McCulloch's ed., p. 69.

have risen greatly throughout nearly the whole of that period." [1]
William Pitt, again, in a pamphlet published by the Board in
1812 on the " Food Produced from Arable and Grass Land," says
that through the " increased luxury of the times more beef and
mutton and butter are used than formerly, even by equal numbers,
and consequently more inducement to throw all the best corn to
grass " (p. 35).   William Culley adds in a footnote that " In the
Northern Counties more rent per acre is given for ploughing
than for grazing farms . . . more rent is given for grazing than
for arable farms in the Southern Counties." If this was so
when famine prices were paid for wheat, how much more in
normal times ?

It is said, in the second place, that " the new agriculture gave
more employment to labour than the old." No doubt such an
improvement as the substitution of well-hoed turnips for a
fallow, the sowing of grass seeds with barley so as to produce a
second crop, or feed for cattle after the barley was carried, both
gave increased employment to labour, and tended to increased
prosperity for the labouring as well as other classes.   But these
changes, as we have seen, and as Dr. Cunningham himself
points out, might take place independently of enclosure, and might
not follow if enclosure did take place.   Whether they usually
did follow upon enclosure is a question that has to be settled by
an appeal to contemporary evidence.   In taking this evidence
reference must always be carefully made to the *time* and the
place.

The Board of Agriculture's General Report on Enclosures
(1808) quotes with approval an anonymous pamphlet published
in 1772 : " The advantages and disadvantages of enclosing waste
lands and common fields," by " A Country Gentleman."   This
tract appears to be a very able and impartial attempt to estimate
the effects of enclosure on all the classes interested.   The way in
which Acts then originated, and the manner in which proposals
were received, is described thus :—

" The landowner, seeing the great increase of rent made by
his neighbour, conceives a desire of following his example ; the

[1] " General Report on Enclosures," p. 41.

village is alarmed; the great farmer dreads an increase of rent, and being constrained to a system of agriculture which neither his experience nor his inclination tempt him into; the small farmer, that his farm will be taken from him and consolidated with the larger; the cottager not only expects to lose his commons, but the inheritable consequence of the diminution of labour, the being obliged to quit his native place in search of work; the inhabitants of the larger towns, a scarcity of provisions; and the Kingdom in general, the loss of inhabitants " (p. 1).

The general conclusion seems to be that all these anticipations and fears, with the exception of the last two—a scarcity of provisions for large towns, and a general loss of inhabitants for the kingdom, are well founded. With regard to the landowner and tithe-owner :—

"There can be no dispute that it is the landowners' interest to promote inclosures; but I verily believe, the improprietor of tithes reaps the greatest proportional benefit, whilst the small freeholder, from his expenses increasing inversely to the smallness of his allotment, undoubtedly receives the least " (p. 25).[1]

Of the small farmer :—"Indeed I doubt it is too true, he must of necessity give over farming, and betake himself to labour for the support of his family " (p. 31).

With regard to the increase or diminution of employment for labourers, he gives the following statistical table, an estimate based on his observation :—

1,000 Acres of	Before Enclosure gives Employment to	After Enclosure gives Employment to
A Rich Arable Land	20 families	5 families
B Inferior Arable	20 ,,	$16\frac{1}{4}$,,
C Stinted Common Pastures ...	$\frac{1}{2}$ a family	5 ,,
D Heaths, Wastes, etc.	$\frac{1}{2}$,,	$16\frac{1}{4}$,,

---

[1] This is badly expressed. He refers to the fact that a small allotment is more expensive to fence, proportionally to its size, than a large one.

It will be seen that his observation is that enclosed arable employs 16¼ families per 1000 acres, open field arable 20 families per 1000 acres; that common pastures, heaths, wastes, etc., employ only 1 family per 2000 acres; but enclosed pasture employs 5 families per 1000 acres. It will also be seen that his observation is that after enclosure rich land becomes pasture, inferior land arable.[1]

With regard to the effect of this on population, he names in one passage[2] Northamptonshire, Leicestershire and Lincolnshire perhaps, as containing "an infinitely greater proportion of common fields, while Northumberland, Westmoreland and Yorkshire exceed in moors, heaths and commons," and in another he mentions Oxfordshire, Buckingham, Northamptonshire and part of Leicester as counties in which rich arable land would be the main subject of an Enclosure Act. A typical parish in this district might include 1000 acres of rich arable land, 500 acres of inferior arable, 500 acres of stinted common, with no heath or waste. Before enclosure it would provide employment for 30¼ labouring families according to the table, after enclosure to 15⅝. If eight such parishes were enclosed, 117 families would be sent adrift—families of poor and ignorant labourers, looking for new homes under all the disabilities and difficulties springing from Acts of Settlement, and a Poor Law administration based on the assumption that those who wander from their native place are all that is implied in the words "vagrants" and "vagabonds." Not eight, but a hundred and twenty-six Acts for enclosing common fields were passed for the four counties he names in the ten years 1762—1772, immediately

---

[1] This is in harmony with all other eighteenth century information with regard to the Midland Counties. As one example we may cite the Vale of Belvoir, the north-eastern corner of Leicestershire. Here, in consequence of enclosure, "all the richest land in the vale, formerly under tillage, was laid down in grass, but the skirtings of the Vale, formerly sheep-walk, were brought into tillage." The landlord, the Duke of Rutland, forbade any land worth more than a guinea per acre to be tilled. The enclosure of the twelve parishes in the Vale took place between 1766 and 1792. (William Pitt, " Agriculture of Leicestershire," 1809.)

[2] Page 43.

preceding the publication of this pamphlet. Assuming the accuracy of the "Country Gentleman's" statement, this would mean that some 1800 odd families, comprising about 9000 individuals, would, in consequence of enclosure, be sent adrift in that short period in the four counties. The quotations given below from three other authors, indicate that even this was an under-statement. The process continued without intermission for many years afterwards.

A specially interesting tract, published in 1786, entitled "Thoughts on Inclosures, by a Country Farmer," gives a detailed account of the results of one case of enclosure. The locality is not named, but it is pretty clear that it was within this Midland country in which enclosure was attended by the conversion of arable to pasture.

On the general question the writer says :—" To obtain an Act of Parliament to inclose a common field, two witnesses are produced, to swear that the lands thereof, in their present state, are not worth occupying, though at the same time they are lands of the best soil in the kingdom, and produce corn in the greatest abundance, and of the best quality. And by inclosing such lands, they are generally prevented from producing any corn at all, as the landowner converts twenty small farms into about four large ones, and at the same time the tenants of those large farms are tied down in their leases not to plough any of the premises, so lett to farm,[1] by which means of several hundred villages, that forty years ago contained between four and five hundred inhabitants, very few will now be found to exceed eighty, and some not half that number ; nay some contain only one poor decripid man or woman, housed by the occupiers of lands who live in another parish, to prevent them being obliged to pay towards the support of the poor who live in the next parish" (p. 2).

The profit of enclosing, he maintains, was dependent upon simultaneous conversion into pasture, for "In some places the lands inclosed do not answer the ends of pasturage, and in

---

[1] See note 1 on next page.

that case tillage is still to be pursued; because the rents cannot be raised so high as in respect of pasturage, therefore the landowner has not the advantage as in case the land turns out fit for pasturage, and is oftener the loser by that proceeding than the gainer."[1]

The particular enclosure he cites is that of a parish enclosed about forty years previously. Before enclosure it contained eighty-two houses, of which twenty were small farms and forty-two were cottages with common rights. It had 1800 acres of common field arable, 200 acres of rich common cow pasture, and 200 acres of meadow, commonable after hay harvest. The common pasture fed two hundred milch cows and sixty dry ones till hay harvest, at which time they were turned into the meadows, and their place taken by about one hundred horses. Twelve hundred sheep were fed on the stubbles.

The gross produce of the parish before enclosure he values as follows:—

	£	s.	d.
1,100 quarters of wheat at 28s. per quarter	1,540	0	0
1,200 quarters of barley at 16s. per quarter	960	0	0
900 quarters of beans at 15s. per quarter	675	0	0
250 todds of wool at 16s. per todd ...	200	0	0
600 lambs at 10s. each	300	0	0
5,000 lbs. of cheese at 1½d. per lb. ...	31	5	0
6,000 lbs. of butter at 5d. per lb. ...	125	0	0
100 calves at 20s. each	100	0	0
150 pigs at 12s. each	90	0	0
Poultry and eggs...	80	0	0
	£4,101	5	0

The quantities estimated are eminently reasonable, and in harmony with other statements available with regard to the produce of the common fields of the Midlands; the prices also are clearly not over-stated.

[1] Arthur Young ("Eastern Tour," 1771, p. 96) remarks that in Leicestershire "Landlords in general will not allow an inch to be ploughed on grazing farms."

As the result of enclosure the twenty farms were consolidated into four, the whole area was devoted to grazing, sixty cottages were pulled down or otherwise disappeared, and the necessary work was done by four herds (one for each farm) at £25 a year each, board included, and eight maidservants at £18 a year each, board included.

The gross produce of the parish after enclosure was :—

					£	s.	d.
Fat beasts	...	...	...	...	960	0	0
Sheep and lambs...		...	...	...	760	0	0
Calves	...	...	...	...	165	0	0
Wool	...	...	...	...	235	0	0
Butter	...	...	...	...	190	0	0
Cheese	...	...	...	...	100	0	0
Horses	...	...	...	...	250	0	0
					£2,660	0	0

But while the gross produce was thus reduced by about one-third, the gross rent was raised from £1137 17s. 0d. to £1801 12s. 2d.[1]

Though unfortunately the parish is not identified, and the witness is anonymous, the whole statement appears to have been carefully and exactly made. In this case we have no fewer than sixty families of small farmers or agricultural labourers expelled from their homes in a single parish of about 2300 acres.

An even more striking example of local depopulation caused by enclosure is supplied by the Rev. John Howlett, one of the strongest advocates of enclosure. He quotes from a private correspondent: "As to Inclosure, I can mention two villages in this County (Leicestershire) within two miles of each other, Wistow and Foston,[2] which formerly contained thirty-four or

---

[1] According to the "Country Gentleman's" calculations, the gross produce of the 1800 acres of common field and 200 acres of common pasture would be before enclosure £4419 8s., and after, £3000, which agrees very closely with the "Country Farmer's" statement, the absolute amounts being greater, the ratio between them practically identical.

[2] Each of these was enclosed without an Act of Parliament.

thirty-five dwellings, but by enclosure Foston is reduced to three habitations: the parsonage house accommodates one family, and the two other buildings are occupied by shepherds, who manage the stock for their different renters, as the whole of the parish belongs to one person. And as to Wistow, the thirty-four mansions have vanished in a very few years, and no dwelling remains but the late Sir Charles Halford's hall house, who owns the lordship; and these are called improvements, for double or treble rents ensue." ("Enclosures and Depopulation," p. 12.)

What became of these farmers and labourers? The "Country Farmer" says: "Many of the small farmers who have been deprived of their livelihood have sold their stock-in-trade and have raised from £50 to £100, with which they have procured themselves, their families, and money, a passage to America."

John Wedge, the Board of Agriculture reporter for Warwick, says seven years later: "About forty years ago the southern and eastern parts of this county consisted mostly of open fields. There are still about 50,000 acres of open field land, which in a few years will probably all be inclosed. . . . These lands being now grazed want much fewer hands to manage them than they did in the former open state. Upon all enclosures of open fields the farms have generally been made much larger; from these causes the hardy yeomanry of country villages have been driven for employment to Birmingham, Coventry, and other manufacturing towns."[1] Such information, given by the representative of an enclosure-advocating corporation, circulated among the members for correction before final adoption, is unimpeachable evidence for the particular time and place.

The rising industries of Birmingham and other Midland towns found employment, no doubt, for many of the exiles from the villages. On the whole, the ruling opinion seems to have found all this very satisfactory. The gross produce of food by these Midland parishes might be diminished on enclosure, but the net produce, as was shown by the increase of rent, certainly

John Wedge, "Warwickshire" p. 40 (1793).

increased, and an abundant supply of labour was furnished for
those metal working industries which were of the greatest
importance in times of war.[1]   When we think of the horrible
sanitary conditions of English towns during the eighteenth
century, of Fielding's description of the London lodging-houses,
of Colquhoun's attempts at a statistical account of London
thieves, of Hogarth's pictures, which interpret for us the meaning of the terrible fact that right through the eighteenth century
the deaths " within the bills of mortality " regularly far exceeded
the births, we feel that there was another side to the shield,
though possibly the sanitary and social condition of Midland
towns was less terrible than that of London.

The connection between enclosure of common fields and rising
poor rates in the eighteenth century is illustrated repeatedly in
Eden's " Condition of the Poor."

In Buckinghamshire we find the two neighbouring parishes of
Maids Morton and Winslow.   The former contained 30 acres of
old enclosure, 60 to 70 acres of commons, and the rest of the
parish, about 800 acres, was common field.   The poor-rates in
the years 1792 to 1795 were 3s. 6d., 3s., 3s., 3s. 6d.   There
were " several roundsmen."   Wages were nominally 1s. to
1s. 2d. per day, but piecework was general, and 1s. 3d. to 1s. 6d.
was generally earned.   The rent of farms varied from £17 to
£90 per farm, and from 18s. to 20s. per acre.

Winslow contained 1400 acres, and was entirely enclosed in
1744 and 1766.   Only 200 acres remained arable.   The farms
varied from £60 to £400 per annum each, the wages were 6s. to
7s. per week, " most of the labourers are on rounds," and the
poor rates from 1792 to 1795 were 5s. 8d., 4s., 5s., and 6s.
" The rise of the Rates is chiefly ascribed to the Enclosure of
common fields ; which it is said has lessened the number of
farms, and from the conversion of arable into pasture, has much
reduced the demand for labourers.   An old man of the parish
says, before the enclosures took place, land did not let for 10s.
per acre."   (Vol. II., pp. 27—33.)

---

[1] 1756—1763, 1775—1784, 1792—1815 were times of war.

In judging the rise of poor rate, it must not be forgotten that where the rent rises at the same time as the nominal rate, the sum of money actually raised for Poor Law purposes is increased in a greater ratio than the nominal poor rate. If, for example, by enclosure the rental of a parish is increased 50 per cent., but the poor rate doubled, the yield of the poor rate is increased threefold. And if a considerable number of labourers are driven elsewhere, the amount of destitution produced by the change is far greater even than that indicated by a threefold increase in the amount of relief given.

The latter side of the process is illustrated in the case of Deddington in Oxfordshire. Here, " the high rates in this parish are ascribed to the common field of which the land principally consists; whereas the neighbouring parishes have been enclosed many years, and many small farms in them have been consolidated ; so that many small farmers with little capitals have been obliged, either to turn labourers or to procure small farms in Deddington, or other parishes that possess common fields. Besides this, the neighbouring parishes are, many of them, possessed by a few individuals, who are cautious in permitting new comers to obtain a settlement." (Vol. II., p. 891.)

In Leicestershire the complaint is naturally more loud and general. In the account of Kibworth Beauchamp we read as follows :—

" No account of the Rates in any of the divisions, previous to the enclosure of the common fields, can be obtained ; but it is said that they were not one-third of what they are at present ; and the people attribute the rise to the enclosures ; for they say ' That before the fields were enclosed, they were solely applied to the production of corn ; that the poor had then plenty of employment in weeding, reaping, threshing, etc., and could also collect a great quantity of corn by gleaning ; but that the fields being now in pasturage, the farmers have little occasion for labourers, and the poor being thereby thrown out of employment, must of course be employed by the parish.' There is some truth in these observations : *one-third or perhaps one-fourth* of the number of hands which were required twenty years ago, would now be sufficient, according to the present system of agriculture, to perform all the farming work of the parish."

He adds that if it were not for the fact that many labourers were getting employment in canal cutting, the rates would be much higher still, and "the tradesmen, small farmers, and labourers are very loud in their complaints against those whom they call monopolising farmers and graziers, an evil which, they say, increases every year." (Vol. II., p. 383.)

In Northamptonshire we find the case of Brixworth, enclosed in 1780, a parish of 3300 acres. Before enclosure it consisted almost entirely of common fields. At the time of Eden's writing, sixteen years later, only one-third remained arable. The expenditure on the poor in 1776, before the enclosure, was £121 6s., in the six years 1787 to 1792 it averaged £325 (Vol. II., p. 529). Again, with regard to local urban opinion, he notes that "the lands round Kettering are chiefly open field : they produce rich crops of corn. The people of the town seem averse to enclosures, which they think will raise the price of provisions, from these lands being all turned to pasture, when inclosed, as was the case in Leicestershire, which was a great corn country, and is now, almost entirely, converted into pasture."

Arthur Young, a little more than twenty years previously (in "Political Arithmetic," published in 1774), while arguing in favour of enclosure on the depopulation count, makes an admission against it with regard to pauperism. "Very many of the labouring poor have become chargeable to their parishes, but this has nothing to do with depopulation; on the contrary, the constantly seeing such vast sums distributed in this way, must be an inducement to marriage among all the idle poor— and certainly has proved so." (Pp. 75, 76.)

As a general rule it may be said that where after enclosure pasturage was increased at the expense of tillage, rural depopulation resulted; where the amount of land under tillage was increased the rural population increased. Further, that enclosure in the northern and western parts of England in the seventeenth and eighteenth centuries increased the area under tillage; that the balance between the production of bread and meat for the whole country, so disturbed, was maintained by the conversion into pasture, on enclosure, of much of the "champion" corn growing land, particularly in those midland counties nearest to the northern and western ones in which the complementary change was taking place. By means of the Enclosure Acts, interpreted by the light of the above statements, we can trace these two compensating movements through the eighteenth century.

The following passage in Arthur Young's "Political Arithmetic," published in 1774, at the time, that is, when he was an eager advocate not only of enclosure of all sorts, but also of the engrossing of farms and the raising of rents, sums up the two movements:—

"The fact is this: in the central counties of the kingdom, particularly Northamptonshire, Leicestershire, and parts of Warwick, Huntingdonshire, and Buckinghamshire, there have been within thirty years large tracts of the open field arable under that vile course, 1. fallow, 2. wheat, 3. spring corn, inclosed and laid down to grass, being much more suited to the wetness of the soil than corn." Here he admits local depopulation takes place, though he claims that a greater *net* produce is, as the result of enclosure, supplied by such districts to the rest of the kingdom. But then, he asks with regard to the opponents of such enclosure, "What will they say to the inclosures in *Norfolk, Suffolk, Nottinghamshire, Derbyshire, Lincolnshire, Yorkshire* and all the northern counties? What say they to the sands of *Norfolk, Suffolk and Nottinghamshire,* which yield corn and mutton from *the force of* INCLOSURE *alone?* What say they to the Wolds of *York* and *Lincoln,* which from barren heaths at 1s. per acre, are *by* INCLOSURE *alone* rendered profitable farms? Ask *Sir Cecil Wray* if without Inclosure he could advance his heaths by sainfoine from 1s. to 20s. an acre:—What say they to the vast tracts in the peak of Derby which *by* INCLOSURE *alone* are changed from black regions of ling to fertile fields covered with cattle? What say they to the improvements of moors in the northern counties, where

INCLOSURES alone have made these countries smile with culture which before were black as night ? "

He then proceeds to ridicule the view of his opponents, that the enclosure of waste, though desirable in itself, should as far as possible be so conducted as to create small farms and small properties, a view with which in later years, and after his tour in France, he very much sympathised. Into the merits of this controversy we need not go; what we have to note here is Arthur Young's evidence to the fact that from about 1744 to 1774 there was simultaneously proceeding a rapid enclosure of waste in Norfolk, Suffolk, Nottinghamshire, Derbyshire, Yorkshire, and Lincolnshire and the northern counties, by which the acreage under tillage was vastly increased, and a compensating enclosure of arable common fields in Northamptonshire, Leicestershire, Warwickshire, Huntingdonshire and Buckinghamshire, involving the conversion of arable to pasture, of small farms into much larger ones, and of the peasantry into urban labourers.

It only remains to be added that the former movement, if it was on at all as great a scale as Arthur Young gives us to understand (and I don't see why one should doubt this) must have proceeded largely, if not mainly, without the intervention of Parliament. This is in the first place antecedently probable. Secondly, whereas between 1727 and 1774 there were 273 common field parishes enclosed by Acts of Parliament in the five counties of Northamptonshire, Leicestershire, Warwick, Huntingdonshire and Buckinghamshire, the commons, fens, moors, etc., attached to only 109 parishes in Norfolk, Suffolk, Nottinghamshire, Derbyshire, Lincolnshire, Yorkshire, Durham and Northumberland were so enclosed. Unless the area of about 100,000 acres thus enclosed in these 109 parishes was merely a fraction of the total area of waste enclosed by all sorts of methods in this latter group of counties, Arthur Young was misleading his readers, for he certainly intends to give the impression that the enclosure of arable fields in the Midlands was on a much smaller scale than the reclamation of heaths, moors and fens in the northern and eastern counties. Thirdly, with regard to Norfolk, Arthur Young specifies enclosure without Acts of Parliament as one of the causes of the great agricultural improvement in parts of Norfolk ("Eastern Tour," 1771, Vol. II., p. 150) :—" From forty to sixty years ago, all the Northern and Western and a great part of the Eastern tracts of the country were sheep-walks, let so low as from 6d. to 1s. 6d. and 2s. an acre. Much of it was in this condition only thirty years ago. The great improvements have been made by reason of the following circumstances :—(1) By inclosing without assistance of Parliament."

Six other reasons follow, then the remark : "Parliamentary enclosures are scarcely ever so complete and general as in Norfolk," i.e., as the enclosures without the assistance of Parliament in Norfolk. I have only been able to find eleven Acts of Enclosure for Norfolk before 1771 ; seven of these were for the enclosure of common field parishes, and four for the enclosure of waste. In other words, the Parliamentary enclosure of these sheep-walks at the time when Arthur Young wrote had proceeded to a merely trifling extent.

We have, then, by Arthur Young's confession, in the five counties of Northampton, Leicester, Warwick, Huntingdon, and Buckingham enclosure admittedly accompanied by decay of tillage and rural depopulation. From "A Country Gentleman's" list we can add Oxfordshire and parts of Lincolnshire. That the same prevailing economic motive operated in Bedfordshire can be shown from Arthur Young's "Tour through the North of England." The country in June, 1768, from St. Neots to Kimbolton was in general open—" the open fields let at 7s. and 7s. 6d. per acre, and the inclosed pastures about 17s. Hence we find a profit of 10s. an acre by inclosing and laying to grass." He might here ask, as he does with regard to the district in Buckinghamshire between Aylesbury and Buckingham, which he found in 1771 in the condition of open field arable, under a course of fallow, wheat, beans, fallow, barley, beans. "As to the landlords, what in the name of wonder can be the reason of their not inclosing ! All this vale would make as fine meadows as any in the world."

As for Gloucestershire, William Marshall ("Rural Economy of Gloucestershire," 1789, p. 21), estimates the rents in the Vale of Evesham at 10s. to 15s. per acre for common field arable, 10s. to 20s. per acre for enclosed arable, and 20s. to 50s. per acre for enclosed pasture. Here again there can be no doubt that enclosure implied laying down at least all the good land in grass.

A Select Committee of the House of Commons appointed to consider the high prices of food in December, 1800 (1800 and 1801 being famine years), made enquiry, by the help of the parish clergy, into the increase or decrease of land under different crops, and of cattle, sheep, and pigs in the districts which had been enclosed in the previous 45 years by private Acts (*i.e.*, since 1755). The total result showed a net gain in area under wheat in 1,767,651 acres enclosed of 10,625 acres; the area under wheat being before enclosure 155,572 acres; after, 165,837 acres. But these figures included all sorts of enclosure. The Board of Agriculture ("Gen. Report," pp. 39 and 232), by leaving out cases where waste only was enclosed, obtained the following result for cases of enclosure of all commonable lands, under Acts passed between 1761 and 1799, in parishes where commonable arable was included. Taking the counties in groups we have:—

	Wheat Acreage Increased		Wheat Acreage Decreased	
	in Cases.	by Acres.	in Cases.	by Acres.
MIDLAND COUNTIES.				
Rutland	0	—	10	596
Warwick	2	93	30	2,871
Leicester	11	453	63	4,340
Northampton	11	450	75	7,016
Nottingham	14	923	28	1,823
Oxford	8	285	11	508
Buckingham	6	161	32	3,085
Bedford	7	668	23	1,801
Total	59	3033	262	22,036

	Wheat Acreage Increased		Wheat Acreage Decreased	
—	in Cases.	by Acres.	in Cases.	by Acres.
EASTERN COUNTIES.				
Norfolk	8	627	1	10
Suffolk	3	150	0	
Huntingdon	7	469	9	530
Cambridge	7	895	2	184
Essex	1	40	0	
Hertford	3	174	1	7
Total	29	2,355	13	731
NORTHERN COUNTIES.				
Northumberland ...	2	80	1	93
Durham	1	20	2	172
Yorkshire	40	3,411	22	1,991
Lincoln	48	2,422	41	2,843
Derby	3	60	10	345
Total	94	5,993	76	5,444
SOUTHERN COUNTIES. (South of Thames).				
Berkshire	5	312	3	249
Wiltshire	12	884	11	528
Hampshire	6	256	2	90
Dorset	4	105	5	177
Somerset	1	50	1	33
Sussex	1	180	0	
Total	29	1,787	22	1,077
WESTERN COUNTIES.				
Gloucester	17	948	20	988
Hereford	1	40		
Shropshire	2	115		
Staffordshire	—	—	1	300
Worcester	9	345	3	155
Total	29	1,448	24	1,343
GRAND TOTAL ...	239	14,507	407	30,894

In estimating the significance of these figures it must be borne in mind that the figures for acreage in wheat after enclosure were collected at a time of famine prices for wheat. Probably many thousands of acres of old arable common field, which had been enclosed and laid down in grass, in each of these counties, were again ploughed under the stimulus of wheat prices exceeding 100*s*. per quarter.

So much with regard to the connexion between depopulation and enclosure in the second half of the eighteenth century. With regard to the first half, the following account is supplied by a certain John Cowper, " Inclosing Commons and Common field lands is contrary to the interest of the Nation " (1732) :—

" When these commons come to be inclosed and converted into pasture, the Ruin of the Poor is a natural consequence; they being bought out by the lord of the *Manor*, or some other person of substance.

" In most open field parishes there are at a medium 40 farmers and 80 cottagers who hold their lands in common, and have right of commonage one with another. Suppose each person employs 6 labourers, we have in all 660 persons, men, women and children, who besides their Employment in Husbandry, carry on large branches of the Woollen and Linnen Manufactures."

With regard to the plea that hedging and ditching will employ many hands, he says: " This is so contrary to constant experience, that it hardly deserves to be taken notice of. I myself, within these 30 years past, have seen above 20 Lordships or Parishes inclosed, and everyone of them has been in a manner depopulated. If we take all the inclosed Parishes one with another, we shall find hardly ten inhabitants remaining, where there were an hundred before Inclosures were made. And in some parishes 120 families of Farmers and Cottagers, have in a few years been reduced to four, to two, aye, and sometimes to but one family. And if this practice of inclosing continues much longer, we may expect to see all the great estates ingrossed by a few Hands, and the industrious Farmers and Cottagers almost intirely rooted out of the kingdom. Raising Hedges and sinking ditches may indeed employ several hands for a year, or hardly so

long, but when that is once over, the work is at an end. . . .
Owners of inclosed Lands, if they have but a little corn to get in,
are already forced to send several miles to open field parishes for
Harvest men."

Six open field farms, averaging 150 acres each, and the little
holdings of twelve cottagers, would be let together, after enclosure,
as one grazing farm, and the total rent thus be raised from £300
to £600. But whereas one acre of arable land would previously
have produced 20 bushels at 3s. per bushel, a gross return of £3;
after enclosure it would contribute to the fattening of a bullock to
the extent of 25s. The gross produce is decreased; but the net
produce is increased. Of the £3 produced by the acre of common
field under wheat, 50s. would go in expenses, leaving 6s. 8d. to
the landlord and 3s. 4d. to the tenant. Of the 25s. produced by
the same acre enclosed under grass, 13s. 4d. would go to the
landlord, 11s. 8d. to the grazier.

It is interesting in passing to note the association of common
field agriculture with manufacture in the domestic stage indicated
by this passage.

We have also direct evidence of the same movements in the
seventeenth century. On the one hand Walter Blyth ("The
English Improver," 1649, p. 40) has the passage:—"Consider but
the Woodlands, who before Enclosure, were wont to be relieved by
the Fieldon, with corne of all sorts. And now growne as gallant
Corne Countries as be in England, as the Western part of
Warwickshire, and the northern parts of Worcestershire,
Staffordshire, Shropshire, Derbyshire, Yorkshire, and all the
countries thereabouts." On the other hand, from the controversy
between the two John Moores on the one hand, and Joseph Lee
and an anonymous controversialist on the other, we can pick out
certain statements of matters of fact that passed uncontradicted.

This controversy arose out of the enclosure of Catthorp, a
parish in the extreme south-west corner of Leicestershire,
bordering on Northamptonshire and Warwickshire. Lee was
the parish priest of Catthorp, and a party to the enclosure. In
his "Vindication of Regulated Inclosure," he gives a list of
fifteen parishes within three miles of Catthorp which had been

enclosed. He also gives a list of nineteen parishes, enclosed from twenty to fifty years, in which depopulation had not yet taken place. This second list, as John Moore remarks, " they were forced to fish up out of the counties of Leicester, Warwick, Northampton, etc.," and it is significant that two only of the fifteen parishes enclosed near Catthorp are asserted by Lee not to have been attended by depopulation. If we go a little earlier we find in 1607 an insurrection against enclosures, followed by a searching enquiry by James I.'s government, and no doubt by renewed vigilance, for a while, in the enforcement of the Depopulation Acts. It may be regarded as axiomatic that in a corn-growing country,[1] enclosure which does not diminish tillage, does not provoke riot and insurrection.

While, however, enclosure which does not diminish the land under tillage does not, as a rule, cause rural depopulation, it is a rule not altogether without exception. One of the most striking passages in Cobbett's " Rural Rides " is that written in August, 1826, in which he describes the valley of the Wiltshire Avon :—

"It is manifest enough, that the population of this valley was, at one time, many times over what it is now; for, in the first place, what were the twenty-nine churches built for ? The population of the twenty-nine parishes is now but little more than one-half of the single parish of Kensington,[2] and there are several of the churches bigger than the church at Kensington. . . . In three instances, Fifield, Milston, and Roach-Fen, the *church porches* would hold all the inhabitants, even down to the bed-ridden and the babies. What then, will any man believe that these churches were built for such little knots of people ? . . . But, in fact, you plainly see all the traces of a great ancient population. The churches were almost all large, and built in the best manner. Many of them are very fine edifices; very costly in the building; and, in the cases where the body of the

---

[1] Riots may occur on the enclosure of waste, where the enclosed waste gave a livelihood to a considerable specialised population, as in Hatfield Chase and the Fens. See Dr. Cunningham's " Growth of English Industry and Commerce," Vol. II., pp. 187, 188.

[2] Just above he states it at 9,116.

church has been altered in the repairing of it, so as to make it smaller, the tower, which everywhere defies the hostility of time, shows you what the church must formerly have been. . . . There are now no less than nine of the parishes out of the twenty-nine, that have either no parsonage houses or have such as are in such a state that a parson will not, or cannot, live in them. . . . The land remains, and the crops and the sheep come as abundantly as ever ; but they are now sent almost wholly away. . . . In the distance of about thirty miles, there stood fifty mansion houses. Where are they now? I believe there are but eight, that are at all worthy of the name of mansion houses. . . . In taking my leave of this beautiful vale I have to express my deep shame, as an Englishman, at beholding the general extreme poverty of those who cause this vale to produce such quantities of food and raiment. This is, I verily believe it, the worst-used labouring population upon the face of the earth."[1]

When Cobbett wrote, the process of Enclosure for this corner of Wiltshire was practically complete. Thomas Davis, whose account of the agriculture of Wiltshire is the most interesting of the whole series of county surveys, wrote when the process was in its early stage, and wrote predicting depopulation. He says, " The greater part of this country was formerly, and at no very remote period, in the hands of great proprietors. Almost every manor had its resident lord, who held part of the lands in demesne, and granted out the rest by copy or lease to under tenants, usually for three lives renewable. A state of commonage, and particularly of open common fields, was particularly favour-able to this tenure. . . . The north-west of Wiltshire being much better adapted to inclosures and to sub-division of property, than the rest, was inclosed first; while the south-east, or Down district, has undergone few inclosures and still fewer sub-divisions."

The common field system was called "tenantry."[3] The tenants ordinarily were occupiers of single "yardlands," rented

[1] "Rural Rides," 1830 edition, pp. 375—390.
[2] Thos. Davis, Wiltshire, p. 8.
[3] *Ibid.*, p. 14.

at about £20 a year each. A typical yardland consisted,[1] besides
the homestead, of 2 acres of meadow, 18 acres in the arable
fields, usually in 18 to 20 pieces, a right on the common meadows,
common fields, and downs for forty sheep, and as many cattle as
the tenant could winter with the fodder he grew.[2] His forty
sheep were kept with those of his neighbours, in the common
flock of the manor, in charge of the common shepherd. They
were taken every day to the downs, and brought back every
night to be folded on the arable fields, the usual rule being to
fold one thousand sheep on a "tenantry" acre (but ¾ of a
statute acre) per night. In breeding sheep regard was had to
what may be termed folding quality (*i.e.*, the propensity to drop
manure only after being folded at night) as much as to quality or
quantity of wool or meat.[3]

On the enclosure of such a manor the common flock was
broken up, and the position of the small farmer became untenable.
It is true, says our author, that he has the convenience of having
his arable land in fewer pieces; but if he has his 18 acres all in
one piece instead of in 20, he cannot plough them with fewer
than the three horses he previously ploughed with. Then he
has no enclosure to put his horses in; he no longer has the
common to turn them on. His right on the down would entitle
him to an allotment of sheepdown of about 20 acres, perhaps
two miles from home. This is too small for him to be able to
take it up, so he accepts instead an increase of arable land. But
now he has no down on which to feed his sheep, no common
shepherd to take charge of his sheep, which are too few to
enable him individually to employ a shepherd. He, therefore,
must part with his flock and then has no sheep to manure his land;
further, having no cow-common, and very little pasture land,

---

[1] Contrast with such farms those described by Cobbett 30 years later : "At one
farm 27 ricks, at another 400 acres of wheat stubble in one piece, at a third a
sheepfold about 4,000 sheep and lambs, at a fourth 300 hogs in one stubble, a
fifth farm at Milton had 600 qrs. of wheat, 1,200 qrs. of barley of the year's
crop, and kept on an average 1,400 sheep " (pp. 363, 4, 5). " The farms are all
large " (p. 361).

[2] *Ibid.*, p. 15.

[3] *Ibid.*, p. 61.

he cannot keep cows to make dung with his straw. Lastly, the arable land being in general entirely unsuited to turn to grass, he is prevented from enclosing his allotment, and laying it down in pasture.[1] Obviously in such circumstances the small farmer, after for a few years raising diminishing crops from his impoverished arable land, must succumb, and in some cases help as a labourer to till his fields for another man, in other cases drift to the towns or enlist.

The contemporaneous decay of rural manufacturing industry,[2] of course, greatly aggravated the depopulating effects of enclosure. It may even have precipitated enclosure by weakening the position of the small farmer during the period of the French wars : during a time, that is, in which a combination of causes, apart from enclosure, was favouring the extension of large farms at the expense of small farms.[3]

In the south-east of Wiltshire, then, enclosure was followed by no increase of pasture farming, but it was followed by local depopulation. Whether the depopulation was merely local, or national as well, would depend upon whether, after enclosure, the total production of food of the parish were increased or diminished. Thomas Davis tells us that in many cases it was diminished, the reason, no doubt, being that there was a lack of farmers with sufficient enterprise and control of capital to absorb the small farms, as their occupiers began to drift towards bankruptcy. That such a result as this was felt to be an impending danger is shown by his statement :—" In some late inclosures allotments of arable land to small farmers have been set out adjoining to each other, directing the same to remain in an uninclosed state with a common right of sheep-feed over the

---

[1] *Ibid.*, p. 80.

[2] " The villages down this Valley of Avon, and indeed, it was the same in almost every part of this county, and in the North and West of Hampshire also, used to have great employment for the women and children in the carding and spinning of wool for the making of broadcloth. This was a very general employment for the women and girls, but it is now wholly gone." (Cobbett, "Rural Rides," p. 385, 1830 edition, written August, 1826.)

[3] These causes were (*a*) the great fluctuations in prices of agricultural produce ; (*b*) the custom of using poor relief as a supplement to agricultural wages. The way in which these operated is ably dealt with by Dr. Cunningham.

whole, and a common allotment of down land and another of water-meadows, and some inclosed pasture to each if necessary."

In this district, consisting of open downs, stretching for miles along the summits and higher slopes of the chalk hills; intersected by winding rivers bordered by flat alluvial land of naturally rich pasture, but converted by irrigation into the famous Wiltshire water meadows, the long lower slopes of the hills, as it were, decreed by nature to be noble corn fields, cultivation had to be on a large scale; the unit of cultivation had to be a piece of land of reasonable width, stretching from the river to the summit of the downs. Hence small farms could not exist without some degree of organised mutual help. When that organisation, which in this district was furnished by the common field system, was terminated by Enclosure Acts, consolidation of farms became necessary.

Nowhere else are these conditions present in quite so fully developed a degree as in Wiltshire, which contains the central hub from which radiate the three great belts of chalk down, the South Downs, the North Downs, and the range containing the Chilterns, the chalk hills of Hertfordshire, the Gog-Magogs of Cambridgeshire, and their continuation into Norfolk. But the most essential feature of Wiltshire agriculture, viz., the combination of sheep down and arable field, may be said to be characteristic of all this country. This is the country from which in the sixteenth century came the great indignant outcry against enclosure, which in More's "Utopia" enters into the classic literature of our country. When it is remembered that the economic motive of enclosure then was the high price of wool, that private individuals are stated to have owned flocks of ten thousand, twenty thousand, and even of twenty-four thousand sheep, it is easy to conceive of whole parishes being converted into great sheep runs.

[1] Preamble to 25 Henry VIII. c. 13.

CHAPTER XI.

" The Poor at Enclosure do Grutch
Because of abuses that fall."
TUSSER, " Champion and Several."

DURING the nineteenth century the controversy with regard to
enclosure did not turn upon the question whether it did or
did not injure the mass of the rural poor of the locality, in
their capacity of agricultural labourers, by depriving them of
employment ; but whether it injured them by depriving
them without compensation of rights which they had enjoyed
before enclosure, but which could not be legally established;
and whether poor owners of common rights have received
compensation : the question, in fact, whether the poor are
justified in " Grutching at Enclosure," because of real abuses
in the method of carrying it out.   On this question no distinction
need be drawn between the two classes of Enclosure Acts.

I do not think that much complaint can be made with regard
to the administration of the Enclosure Acts since 1876 by the
Board of Agriculture.   By the provision of adequate allotment
grounds and recreation grounds compensation is made to those
villagers who can claim no specific rights of common ; and
though no doubt many of the owners of single common rights
are dissatisfied with the plots of land assigned to them, there
seems to be no reason for doubting that the Commissioners
appointed have endeavoured to deal with rich and poor with
equal fairness.   Further, a great deal of the work of the Board
in its capacity of Enclosure Commissioners has been the regulation of commons ; and to a certain degree they have become a
body for preserving instead of destroying commons.   They may
even be described as the most potent force for the preservation

of existing common-fields, simply by insisting on a certain method in the division and allotment, which may be too expensive.

But this verdict of "Not guilty" only applies to the enclosure authority since it was chastened and corrected by the movement for the preservation of commons. All the early reports of the Enclosure Commissioners, or the Enclosure, Tithe and Copyhold Commissioners give abundant evidence of the hard, legal spirit in which the claims of cottagers were considered, and the slight reasons which were considered good enough for refusing recreation grounds and allotments. The twenty-seventh annual report—the *apologia* of the Commissioners—pleads, as we have seen above, that 8,000,000 acres of commons, and 1,000,000 acres of commonable arable fields or meadows still existed, which was absurdly inaccurate, and that "of all modes of tenure in a fully peopled country there is none more prejudicial to improved culture than that of holding in common." Again, the thirty-second report makes a great deal of the fact that the 590,000 acres of common and commonable land dealt with since the Act of 1845 had been distributed among 26,000 separate owners; which, however, only proved that the number of people who owned rights over unenclosed land had been greater than the number of owners of a corresponding area of enclosed land— but whether that was because commons and common fields favoured the creation or preservation of small properties (as it certainly does in many cases), or whether because a multiplicity of owners favours the preservation of commons and common fields (which is always the case), no credit was due to the General Enclosure Act, or to the body administering it.

We find that between 1845 and 1875, out of a total area of 590,000 acres divided and allotted, just 1758 acres were set aside for recreation grounds, and 2195 acres for field gardens and allotments. The administration of the Act since 1877 is, therefore, a very severe condemnation of its administration in the earlier period.

We have seen in the case of Ewelme and the neighbouring parishes, how the cottagers were injured on enclosure, by losing their source of fuel, without getting any compensation. I am indebted to Mr. John Swain for the following description of the effects of enclosure of a Welsh mountain.

"The parish of ——, in the county of Montgomeryshire, is about five miles long by two miles broad. It consists for the most part of a hill, lying between a river and one of its tributaries. The hill rises to about 900 feet above sea level, and contains no unenclosed land. We have, therefore, in this parish, two strips of low-lying meadow land, land of a moderate quality on the hill slopes, and rough pasture land near the summit. On this hill most of the cottage holdings are to be found, usually in some sheltered hollow near a spring or a running stream. . . .

"Previous to the Enclosure Act, passed early in the nineteenth century, the greater part of the hill was open. The farms occupied the bottom lands, and the foot of the hill, up which they crept, their boundary fences forming an irregular line on the hillside, being higher or lower as the nature and quality of the land tempted enclosure. The unenclosed portion of the hill was used as a common pasture by all the farmers whose land adjoined it, and the amount of stock each one was allowed to feed on it was roughly regulated by the size of his holding.

"About 120 years ago a number of the poorer peasantry began settling on this common land. There was a general understanding that if a house was raised during the night so that the builders were able to cause smoke to issue from the chimney by sunrise, they thereby established a right of possession which none could gainsay. Timber in the neighbouring woods was abundant and cheap, so an intending squatter had little difficulty in procuring the material for building his cottage. With the help of his friends he procured sufficient wood for the framework, and then selected a convenient site in a sheltered spot with a southern aspect, and marked down the foundations of his future dwelling. When all preparations were made he gathered together all the help he could, and in the dusk of the evening had all his materials conveyed to the selected spot. Rough stonework was laid to form the foundations and chimney end of the cottage, and then the framework was quickly set up.

The panels were interwoven with stout laths, and covered with clay, over which was smeared a coating of lime-plaster, while a roof of thatch completed the edifice. Windows were not for a time considered necessary, but the entrance was carefully secured by a stout door. Then just as the dawn was breaking, a fire was kindled on the hearth, and the curl of smoke above the rude chimney told the workers that they could now relax their efforts. . . .

" A dwelling-house having been erected, the next step was to appropriate a few acres of land surrounding it. . . . The difficulty of obtaining sufficient land for the keep of a cow was no more than the labour of enclosing and reclaiming it.

" In this way some thirty or forty families were settled in cottages built by themselves, around which were three or four fields, where for many years they lived in undisturbed possession. By patient labour the gorse and fern were got rid of, trees were planted round the cottage, or allowed to grow where they sprang up in suitable places in the hedgerows; by cultivation and manuring the herbage was improved.

" With the Enclosure Act there came a disturbance of this state of affairs. The partition of the unappropriated land seems to have been carried out fairly, by adding to each farm a quantity of land in proportion to the amount of pasturage the occupier enjoyed on the common. . . . When, however, we come to consider the case of the cottager, his treatment was by no means fair. Enclosures of over twenty-one years' standing were not interfered with, and their owners were left in undisturbed possession, but such as had been enclosed for a shorter period were claimed by the Lord of the Manor, who lived some twelve miles away, and possessed little or no land in the parish. He advanced his claim cautiously, asking only a nominal rent, and as unlettered peasants felt the inequality of a contest in the matter, this rent was paid. Consequently more than half the cottage holdings fell into his hands, and the poor occupiers were deprived of the ownership of the dwellings they had erected, and of all the improvements they had put into the land they had enclosed. None of them had to leave their holdings,· and the rent at first charged was trifling; but except in cases where life-leases were granted, the cottagers had lost all their rights, and they and their holdings were left entirely in the hands of a large landowner."

The Enclosure Act, of course, prevented the creation of any more cottage holdings. The fertility of the soil in these small holdings, Mr. Swain says, is enormously greater than that of the land, naturally similar, on the other side of the hedge. Usually the cottager gets a neighbouring farmer to plough half an acre of his holding for him, paying for this service in labour at harvest time; and keeps the rest, except the garden plot, under grass. The average size of the holding is about six acres; which is found sufficient for two cows, a heifer, a calf, several pigs, thirty fowls, and a dozen ducks. The produce supplies all the vegetables, fruit, milk, butter, eggs and bacon consumed by the family, and brings in the following money returns, on Mr. Swain's calculations :—

	£	s.	d.
One cow and one calf sold per annum (the other calf being reared to replace the cow sold)	14	0	0
Six pounds of butter per week, at 1s. per lb.	15	12	0
1 pig, sold at a net profit of	2	10	0
20 fowls	2	5	0
400 eggs (allowing 600 for home consumption)	1	8	0
	£35	15	0

As Mr. Swain writes from an intimate personal knowledge, I have no hesitation in accepting his statement as approximately accurate.

The injury to the cottagers does not end with the prevention of the creation of fresh holdings, and the transfer of the ownership of most of those already existing to the lord of the manor. For the landlord, managing his estate in the ordinary way, through the intermediaries of steward and agent, is almost invariably led into merging such small holdings into larger farms, in spite of the high rents which would often be gladly paid.

It will be seen that these two cases are in the nature of things typical. Similar hardships may be regarded as the almost inevitable effect of any enclosure which included any considerable quantity of waste land ; and if the enclosure is necessary or highly desirable, some compensating advantages ought to be provided for the inhabitants as such. The smallness of such provision between 1845 and 1875 is very significant. And it makes one seriously doubt whether in their zeal for furthering improved culture, the Commissioners were as considerate as was desirable to the cottager who had a legal common right. But on that point we can apply no statistical test.

If we turn from enclosures since 1845 to enclosures before, we have a verdict from the old Board of Agriculture in its General Report on Enclosures published in 1808, which, so far as it is biassed, is biassed entirely in favour of enclosure. It says : " The benefit (of enclosure) in this case (to the poor) is by no means unmixed."

The loss of fuel is declared to be the chief injury ; and besides, " In some cases many cows had been kept without a legal right, and nothing had been given for the practice."

" In other cases, where allotments were assigned, the cottagers could not pay the expense of the measure, and were forced to sell their allotments."

" In others they kept cows by right of hiring their cottages, or common rights, and the land going, of course, to their proprietor, was added to the farms, and the poor sold their cows. This is a very common case."[1]

The results are given of an investigation into the results of sixty-eight Enclosure Acts, chiefly in the Eastern Counties ; testimony having been obtained from the clergy and others considered to be impartial witnesses. In fifteen cases it is asserted that the poor were not injured by the enclosure ; in fifty-three cases

[1] " General Report on Enclosures," pp. 12, 13.

that they were. The general tenour of the statement in these cases is to the effect that the condition of the poor has become very much worse, that they have lost all their cows,[1] and they no longer are able to buy milk for their children. Here are a few of the more striking descriptions :—

Ackworth, Yorkshire. The parish belonged to near 200 owners; nearly the whole of whom have come to the parish since the enclosure, or changed the quantity of their lands.

Todenham, Gloucester. Nothing increased but the poor. Eight farmhouses filled with them.

Tingewick, Bucks. Milk to be had at 1d. a quart before ; not to be had now at any rate.

Passenham, Northamptonshire. (The poor) deprived of their cows, and great sufferers by the loss of their hogs.

Tulvy, Bedfordshire. Cows lessened from 110 to 40.

Letcomb, Berkshire. The poor can no longer keep a cow, and they are therefore now maintained by the parish.[2]

Alconbury, Huntingdon. (1791, c. 70.) Several who kept cows before were, upon enclosure, forced to part with them, and have kept none since. The cottage allotments going to the landlords were thrown together, and the inhabitants left without cows or land. Those who had allotments given in lieu of their rights, not being able to enclose them,[3] were forced to sell, and became as the rest in this respect. Before enclosure milk could readily be bought, poor people could lay out a half-penny or a penny every day, but nothing of the sort could be got since.[4]

With regard to Buckingham in general, we have the following statement from a later survey for the Board of the County :—

" The poor and persons with little capital (such as butchers, common shepherds, etc.) derive benefit from open fields and commons, by being enabled to keep horses, cows, and sheep. . . . It will be difficult to prove that in any case the poor have been benefited (by enclosure). No instances of benefit on this score

[1] This is specifically asserted in 17 cases.
[2] " General Report on Enclosures," pp. 150—152.
[3] Because of the expense.
[4] " General Report," p. 154.

have been stated to me. On the contrary, an increase of poor (*i.e.*, of paupers) has been the general complaint."

Similar evidence is given by two professional Enclosure Commissioners. Mr. Forster, of Norwich, "lamented that he had been accessory to injuring 2000 poor people, at the rate of twenty families per parish. Numbers in the practice of feeding the commons cannot prove their right; and many, indeed most who have allotments, have not more than one acre, which being insufficient for the man's cow, both the cow and land are usually sold to opulent farmers. The right sold before the allotment produced much less than the allotment after it, but the money is dissipated, doing them no good when they cannot vest it in stock." [1]

Mr. Ewen, another Commissioner, " observed that in most of the enclosures he has known the poor man's allotment and cow are sold five times in six before the award is signed." A third Commissioner, Mr. Algar, declared that he made it a practice to give an allotment whenever a cottager could merely prove that he had been in the practice of cutting turf. But one wonders whether Mr. Algar did not find this custom of his prejudicial to the demand for his professional services.

In estimating the weight of this evidence, both as to depopulation and as to injury to the poor, it must be borne in mind that it is taken almost entirely from the mouths of advocates, and mostly very enthusiastic advocates, of enclosure. They are admissions of men who feel that the general case in favour of enclosure is so strong that they may well candidly admit the existence of some drawbacks. Of course, some advocates of enclosure are not disposed to make any admissions at all. Many urge the moral evils engendered by waste lands, as : " Where wastes and commons are most extensive, there I have perceived the Cottagers are the most wretched and worthless; accustomed to relie on a precarious and vagabond subsistence from land in a state of nature, when that fails they recur to pilfering, and thereby become a nuisance to their honest and

---

[1] " General Report," p. 157.

industrious neighbours; and if the father of a family of this sort is withdrawn from society for his crimes, his children become burthensome to the parish. It may truly be said that for cottagers of this description the game is preserved, and by them destroyed; they are mostly beneath the law and out of reach of detection; and while they can earn four or five shillings, and sometimes more, in a night, by poaching, they will not be satisfied with 10d. or 1s. a day for honest labour."[1] A not unusual style of argument is the following :—

"To deprive the poor of that benefit, which, in their present state, they derive from the waste lands, must no doubt, at first view, sound harsh. But it ought to be remembered that in this wealthy county, where there is so much work to be done, and so few hands comparatively to do it, there are few poor that do not deserve to be so. Those persons who are disqualified to provide for the calls of human nature by the feebleness of infancy, the crushing hand of disease, or the infirmities of old age, cannot be said to be poor, because *all* the landed property, situate within their respective parishes, is always liable to be charged with their maintenance."[2]

After reading of the good fortune of these Herefordshire labourers, so much in demand in a wealthy county that the benefits derived from wastes and commons are of little concern to them, one naturally inquires, what were their wages? Day labourers earned in summer, "6s. a week and a gallon of drink to each man";[3] in winter, 5s. a week and three quarts; in harvest, 14d. a day and meat and drink : the hours of labour being in harvest time and in winter as early and as late as they could see; in summer, not harvest, from 6 to 6. Leaving out the cider, this works out at a penny an hour, and a penny in 1794 would not buy very much more of the ultimate necessaries of life in Herefordshire than it will to-day.

There seems, underlying John Clark's words, a notion that if any injury is done to the poor by enclosure, proper and sufficient

---

[1] D. Walker, "Hertfordshire" (1794), p. 53.
[2] John Clark, ' Hereford " (1794), p. 27.
[3] *Ibid.*, p. 29. " Drink " of course means cider.

compensation will be made in the ordinary course to the persons injured out of the poor-rates. The logical deduction is that the profits of enclosure should contribute to the poor-rates, and I have noted thirteen enclosures of wastes and commons in which this was done. Another logical deduction was that the poor rate in parishes in which waste was enclosed was, in part at least, a species of common property belonging to the poor ; and to deprive them of this property was robbery, unless the commons were restored. This view was vigorously expressed by Cobbett in his "Political Register," at the time of the introduction of the Poor Law of 1834, and from him became part of the traditional stock of political ideas handed down through the Chartists to the Labour movement of recent times.

Arthur Young, in a pamphlet published in 1801,[1] not only insists upon the injury to the poor from Enclosure Acts as ordinarily drawn and put into execution, but pleads for enclosure on methods which would tend to the social elevation of the labourer. His proposals, which strike one as, for the time, wise and statesmanlike, though they ignore some considerations which would be of great importance to-day, were :

(1) That in the case of small commons in the midst of an enclosed country, labourers should be allowed to absorb the whole by gradual encroachments, thus building up small properties for themselves.

(2) In the case of extensive wastes, procedure must be by Act of Parliament, but all Acts should secure enough land for every cottager to keep a cow both summer and winter, such land to be *inalienable from the cottage, and the ownership to be vested in the parish.*

I have found one Act which realises Arthur Young's ideal of an Enclosure Act. It was passed in 1824 for Pottern in Wiltshire, and though it was an Act for the enclosure of a common only, no commonable meadow or common field being included, I give its provisions here on account of its intrinsic interest.

The ownership of the whole common was vested in the Bishop

---

[1] "Enquiry into the propriety of applying wastes to the better support and nourishment of the poor."

of Salisbury, who was lord of the manor, the vicar and church-wardens, in trust for the parish.   The trustees were required to lease it in small holdings, with or without rent, to poor, honest, and industrious persons, who had not, except in cases of accident or illness, availed themselves of Poor Law relief.

The following Acts, all (except that for Earsham) for " extinguishing village communities," *i.e.*, for enclosing all the commonable lands of the parishes or townships, which in each case include commonable arable fields, have special provisions to safeguard the interests of the poor :—

1757, c. 53.   Wimeswould, Leicestershire.   Cottagers who have no land are to have a share together within one fence, which they may afterwards separately enclose if they like.   This is specially interesting as anticipating the modern practice of providing allotments for such cottagers.

1767, c. 49.   Carlton in Lindrick, Nottingham.   Three acres (out of a total of 2492 acres) are to be set aside for building cottages for the benefit of the poor.

1779, c. 89.   Evenley or Bury Manor, Northampton.   Lands to the value of £10 per annum (out of £1200) are to be set aside for the most deserving poor not receiving poor-relief.

1785, c. 56.   Eight parishes in Wiltshire enclosed by one Act.   Not more than ten acres in each parish is to be set aside, free of taxes, for fuel for the poor.

1805, c. 19.   Palling, Norfolk.   One-twentieth of the whole area is to be vested in the lord of the manor, vicar, and overseers, in trust for the poor, for common of pasture and fuel.

1807, c. 18.   Herringswell, Suffolk.   An allotment is to be made for fuel for the poor.

1809, c. 7.   Barton Turf, Norfolk.   Thirty acres is to be reserved for common for the poor.

1810, c. 55.   Great Sheepey, Leicestershire.   *Every cottage to have not less than 3 acres allotted to it.*

1812, c. 3.   Little Brandon, Norfolk.   Ten acres to be set aside for the benefit of the poor, partly to be used as common for fuel, or to be leased to pay for fuel ; another part to provide a common pasture for the poor inhabitants; while the *remainder* (how much? one wonders) was to be leased in aid of the poor-rates.

1812, c. 17.   Earsham, Norfolk.   Five acres to be set aside to be leased to buy fuel for the poor.

Also in the Acts for Northwold, Norfolk (1796, c. 14), Lower Wilbraham, Cambridge (1797, c. 89), and Barnady, Suffolk, allotments were made inalienable from the cottages for which they were assigned.   At Northwold land capable of supplying annually 12,000 turves per annum was reserved as a common turbary for the poorer owners of common rights.[1]

This list of Acts containing special provisions for the benefit of the poor is not a complete one, but if it were it would not, I believe, include more than one per cent. of the Enclosure Acts passed prior to 1845.   Arthur Young did not over-state the case when he wrote : " By nineteen Enclosure Acts out of twenty, the poor are injured, in some grossly injured. . . . The poor in these parishes may say, and with truth, *Parliament may be tender of property, all I know is, I had a cow, and an Act of Parliament has taken it from me.*" [2]

---

[1] I must here refer to the extraordinary Act by which Pickering Moor (York-shire, West Riding) was enclosed in 1785 and divided equally among all owners of common rights, the poorest cottager owning an ancient cottage getting as much as the largest landowner.   Before enclosure the yeomen of Pickering had pastured such animals on the moor as they could provide with winter keep. The great tithes were rented by an enterprising lessee, who conceived the idea of parcelling the moor into small farms which would grow corn and yield tithes. In spite of the disinclination of the yeomen to any change, he procured the passing of an Enclosure Act, in which it was declared that the moor was equally the property of all ancient cottages and messuages, and was required to be divided equally among the owners of all of these.   A peculiar clause in the Act enacted that no part of the moor should be " deemed barren in respect of tithes." The larger yeomen felt themselves to be cheated, and were very indignant, but through inertness and lack of co-operation they failed to take steps to prevent the Act being executed.   This they presumably might have done by an appeal to Quarter Sessions.

[2] " Enquiry into the propriety of applying wastes to the better support and maintenance of the poor," 1801, p. 42.

CHAPTER XII.

THREE ACRES AND A COW.

THAT the poor were not always the only sufferers from an Enclosure Act, is shown by the account given by the General Report on Enclosures of the way in which farmers were affected. After referring to the idea that opposition from farmers is usually to be ascribed to ignorant prejudice, the report proceeds :—

" In many instances they have suffered considerably for four, five, or six years. From the first starting the project of an Enclosure Act to the final award, has, in numerous cases, taken two, three, four, and even five or six years ; their management is deranged ; not knowing where their future lands will be allotted, they save all their dung till much of it is good for little ; they perform all the operations of tillage with inferior attention ; perhaps the fields are cross-cropped and exhausted, and not well recovered under a course of years. Rents are greatly raised and too soon ; so that if they do not absolutely lose five years they at least suffer a great check. In point of profit, comparing the old with the new system, attention must be paid to their capitals ; open field land is managed (notwithstanding the inconvenience of its pieces) usually with a less capital than enclosures ; and though the *general* profit of the latter exceeds that of the former, yet this will entirely depend on the capital being adequate. In cases where the new enclosures are laid down to grass, all this becomes of tenfold force ; to stock rich grass lands demands a far greater sum than open field arable ; the farmer may not possess it ; this has often happened, and drove them to seek other investments, giving way to new-comers more able to undertake the new system introduced ; and if profit be measured by a percentage on the

capital employed, the old system might, at the old rents, exceed
the profits of the new; and this is certainly the farmers' view
of the comparison. He also who had given the attention of a
life to the regular routine of open field arable, without 10 acres
of grass ever having been in his occupation, may find himself
much at a loss in the regular purchase and sale of live stock,
the profit of which depends so much on habitual skill. Add to
all this the previous circumstance of laying down to grass, the
business of all others of which farmers know the least, of which
I have many times seen in new enclosures striking instances;
and if all these points be duly considered, we shall not find
much reason to be surprised at the repugnance shown by many
farmers to the idea of enclosing." (Pp. 31, 32.)

While the whole of this description of the ordeal that the
farmers had to pass through is interesting, the point I desire
here to emphasize is the need of a larger capital after enclosure.
Those who had the requisite skill, knowledge, energy and
capital survived the crisis; they were able to take up the farms
which their weaker neighbours were compelled to relinquish;
to send, in almost every case, a larger *surplus* of food from the
lands of the parish to maintain the state and power of England,
and to pay higher rents. In perhaps the majority of cases they
raised a larger gross produce, and provided maintenance and
employment for a larger population than before. In some cases
even (though these were rare exceptions) the labouring population gained in material prosperity as well as in numbers. But
in any case the relationship between employer and employed
was notably altered.

In the open field village the entirely landless labourer was
scarcely to be found. The division of holdings into numerous
scattered pieces, many of which were of minute size, made it
easy for a labourer to obtain what were in effect allotments in
the common fields. If he had no holding, he still might have a
common right; if no acknowledged common right, he might
enjoy the advantage of one in a greater or less degree. From
the poorest labourer to the richest farmer, there was, in the
typical open field village, a gradation of rank. There was no

perceptible social gap between the cottager who worked the greater part of his time for others, and for the smaller part of his time on his own holding, who is therefore properly termed a labourer, and his neighbour who reversed that distribution of time, and is therefore to be deemed a farmer. It was easy for the efficient or fortunate man to rise on such a social ladder ; equally easy for the inefficient or unlucky to slip downwards.

After enclosure the comparatively few surviving farmers, enriched, elevated intellectually as well as socially by the successful struggle with a new environment, faced, across a deep social gulf, the labourers who had now only their labour to depend upon. In the early part of the nineteenth century, at any rate, it was almost impossible for a labourer to cross that gulf; on his side the farmer henceforward, instead of easily becoming a farm labourer if bankrupt, would rather try his fortune in the growing industrial towns.

Our " Country Farmer " gives us a vivid picture of one side of the social change ("Thoughts on Enclosure," p. 21). Of the farmer after enclosure he says :

" Their entertainments are as expensive as they are elegant, for it is no uncommon thing for one of these new created farmers to spend ten or twelve pounds at one entertainment ; and to wash down delicate food, must have the most expensive wines, and these the best of their kind ; and to set off the entertainment in the greatest splendour, an elegant sideboard of plate is provided in the newest fashion. As to dress no one that was not personally acquainted with the opulent farmer's daughter can distinguish her from the daughter of a Duke by her dress, both equally wishing to imitate something, but they know not what.

" View the farmer before the land was inclosed, and you will find him entertaining his friends with a part of a hog of his own feeding, and a draught of ale brewed from his own malt presented in a brown jug, or a glass, if it would bear it, which was the utmost of his extravagance : in those happy days you might view the farmer in a coat of the growth of his flock ; and spun by his industrious wife and daughters, and his stockings produced from the same quarter of his industry, and his wife and daughters clad from their own hands of industry and their own flock."

As for the other side of this social change, the labourer's side, it seemed so serious an evil to many even of the progressive landlords and agriculturists who strongly advocated enclosure, that they busied themselves to find a remedy.

In 1897 the Board of Agriculture drew the attention of its members to a typical case. Mr. Thomas Bernard communicated an "Account of a Cottage and Garden near Tadcaster." The cottager had held two acres of land and a common right at Poppleton for nine years, and there had lived comfortably and brought up six children. The enclosure of the parish turned him adrift, but he prevailed upon a landlord to let him have a piece of roadside waste for a garden, saying, "I will show you the *fashions* on it." The landlord was so delighted afterwards with the way in which this garden was cultivated, that he offered the man to let him have it rent free. Particular attention was directed to the man's reply :—"Now, sir, you have a pleasure in seeing my cottage and garden neat: and why should not other squires have the same pleasure in seeing the cottages and gardens nice about them ? The poor would then be happy and would love them and the place where they lived ; but now every nook of land is let to the great farmers ; and nothing left for the poor but to go to the parish." ("Communications to the Board," Vol. I. p. 404.)

It was by "going to the parish" that the labourer could bring home to the landlord the idea that the spirit of ambition and self-reliance fostered by the possession of two acres and a common right was of value to the nation. The national emergency due to the famine prices of food during the French War, which produced the complete change in the spirit of the administration of the Poor Law associated with the "Speenhamland Act of Parliament," also forced into public attention the desirability of both providing agricultural labourers with some other supplement to their wages, and of encouraging them to avoid pauperism.

We accordingly find the Board of Agriculture offering for 1800 three gold medals :—

" To the person who shall build on his estate the most cottages for labouring families, and assign to each a proper portion of land, for the support of not less than a cow, a hog, and a sufficient garden—the Gold Medal."

" To the person who shall produce the most satisfactory account of the best means of supporting cows on poor land in a method applicable to cottagers—the Gold Medal," (doubts having been raised with regard to the practicability of cottagers keeping cows except on rich soil).

" The Board having received information that the labouring poor of Rutland and Lincolnshire, having land for one or two cows, and a sufficiency of potatoes, have not applied, in the present scarcity, for any poor law relief ; and it appearing to be a great national object to spread so beneficial a system, the Board will give to the person who shall explain, in the most satisfactory manner, the best means for rendering this practice as general through the kingdom as circumstances will admit—the Gold Medal." (" Communications," Vol. II.)

Each of these medals was again offered in subsequent years.

The question appears to have been first brought before the Board of Agriculture by the Earl of Winchilsea, in a conversation at the Farmers' Club with Sir John Sinclair, President of the Board, in 1795. At Sir John Sinclair's request, the Earl of Winchilsea put his views in writing, and they were submitted to the Board, in the form of a letter, dated Jan. 4th, 1796. This letter is a convincing statement in favour of the case for " three acres and a cow," and deserves the attention of politicians of to-day.

Beginning by stating that he has made further enquiries, since the conversation with Sir John Sinclair, into the practice of agricultural labourers keeping cows, he continues :—" I am more and more confirmed in the opinion I have long had, that nothing is so beneficial, both to them and to the landowners, as their having land to be occupied either for the keeping of cows, or as gardens, according to circumstances. By means of these advantages, the labourers and their families live better, and are consequently more fit to endure labour; and it makes them more contented, and gives them a sort of independence, which makes them set a higher value on their character. . . . When a labourer has obtained a cow, and land sufficient to maintain her, the first thing he has thought of has been how he could save money enough to buy another; . . . there are from 70 to 80 labourers upon my estate in Rutland, who keep from 1 to 4 cows each. . . . I am informed that those who manage well clear about 20d. per week, or £4 6s. 8d. per ann. by each cow."[1]

If the cow died, it was, he says, a great misfortune for the labourer, but he contrived to beg or borrow the money necessary to obtain another cow—"I scarcely ever knew a cow-gait given up for want of ability to obtain a cow, except in the case of old and infirm women."

He classifies the situation of labourers, in order of felicity, as follows:—

(1) Those who have a sufficient quantity of grass enclosed land to enable them to keep one or more cows winter and summer, and a garden near their house; a grass field allotted to a certain number being as advantageous, or nearly so, as separate small enclosures.

(2) Those who have a summer pasture for their cow, and some arable land, on which they grow the winter provision. This is slightly less advantageous than (1), because tilling the arable land takes up more time.

(3) Those who have a right of common for the summer keep of the cow, and a meadow, or arable ground, or the share of a meadow in common, for the winter provision. If it were not that commons are usually over-stocked, this would be equivalent to (1) or (2).

(4) Those who have a right of common, but no cow, and a garden. In this case geese and pigs can be kept.

---

[1] Milk being valued at 1d. per quart; it seems clear also that what is consumed at home is not included in this calculation.

(5) Those who have a right of common and no garden. In this case the value of the right of common depends upon whether fuel is obtained from the common or not.

(6) Those who have several acres of arable land, and no summer pasture for a cow. This, he maintains, is of little value, because of the large expenditure of labour necessary for cultivating the land, but he admits that many would differ from him on this point.

(7) Those who have a garden near the house.

(8) Those who have no land whatever. " This is a very bad situation for a labourer to be placed in, both for his comfort and the education of his children."

Then he continues, in words which seem in general as true and weighty now as when written or as at any time within the last hundred years :—" In countries where it has never been the custom for labourers to keep cows, it would be very difficult to introduce it; but where no gardens have been annexed to the cottages it is sufficient to give the ground, and the labourer is sure to know what to do with it, and will reap an immediate benefit from it . . . there should be as much as will produce all the garden stuff the family consumes, and enough, with the addition of a little meal, for a pig. I think they ought to pay the same rent that a farmer would pay for the land, and no more. I am persuaded that it frequently happens that a labourer lives in a house at 20s. a year rent, which he is unable to pay, to which, if a garden of a rood was added, for which he would have to pay five or ten shillings a year more, that he would be enabled, by the profit he would derive from the garden, to pay the rent of the house, etc., with great advantage to himself.

"As I before mentioned, some difficulties may occur in establishing the custom of labourers keeping cows in those parts of the country where no such custom has existed; wherever it has or does exist it ought by all means to be encouraged, and not suffered to fall into disuse, as has been the case to a great degree in the midland counties, one of the causes of which I apprehend to be, the dislike the generality of farmers have to seeing the labourers rent any land. Perhaps one of their reasons for disliking this is, that the land, if not occupied by the labourers, would fall to their share ; and another, I am afraid, is, that they rather wish to have the labourers more dependent upon them, for which reasons they are always desirous of hiring the house and land occupied by a labourer, under pretence, that by that means the landlord will be secure of his rent, and that they will keep the house in repair. This the agents of estates are too apt to give in to, as they find it much less trouble to meet six than sixty tenants at a rent day, and by this means avoid the being sometimes obliged to hear the wants and complaints of the poor." . . . The landlord naturally yields to this pressure . . . "and it is in this manner that the labourers have been dispossessed of their cow-pastures in various parts of the midland counties. The moment the farmer obtains his wish, he takes every particle of the land to himself, and relets the house to the labourer, who by this means is rendered miserable, the poors rate increased, the value of the estate to the land-lord diminished, and the house suffered to go to decay . . . Whoever travels through the midland counties, and will take the trouble of enquiring, will generally receive the answer, that formerly there were a great many cottagers who kept cows, but that the land is now thrown to the farmers ; and if he enquires still further, he will find that in those parishes the poors rates have increased in an amazing degree, more than according to the average rise throughout England."

Sir John Sinclair,[1] President of the Board of Agriculture, did not agree that a plot of a few acres of arable land was, by itself, of little value to the agricultural labourer. He estimates that two cows can be kept on $3\frac{1}{4}$ acres of arable land, and that the net produce, valuing milk at 1d. per quart, would amount to £21 per annum, about as much as the man's wages. He advocated spade labour, and recommended that the cottager should rather hire men to dig for him, than get the land ploughed. In confirmation of this opinion Sir Henry Vavasour cited an example of a cottager holding 3 acres who kept two cows and two pigs. The

---

[1] "Communications to the Board of Agriculture," Vol. IV., p. 358.

butter alone paid the rent, and the gross produce was estimated at £54 per annum, exclusive of milk and vegetables consumed at home.

It is of course practically impossible to calculate how much effect this landowners' agitation for the policy of "Three acres and a cow" had on the number of such cottage holdings. Lord Brownlow [1] writes: "In all open field lordships there have always been pastures in which the cottagers have had their share of benefit; but the practice of enabling cottagers to keep cows in inclosed parishes, is in my neighbourhood rare, and of recent date." Accounts are sent of cottage holdings provided by the Earl of Carrington, and of large allotments provided by Mr. Thomas Estcourt; but I cannot say how extensively their example was followed.

Mr. W. E. Bear's report to the recent Labour Commission, on the agricultural labourers of the Southwell Union, contains the following passage, in which we probably see some fruits of the Earl of Winchilsea's movement:—"Small holdings, of three to ten acres commonly, are let with cottages in a few parishes, and called 'cottagers.' This custom appears to be a very old one, dating back far beyond the time when the term 'three acres and a cow' was invented. In Ossington, Mr. Richardson told me, it was 50 years old or more; but he said it was falling into disuse. I found some 'cottagers' in Averham, Ossington and Hockerton, and heard of them in another parish or two. They usually consist of grass land, and are best so, as the labourer can leave his wife to manage the cow or two kept on them, and work for wages regularly. In Averham some of these small holdings have been given up, apparently because they were partly arable, and occupiers found that they could not keep regular places and also attend to their land. But where the land is all pasture, they are excellent institutions, providing families with milk, and adding to the incomes by means of milk or butter, poultry, eggs and pork sold. These little holdings are let from £2 10s. to £3 an acre, including the cottage " (par. 51 A).

---

[1] " Communications to the Board of Agriculture, Vol. IV., p. 367.

The same Commissioner found in Leicestershire a system of common cow-runs for cottagers which also probably dates from the eighteenth century, being in some way a survival from the common field system. He describes it as follows :—

" There are cow plots let with cottages in several parishes. Some have already been referred to as existing on the Earl of Dysart's estate. One example is to be found at Saxby, where cow runs of 6 a. 3 r. 12 p., each in common, are let with a cottage and garden at £10 per annum. At Grimston I visited some which are let by Mr. Wright or Mr. Reckitts, who appear to be somehow connected on the same estate. . . . Some of these cow-plots are 3½ acres in extent, and their holders are allowed to keep only one cow, as three or more of them occupy a pasture in common, having a portion of their 3½ acres each year to mow and another portion to feed. The rent, including cottage and garden, is £10. There are some other cow plots of 8 acres on which two or three cows are kept, the rent being £15. In these cases, too, the pasture is common to several holders, each one having a piece to mow, while they run their cows together on the portion devoted to grazing. As an example of the advantage which a cow plot may sometimes be to a labourer and his family, I may mention the case of a widow who has 3½ acres and a very good cottage for £10 per annum. Last year she had an exceptionally good cow, and she sold milk at the rate of 6d. a gallon, amounting to £15 10s., fattening a calf which sold at £4 10s. ; altogether the return was £20, besides what milk was consumed in the cottage."

Another probable survival of the Earl of Winchilsea's movement is thus described by Mr. Rider Haggard :—

" The system of cottage holdings was introduced about a hundred years ago on the Burley estate" (Rutlandshire) " and was copied by the late Lord Tollemache, who was brother-in-law of the late Mr. Finch. It is in force in the parishes of Burley, Egleton, Hambleton and Greetham. In 1901 there lived in those parishes forty-three small occupiers, whose acreage varied from 5 acres to 40 acres, the holdings being all grass. Originally there were many more, the Hambleton cow pasture, which is 102 acres in estate, being divided into 80 cow commons. Some of the holders occupy two or more small fields, but the general custom has been for tenants to graze large fields in common, and to have separate small fields reserved for mowing hay in the winter. In the fields which are grazed in common, five roods have been taken as sufficient to keep a cow." ("Rural England," Vol. II. p. 260.)

CHAPTER XIII

IN this table the cross-heading A includes Acts up to and including the year 1801, in which year a general Act facilitating enclosure was passed; cross-heading B, Acts from 1802-1845; cross-heading C, enclosures under the General Enclosure Act of 1845 and subsequent amending Acts. No Act or enclosure is included unless the enclosure was partly of arable common field, but in some few cases, as will be seen from the Appendix giving the chief particulars of each Act, the arable land formed only a trifling part of the area dealt with.

Where the area enclosed is not stated, and cannot even be approximately inferred from the wording of the Act, it is estimated on the assumption that the average area per Act where the area is not stated, is the same as for Acts relating to the same county where the area affected is stated, enclosures under the Act of 1845 being left out of account. This method, I believe, gives more satisfactory results than any other would; but it must be confessed that in the case of Norfolk the Acts in which the area is not stated are so many, and those in which it is stated are so few, that the average obtained is not trustworthy. In this case I believe the figure arrived at is too large. The counties are arranged in order of prevalence of Parliamentary enclosures.

	Area stated.		Area not stated.		Total.		Percentage of Area of County.
	Acts.	Acres.	Acts.	Acres.	Acts.	Acres.	
NORTHAMPTON.							
Period A	137	237,211	6	10,306	143	247,517	
,, B	40	66,807	7	12,023	47	78,830	
,, C	3	4,704	—	—	3	4,704	
Total	180	308,722	13	22,329	193	331,051	51·5

	Area stated.		Area not stated.		Total.		Percentage of Area of County.
	Acts.	Acres.	Acts.	Acres.	Acts.	Acres.	
HUNTINGDON.							
Period A	30	50,147	7	11,392	37	61,539	
,, B	25	39,364	2	3,255	27	42,619	
,, C	3	3,855	—	—	3	3,855	
Total	58	93,366	9	14,647	67	108,013	46·5
RUTLAND.							
Period A	20	33,857	2	3,323	22	37,180	
,, B	2	2,700	—	—	2	2,700	
,, C	6	7,344	—	—	6	7,344	
Total	28	43,901	2	3,323	30	47,224	46·5
BEDFORD.							
Period A	30	55,470	13	21,229	43	76,699	
,, B	21	27,810	15	24,495	36	52,305	
,, C	5	8,309	—	—	5	8,309	
Total	56	91,589	28	45,724	84	137,313	46·0
OXFORD.							
Period A	54	96,596	22	35,277	76	131,873	
,, B	20	22,064	22	35,277	42	57,341	
,, C	18	23,578	—	—	18	23,578	
Total	92	142,238	44	70,554	136	212,792	45·6
YORKS, EAST RIDING.							
Period A	108	227,009	6	12,148	114	239,157	
,, B	25	42,277	7	14,173	32	56,450	
,, C	4	5,193	—	—	4	5,193	
Total	137	274,479	13	26,321	150	300,800	40·1
LEICESTER.							
Period A	124	175,280	9	12,437	133	187,717	
,, B	10	9,896	2	2,764	12	12,660	
,, C	—	—	—	—	—	—	
Total	134	185,176	11	15,201	145	200,377	38·2

	Area stated.		Area not stated.		Total.		Percentage of Area of County.
	Acts.	Acres.	Acts.	Acres	Acts.	Acres.	
CAMBRIDGE.							
Period A	20	45,230	3	5,789	23	51,019	
,, B	21	33,885	55	106,128	76	140,013	
,, C	9	8,298	—	—	9	8,298	
Total	50	87,413	58	111,917	108	199,330	36·3
BUCKINGHAM.							
Period A	47	71,323	23	35,834	70	107,157	
,, B	20	33,090	10	15,580	30	48,670	
,, C	6	7,014	—	—	6	7,014	
Total	73	111,427	33	51,414	106	162,841	34·2
NOTTINGHAM.							
Period A	64	112,880	18	29,217	82	142,097	
,, B	17	18,596	7	11,362	24	29,958	
,, C	3	3,269	—	—	3	3,269	
Total	84	134,745	25	40,579	109	175,324	32·5
NORFOLK.							
Period A	28	71,904	36	76,066	64	147,970	
,, B	16	21,966	114	240,877	130	262,843	
,, C	6	12,173	—	—	6	12,173	
Total	50	106,043	150	316,943	200	422,986	32·3
LINCOLN.							
Period A	175	354,048	15	29,240	190	383,288	
,, B	53	90,398	11	21,443	64	111,841	
,, C	2	1,331	—	—	2	1,331	
Total	230	445,777	26	50,683	256	496,450	29·3
BERKSHIRE.							
Period A	12	13,651	23	28,980	35	42,631	
,, B	33	42,652	20	25,200	53	67,852	
,, C	10	9,119	—	—	10	9,119	
Total	55	65,422	43	54,180	98	119,602	26·0

	Area stated.		Area not stated.		Total.		Percentage of Area of County.
	Acts.	Acres.	Acts.	Acres.	Acts.	Acres.	
WARWICK.							
Period A	85	116,919	6	7,909	91	124,828	
,, B	12	10,950	8	10,546	20	21,496	
,, C	3	3,235	—	—	3	3.235	
Total	100	131,104	14	18,455	114	149,559	25·0
WILTSHIRE.							
Period A	18	30,949	47	80,211	65	111,160	
,, B	27	45,849	30	51,199	57	97,048	
,, C	6	3,925	—	—	6	3,925	
Total	51	80,723	77	131,410	128	212,133	24·1
GLOUCESTER.							
Period A	53	78,645	30	37,724	83	116,369	
,, B	18	20,616	30	37,724	48	58,340	
,, C	11	4,419	—	—	11	4,419	
Total	82	103,680	60	75,448	142	179,128	22·5
MIDDLESEX.							
Period A	5	11,854	3	4,114	8	15,968	
,, B	12	12,251	5	6,913	17	19,164	
,. C	1	625	—	—	1	625	
Total	18	24,730	8	11,027	26	35,757	19·7
WORCESTER.							
Period A	29	36,942	10	11,317	39	48,259	
,, B	9	6,066	24	27,161	33	33,227	
,, C	7	4,009	—	—	7	4,009	
Total	45	46,017	34	38,478	79	85,495	16·5
DERBY.							
Period A	37	45,028	9	13,312	46	58,340	
,, B	25	46,675	—	—	25	46,675	
,, C	—	—	—	—	—	—	
Total	62	91,703	9	13,312	71	105,015	15·9

	Area stated.		Area not stated.		Total.		Percentage of Area of County.
	Acts.	Acres.	Acts.	Acres.	Acts.	Acres.	
HERTFORD.							
Period A	11	20,524	4	6,103	15	26,627	
„ B	8	8,464	5	7,628	13	16,092	
„ C	17	10,775	—	—	17	10,775	
Total	36	39,763	9	13,731	45	53,494	13·1
YORKS, WEST RIDING.							
Period A	67	82,389	17	23,736	84	106,125	
„ B	55	88,453	7	9,774	62	98,227	
„ C	4	2,102	—	—	4	2,102	
Total	126	172,944	24	33,510	150	206,454	11·6
DORSET.							
Period A	9	13,704	8	8,533	17	22,237	
„ B	23	20,426	8	8,532	31	28,958	
„ C	6	3,786	—	—	6	3,786	
Total	38	37,916	16	17,065	54	54,981	8·7
SUFFOLK.							
Period A	4	6,400	6	9,876	10	16,276	
„ B	14	13,356	24	39,505	38	52,861	
„ C	5	2,450	—	—	5	2,450	
Total	23	22,206	30	49,381	53	71,587	7·5
HAMPSHIRE.							
Period A	12	15,459	23	25,649	35	41,108	
„ B	13	12,856	8	10,664	21	23,520	
„ C	4	1,512	—	—	4	1,512	
Total	29	29,827	31	36,313	60	66,140	6·4
SURREY.							
Period A	4	5,140	2	2,562	6	7,702	
„ B	11	14,078	5	6,406	16	20,484	
„ C	5	2,796	—	—	5	2,796	
Total	20	22,014	7	8,968	27	30,982	6·4

	Area stated.		Area not stated.		Total.		Percentage of Area of County.
	Acts.	Acres.	Acts.	Acres.	Acts.	Acres.	
YORKS, NORTH RIDING.							
Period A	24	33,257	9	15,279	33	48,536	
„ B	14	31,171	3	5,093	17	36,264	
„ C	2	1,034	—	—	2	1,034	
Total	40	65,462	12	20,372	52	85,834	6·3
HEREFORD.							
Period A	5	3,920	1	708	6	4,628	
„ B	6	3,870	14	9,915	20	13,785	
„ C	3	378	—	—	3	378	
Total	14	8,168	15	10,623	29	18,791	3·6
SOMERSET.							
Period A	12	16,225	3	2,644	15	18,869	
„ B	23	14,623	4	3,525	27	18,148	
„ C	—	—	—	—	—	—	
Total	35	30,848	7	6,169	42	37,017	3·5
STAFFORD.							
Period A	10	10,924	1	996	11	11,920	
„ B	7	6,001	3	2,987	10	8,988	
„ C	—	—	—	—	—	—	
Total	17	16,925	4	3,983	21	20,908	2·8
ESSEX.							
Period A	4	6,551	—	—	4	6,551	
„ B	4	6,190	3	4,777	7	10,967	
„ C	10	4,652	—	—	10	4,652	
Total	18	17,393	3	4,777	21	22,170	2·2
SUSSEX.							
Period A	1	1,400	—	—	1	1,400	
„ B	18	13,537	4	3,145	22	16,682	
„ C	2	248	—	—	2	248	
Total	21	15,185	4	3,145	25	18,330	1·9

	Area stated.		Area not stated.		Total.		Percent-age of Area of County.
	Acts.	Acres.	Acts.	Acres.	Acts.	Acres.	
NORTHUMBERLAND.							
Period A	4	9,657	—	—	4	9,657	
„ B	4	12,691	—	—	4	12,691	
„ C	—	—	—	—	—	—	
Total	8	22,348	—	—	8	22,348	1·7
CUMBERLAND.							
Period A	1	4,000	1	2,175	2	6,175	
„ B	3	4,700	—	—	3	4,700	
„ C	—	—	—	—	—	—	
Total	4	8,700	1	2,175	5	10,875	1·1
DURHAM.							
Period A	5	4,437	—	—	5	4,437	
„ B	1	200	—	—	1	200	
„ C	—	—	—	—	—	—	
Total	6	4,637	—	—	6	4,637	0·7
WESTMORELAND.							
Period A	—	—	—	—	—	—	
„ B	4	3,237	—	—	4	3,237	
„ C	—	—	—	—	—	—	
Total	4	3,237	—	—	2	3,237	0·6
CHESHIRE.							
Period A	—	—	—	—	—	—	
„ B	2	3,326	—	—	2	3,326	
„ C	—	—	—	—	—	—	
Total	2	3,326	—	—	2	3,326	0.5
MONMOUTH.							
Period A	1	780	—	—	1	780	
„ B	—	—	—	—	—	—	
„ C	3	513	—	—	3	513	
Total	4	1,293	—	—	4	1,293	0·4

	Area stated.		Area not stated.		Total.		Percentage of Area of County.
	Acts.	Acres.	Acts.	Acres.	Acts.	Acres.	
SHROPSHIRE.							
Period A	3	1,670	—	—	3	1,670	
,, B	2	1,140	—	—	2	1,140	
,, C	—	—	—	—	—	—	
Total	5	2,810	—	—	5	2,810	0·3

Lancashire, Kent, Devon and Cornwall have no Acts for Enclosure of Common Fields.

CHAPTER XIV.

ON the map of England, in Chapter VII., enclosures of common field parishes by Act of Parliament before the General Enclosure Act of 1801 are shaded vertically, such enclosures from 1802 to 1845 are dotted, and subsequent enclosures under the General Enclosure Act of 1845 are black. In other words, all the shaded area represents the area of parishes which had arable common fields up to the year 1700, all the dotted and black area represents the area of parishes which had arable common fields up to 1801, and all the black area represents the area of parishes which had arable common fields up to 1845.

What about the area which is not shaded at all ?

An inspection of the map yields certain striking results.

In the first place, we see that the shaded districts lie in a broad band across England from north-east to south-west, from the East Riding of Yorkshire to Dorset and the east part of Somerset.

Secondly, we see that there is a perfectly sharp line of demarcation between the shaded and the non-shaded area, running through Suffolk, Essex, passing through London, and along the border between Surrey and Kent. This line becomes indefinite as it passes through the Weald of Surrey and Sussex, but its termination can be traced in the part of Sussex which lies on the southern slope of the South Downs. In the white area to the south-east of this line there are but two shaded patches—the parishes of Iken and Orford, in Suffolk, situated close together, in the peninsula formed by the estuaries of the rivers Alde and Deben.

Thirdly, we can trace an equally sharp line of demarcation between the shaded and the non-shaded area in the south-west, running from the Bristol to the English Channel, across Somerset and Dorset.   South-west of this line there is no shaded patch— *i.e.*, there is no case of common field enclosed by Act of Parliament.

Fourthly, on the north-west side of the shaded belt, towards Wales and Scotland, there is no sharp line of demarcation between the shaded and the non-shaded area, but as one travels further and further from the central axis of the shaded area to the north-west, the shaded patches become sparser and sparser ; but still some shaded patches are to be found in every English county on this side of the shaded belt, except Lancashire.

Fifthly, it is to be noticed that along the central axis of the shaded belt the vertical shading—indicating enclosure by Act of Parliament in the eighteenth century—greatly predominates, and most of all the shading is overwhelmingly vertical in the very centre of the shaded area.   Dotted and black patches, indicating Parliamentary enclosure in the nineteenth century, and particularly black, indicating the latest group of Parliamentary enclosures, show more prominently in the edges or fringes of the coloured area.   In other words, when the great movement of Parliamentary Enclosure began in the eighteenth century, its chief field was the very centre of the district over which it ultimately spread.

It is obvious that there must be certain broad historical reasons for these striking facts.   The map, in fact, presents to us a series of definite puzzles for solution.

1. How and when was the south-eastern corner of England enclosed ?

2. How and when was the south-western corner enclosed ?

3. How and when was the great district in the north-west, in which Parliamentary enclosure is the exception, enclosed ?

4. How and when were the numerous parishes within what we may call the Parliamentary Enclosure belt, which escaped Parliamentary enclosure, enclosed ?

And lastly, there is the question which sums these up, and presents the problem on the other side—

5. Why were special Acts of Parliament necessary for the

enclosure of some three thousand of the English parishes, in the geographical position indicated by the map?

And it is important that it should be clearly understood that this is the more natural way of putting the question, because the surprising fact is not that the common field system should gradually and quietly disappear in parish A, but that it should persist in parish B, until ended by the very expensive and troublesome measure of a special Act of Parliament.

In order to proceed as far as possible from the known to the unknown, we will first consider the various methods of common field enclosure operating within the belt of Parliamentary Enclosure of common fields. But before beginning this enquiry, attention may be drawn to a ray of light which the map throws upon the social history of England in the Tudor period. The reader of the history of that period is tempted to suppose that the districts from which the greatest complaints, and still more riots and insurrections, arose against enclosures, were those in which enclosure was proceeding most rapidly. Now, the most formidable of these popular agitations began in the reign of Edward VI. in Somersetshire, and spread northwards and east-wards, growing in intensity, till it reached its climax in Ket's rebellion in Norfolk.[1] The earlier complaints also come from counties within the Parliamentary Enclosure belt—Oxford, Buckingham, Wiltshire and others. The map suggests that a possible interpretation of these popular movements is, that an industrial and economic change involving normally the enclosure of common fields was in the fifteenth and sixteenth centuries gradually spreading over the southern and midland counties; that in some parts it met with little or no resistance; but that in other parts popular resistance was roused to some features of this change, including the enclosure of arable fields, and

---

[1] "Can it be denied that the fyrst rysynge this yeare was in Somersetshire, ffrom Somersetshire it entred into Gloucettershire, Wylshire, hampshire, Sussex, Surrey, Worcestershire, Essex, hertfordshire, and dyuers other places?" (John Hale's Defence, "The Commonweal of this Realm of England," Miss Lamond's edition, p. lviii.) This is to prove that the rising was not caused by the Enclosure Commission of 1549. The Commissioners were sent to Oxford, Berkshire, Warwick, Leicester, Buckingham, and Northampton.

that popular resistance was in a very great degree successful in causing the postponement of such enclosure. Briefly, a special outcry against enclosure in a particular locality shows, not necessarily that enclosure was proceeding with special rapidity there, but possibly that there it was specially obnoxious; and being there specially obnoxious, proceeded more slowly than elsewhere.

Enclosure by Principal Landlord.

But to return to our own subject. We have shown that enclosure by Act of Parliament was greatly to the landlord's interest; but it is perfectly obvious that the landlord's interest was much more served by an enclosure without all the expense, loss of time, labour and anxiety involved in Parliamentary proceedings. Obviously, therefore, if one landlord could acquire all the open and commonable land in the parish, he would enclose without an Act of Parliament. The only difficulty in his way would be in arranging leases so that they should all fall in simultaneously, or, failing this, in overcoming the resistance of any tenant whose lease gave him the power of resisting, if he were unwilling to agree. We have noticed that even in recent years the common fields of Yelden in Bedfordshire have disappeared in this way; that the Duchy of Cornwall in 1876 bought out all the copyholders holding lands in Fordington Field; that Earl Manvers is similarly acquiring by degrees all the common rights in the common fields of Laxton, and the Ecclesiastical Commissioners are endeavouring in this way to procure the enclosure of Elmstone Hardwicke; that Stratton and Grimstone were thus enclosed since 1900, and that the common fields of several Berkshire parishes have thus disappeared within the last half-century. The same process can be watched on a much larger scale with regard to common rights over commons proper. The buying up of the rights of commoners over Dartmoor by the Duchy of Cornwall is one striking example; similar purchases of common rights over the

Wiltshire downs on a very large scale have come into notice through the approach to Stonehenge being affected.

The enclosure of common fields in this way is proceeding slowly merely because the remains of common fields are now so small.

And it is obvious that through the last two hundred years the restraints of law and public opinion upon the freedom of the country squire or great landowner, in doing as he likes with the villages under his control, have been gradually and continuously strengthened. In looking back over the nineteenth and eighteenth centuries, we are looking back at a greater and greater proportion of local autocratic power accompanying any given degree of local pre-eminence in wealth and landed property.

If we look back to the beginning of the eighteenth century we find the principles generally accepted by the landowning class with regard to the general management of their estates, and particularly with regard to common fields, thus clearly laid down by Edward Lawrence in " The duty of a Steward to his Lord":—

Article XIV. " A Steward should not forget to make the best Enquiry into the Disposition of any of the Freeholders within or near any of his Lord's Manors to sell their Lands, that he may use his best Endeavours to purchase them at as reasonable a price as may be for his lord's Advantage and Convenience . . . especially in such Manors where Improvements are to be made by inclosing Commons and Common fields . . . If the Freeholders cannot all be persuaded to sell yet at least an Agreement for Inclosing should be pushed forward by the Steward " (p. 9).

" The Steward should not suffer any of the Lord's lands to be let to Freehold Tenants within or near his Lord's Manor " (p. 34).

" The Steward should endeavour to lay all the small Farms, let to poor indigent People, to the great ones " . . . but "It is unwise to unite farms all at once, because of the odium and increase of Poor-rates. It is much more reasonable and popular to stay till such farms fall into Hand by Death " (p. 35).

And to facilitate this process, " Noblemen and Gentlemen should endeavour to convert copyhold for lives to Leasehold for lives " (p. 60).

The significance of this last recommendation may be illustrated by the passage in William Marshall's account, in " Agriculture of Gloucestershire," published about sixty years afterwards, of the Cotswold Hills :—

" Thirty years ago this district lay almost entirely in an open state; namely in arable common field, sheep-walk, and cowdown. At present it may be said to be in a state of inclosure, though some few townships yet remain open.

" The difficulties of Inclosure were not, in this case, numerous or great. The sheep-walks and cowdowns were all of them stinted by ' yardlands ' in the arable fields : there was not, perhaps, one unstinted common on these hills. They were, formerly, many of them, or all of them, occupied by leasehold tenants for three lives renewable. A species of tenancy I have not met before. Many of these leaseholds had fallen in. The removal of those which remained, was " (sic: he means, of course, "removed ") " the main obstacle of inclosure."

Because the number of Acts for Enclosure gradually increases through the eighteenth century, and reaches its maximum at the opening of the nineteenth century, it has been hastily assumed by some that the process of enclosure was similarly accelerated. But it is on a priori grounds at least as probable that there was no acceleration in the rate of extinction of common fields, only a gradual change in the prevailing method of procedure.

Thus very few Acts of Enclosure are extant previous to 1727, the year in which Edward Lawrence recommends to Stewards and Landlords a vigorous enclosure campaign. That that campaign was being carried on at the time can be shown by two contemporary extracts from writers on opposite sides. The Rev. John Laurence of Yelvertoft, in the " New System of Agriculture," 1726, writes :—

" The great quantities of ground that have been of late and are daily inclosing, and the increase of Rent that is everywhere made by those who do inclose, sufficiently demonstrate the benefit and use of Inclosures. In the Bishopric of Durham nine parts in ten are already inclosed " [1] (p. 45).

John Cowper, in " Inclosing Commons and Common fields is contrary to the interest of the Nation " says:—"I myself within these 30 years past" (*i.e.*, 1702—1732), "have seen above twenty Lordships or Parishes inclosed . . . I have been informed by an eminent Surveyor that one third of all the land of England has been inclosed within these 80 years."

Perhaps what the eminent Surveyor said to John Cowper is not very convincing evidence. But in considering the estimate of the amount of enclosure in the "last 80 years," *i.e.*, from 1652, the first year of peace after the Civil War, to 1732, the time when John Cowper wrote, we have to bear in mind, firstly, that there was an important enclosure movement going on in the Commonwealth period ; and secondly, that in 1660, with the Restoration, the country gentry came by their own again. The King's ministers during the reigns of Charles II., James II., William III. and Anne would scarcely have dared, even if they had desired, to check any proceedings on the part of landowners, with the object of raising rents. The whole policy of Parliament was, in fact, in sympathy with this object, as may be seen from all the legislature affecting agriculture.

For the first part of this period there is further evidence of the progress of enclosure in John Houghton's "Collection for the Improvement of Husbandry and Trade." In repeated issues he strongly advocates Enclosure; in that for September 8, 1681, he says : " Oh that I had sufficient influence to put it" (*i.e.*, a General Enclosure Act) " to the trial, if it did not succeed I'd be content not to be drunk this seven years " . . . "Witness the many enclosures that have of late been made, and that people are daily on gog on making " (pp. 15, 16). It will be remembered that a General Enclosure Act for Scotland was passed in 1695.

---

[1] This statement is confirmed by the Board of Agriculture reporter : " In this county the lands, or common fields of townships, were for the most part inclosed soon after the Restoration." (Joseph Granger, " Agriculture of Durham," 1794.)

To sum up, it is clear that the Parliamentary enclosure of a given parish indicates that the lord of the manor, or principal landlord, had not secured such a complete or preponderating influence over the parish as to enable him to effect an enclosure without an Act of Parliament.

ENCLOSURE BY YEOMEN.

And yet, on the other hand, it does not appear that the absence of any lord of the manor, or of any single landowner superior in wealth to the others in the parish was favourable, through the seventeenth, eighteenth and nineteenth centuries, to the continuance of common fields, except where many of the properties were extremely small.

We have seen that the Ecclesiastical Commissioners, in Elmstone Hardwicke, while desiring themselves to enclose the parish, discourage enclosure by the tenants on their own account, by raising the rents to a prohibitive extent. Similarly Edward Lawrence in 1727, while urging, as we have seen, the steward to procure a general enclosure of his lord's manor, declares that it is the duty of the steward, particularly if his lord is the owner of the Great Tithe, to prevent gradual enclosure by yeomen— "He should be ever on his watch to prevent (if possible) the Freeholders inclosing any part of their land in the common fields (Article xxiv.)." "Partial enclosure should never be permitted without a general agreement to do the whole."

The objection of the Tithe Owner to enclosures in the common fields was that by increasing the pasture, and decreasing the arable area, they diminished the produce of grain and so diminished the tithe. John Houghton (September 16, 1681, p. 16) also refers to the objection of the tithe owning clergy to enclosure. And this objection was probably one of the strongest forces against enclosure at that time.

Again, going back a century and a quarter, John Norden's " Book of Surveying," published about 1600, in one place recommends general enclosure, on the ground that " one acre enclosed is woorth one and a half in Common, if the ground be fitting thereto" (Book III., p. 97), in another declares "Also enclosures of common fields, or meddowes in part, by such as are most powerful and mighty, without the Lord's licence, and the Tenants' assents, is more than may be permitted" (*ibid.*, p. 96).

The reason of course is, firstly, that the holder of lands in common fields or common meadows, who fenced his holding, or parts of it, thereby prevented the other holders from exercising their rights of pasturing their cattle upon the fenced portions, without giving up his recognised right to pasture cattle on his neighbours' holdings, very likely indeed turning out all the more cattle in the summer and autumn, because better supplied with winter feed ; and, secondly, because the shade of his hedges, if he set quickset hedges, injured his neighbours' crops. In "Select pleas in the Manorial Courts" we find numerous cases of complaints against manorial tenants for attempting to make hedges, banks, or such barriers.

At Bledlow, in Northamptonshire, "it is presented that John Le Pee has unlawfully thrown up a bank" in 1275 (p. 23). In Hemingford (Huntingdon) that "William Thomas Son has planted willows in the bank unlawfully" in 1278 (p. 90), and in the same manor "Elias Carpenter has wrongfully planted trees on a boundary" (p. 92). In Weedon Beck (Northamptonshire) in 1296 "Walter Mill complains of John Brockhole and says that he has raised a wall and hedge between their tenements to his damage."

One is tempted to associate the early and complete enclosure of Kent, without Acts of Parliament, with the proverbial wealth and importance of the Kentish yeomen, and the custom of Gavelkind (*i.e.*, the equal inheritance of landed property by all sons), which necessarily tended to multiply small properties.

William Marshall's description of the enclosure of the Vale of Pickering, the most fertile part of the North Riding of Yorkshire, occupying the southern slopes of the Yorkshire Wolds, shows a similar association. In "Rural Economy of Yorkshire," published in 1788, we read :—"A century ago the marginal townships lay perhaps entirely open, and there are vestiges of common fields in the area of the vale. The West Marshes, church property, have been longer under inclosure; and the central townships were probably inclosed long before those of the margin; the soils of that part being adapted to grass; and while the surrounding country lay open, grass land was of singular value. At present the entire vale may be said to be in a state of inclosures (p. 17).

" Lands are much in the hands of small owners, in general, in the occupation of yeomanry; a circumstance, this, which it would be difficult to equal in so large a district " (p. 19).

He notices (p. 20) that it was the custom to divide lands among all the children, and (p. 24) that the custom of sale of tenant right existed.

" In the present century, more especially in the last fifty years, enclosure has made a rapid progress. . . . In my own remembrance more than half the vale lay open " (p. 50).

The township of Pickering itself lay open at the beginning of the century. It then had 2376 acres of common field arable, stinted pastures, and 3700 acres of common. " The common fields and common meadows have been gradually contracting by amicable changes and transfers, and are now, in a manner, wholly inclosed. The stinted pastures have, at different times, been inclosed 'by commission,' namely, by the unanimous reference to arbitrators." [1]

In general, it may be said, that the Parliamentary enclosure of a given parish indicates that the manorial authority was exercised during a long period antecedent to the enclosure, to prevent gradual enclosure by individual tenants; and that the existence of important rights and properties belonging to the lord of the manor prevented a common agreement to enclose by

---

[1] An older description of piecemeal enclosure is given by John Houghton : " Would they who plough in champain grounds but change their little parcels ; would they who have 6 or 8 acres together make a ditch of 6 or 7 foot wide and deep, and fill it if they would with water, and carry away the bank that it might not be thrown in again, hedges might chance to thrive, and in 2 years (tho' they to please the people might at certain times lay it open) they would raise more money than they use to do in six." (Collections, September 16th, 1681, p. 16.) This gives me a pretty fair idea both of the profit and of the unpopularity of such enclosure at the time.

the actual cultivators of the soil from being reached and put
into execution.

It may also be noticed that in a parish or township where
there is no one principal landlord, but a number of landowners
owning moderate properties, there is comparatively little
likelihood of the net profit of an Enclosure Act seeming to any
one owner worth the trouble of initiating a movement to
promote one; and a comparatively greater likelihood of some
owner or owners being found disposed, from private grudges or
on public grounds, to oppose the proceedings.

This distribution of property in a common field parish
increases the probability that enclosure will proceed in a piecemeal fashion, instead of by an Act.

Enclosure under the General Acts of 1836 and 1840.

In 1836 a general Act (c. 115) was passed "to facilitate the
Inclosure of Open and Arable Fields in England and Wales."
By this Act two-thirds in number and value of the proprietors
of lands and common rights in Arable Common Fields could
appoint Commissioners for Enclosure, provided such fields were
not within ten miles of the centre of London, or three miles
from the centre of some town of over 100,000 inhabitants, or
within certain smaller distances of smaller towns. Enclosure
so effected was only recorded locally. Awards had to be
deposited in the parish churches; but no confirming Act was
needed. If seven-eighths in number and value of the proprietors
were agreed upon enclosure, it was not necessary for them even
to appoint Commissioners, if they could come to an agreement as
to the redistribution of properties.

In 1840 an amending Act (c. 31) was passed, providing that
persons who took possession of the allotments awarded them in
enclosures under the Act of 1836 must be deemed to have waived
the right of appeal from the award. The scope of the Act of
1836 was also extended to Lammas meadows.

As these Acts were in operation from 1836 to 1845, the
enclosures effected by special Acts of Parliament during this

period must have been greatly outnumbered by those effected during that period without being recorded by the central Government. Between 1845 and 1852 the enclosure of lands which were neither commonable all the year round nor subject to any common rights not regulated by a stint, could be effected by the Enclosure Commissioners without being reported to Parliament; but after 1852 the Enclosure Commissioners had to report all their proceedings.

ENCLOSURE IN CORN-GROWING AND PASTORAL DISTRICTS.

The arable common fields, and in consequence the commonable meadows with intermixed ownership, which were situated in districts predominantly pastoral, tended, other things being equal, to be divided and enclosed earlier than the common fields in the predominantly corn-growing districts. For this there are various reasons :—

Firstly, as may be seen from the maps of Castor and Ailesworth, of Laxton, of Braunton (p. 250), or of any maps of any common-field parishes, piecemeal enclosure tends to begin in the arable fields (*a*) close to the village, and (*b*) on the outermost margin of the fields. The greater the extent of the fields, the longer, *ceteris paribus*, will it be before piecemeal enclosure completely obliterates them.

Secondly, enclosure in a pastoral district does not arouse the same resentment and popular resistance that it does in a corn-growing district. This is easily seen from all the controversial writings of the whole period during which enclosure has been a matter of controversy, up to about the middle of the nineteenth century. It was not enclosure as enclosure that offended, but enclosure as causing, or as being intended to result in, the laying down of arable land in grass; as being, in the words of Joseph Bentham of Kettering, "the inhuman practices of madded and irreligious depopulators"[1] which robbed the king of subjects and the country of corn and cattle. Those who enclosed were "monsters of men, dispeoplers of towns, ruiners

---

[1] "The Society of the Saints," p. 67.

of the commonwealth as far as in them lyeth, occasioners of beggars and beggery, cruell inclosiers, whose Adamantine hearts no whit regard the cries of so many distressed ones." [1] Such denunciation would be out of place, and the passions which gave rise to it would never have arisen, in a predominantly pastoral district, because there would be in such a district comparatively few persons thrown out of employment even if the enclosure were of the arable fields only; and because it is scarcely possible that while enclosure of the arable fields was going on, there would not be simultaneous enclosure of waste land, which would have to be repeatedly ploughed and tilled even if the intention were to ultimately convert it into permanent pasture.   In other words, while enclosure in a predominantly corn-growing district is associated with "depopulation," in a pastoral district it is associated with increased employment, increased local population, a larger production of food, and on the whole increased local prosperity.   Thus, though there was a rebellion in Devon and Cornwall in 1549, the same year as Ket's rebellion, enclosure was not one of the complaints of the rebels.   And this was not because enclosure had not begun in Devon and Cornwall, because, as a matter of fact, enclosure had advanced further in Devon and Cornwall than in most other counties. The attitude of the Cornishmen is thus expressed by Carew :— " They fal everywhere from Commons to Inclosure, and partake not of some Eastern Tenants envious dispositions, who will sooner prejudice their owne present thrift, by continuing this mingle-mangle, than advance the Lords expectant benefit, after their terme expired." [2]

Thirdly, there was, during one period in the sixteenth century, a law specially guarding the corn-growing districts from enclosure, from which other districts were exempt.

The Statute 7 Henry VIII., c. 1, was the Depopulation Act in force for the 20 years 1516—1536.   It derives special importance from the Inquisition into Enclosures which followed its enactment, in 1517.   It applies only to parishes " Whereof the more

---

[1] " The Society of the Saints," p. 98.   [2] Carew," Cornwall " (1600), p. 30.

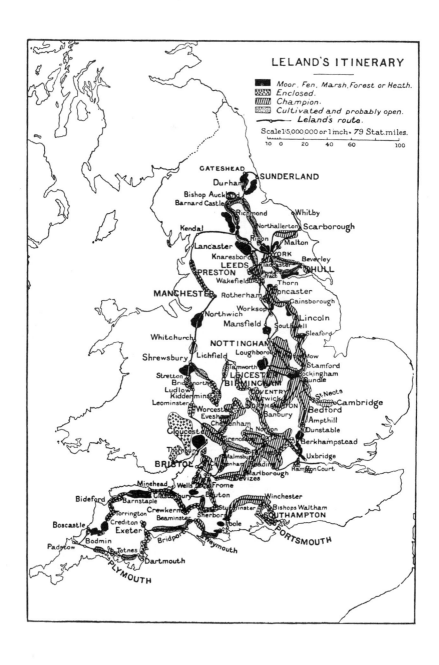

LELAND'S ITINERARY

Moor, Fen, Marsh, Forest or Heath.
Enclosed.
Champion.
Cultivated and probably open.
Leland's route.

Scale 1:5,000,000 or 1 inch = 79 Stat. miles.
10 0   20   40   60   100

GATESHEAD
Durham   SUNDERLAND
Bishop Auckland
Barnard Castle
Richmond   Whitby
Kendal   Northallerton Scarborough
Lancaster   Ripon Malton
Knaresbro   YORK   Beverley
LEEDS   HULL
PRESTON   Wakefield Thorn
MANCHESTER Rotherham Doncaster
Northwich Worksop   Gainsborough
Mansfield Southwell Lincoln
Whitchurch   Sleaford
Shrewsbury Lichfield NOTTINGHAM
Stretton   Loughborough Mow
Bridgnorth Tamworth   Stamford
Ludlow   LEICESTER Rockingham
Kidderminster BIRMINGHAM Undle
Leominster COVENTRY   St. Neots
Worcester Warwick   Cambridge
Evesham   NORTHAMPTON Bedford
Cheltenham Banbury   Ampthill
Gloucester   Norton Dunstable
Tewkesbury Cirencester Berkhampstead
BRISTOL   Malmsbury Uxbridge
Minehead Wells Bath Reading Hampton Court
Barnstaple Glastonbury Marlborough Winchester
Bideford   Bruton   Devizes Bishops Waltham
Boscastle Torrington Crewkerne Sherborn SOUTHAMPTON
Crediton Beaminster Sturminster Poole
Padstow   Exeter   Bridport PORTSMOUTH
Bodmin   Totnes   Weymouth
PLYMOUTH Dartmouth

part was or were used and occupied to tillage and husbandrie " ; and it required the land to be tilled "after the maner and usage of the countrey where the seyd land lyeth." This restriction drops out of the next Depopulation Act, 27 Henry VIII., c. 22, passed in the year 1536.

In the year 1536 Leland, the King's Antiquary, began his Itinerary, which lasted till 1542. Whether in consequence of special instructions or not, he almost everywhere notes the condition of the country he traverses with regard to enclosure. A summary of his observations is shown in the form of a map ; Devon, Cornwall, West Somerset, South Wales, Hereford, Worcester, the north-west of Warwick, South Lancashire, the country round Southampton, and near Hampton Court, with parts of Yorkshire, are shown to be the most enclosed districts which are described ; and the districts described by Leland as champaign are those which were later largely enclosed by Act of Parliament.

The general movement of agricultural progress, it may safely be assumed, up to Leland's time, was from the south-east of England northwards and westwards. The extreme south-east corner was certainly very early enclosed, as one would naturally expect, but we also find remote western districts, where one would naturally expect to find old customs linger comparatively late, precede the central districts in the abandonment of the "village community," by many years. [1]

Whether much of the enclosure which Leland saw in 1536 had been the work of the previous twenty years, it is of course impossible to say ; but making any reasonable allowance for progress in hedging and ditching in the western counties where

---

[1] How long the enclosure of certain western counties preceded the enclosure of the east midlands, is shown by comparing the two following extracts. Of the former, Joseph Lee, in "A Plea for Regulated Inclosure," published 1656, asks, "Are not many places in England, Essex, Hereford, Devonshire, Shropshire, Worcester, wholly enclosed?" (p. 31). Of the latter the "General Report on Enclosures," published 152 years later, "A village of farmers and labourers surrounding a church and environed by three or four and in a few cases by five open fields, form the spectacle of Cambridge, Huntingdon, and Northampton shires, as much as on the Loire and on the plains of Moscow" (p. 25).

agriculture was mainly pastoral during those twenty years, and assuming that the Act of 1516 had effectually stopped enclosure in that period in the corn-growing districts, one can hardly resist coming to the conclusion that if Leland had made his journey in 1516 he would then also have found enclosure most advanced in those districts which were most enclosed in 1536.

What we have, then, to ask is whether the priority of enclosure in the western counties is to be attributed entirely to the fact of their being devoted more to grass and less to tillage, or whether there was some difference in the primitive village community of the west which caused cultivated land to pass more easily into the condition of exclusive ownership and separate use. Obviously we must look for the answer to this question beyond the boundaries of England. To understand the differences between the village life of those parts of England which were once the Danelagh, Mercia and Wessex, from those which were then West Wales and Strathclyde, which may be regarded as at least semi-Celtic, we must examine the purely Celtic type of village community.

But it must also be noticed that there is one characteristic feature of the typical English village community, namely the importance attached to the right of common pasturage on the fallow field, and in the other arable fields after harvest, which would probably never have developed in any part of the country where only a small proportion of the land was ploughed. There would be too little profit and too much inconvenience attached to the exercise of the right for it to have a chance of being established, or if established, of persisting.

Lastly, it seems to me impossible to account for the perfect definition of the two boundaries between parishes early enclosed, without special Acts, and parishes enclosed late by special Acts, the one in the south-east, passing through Suffolk, Essex, and between Surrey and Kent, and the other in the south-west, passing through Somerset and Dorset, except on the assumption that the enclosure movement beginning in these two corners of England, was suddenly checked when it had reached the limits indicated, by the Tudor series of Depopulation Acts, and by the Inquisitions and other measures taken to enforce them.   These Acts specially stipulated for the continuance of the ancient customary methods of tillage.   A summary of their provisions which affect enclosure will be found in Appendix D.

CHAPTER XV.

It is a familiar fact that the early open field system of agriculture of Scotland, Wales, and Ireland, known as run-rig or rundale, differed in some important features from the common field system of England.

The mere fact suggests a series of questions with regard to the relationships between common field and run-rig; whether, for instance, the more complex common field system was evolved from the more simple and primitive run-rig system; or supposing the two not connected, whether a boundary can be defined on one side of which the early agriculture was of the English type and on the other of the Celtic type; and again, if so, which parts of England lie on the Celtic side of the boundary, and which, if any, of Wales and Scotland lie on the English side.

Obviously before considering such questions it is necessary to have a clear grasp of the nature of run-rig, and of the differences between it and the English system.

In the year 1695 the Scotch Parliament passed an Act allowing anyone " coterminous heritor " owning a share in a " commonty " to have his portion separate from the rest, and to enclose it; and a series of cases established a defined system of computing the share of the " commonty " to which the lord of the manor as such was entitled in lieu of manorial rights. This caused the process of the separation of intermixed properties in open fields to proceed without the intervention of special Acts of Parliament, except for Royal burghs. Also while in England under Enclosure Acts or agreements to enclose the three processes of (a) the separation of intermixed and intercommonable properties, (b) the separation of intermixed and intercommonable holdings, and (c) the hedging or fencing of the separated properties, were accomplished by one continuous series of actions on the part of those concerned, in Scotland it was otherwise. The separation of properties where necessary was first accomplished, and for long afterwards the system of run-rig was followed by groups of tenants on the same estate. After run-rig had been abandoned, the separate holdings remained open and unenclosed, and the process of building dykes or planting hedges was carried out at a later date, and by slow degrees.

The abandonment of run-rig was general, according to the reports to the Board of Agriculture, in the lowlands of Scotland about the year 1730. In the county of Perth up to the year 1744 " the land was always occupied in run-rigg, either by the different tenants on the same farm, and sometimes by coterminous heritors. The houses were in clusters for the mutual protection of the inhabitants." (James Robertson, D.D., " Agriculture of the Southern District of Perth," 1794, pp. 22, 23.) In the northern and Highland counties the transition was naturally later. Sir John Sinclair ("General View of the Agriculture of the Northern Counties and Islands of Scotland") describes the cultivated land of the Islands as being open almost everywhere, except in the case of the " mains " or manor farms, the glebe lands, and the farms of a few principal tacksmen. Of Caithness he says, " The greater part of the arable land in this county is occupied by small farmers who possess it in *run-rig*, or in *rig and rennal*, as it is here termed, similar to the common fields of England, a system peculiarly hostile to improvement " (p. 207). But in the Orkneys " Much of the land that formerly lay in the state known in Scotland under the name of run-rig land has been divided, but much still remains in the same situation " (p. 227) ; and the process of enclosing had begun even in the Shetlands (p. 252).

Turning westwards, we find that in the inner Hebrides 1850 was the date at which the run-rig system finally died out, in a manner and under conditions which will demand further attention. But it survived in the Outer Hebrides to a considerably later date. A very full and interesting description by Mr.

Alexander Carmichael is given in Skene's "Celtic Scotland,"
Vol. III. chapter x.

"Old systems are tenacious. They linger long among a rural
people and in remote places. Of these is the land system of run-
rig (Mor Barann) which characterises more or less the land
system of the Western Isles. The outer Hebrides are called the
Long Island. They are a series of islands 119 miles in length,
and varying from half-a-mile to twenty miles in breadth. This
kite-like chain of forty inhabited and upwards of a hundred and
fifty uninhabited islands contains a population of 40,000. Much
of this land is held by extensive tacksmen on leases (Fir Baile),
and there being no intermediate tenantry, the rest of the land
is occupied by small tenants at will without leases. These
number 4,500, the majority of whom fish as well as farm.

"The country is divided into townlands of various extent.
The arable land (Fearann Grainsich) occupied by the small
tenants of these townlands is worked in three ways—as crofts
wholly, as crofts and run-rig combined, and as run-rig wholly.
In Lewis and Harris the arable land is wholly divided into crofts ;
in Uist and Barra the arable land is divided in part into crofts,
and in part worked in run-rig ; while in the townlands of Hosta,
Coolas Paipil, and the island of Heisgeir in North Uist, the
arable land is worked exclusively upon the run-rig system of
share and share alike. The grazing land of the tenants of each
townland throughout the Long Island is held in common (in
Lewis called Comhpairt).

"The soil varies from pure sand to pure moss. Along the
Atlantic there is a wide plain of sandy soil called *Machair*. This
merges into a mixture of sand and moss (Breacthalamh, or
mottled soil), which again merges into pure moss (Mointeach)
towards the Minch. As the soil is dry and sandy, if the summer
is dry the crop is light. On the other hand, if the summer is
moist the crop is heavy and good. In order that all may have
an equal chance, the *Machair* belonging to them is equally
divided among the tenants of the township. Obviously the man
who is restricted to his croft has fewer advantages than the
man who, together with his croft, has his share of the *Machair*,

and still fewer advantages than the man who has, rig for rig with his neighbours, the run of the various soils of his townland, which gives name to the system. Consequently a wet or dry season affects the tenant of the croft system more than the tenant of the combined system, and the tenant of the combined system more than the tenant of the run-rig system.

" The townland of Hosta is occupied by four, Ceolas Paipil by six, and the island of Heisgeir by twelve tenants. Towards the end of autumn, when harvest is over, and the fruits of the year have been gathered in, the constable calls a meeting of the tenants of the townland for Nabachd (neighbourliness). They meet, and having decided upon the portion of land to be put under green crop next year, they divide it into shares according to the number of tenants in the place, and the number of shares in the soil they respectively possess. Thereupon they cast lots, and the share which falls to a tenant he retains for three years. A third of the land under cultivation is thus divided every year. Accordingly the whole cultivated land of the townland undergoes revision every three years. Should a man get a bad share he is allowed to choose his share in the next division. The tenants divide the land into shares of uniform size. For this purpose they use a rod several yards long, and they observe as much accuracy in measuring their land as a draper in measuring his cloth. In marking the boundary between shares, a turf (Torc) is dug up and turned over the line of demarcation. The *torc* is then cut along the middle, and half is taken by the tenant on one side, and half by the tenant on the other side, in ploughing the subsequent furrow ; similar care being afterwards exercised in cutting the corn along the furrow. The tenant's portion of the run-rig is called Cianag, and his proportion of the grazing ground for every pound he pays Coir-sgoraidh.

" There are no fences round the fields. The crop being thus exposed to injury from the cattle grazing along the side, the people have a protecting rig on the margin of the crop. This rig is divided transversely into shares, in order to subject all tenants to equal risks. . . . Occasionally, and for limited bits of ground, the people till, sow, and reap in common, and divide the produce into shares and draw lots. This is called *Comachadh*, promiscuous. The system was not uncommon in the past, though now nearly obsolete.

"In making their own land arrangements for the year, the tenants set apart a piece of land towards the support of the poor. . . .

"In reclaiming moor-land the tenants divide the ground into narrow strips of five feet wide or thereby. These strips, called lazy-beds (Feannagan, from feann, to scarify), the tenants allot among themselves according to their shares or crofts. The people mutually encourage one another to plant as much of this ground as possible. In this manner much waste ground is reclaimed and enhanced in value, the ground hitherto the home of the stonechat, grouse, snipe and sundew, is made to yield luxuriant crops of potatoes, corn, hay and grass. Not unfrequently, however, these land reclamations are wrested without acknowledgment from those who made them.

"The sheep, cattle and horses of the townland graze together, the species being separate. A tenant can only keep stock conformably to his share in the soil. He is however at liberty to regulate the proportions of the different kinds, provided that his total stock does not exceed his total grazing rights. He can keep a greater number of one species and a corresponding smaller number of another. Or he can keep a greater number of the young, and a corresponding less number of the old of the same species, or the reverse. About Whitsuntide, when the young braird appears, the people remove their sheep and cattle to the grazing ground behind the arable land. This is called clearing the townland. The tenants bring forward their stock (Leibhidh) and a souming (Sumachadh) is made. The *Leibhidh* is the tenant's stock, the *Sumachadh* the number he is entitled to graze in common with his neighbours. Should the tenant have a croft, he is probably able to graze some extra stock thereon, though this is demurred to by his neighbours. Each 'penny' of arable lands has grazing rights of so many soums. Neither, however, is the extent of land in the penny, nor the number of animals in the soum uniformly the same."

A soum consists of a cow and her progeny; in some places the cow and her calf only: in some a cow, her calf, her one-year-old progeny (called a *stirk*) and her two-year-old *quey;* in other places again, the cow, calf, stirk, quey and a three-year-old heifer. At four years old the heifer becomes a cow, and so originates a fresh soum.

In making souming calculations, it is assumed that one cow is equal to two queys or to four stirks or to eight calves, or to one heifer and one stirk. Also one cow is equal to eight sheep, or to twelve hoggs (one-year-old sheep) or to sixteen lambs or to sixteen geese. One mature horse is equal to two cows; also to eight foals, or to four one-year-old colts or fillies, or to two two-year-olds, or to one three-year-old and one colt or filly. The cow is entitled to her calf; and if one tenant has two cows without calves they are entitled to take one stirk instead.

Those tenants who are found at the souming to have overstock must either buy grazing from a tenant who has understock or may be allowed by the community to let the overstock remain on the grass till he can dispose of it. In that case payment must be made, according to a recognised code, into a common fund which is used to buy bulls or tups or for some other common purpose. The souming is amended at Lammas, and again at Hallowtide.

In Lewis and Harris similar arrangements with regard to stock obtain among the *crofters*, the amount of stock allowed to each crofter being regulated according to the rent paid.

During the early summer the herds are put at night into enclosures, according to the species, and two tenants, chosen in rotation, keep watch to prevent them from straying over the open fields. If they escape, the watchmen are fined and have to make any damage good, but the fines, and the amount assessed for damages, both go into the common fund.

Early in June, the tillage being finished, the people go to the hill grazing with their flocks. The scene is vividly described by Mr. Carmichael, the general excitement, the men shouting directions, the women knitting and chatting, the children scampering about. Sheep lead the procession, cattle come next, the younger ones preceding the older, the horses follow. Implements and materials are carried to repair the summer huts. When the grazing ground is reached the huts are repaired, fires lit, and food cooked. The people bring forward their stock into an enclosure, and the constable and another man stand at the gate of the enclosure and count each man's stock separately to see that he has brought only his proper souming. Then the cattle are turned out to graze, and the "Shealing Feast" is celebrated by the singing of hymns and the eating of cheese. The summer huts are of a beehive shape, and are sometimes constructed of stone, and sometimes of turf and frail materials.[1]

Each tenant under the run-rig system is responsible for his own rent only. Formerly the rent was paid partly in money, partly in meal, partly in butter and cheese, and partly in cattle.

The common functionaries, the shepherd, cattleherd and marchkeeper, are paid by their co-tenants for their services in seaweed, land and grazing. The business of the marchkeeper is to watch the open marches of the townland and prevent trespass. He may also have the duty of watching the shore to see when the seaweed is cast upon it. Then he erects a pole with a bunch of seaweed at the end, and the people come down to the shore to collect the weed for manure. No tenant is permitted to take seaweed till his neighbours arrive, unless the custom prevails of collecting the weed in common, dividing it into shares and casting lots.

When required by the proprietor or the people, the constable convenes a meeting of the inhabitants. At such meetings the questions in dispute are settled, after full discussion, by votes; lots are drawn if the votes are equal.

"The closer the run-rig system is followed, the more are

---

[1] The ruins of beehive huts all over Dartmoor, and of enclosures like Grims-pound, are conceivably evidence of similar customs in Devonshire. Now, however, the care of the cattle pastured on Dartmoor by the occupiers of adjacent farms, is a distinct occupation. Those who follow it are called "Moor-men."

the unwritten customs and regulations observed. The more intelligent tenants regret a departure from them. . . .

" The houses of the tenants form a cluster. In parts of Lewis the houses are in a straight line called *Straid*, street, occasionally from one to three miles in length. They are placed in a suitable part of the townland, and those of the tenants on the run-rig system are warm, good and comfortable. These tenants carry on their farming operations simultaneously, and not without friendly and wholesome rivalry, the enterprise of one stimulating the zeal of another. . . .

" Not the least pleasing feature in this semi-family system is the assistance rendered by their neighbours to a tenant whose work has fallen behind through accident, sickness, death, or other unavoidable cause. . . .

" Their mode of dividing the land and of equalising the stock may seem primitive and complex to modern views, but they are not so to the people themselves, who apply them amicably, accurately and skilfully. The division of the land is made with care and justice. This is the interest of all, no one knowing which place may fall to himself, for his neighbour's share may become his own three years hence.

" Whatever may be the imperfections, according to modern notions, of this very old semi-family system of run-rig husbandry, those tenants who have least departed from it are the most comfortable in North Uist, and, accordingly, in the Outer Hebrides."

Mr. Carmichael informs me that the whole of this description held good at least up to May, 1904.

The brief descriptions and other references to the run-rig system of the agricultural writers whom Sir John Sinclair and Arthur Young enlisted in the service of the Board of Agriculture at the end of the eighteenth, and the beginning of the nineteenth century, are sufficient to show that in all essential features it was fundamentally identical in different parts of Scotland. Sir John Sinclair's own description is meagre and unsympathetic : " Were there twenty tenants and as many fields, each tenant would think himself unjustly treated unless he had a proportionate share in each. This causes treble labour, and as they are perpetually crossing each other, they must be in a state of constant quarrelling and bad neighbourhood. In order to prevent any of the soil being carried to the adjoining ridge, each individual makes his own ridge as high as possible, which renders the furrow quite bare, so that it produces no crop, while the accumulated soil in the middle of the ridge is never stirred deeper than the plough. The proprietors begin to see the inconveniences of this system, and in general intend to remedy it, by dividing the land into regular farms."[1]

This is obviously a description of run-rig in a state of decrepitude; the communal spirit has died out of it, and apparently the practice of periodic redivision of the land has fallen into desuetude. In another passage[2] we find a variation of the method of guarding the crops which again, when compared with Mr. Carmichael's description of the "promiscuous rig," appears to show the decay of the system. "The tenants have a miserable sort of fence, made of turf, which separates their arable land from the adjoining waste; but it requires constant repairs, and when the corn is taken off the ground, is entirely neglected, and the country becomes one immense common, over which immense numbers of cattle are straggling in search of food, greatly to the injury of the soil."

William Marshall, the rival as an agricultural writer and bitter critic of Arthur Young, supplied the "General View of the Agriculture of the Central Highlands of Scotland." He supplies us with one significant hint, if we need it, with regard to the fundamental basis of run-rig: "Not the larger farms only, but each subdivision, though ever so minute, *whether* '*plow-gait*,' '*half-plow*,' or '*horse-gang*,' has its pittance of hill and vale, and its share of each description of land, as arable, meadow, green pasture and muir " (p. 29). By the way, even smaller farms than the " horse-gang," *i.e.*, one quarter of the arable land which could be ploughed by a four-horse plough,

---

[1] "General View of the Agriculture of the Northern Counties and Highlands of Scotland," p. 205.

[2] *Ibid.*, p. 207. This passage and the next occur in the description of Caithness, but they appear to be intended to apply to the whole district.

together with the corresponding proportion of meadow, pasture and moor, were to be found on the Royal burghs where inter-mixed ownership was exempt from the operation of the Act of 1695.   On these the smallest farms consisted of a " horse's foot " of land, i.e., one sixteenth part of a " plow-gait."

Dr. James Robertson defines run-rig as " Two or three or perhaps four men yoking their horses together in one plough, and having their ridges alternately in the same field, with a bank of unploughed land between them, by way of march." [1]

James McDonald, writing in 1811 a later report on the Agriculture of the Hebrides, published in 1811, gives an account of the beginning of the disappearance of run-rig in those islands. " Mr. Maclean of Coll insisted upon some of his tenants dividing among them the land which they formerly held in common, or run-rig, and which they were accustomed for ages to divide annually by lot, for the purposes of cultivation.   They obeyed with great reluctance, and each tenant had his own farm to himself.   Three or four years' experience has convinced them now that their landlord acted wisely. . . .   The same thing happened on various other estates, and especially in Mull, Tyree and Skye " (p. 133). But the general disappearance of run-rig in these islands took place about the middle of the nineteenth century, and was the consequence of the temporary prosperity produced by the rise of the kelp industry.   This led to extreme subdivision of holdings by sub-letting, the body of small crofters so created relying in the main upon the kelp industry for a livelihood, and using their crofts as a subsidiary means of subsistence (Skene, " Celtic Scotland," Vol. III., ch. x.).

It is clear that the two essential features of run-rig are (1) that it is based upon co-aration, several farmers yoking their horses to one plough, and tilling the land in partnership ; just as the English common-field system was also based upon co-aration, with the difference that in England, in general, at the time that co-aration was practised, the plough was generally drawn by eight oxen instead of by four horses.

---

[1] " Agriculture of the Southern Districts of Perth " (1794).

(2) That run-rig has a special distinctive feature in the periodical division and re-division of the land, and that in the Hebrides, at least, this feature survived after co-aration had become obsolete.[1] In this respect the Scotch agricultural community resembles that of Great Russia, where also the periodical re-division of the open fields, so as to make the shares proportional to the working power of each family, persists after co-aration has disappeared.

That throughout the British Isles, and indeed throughout Northern Europe, the earliest tillage of the soil by ploughs was accomplished by the method of co-aration, scarcely admits of doubt ; nor is it easy to doubt that before the possibility of improving the crop by manure was discovered, there was no permanent occupation by one of the partners in the ploughing, of any particular set of strips so ploughed.

But it is also obvious that whereas we know that in some places, as in the Hebrides and in Russia, the idea of common occupation of the land persisted, after co-aration had ceased, and displayed itself in the form of periodic or occasional re-division of the arable land, it is equally possible for the permanent occupation of certain strips of land to be definitely allotted to some individuals, while the practice of co-aration is still persistent among other individuals of the same community. In the latter case when individual cultivation begins, the peasant who drives his own plough team, drives it over the same set of strips of land as had previously been ploughed by the common plough ; he feels more than ever that they are his own, and that he must guard them against encroachment ; though, perhaps, he is not averse, when occasion offers, to widen his strips at the expense of his neighbours. The consequence is that by the time individual cultivation has entirely superseded co-operative ploughing in any particular village, freeholds and copyholds are definitely arranged as we know them in the English common fields.

---

[1] Mr. A. N. Palmer, in his important work, " A History of Ancient Tenures of Land in the Marches of N. Wales," expresses the opinion that co-aration and the shifting of land disappeared simultaneously in North Wales, and had come to an end by the reign of Henry VI. (p. 36, note).

Particularly is this likely to be the case if a long interval of time elapses between the first beginning of individual ploughing and the last disappearance of combined ploughing.

If on the other hand the practice of periodic re-allotment of the land persists up to the time when co-aration ceases, it will obviously be natural for the peasants when they dissolve their plough-partnership, to allot their land to one another with some regard for convenience as well as equity.   They will naturally— as Sir John Sinclair noticed they did—allot to each household a share in each particular sort of soil which had previously been cultivated in common, but each man's share in each field is likely to be allotted to him in one piece, or at least in a few, and not in a number of strips intermixed with those of his neighbours.   Then when at a later period hedging and ditching begin, each man has his land in a form convenient for enclosure; and by enclosing it he forms a series of irregular fields, roughly square, or when oblong, with the length not many times exceeding the width.   No throwing of the parish into the melting pot, either by a private Act of Parliament or by a voluntary submission to a Commission, was necessary in order to effect enclosure.

On the one hand, then, it is obvious that the great inequality of the holdings held by servile and semi-servile tenures from the time of Domesday onwards, was favourable to the creation of the conditions necessary to make piecemeal enclosure difficult.   The *socmanni* or *francigenae*, who held a whole carucate or ploughland apice, presumably also had, as a rule, a whole ploughteam, and were able to plough for themselves, while their neighbours, who held yardlands and half-yardlands, *i.e.*, one-quarter or one-eighth of a ploughland, could only have their lands ploughed by the common village ploughs.   As soon as the *socmanni* and *francigenae* began to permanently improve the soil, as for instance by marling, the beneficial results of which were believed in the eighteenth century to last for at least twelve years, they would naturally become a practically insuperable obstacle not only to any re-division of the land, but also to any minor variation in the exact position of the ridges which comprised the different holdings. Once one such holding was definitely located, the fixing of all other holdings which were intermixed with it would follow: every increase of certainty would be an encouragement to any given tenant to improve his land, and every expenditure of effort by a tenant on permanent improvement would be an additional motive to him to resist any changes in the position of his ridges.

On the other hand, in the case of land first brought into cultivation at a later date, when servile tenures had become obsolete, by "tenants at will" of the lord of the manor, the assured continued occupation of a defined set of ridges in land so reclaimed would not arise, even if the original tenants practised co-aration; and if the original cultivators worked independently, of course no intermixture of holdings would ever arise on such holdings.

Hence the very close connection between copyholds, *i.e.*, the commuted servile tenures, and common fields, which was observed as long as common fields were numerous.

To sum up, it is clear that on *a priori* grounds there are certain defined conditions in which alone we can expect to find the peculiarly English type of open-field arable, the type which most obstinately resists dissolution, persisting until destroyed by (*a*) the absorption of all properties into the hands of a single owner, or (*b*) a general valuation and redistribution of properties and holdings. These are that the land must originally have been tilled by the method of co-aration, and that co-aration must have persisted until after some at least of the holdings had become a definite set of strips of land, the position of which was not shifted from year to year. These conditions, as Seebohm shows, are the characteristics of the typical English village community. But they are not to be found in open arable fields of the Celtic type of run-rig; and they are not to be expected in lands first brought into cultivation after the disappearance of serfdom.

We may therefore expect to find enclosure of arable land proceeding easily, without the necessity for special Acts of Parliament, and at a comparatively early stage of social evolution, on the one hand in Devon and Cornwall, the counties bordering on Wales, and in Cumberland, Westmoreland and Lancashire; and on the other hand in districts like the Weald of Surrey, Kent and Sussex.

That this inference agrees with the facts will be shown in detail.

Traces of run-rig, however, both in the form of characteristic terms, and of records of local custom, are not confined entirely to the counties within or near the borders of Wales or West Wales. The Act (1770 c. 59) for Matton in Lincolnshire has for its object to enclose certain commons and " forty-five acres or thereabouts of antient Toftheads and small Inclosures called the Town Rig." To the Act for Barton in Westmoreland (1819 c. 83), which encloses " certain open common fields or town fields," which mentions " the dales or parcels of land in the said common fields or town fields," there is a parallel in the Act (1814 c. 284), for Gateshead in Durham to enclose " certain common or town fields, and other commonable lands and grounds." These phrases are all reminiscent of the fact that lands held, or which had previously been held, in run-rig in Scotland, or in rundale in Ireland, are known as town lands. [1]

Much more striking, however, is the local custom at Stamford, described in the following passage by Arthur Young : " Lord Exeter has property on the Lincoln side of Stamford, that seems held by some tenure of ancient custom among the farmers, resembling the *rundale* of Ireland. The tenants divide and plough up the commons, and then lay them down to become common again ; and shift the open fields from hand to hand in such a manner, that no man has the same land two years together ; which has made such confusion that were it not for ancient surveys it would now be impossible to ascertain the property " (" General View of the Agriculture of Lincolnshire," p. 27).

[1] " The Town Fields " indifferently with " The Common Fields " is the name by which the ancient arable area of Wrexham is called in old deeds, and the same name is applied to the ancient common fields in many places in North Wales. (See A. N. Palmer, " History of Ancient Tenures of Land in the Marches of North Wales," pp. 1, 2.)

William Marshall's comment is perhaps worth adding: "In regard to commons, a similar custom has prevailed, and indeed still prevails, in Devonshire and Cornwall; and with respect to *common fields*, the same practice under the name of 'Run-rig' formerly was common in the Highlands of Scotland, and, perhaps in more remote times, in Scotland in general."

Lastly, it is to be noticed that there is no mention in any description of run-rig of the arable fields being used as a common pasture after harvest, or during a fallow year. We shall find later the same absence of this custom characteristic of English Common Field, from open arable fields in Cumberland, Westmoreland, Lancashire, Wales and Devonshire; *i.e.*, from the Celtic part of England and Wales. This may, of course, be a mere coincidence, and the true explanation may in each be that the stubble was not needed for pasture. But in any case the absence of rights of pasture over arable fields removes a great obstacle to piecemeal enclosure.

EVERY YEAR LANDS.

In the chapter on Norfolk agriculture it is shown that the distinction between Infield and Outfield, which was characteristic of the agriculture of the Lothians, was also characteristic of the agriculture of Norfolk; and that a great part of the uninclosed intermixed arable land was not subject to rights of common, and was made to bear a crop every year, such land being known as Every Year lands, Whole Year lands, or Infields.

Here again we were obliged to look to Scotland for further light upon the customs of an English county, but in this case we cannot attribute the resemblance between the customs of Norfolk and the east of Scotland to a common Celtic influence. The hypothesis would be a difficult one, and a different explanation presents itself.

Seebohm points out that the ancient characteristic agriculture of Westphalia, East Friesland, Oldenburg, North Hanover, Holland, Belgium, Denmark, Brunswick, Saxony and East Prussia, a vast area comprising all districts from which the

Anglo-Saxon conquerors of Britain are believed by any historians to have come, is that known among German scholars as "Einfeld-wirthschaft," the "one field system." Crops, usually of rye and buckwheat, are continually grown year after year, in the strips in the open fields, the fertility being maintained by marling and the application of peat manure.[1]

It is therefore natural to attribute the whole year or every year lands of Norfolk, and the infields of Scotland, alike, to the influence of Saxon, Anglian or Danish conquest and settlement. If it is asked why the same agricultural feature was not more widely produced, the obvious answer is that when people of different races are mixed together in the occupation of the same villages, it is by no means certain that the agricultural customs which will afterwards prevail will be those of the conquerors, or of the race which is in the majority. The customs of the first occupiers had been modified by the environment, and had to some extent modified the environment, till something like harmony was created. After a conquest by another race, if any of the conquered race remain, the *easiest* course is to continue the existing mode of husbandry. It is more likely that the customs of the conquered race should remain as the basis of the future practice, though altered to some extent in form and more in spirit, than that the previous customs of the conquerors, which they had followed in other circumstances on a different soil and amidst other surroundings, should be imposed on the conquered people.

The following are the Acts for places outside Norfolk which specify the existence of Whole Year lands, Every Year lands, or Infields.

1740, c. 19. Gunnerton, *Northumberland*. This Act is to enclose 1300 acres of Ingrounds, and 1000 acres of Outgrounds.

1752, c. 27. Enclosing Wytham on the Hill, Infield, *Lincoln-shire*.

1761, c. 32. Enclosing Norham Infields. Norham was nominally in *Durham*, but it is on the Scottish border.

---

[1] "The English Village Community," p. 372.

1807, c. 18. Herringswell, *Suffolk*. "Divers old inclosed meadow and pasture grounds, and old inclosed whole year or every year arable lands, open or common fields, half year or shack lands, common meadows, heaths, warrens, fens, commons, and waste grounds."

1811, c. ccxix. Great Waddingfield c. Chilton and Great Coniard, *Suffolk*, "divers open fields called Whole Year lands and Half Year lands."

1813, c. 29. Icklingham, *Suffolk*. "Open and Common fields, Infields or Every Year lands, Common Meadows, Heaths, Commons and Wastes.

1819, c. 18. Yelling, Huntingdon, "Whole year lands."

Further, Arthur Young ("Agriculture of Suffolk," appendix, p. 217) tells us that the parish of Burnham, near Euston, in Suffolk, contained in 1764—

Infield arable, inclosed ...	...	...	381	acres,
Outfield arable ...	...	...	...	2626	,,
Meadow and Pasture ...	...	...	559	,,
Heath or Sheep-walk ...	...	...	1735	,,
	Total		5302	

And William Marshall (" General View of the Agriculture of the Central Highlands of Scotland," 1794, p. 38) remarks : "The every year lands as they are called, of *Gloucester*, may be said to be clean compared with those of Breadalbane." Now, William Marshall knew the agriculture of Gloucestershire well; and he was an extremely accurate observer, and more interested in the local variations of common field cultivation than other agricultural writers of his time ; his authority may therefore be considered good enough to establish the existence of lands known as every year lands in Gloucestershire.

It is also to be noticed that Acts of Enclosure for Gloucester and Oxford frequently specify, not " open and common fields " but " an open and common field," perhaps of between two and three thousand acres; and further, as we have previously noted, the Board of Agriculture reporter for Oxfordshire says: "In divers uninclosed parishes the same rotation prevails over the whole of the open fields; but in others, the more homeward or bettermost land is oftener cropped, or sometimes cropped every year." Of Gloucestershire, William Marshall says: "In the neighbourhood of Gloucester are some extensive Common fields which have been cropped, year after year, during a century, or perhaps centuries, without the intervening of a whole year's fallow. Hence they are called Every Year's land. Cheltenham, Deerhurst, and some few other townships, have also their Every Year's lands." On these lands no regular succession of crops is observed, except that "a brown and a white crop—pulse and corn—are cultivated in alternacy" ("Rural Economy of Gloucestershire," Vol. I., p. 65).

It may be suggested, further, that a four-year course, such as we have seen was customary in many places, might possibly have originated from the custom of cropping the land every year. The difficulties of maintaining the fertility of the land, and of keeping it clean, under perennial crops, might very well have been found insuperable before the introduction of turnip culture, and the natural remedy, suggested by the two- or three-year course in neighbouring parishes, would be a periodic fallow. It is, however, so far as any evidence that can be supplied from the eighteenth and nineteenth centuries goes, equally possible that the four-year course was a modification of the three-year course, or that the two-, three- and four-years systems are all equally ancient; and that the varying customs, not only of systems of tillage, but also of occupation of meadow land and regulation of common of pasture, as found in different parts of the country, have grown up in each district as the result of the inter-action of Keltic, Anglo-Saxon, and Norse tradition.

If we take this view, which appears to me antecedently probable, we can see in the Midland or Mercian system a complete blend of Anglo-Saxon and Keltic custom, in which the specific features of both of the original strains are lost, and an intermediate, but perfectly distinct, type of village community resulted. The Wessex system, both in its feature of lot or rotation meadow,

and in the customs of individual cultivation of land for common
benefit, as in the sowing of clover by each occupier to be fed on
by the village flock, compared with the Mercian system, shows a
much closer affinity with Keltic run-rig; while the Norfolk
customs are quite easily accounted for as the result of a fresh
infusion of Teutonic tradition, re-introducing the original one-
field system into villages where that system had previously been
blended with Keltic custom.

CHAPTER XVI.

A CERTAIN amount of light upon the question when the common field system lost its vitality, its advantages being completely overshadowed by its disadvantages, so that only the obstructive forces which we have considered prevented its disappearance, is furnished by the fact that the original settlers of New England, who presumably derived their ideas of agriculture from the eastern counties of England, reproduced in America a form of the English village community. No doubt their poverty and early difficulties compelled them to revert to a further degree of dependence on mutual help, and so perhaps the form of community which they there established may have been of a more primitive type than that which they had left behind, and allowance must be made for this possibility ; and also for the possibility of effects of the sojourn of the Pilgrim Fathers in Holland.

The following accounts of the New England common fields are taken from two papers by Mr. Herbert B. Adams :—

" Vestiges of the old Germanic system of common fields are to be found in almost every ancient town in New England. In the town of Plymouth there are to this day some 200 acres of Commons known as Town Lands. This tract is largely forest, where villagers sometimes help themselves to wood in good old Teutonic fashion. . . . In the old town of Sandwich, near Cape Cod, at the point where the ship canal was projected in 1880, there is a little parcel of 130 acres known as the Town Neck. This is owned by a company of twenty-four proprietors, the descendants and heirs of the first settlers in the town, and this tract is managed to this day as a common field. Originally the Town Neck with other common lands belonged to the whole town. In the MS. town records of Sandwich I find under date May 22, 1658, this vote : ' If any inhabytant wanteth land to plant, hee may have some in the Towne Neck, or in the Common for six yeare and noe longer.' Later, in 1678, April 6, townsmen are given liberty to improve Neck lands 'noe longer than ten yeares . . . and then to be at the townsmen's ordering again.' In the year 1695, the use of the Town Neck was restricted to the heirs of the original proprietors, and the land was staked out into 38 lots. The lots were not fenced off, and the whole tract continued to lie under the authority of the entire body of proprietors, like the arable fields of a German village community. In 1696, April 4, it was agreed that the Town Neck should be improved for the future by planting and sowing as a common field, until the major part of those interested should see cause otherwise to dispose or improve the same. The common fence was to be made up, and a gate to be provided by the first of May. A field driver or hayward was to keep the Town Neck clear of creatures and to impound for trespass. In 1700 it was voted that the Neck be cleared of creatures by the 16th of April, and that no part of the land be improved by tillage other than by sowing.

" And thus from the latter half of the 17th century down to the present day (May 9, 1881) have the proprietors of Sandwich Town Neck regulated the use of their old common field. Every year they have met together in the Spring to determine when the fences should be set up and how the pasture should be stinted. The old Commoners' records are for the most part still in existence as far back as the year 1693, and before this time the town records are full of agrarian legislation, for the Town Neck was then virtually town property. There arose in Sandwich and in every New England village community the same strife between old residents and new comers, as between the Patricians and Plebeians of ancient Rome. The old settlers claimed a monopoly of public land, and the new comers demanded a share. In most old New England towns the heirs of original settlers or of citizens living in the community at a specified date retained a monopoly of the common lands for many years until finally compelled by force of public opinion to cede their claims to the town. In Sandwich, however, a vestige of the old system has survived to this day. Every Spring, for many years, has appeared a public notice (I saw one in the *Seaside Press*, May 8, 1880) calling together the proprietors of the Town Neck at some store in the village to choose a moderator and a clerk, and to regulate the letting of cow rights for the ensuing year. . . .

"There were for many years in the town of Salem certain common fields owned by associated proprietors just as in the case of Sandwich Town Neck. Such were the north and south fields in Salem. The old Commoners' records of the south fields are still preserved in the library of the Essex Institute, and date as far back as 1680. Under the date of October 14th of that year, I find the following: ' Voted that the proprietors have liberty to put in cattle for herbage—that is to say 6 cows, 4 oxen, 3 horses or yearlings, or 24 calves to 10 acres of land, and so in proportion to greater or less quantities of land; and no person shall cut or strip their Indian corn stalks after they have gathered their corn, on penalty of forfeiting herbage.'

" The so-called great pastures of Salem, some 300 acres, are to this day owned and managed by a small company of proprietors in common, of whom Dr. Wheatland of the Essex Institute has been for some years the clerk. He has in his hands the records of the proprietory, extending back for many years.

" These records are full of old time regulations in regard to common fencing, common pasturage, cow commons, sheep commons and the like." (" The Germanic Origin of New England Towns " p. 33.)

Perhaps still more conclusive are the following decrees of the legislative body of Massachusetts, which Mr. Adams quotes. In the spring of 1643 the Massachusetts General Court ordered " For preventing disorder in corn feilds wch are inclosed in common . . . that those who have the greater quantity in such fields shall have power to order the whole, notwithstanding any former order to the contrary, & that every one who hath any part in such common feild shall make and maintaine the fences according to their severall quantities."

But in the autumn of the same year, the Act was passed :— " Whereas it is found by experience that there hath bene much trouble and difference in severall townes about the Manner of planting, sowing, & feeding of common corne ffeilds & that upon serious consideration wee find no general order can provide for the best improvement of every such common feild, by reason that some consists onely of plowing ground, some haveing a great part fit onely for planting, some of meadowe and feeding ground ; also so that such an order as may be very wholesome & good for one feild may bee exceeding preiudiciall & inconvenient for another, it is therefore ordered, that where the commoners cannot agree about the manner of improvement of their feild, either concerning the kind of graine that shalbee sowen or set therein, or concerning the time and manner of feeding the herbage thereof, that then such persons in the severall townes that are deputed to order the prudenciall affaires thereof, shall order the same, or in case where no such are, then the maior portion of the freemen, who are hereby enioyned wth what convenient speed they may to determine any such difference as may arise upon any information given them by the said commoners ; & so much of any former order as concerns the improvement of common feilds & that is hearby provided for, is hearby repealed." (" Village Communities of Cape Ann and Salem.")

CHAPTER XVII.

THE PROGRESS OF ENCLOSURE WITHOUT PARLIAMENTARY SANCTION.

A. FROM 1845 ONWARDS.

ANY statistical account of enclosure without Parliamentary sanction must necessarily be vague in comparison with the statements which it is possible to make of enclosure by Act of Parliament, and must consist of inferences from evidence of varying value. And, naturally, the evidence in general becomes scantier in proportion as the period investigated is more remote.

The Tithe Commutation maps and awards afford the richest mine of information for the period since 1836. We have seen that according to the analysis of them published by the Copyhold, Enclosure and Tithe Commission in 1873, they indicated the existence at that date of 264,307 acres of common fields. We have already seen how untrustworthy this estimate is if taken for a basis for calculating the area of existing common fields, how inaccurate it was even at the date at which it was published. But one great source of inaccuracy in it, as we have seen, is the assumption that no enclosure, other than by Act of Parliament, took place after the date of Tithe Commutation. If we could eliminate all other errors, and also get a perfectly accurate statement of the area of existing common fields, we should then know how much enclosure of common fields has taken place without Parliamentary intervention since the date of Tithe Commutation. This date, of course, is different in different parishes, but the average date is about 1845.

To eliminate all other errors it would be necessary to go over all the work again, a task which would take a single investigator several years of continual labour, and would not then be accomplished unless the investigator were himself infallible. We must therefore be content with an approximate correction.[1]

The tithe maps and awards deposited with the Tithe Commission cover about three-quarters of the area of England and Wales. The amount of common field in the other quarter is estimated on the assumption that in each county the part for which there are no tithe awards in the custody of the Tithe Commission contained the same proportion of common field as the part for which title awards existed. The common fields thus estimated amount to about two-fifths of the total estimate. If the particulars given in the return for the different counties were added up, we should get the statement :—

	Common Field Lands. Acres.
Areas ascertained from the tithe documents	163,823
Estimated additional areas	100,484
	264,307

We have seen that assuming the total of 163,823 acres is correctly " ascertained," the estimate of 100,484 acres for the other parishes is very excessive, because the most frequent reason for no title documents existing in the custody of the Tithe Commission is that the commutation of tithes was effected before 1836 by a local Enclosure Act, which swept away the common fields.

In consequence, counties which were mainly enclosed by Acts of Parliament are very partially covered by the tithe documents; counties which have few or no Acts for enclosure

---

[1] There are no less than 11,783 separate sets of awards and apportionments, each with its map. The maps vary in size from about six or seven to over a hundred square feet each. The apportionments are bulky rolls of parchment.

of common fields are nearly entirely so covered. For example, we have—

—	Percentage of Area enclosed by Acts.	Area Covered by Tithe Documents.	Area not so Covered.
COUNTIES OF PARLIAMENTARY ENCLOSURE.			
Northampton... ...	51·5	148,066	485,220
Rutland	46·5	37,728	54,968
Huntingdon	46·5	83,856	146,630
Bedford	46·0	104,357	191,159
Oxford...	45·6	214,889	252,417
East Riding, Yorkshire	40·1	263,473	479,228
Leicester	38·2	158,889	352,539
COUNTIES WITH LITTLE OR NO PARLIAMENTARY ENCLOSURE.			
Devon...	*Nil.*	1,611,710	46,039
Cornwall	*Nil.*	851,486	6,122
Kent	*Nil.*	973,726	29,246
Shropshire	0·3	788,108	64,385
Monmouth	0·4	329,430	16,292
Cheshire	0·5	599,904	115,931

Fortunately there is another possible way of calculating the probable area of common field land which would have been found in the parishes not covered by tithe documents, if it had been investigated at about the same date.

Out of the seventy-five parishes enclosed by Act of Parliament since 1850—*i.e.*, at a later date than almost all of the tithe documents—the Tithe Commission had the maps and awards of seventy-one—all, that is, but four. Common fields subsequently enclosed were to be found in these two classes of parishes in the proportion of 71 to 4 ; it is a fair inference that the total area of common fields, whether subsequently enclosed or not, was distributed in the same proportion.

On this assumption we should have the following calculation :—

	Common Field Lands.
	Acres.
Areas ascertained from the tithe documents	163,823
Estimated additional areas...	9,229
Total	173,052

No probable error in the additional estimate in this calculation would have an appreciable effect on the total.

Next, as we have noticed above, the " areas ascertained " require correction. This it is much more difficult to supply satisfactorily; all that we can do is to determine—(1) whether the number given is likely to err by excess or by defect; (2) whether the error is likely to be large.

The main purpose of the return was to establish the total amount of waste land subject to common rights, and the proportion of such land likely to be capable of cultivation. This part of the work was done with great care, and particularly with great care not to include any land which was not certainly subject to common rights. The final figure arrived at was certainly considerably in defect through the documents on which it was based failing to mention common rights in all cases where they existed.

The part of the return relating to common field lands, on the other hand, was considered of less importance; the explanatory letter says with regard to them :—

" The common field lands are generally distinguishable by the particular manner in which they are marked on the tithe maps, and their extent has been estimated by these maps." This means that areas on the tithe maps subdivided by dotted lines were assumed to be common field lands. This method had the advantage of comprehensiveness—it is probable that scarcely any common field land escaped notice, if there were a tithe map for the parish in which it existed. I have only detected one error

of omission. The common fields of Eakring were very considerably in excess of the 54 acres at which they were estimated.
But on the other hand it has the disadvantage of including with
common field lands numerous cases of properties or holdings
which were inadequately divided from one another by fences or
hedges, but which were not common fields. But it is very hard
to say precisely what percentage ought to be deducted to allow
for this error. Generalising from all the cases in which I have
been able to put estimates for particular parishes to a test, I
should say that more than one-sixth, but less than one-third of
the total should be deducted. Taking the larger fraction, so as
to leave the remainder under-estimated, rather than over-esti-
mated, we have—

	Acres.
Area of common field lands, by estimate above	173,052
Less one-third	57,684
	115,368
Parliamentary enclosure since 1873 has reduced the area of common fields by	14,842
	100,526

The final remainder represents our corrected estimate of the
area of common fields arable and commonable meadows of
intermixed ownership which would now exist if there had been
no enclosure except by Act of Parliament since about the year
1845. The total area of such fields and meadows actually
existing almost certainly does not exceed 30,000 acres. We
therefore may conclude that not less than 70,000 acres have
been enclosed as the result of the consolidation of farms and
properties and voluntary agreements and exchanges, since about
the year 1845, and that not more than 100,000 acres have been
thus enclosed.

The total area of common fields enclosed by Acts since 1845,
together with such meadows and commons as were enclosed
together with common arable fields, is 139,517 acres.

It would therefore appear that such voluntary methods of enclosure have accounted in this period for an area something between half as large an area as Enclosure Acts and five-sevenths of that area.

The proportion of villages in which common fields have been entirely got rid of by voluntary enclosure during the same period would of course be smaller ; because wherever common fields exist they are subject to continual diminution by gradual enclosure ; and the final application of an Act of Parliament may be merely the *coup de grace*. Curiously, also, it may happen that a practically complete enclosure may be effected, and years later resort be had to an Act, as in the cases of Hildersham (Cambridge), and Sutton (Northampton).

B.   BEFORE 1845.

The agricultural survey of Great Britain carried out by the Board of Agriculture in 1793 furnishes us with much information about the state of enclosure of some counties, and with scraps of information about others.   Where the information is fullest it may take the form of estimates of the total area enclosed or open, or the form of information with regard to particular villages.   By correlating the information thus supplied with that furnished by the Acts themselves, and from other sources, we can in some cases obtain a fairly full account of the enclosure history of a county.

BEDFORDSHIRE.

The " General Report on the Agriculture of Bedfordshire " gives the following estimate of the condition of the county (p. 11) :—

	Acres.
Enclosed meadow, pasture and arable ...	68,100
Woodland	21,900
Common fields, common meadows, commons and waste	217,200
Total ...	307,200

The area of Bedfordshire being 298,500 acres, a slight deduction should be made from the figures under each head. But this does not affect the two striking points about the estimate : (1) that over two-thirds of the area of the county was open, and (2) that the open and commonable land amounted to over 200,000 acres.

The author proceeds: "Every parish which is commonly understood to be open consists of a certain proportion of antient inclosed land near the respective villages, but that proportion, compared with the open common field in each respective parish, does not on an average exceed one-tenth of the whole " (p. 25).

He further says that Lidlington, Sundon and Potton had been recently enclosed. Each was enclosed by Act of Parliament.

We can deal with the above information in two ways: (1) by translating it into terms of parishes, and (2) by dealing with it in terms of acres.

In Bedfordshire very little common indeed existed apart from the open field parishes. This is proved by the fact that from 1700 to 1870 there were only three enclosures of commons, apart from arable common fields, comprising an area of 867 acres, and that the tithe maps only indicated 507 acres more of commons in parishes where there were no common fields. We may safely assume that at least 200,000 acres out of our author's 217,200 acres of open land belonged to open field villages, and that these villages also had, in accordance with his estimate, 20,000 acres of old enclosures, the area of all the open fields parishes in 1764 was, according to the estimate, about 220,000 acres; that of the enclosed parishes about 87,200 acres. If the numbers of the parishes enclosed and open were about in the same proportion, out of the one hundred and twenty-one parishes in Bedfordshire, there should have been eighty-seven open and thirty-four enclosed.

From the list of Parliamentary enclosures in the appendix, it will be seen that seventy-three parishes were enclosed by Acts passed in 1793 and later. There were also seven other parishes in which the tithe documents indicate common fields surviving up to the date of Tithe Commission, making a total of eighty parishes, which we have previously accounted for.

It would follow that about seven parishes were enclosed in Bedfordshire between 1794 and 1845 without any Act. This is in accordance with what we might reasonably expect.

Of the thirty-four parishes which by this argument were enclosed in 1790, seventeen had been enclosed by Acts passed between the years 1742 and 1783, leaving a remainder of seventeen parishes. There is obviously a strong probability that the majority of these were enclosed in the eighteenth century.

But in this calculation I have treated the 21,900 acres of woodland as though it were part of the enclosed parishes. If it be considered to belong indifferently to open and enclosed parishes, the above calculation must be modified. We then have ninety-four parishes open in 1793, and twenty-seven enclosed; fourteen out of the ninety-four would be enclosed without Parliamentary sanction between 1793 and 1845, leaving only ten parishes so enclosed at some unknown date earlier than 1793.

By dealing with the Bedfordshire estimate on the basis of acreage instead of parishes, I arrive at the following statement of the history of the enclosure of Bedford :—

	Acres.
Ancient woodland and waste, which passed directly into individual use, and ancient roads, &c.	43,000
Common fields, meadows and pastures enclosed before 1742	33,000
Ditto enclosed from 1742—1793 by Acts of Parliament	23,883
Ditto ,, ,, ,, ,, not by Acts	26,000
Ditto ,, ,, 1793—1900 by Acts ...	114,430
Ditto ,, ,, ,, ,, not by Acts	58,000
Total	298,313

Arthur Young, in June, 1768, travelled through Bedfordshire to St. Neots, and then close to the boundary between Bedford and Huntingdon to Kimbolton and Thrapston in Northampton-shire. He found from Sandy to St. Neots the country chiefly open, and that it continued so to Kimbolton and Thrapston ; though with regard to the two latter places he mentions enclosed pastures ("Northern Tour," 2nd Ed., Vol. I., pp. 55—59). This, so far as it goes, tends to confirm our conclusions.

I am anxious not to lay any undue stress on the above arithmetical calculations; but I think it is quite clear that up to the year 1742 the condition of the county of Bedford was that indicated by Leland's description.

Leland passed through Bedfordshire in his "Itinerary." From Vol. I., fols. 116—120, we find that from Higham Ferrers in Northamptonshire, about 2 miles from the Bedfordshire boundary, to Bedford (14 miles) was "champaine" from Wellington village, near Bedford, to Antchille Castle (Ampthill), "12 miles almost al by Champayn Grounde, part by corne and part by Pasture, and sum baren hethy and sandy grounde." Then "From Antchille to Dunstable X m. or more. First I passed partely by woddy ground and Enclosures. But after most parte by champaine Grounde. . . . And thens to Mergate al by Champaine a vj miles." And so out of Bedfordshire. A small part of the county was ancient woodland, a smaller part was cultivated land reclaimed from the forest state, which had never passed through the common fields system of cultivation, but almost all was in the condition of the typical open field parish, common field arable, commonable meadows, and common pastures, with a certain amount of enclosure round the villages. It would appear that during the 200 years following Leland's journey only an insignificant amount of progress in enclosure took place in Bedfordshire. This conclusion is not contradicted, but on the other hand it is not strikingly confirmed by Walter Blyth ("The English Improver," 1649), who enumerates as unenclosed "the south part of Warwick and Worcestershire, Leicester, Notts, Rutland, some part of Lincoln, Northampton, Buckingham, some part of Bedfordshire, most part of the Vales of England, and very many parcels in most counties."

One further point may be noticed. In Bedfordshire the

percentage of the total area enclosed by Act of Parliament is exceptionally high—46·0 per cent. We find that when we make allowances for (1) contemporary voluntary enclosure, (2) for ancient woodland and for some land passing directly from the forest state into that of separate ownership and occupation, (3) for some ancient enclosing of land in the immediate vicinity of villages, there is little or no other enclosure remaining to be referred to the period before Parliamentary enclosure began— in this case the year 1742.

NORTHAMPTON, RUTLAND, S.E. WARWICK AND LEICESTER.

These four counties may be said to form a definite group, so far as their enclosure history is concerned. The main facts of their Parliamentary enclosure are shown in the following table :—

	Acreage Enclosed		Percentage of Total Area.
	By 18th Century Acts.	By 19th Century Acts.	
Warwick	124,828	24,731	25·0
Leicester	187,717	12,660	38·2
Rutland	37,180	10,044	46·5
Northampton...	247,517	85,251	51·8

Like Bedford, they are all counties with a high proportion of enclosure by Act of Parliament; but they differ from Bedford in that their enclosure was much more preponderatingly effected in the eighteenth century. The proportion of eighteenth-century Acts is particularly high in Leicester, but the proportion of Acts earlier than 1760 is higher in Warwick than in any other county —twenty-nine out of 114. These counties comprise the district in which the greatest amount of agitation arose against enclosure in the seventeenth century, and that in which the effect of

EAST MIDLANDS

SECTION I.

Enclosed before the General Enclosure Act of 1801.
   ,, between 1802 and 1845.
   ,, under general enclosure Act of 1845.

Scale 1: 1,000,000 or 1 inch = 15.78 Stat. miles.

5 0 5 10 15 20

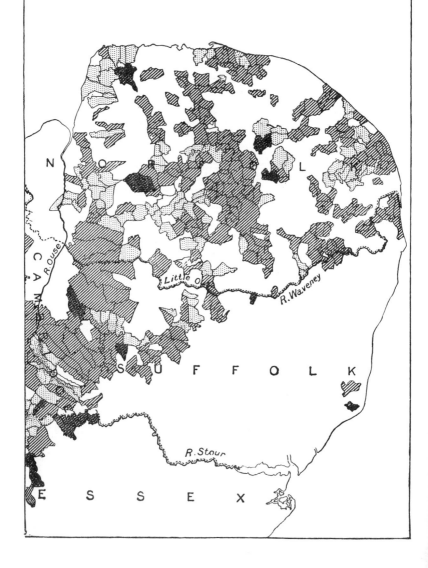

EAST MIDLANDS
SECTION 2.

Enclosed before the General Enclosure Act of 1801.
" between 1802 and 1845
" under general enclosure Act of 1845.
Scale 1: 1,000,000 or 1 inch = 15.78 Stat miles.

5   0   5   10   15   20

N O R F O L K

C A M

R. Ouse

Little O

R. Waveney

S U F F O L K

R. Stour

E S S E X

enclosure in causing depopulation through decay of tillage was most marked in the eighteenth century.

NORTHAMPTONSHIRE.

Northamptonshire has 51·5 per cent. of its area covered by Acts of Parliament for the enclosure of whole parishes, a larger proportion than any other county. There have been passed in addition an important Act for extinguishing foreign rights in Rockingham Forest in 1796, an Act in 1812 for draining and enclosing Borough Fen, and creating a new parish to be called Newborough, and three other Acts for enclosing commons or wastes ; the whole area affected by the five Acts being perhaps 15,000 acres. These being included, the total area which has undergone Parliamentary enclosure reaches 54 per cent. of the area of the county.

James Donaldson, the Board of Agriculture reporter, says that of the 316 parishes, 227 were enclosed by 1793, and eighty-nine were then in open field ; and that "half of the inclosed parishes may be denominated old inclosure."

Of the eighty-nine parishes, open in 1793, eighty-eight have been enclosed by Act of Parliament since ; so that there was only one parish enclosed without Parliamentary intervention from 1793 to 1903, when the last trace of the Northamptonshire common fields was swept away by the enclosure of Sutton. This fact is remarkable, it points to a wide diffusion of ownership of lands and of rights over the land ; and it should be associated with the specially strenuous resistance of Northamptonshire to enclosure in the reign of James I.

The statement that of the enclosed parishes half may be denominated old enclosure, would be more enlightening if one knew exactly what Mr. Donaldson meant by old enclosure. But we find that 113 parishes (which is as near as possible half 227) were enclosed by Acts passed in the period 1765—1792 ; if therefore by " old enclosure " he means enclosure dating back more than twenty-eight years, his statement would imply that there was no enclosure without an Act in that period. Nineteen parishes were enclosed by Act in the five years 1760—1764, eighteen in the period 1749—1759, and four earlier. These Acts altogether account for the enclosure of 153 out of the 227 parishes, and there is evidently a strong balance of probability that the enclosure of the remaining seventy-two took place almost entirely before the middle of the eighteenth century.

LEICESTERSHIRE.

R. Monk, the reporter for Leicester, gives as an Appendix a list of the "Lordships" of that county, with the names of the Lords of the manors, or chief landowners, and the date of enclosure, when he could ascertain it. He only knew of ten open field parishes and of two half open and half enclosed; but, of these, four, Cold Overton, Cole Orton, Whitwick and Worthington, have not since been enclosed by Act of Parliament; they must therefore have been enclosed voluntarily at the end of the eighteenth or in the first half of the nineteenth century; for the tithe documents for these parishes do not indicate any surviving common field. For thirty-five of the parishes not enclosed by Act of Parliament, Monk gives no information; of the following fifteen he gives the date of enclosure :—

Parish.	Enclosed.	Parish.	Enclosed.
Shanktons	1738	Stapleford	1772
Birstall	1759	Shearsby	1773
Beeby	1761	Hathorn	1777
Thurnaston	1762	Ilston	1788
Saxelby	1765	South Kilworth ...	1789
Frisby	1769	Hose...	1791
Stretton Parva ...	1770	Barkston and Plunger	1791

The following fifty-five he merely describes as "enclosed" :—

Allexton	Bittesby	Broughton Astley
Aston Flamville	Blackfordby	Burrow
Barwell	Brooksby	Burton-by-Prestwould

Cadeby	Hether	Stapleton
Carlton	Huncote	Stretton Magna
Coston	Ibstock	Swepston
Cotes	Isley Walton	Thorpe Arnold
Dadlington	Knossington	Thurnby
Dalby-in-the-Wolds	Lockington	Tilton-on-the-Hill
Great Dalby	Loseby	Twycross
Dishly Grange	Market Bosworth	Ullesthorpe
Eastwell	Potters Marston	Welham
Edmundthorpe	Misterton	Little Wigston
Fenny Drayton	Normanton-on-the-	Witherby
Foolesworth	Heath	Woodthorpe
Gaddesby	Odstone	Owston
Garthorpe	Rollestone	Staunton Harold
Galby	Saxby	
Goadby	Snareston	

Wanlip he describes as enclosed lately.

The following forty he describes as " old enclosure," or gives seventeenth-century dates for their enclosure—

Ashby Folville	Elmesthorpe	Ragdale
Great Ashby	Enderby	Scraptoft
Barlston	Foston	Shawell
Buckminster	Freathby	Staunton Wyville
Beaumont Leys	Glen Parva	Stoke Golding
Burbage	Kirkby Beler	Thedingworth
Burton Lazars	Lodington	Thorpe Sacheville
Braunston-by-Kirkby	Muston	Welby
Carleton Curlew	Nailston	Willoughby Waterless
Catthorp	Newton Linford	Wyfordby (or Wiverby)
Cossington	Packington	Wymondham
Cotterback	Peatling Magna	
Little Dalby	Prestwould	

Pickwell, he says, was enclosed in 1628, Shenton in 1646, and Laughton in 1665.

Here, again, in interpreting these statements, we are confronted with the difficulty of determining what antiquity is implied by the term " old enclosure," and also by the difficulty of estimating what proportion of the parishes described merely as " enclosed " belonged to any particular epoch of enclosure.

On the one hand, we note (1) that one-third of the open field parishes known to Monk were enclosed without Acts in the following half-century, (2) that he gives the date of enclosure of fifteen other parishes for which we have no Acts, which were enclosed in the previous half-century. It would therefore appear that a very considerable amount of enclosure was going on, without Acts of Parliament, during the period in which Parliamentary enclosure was proceeding rapidly.

On the other hand, the fact that he can give seventeenth-century dates for the enclosure of three parishes suggests that probably a very large proportion of his " old enclosure parishes " and a fair proportion of his enclosed parishes were enclosed in the seventeenth century.[1]

Pursuing the inquiry backwards, we find our next source of information in Celia Fiennes, a lady of Newtontony, who made a series of rides in the last few years of the seventeenth century. Newtontony is three miles east of Amesbury, amid the open chalk hills, or, as she describes it, in the midst of " a fine open champion country "; and she usually describes the aspect of the country she passes through. She travelled westwards to Land's End, eastwards to Kent, northwards to the Border, and she gives some information with regard to the state of enclosure of most of the English counties. She went through both Bedfordshire and Northamptonshire, but with regard to those two counties gives no information as to their condition of enclosure. As she is more apt to notice the presence than the absence of hedges, this, so far as it goes, confirms our conclusions with regard to Bedfordshire ; and, with regard to Northamptonshire, this small piece of negative evidence tends to the conclusion that that county also was almost entirely open in the beginning of the eighteenth century.

"Leicestershire," she says, " is a very Rich Country—Red land,

---

[1] William Pitt, who made a second survey of the agriculture of Leicestershire for the Board, published in 1809, gives an interesting account of the enclosure of the vale of Belvoir. This, the north-eastern corner of Leicestershire, was enclosed between 1760 and 1800 ; and as a result a complete change in the cultivation took place ; the rich land in the valleys, which had been arable common fields, was laid down in grass, and the tenants forbidden under heavy penalties to plough it ; while the summits of the hills and edges of the vales, which had been sheep-runs, were converted into arable land.

good corn of all sorts and grass, *both fields and inclosures.* You see a great way upon their hills the bottoms full of Enclosures, woods, and different sorts of manureing and herbage " (p. 133).

It is evident that enclosure had considerably advanced ; but it must be noted that " fields " with Celia Fiennes means common fields. It is further to be noted that her description of the enclosures creeping up the hills implies a process of gradual enclosure. Of the neighbourhood of Bosworth (in the west of Leicestershire) she says, " this is a great flatt full of good Enclosures." The western side of Leicestershire was therefore mainly enclosed before 1700, while the north-east was all open till 1760.

But though enclosure was so far advanced in Leicestershire, " their fewell," Celia Fiennes says, " is but cowdung or Coale." The use of cowdung for fuel supplied to advocates of enclosure in the seventeenth and eighteenth centuries one of their chief arguments. Either the hedges of Leicestershire were not yet able to supply enough wood for fuel, or the old custom continued although it was as unnecessary as objectionable. In either case the natural inference is that much of the enclosure of Leicestershire which Celia Fiennes observed, was then recent.[1]

This again is confirmed by Walter Blyth, who in the passage quoted above describes Leicestershire as entirely open, as well as Northampton, Rutland, and the south part of Warwick.

Further detailed information is given by the disputants Joseph Lee, John Moore, and the anonymous writers who joined in the controversy, who debated the ethics of enclosure in the Midlands in the years 1653—1657. John Moore, in his first pamphlet, asks, " Above one hundred touns inclosed in Leicestershire, how few amongst them all are not unpeopled and uncorned ? " Now it is probably fair to read " above

---

[1] Arthur Young found the practice still prevalent in Northamptonshire more than seventy years later : " they collect all the cow-dung from their fields and daub it in lumps, barns, and stables, to dry for fuel " (" Eastern Tour," Vol. I., p. 48). Edward Lawrence speaks of Yorkshire (evidently the East Riding only is meant) and Lincolnshire as the counties where the practice prevailed in 1727 (" The Duty of a Steward to his Lord," Article 3).

one hundred " as " about one hundred " or " nearly one hundred." The names of some of these are supplied by Joseph Lee in his " Vindication of Regulated Enclosure," for he gives (page 5) as examples of enclosure without depopulation the following thirteen parishes in Leicestershire : Market Bosworth, Carlton, Coten, Shenton, Cadesby (Cadeby), Bilson (Billesdon), Twicriss, Higham, Golding (Stoke Golding), Little Glen, Croft, Ashby Magna, and Stapleton, together with Stoke in Northamptonshire, Upton and Barton, which might be either in Northampton or in Warwick, and three others, Nelson, Cosford and Woscot, which I am unable to locate, except that Cosford was near Catthorp, the extreme south corner of Leicestershire ; for Lee further gives a list of fifteen enclosures within three miles of Catthorp, in which Cosford and Coten are included, and also Bigging, Brownsover, Shawell, Streetfield, Over, Cottesbatch, Pultney, Sturmer, Hallfield, Sister (? Siston), Moorebarn, Cotes and Misterton (p. 8).

Of the former set of townships he says : " They have been enclosed some twenty, some thirty, some forty or fifty years." Of the latter he says : " Most of these Inclosures have been plowed within thirty years, and the rest are now about to be plowed."

It would appear, therefore, that enclosure began in Leicestershire at about the beginning of the seventeenth century, and proceeded so rapidly that nearly a hundred townships, mainly situated in the south and west of the county, were enclosed within about fifty years. Enclosure also began in Northamptonshire about the same time, but at not so great a rate. The author of " Considerations Concerning Common Fields and Enclosures," published in 1653, makes a reference to " Mr. Bentham's[1] Christian Conflict " (p. 322), which gives a list of eleven manors in Northamptonshire, enclosed and depopulated. In a later sermon, " A Scripture Word against Inclosures," 1656, John Moore says : " England (especially Leicestershire and the counties round about) stands now as

---

[1] This was Joseph Bentham of Kettering, who published " The Societie of the Saints," in 1638, in which he denounces enclosure with remarkable vehemence.

guilty in the sight of God of the sinnes in the text. They sold the righteous for silver and the poor for a pair of shoes, as Israel did then" (p. 1). A little later he again referred to "Enclosure in Leicestershire and Northamptonshire, and the counties adjacent." This confirms the conclusion reached from the other evidence that Leicestershire was in the centre of the seventeenth-century movement of enclosure of common fields, and that it was in Leicestershire that the movement was most effective.

Rutland.

Rutlandshire has had 46·5 per cent. of its area enclosed by Acts of Parliament, 47,224 acres. Of this area 14,641 acres were enclosed by Acts passed between 1756 and 1773 ; then for twenty years there were no Acts, the next being passed in 1793. By that and subsequent Acts 32,583 acres were enclosed.

John Crutchley, the Board of Agriculture reporter, says that two-thirds of the country was enclosed, one-third unenclosed ("Agriculture of Rutland, 1793," p. 30). As the area (32,583 acres) is just one-third of the total area of Rutlandshire (97,273 acres), Acts of Parliament entirely account for all the enclosure since 1793. Of the area enclosed before 1793 there remains about 50,000 acres, a little more than half the county, unaccounted for.

Part at least must have been enclosed before the beginning of the eighteenth century, for Celia Fiennes says : "Rutlandshire seems more woody and enclosed than some others" (p. 54). It is one of the counties described by Walter Blyth as entirely unenclosed in 1649 ; but, as we have seen, this description is also applied by him to Leicestershire and Northamptonshire, and as it was, especially in the case of the former county, decidedly too sweeping, we cannot infer that no enclosure took place in Rutlandshire before that date.

Leland passed through Uppingham and Stanford ; he found part of the county woody, but he makes no mention of enclosure.

He also gives a very full description of the counties of Leicester and Northamptonshire. Charnwood Forest in Leicestershire, and Rockingham Forest in Northamptonshire, were then very extensive ; but all the remainder of the two counties he describes in general as "champaine," or by words which imply an unenclosed condition. The only mention of enclosure is in the case of two parks in Northamptonshire. (See Appendix C.)

WARWICK.

Warwickshire is divided by the River Avon into two parts of approximately equal area ; the north-western part is a district of ancient enclosure, probably enclosed in the main direct from the forest state ; the south-eastern part has a similar enclosure history to Leicester and Northampton, except that its enclosure took place generally somewhat earlier. One-quarter of the whole county has undergone Parliamentary enclosure, but the proportion so enclosed of the south-eastern part is much larger.

John Wedge, the Board of Agriculture reporter, estimates that in 1793, out of a total area of 618,000 acres, 57,000 was open field land (p. 11). To reduce 618,000 to the true area of the county (577,462 acres), one must deduct 10 per cent. A deduction of 10 per cent. leaves about 51,000 acres of common field. Enclosure Acts since account for 38,444 acres, and in parishes not enclosed by Acts the tithe documents indicate rather over 1000 acres of common field lands. There remains a little over 10,000 acres unaccounted for, which has disappeared between 1793 and the date of tithe commutation.

John Wedge appears to have attempted a list of open field parishes with their area and extent of common field and waste, but only got so far as to supply this information for five parishes (p. 54), each of which has undergone subsequent enclosure by Act of Parliament. He draws attention to the contrast between the two parts of Warwickshire : "About forty years ago the southern and eastern parts of this county consisted mostly of open fields. There are still about 50,000 acres of open field land which in a few years will probably all be enclosed. These lands, being now grazed, want much fewer hands than they did in the former open state. Upon all inclosures of open fields the farms have generally been made much larger. For these causes the hardy yeomanry of country villages have been driven for employment into Birmingham, Coventry, and other manufacturing towns."

About 90,000 acres was enclosed by Act of Parliament in the part of Warwick described between 1743 and 1793. This, together with the 50,000 acres remaining, amounts to rather less than half the area of the division of the county under consideration. As Wedge clearly was of opinion that the greater part of S.E. Warwick was open at the date he mentions, and as there is no reason for thinking he was wrong, it is to be inferred that a considerable amount of non-Parliamentary enclosure was going on in S.E. Warwick during the second half of the eighteenth century.

The extracts above given with reference to Leicester and Northampton also prove that enclosure was going on in this part of the county during the first half of the sixteenth century, though it had so little advanced up to 1649 that Blyth speaks of this part of the county as unenclosed.

Leland gives an extremely full account of the state of enclosure of Warwickshire, which shows that as early as 1540 the north-west part of the county was "much enclosed." It was on one of his later journeys that he explored the county, entering from Oxfordshire. He found, "Banbury to Warwick, twelve miles by Champaine Groundes, fruitful of corne and grasse, and two miles by some enclosed and woody groundes" (Vol. IV., Part 2, fol. 162).

"I learned at Warwick that the most part of the shire of Warwicke, that lyeth as Avon River descendeth on the right hand or ripe of it, is in Arden (for soe is the ancient Name of that part of the shire); and the ground in Arden is much enclosed, plentifull of grasse, but not of corne. The other part of Warwickshire that lyeth on the left hand or ripe of Avon River, much to the south, is for the most part Champion, somewhat barren of wood, but plentifull of corne" (fol. 166 a).

We may add, so as to complete our review of the evidence,

that William Marshall, in his book on the "Agriculture of the Midland District of England" (1790), treats a region of which the town of Leicester was near the centre, comprising the counties of Warwick, Rutland, the north of Leicester and of Northampton, the east of Staffordshire, and the southern extremities of Derby and Nottingham, as an agricultural unit. He says: "Thirty years ago much of this district was in an open state, and some townships still remain open; there are others, however, which appear to have been long in a state of enclosure, and in which, no doubt, the present system of management originated" (p. 8). This does not add to our information about this district, but the fact that Marshall was perfectly correct in his reading of the story told by the aspect of the country is important, because for some other districts his testimony is material.

To sum up, we find that in the north-west of Warwick enclosure was general as early as 1540, while it was practically non-existent in the south-east of that county and in Leicester, Northampton and Rutland. We find that the movement towards enclosure of the "champaine" country began about the year 1600, that it proceeded steadily in spite of great popular resistance through the seventeenth century, but at a much greater rate in Leicester, and probably in S.E. Warwick, than in Northamptonshire, the rate in Rutland being probably slower than in Leicester, but certainly greater than in Northamptonshire, the course of the movement being from west to east; that about half of S.E. Warwick and of Leicester was enclosed when the movement of Parliamentary enclosure began, but less than half of Rutland, and not more than quarter (probably not more than a fifth) of Northamptonshire.

We have seen that the enclosure of Bedford was later than this, and we shall see that the same is true of Cambridgeshire and Huntingdon. In the midlands of England the course of enclosure from 1600 onwards was from west to east.

A word may be added with regard to the methods by which non-Parliamentary enclosure was effected in this district. There was great diversity in Leicestershire from village to village with regard to the diffusion of property, as may be seen from Monk's Appendix, in which he endeavours to give the names of the principal owners in each "lordship." Some were entirely in the hands of a single individual, others had many owners, but in the great majority the land was mainly, but not entirely, owned by the lord of the manor. The description of the enclosure of S.E. Warwick supplied by John Wedge, the consolidation of farms, and the depopulation of the villages, indicates that there enclosure, whether by Act of Parliament or not, was carried through by the authority of the lord of the manor, he being the main landowner.

The method by which this would be done when an Act of Parliament was not resorted to is fully explained by Edward Lawrence ("The Duty of a Steward to his Lord, 1727"), Article XIV.

"A Steward should not forget to make the best Enquiry into the disposition of any of the Freeholders within or near any of his Lord's Manors, to sell their Lands, that he may use his best Endeavours to purchase them at as reasonable a price as may be for his Lord's Advantage and Convenience . . . especially in such Manors where improvements are to be made by inclosing Commons and Common Fields; which (as every one, who is acquainted with the late Improvements in Agriculture must know) is not a little advantageous to the Nation in general, as well as highly profitable to the Undertaker. If the Freeholders cannot *all* be perswaded to sell, yet at least an Agreement for Inclosing should be pushed forward, by the Steward, and a scheme laid, wherein it may appear that an exact and proportional share will be allotted to every proprietor ; perswading them first, if possible, to sign a Form of Agreement, and then to chuse Commissioners on both sides . . . If the Steward be a Man of good sense, he will find a necessity of making use of it all, in rooting out *superstition* from amongst them, as what is so great a hindrance to all *noble* Improvements." The superstition referred to, is that enclosed land is cursed, and doomed in three generations to pass out of the hands of the descendants of the proprietor who enclosed it.

That in the early seventeenth century much of the enclosure was carried out by the power of the lord of the manor is plain from the scraps of information given by John Moore. Thus he tells us that Ashby Magna was enclosed in 1606, and that the lord gave most of his tenants leases for three lives and twenty-one years after("Scripture Word Against Inclosures," p. 9), that being the reason why depopulation had not resulted up to 1656; that in both Misterton and Poultney no house at all was left except the minister's, so that these two manors must have been the property of absentee landlords.

But Catthorpe had no lord of the manor, it consisted of 580 acres divided among eight freeholders and five or six holders of "ancient cottages" who were also Freeholders (Joseph Lee, p. 5). The enclosure was carried out by the agreement of all the owners, except one who objected on conscientious grounds. The way in which these agreements to enclose were effected in parishes where property was divided is thus described by Moore:—
"In common fields they live like loving neighbours together for the most part, till the *Spirit of Inclosure* enter into some rich Churles heart, who doe not only pry out but feign occasions to goe to law with their neighbours, and no reconcilement be made till they consent to Inclosure. So this Inclosure makes thieves, and then they cry out of thieves. Because they sold the righteous for silver, and the poor for a pair of shoes. If it had not been for two or three righteous in many Townes of these Inland Counties, what desolation had there been made ere this time?" (Scripture Word, p. 12).

CAMBRIDGE AND HUNTINGDON.

Much of these two counties anciently consisted of fen and marsh, and of the land now cultivated a great deal never passed through the common field system. But the "upland" of each county was very late in undergoing enclosure.

Vancouver, the reporter for Cambridgeshire, gives an estimate of the areas of lands of different description, which I slightly rearrange below.

—	Unenclosed.	Enclosed.	Doubtful.
	Acres.	Acres.	Acres.
Enclosed arable	—	15,000	—
Open field arable	132,000	—	—
Improved pasture... ...	—	52,000	—
Inferior pasture	—	—	19,800
Improved fen	—	50,000	—
Woodland	—	—	1,000
Waste and unimproved fen	150,000	—	—
Half-yearly meadow land...	2,000	—	—
Highland common ...	7,500	—	—
Fen or moor common ...	8,000	—	—
Heath and sheepwalk ...	6,000	—	—
	305,500	117,000	20,800

Total area, 443,300 acres.

The actual area of Cambridgeshire is 549,723 acres; but Vancouver was an exact and careful observer, and the proportions between the areas assigned to each description were no doubt reasonably accurate. Here we find over two-thirds of the total area unenclosed, and more than eight-ninths of the arable land. It is, of course, possible, probable even, that a larger amount than 15,000 acres of open field arable had undergone enclosure, and that the 52,000 acres of improved pasture includes a good deal of such land, laid down in grass on enclosure. But even if we included the whole, there would only be 67,000 acres of ancient common field arable which had undergone enclosure, compared with 132,000 acres still open.

Vancouver also gives detailed accounts of ninety-eight of the Cambridgeshire parishes, eighty-three of which were open, fifteen enclosed. Of those which were open in 1793, seventy-four have since been enclosed by Act of Parliament, nine have not, viz., Babraham, Boxworth, Downham, Ely, Littleport, Lolworth, Madingley, Soham and Over.

Babraham had 1,350 acres of common field, and Vancouver says that enclosure was desired. It was completely effected before the date of tithe commutation.

Boxworth had 900 acres of common field. " The whole of this parish," says Vancouver, " lies within a ring fence and containing 2,100 acres, is the property of one gentlemen." Vancouver's acres, as we have seen, are large ones; the actual area is 2,526 acres. Enclosure was effected before the date of tithe commutation, and as might be supposed under the circumstances, without an Act.

Downham had, according to Vancouver, 680 acres of common field ; the tithe map indicates 450 acres still remaining.

To Ely he assigns 2,100 acres of common field. This had all gone at the time of tithe commutation.

Of 345 acres assigned to Littleport, a remnant of forty acres survived to be recorded in the tithe map.

The common field land of Lolworth suffered no diminution ; for while Vancouver gives it 650 acres, the tithe map indicates 800 acres. They were enclosed at the time of the Crimean war by common agreement of the owners, without an Act. This was the last surviving common field parish in the vicinity.

In Soham enclosure was nearly as slow. Vancouver assigns it 1,200 acres of common field ; the tithe map 1,100 acres.

Madingley, Vancouver says, had 1,030 acres of common field. These were all enclosed before the date of tithe commutation.

For Over the Board of Agriculture has no tithe documents; but we may add that Horseheath had about 750 acres of common field, out of a total of 1,850 acres, according to the tithe map.

Of the fifteen parishes stated by Vancouver to have been enclosed before 1793, only two were enclosed by Act of Parliament.

The extent of the information obtained from the Acts, the tithe documents, and Vancouver's report is as follows :—

Of the 152 agricultural parishes of Cambridgeshire, we know the date of enclosure of 118, enclosed by Acts of Parliament. These are given in Appendix B.

Of thirteen, viz., Arrington, Childerley, Chippingham, Hatley St. George, Leverington, Newton in the Isle of Ely, Outwell, Tadlow, Tid St. Giles, Upwell-cum-Welney, and Wisbeach St. Mary, we know that they were enclosed without Acts before 1793. The date 1790 is given for Chippingham, and a small remnant of common field survived till 1851 in Newton.

Four parishes were enclosed, not by Acts, between 1793 and the date of tithe commutation—Babraham, Boxworth, Ely and Madingley.

Five parishes which were not entirely enclosed even at the date of tithe commutation have not been enclosed by Act since. These are Lolworth, which then had only about one-fifth of its area enclosed ; Horseheath, which was about half enclosed ; Soham, which had about 1,100 acres of common field and 456 acres of common, out of a total area of nearly 13,000 acres ; and Downham and Littleport, which had respectively 450 and forty acres of common field remaining.

Of one parish, Over, we only know that it was open in 1793.

Of nine parishes, Borough Green, Croydon-cum-Clapton, East Hatley, Papworth St. Agnes, Long Stanton, Westley Waterless, Wisbeach St. Peter, Witcham and Witchford, we only know that they were enclosed before the date of tithe commutation.

Of two, Little Gransden and Stanground, we have no information.

I have before laid stress upon the eastward march of enclosure in the midlands during the sixteenth, seventeenth, and eighteenth centuries, which the following comparison illustrates :—

—	Parliamentary Enclosure.			
	In the 18th Century.		In the 19th Century.	
	Acts.	Acres.	Acts.	Acres.
Warwick	91	124,828	23	24,731
Cambridge ...	23	51,028	85	147,311

Celia Fiennes traversed the county. She describes the part from Littlebery (in Essex) to Cambridge as entirely open (p. 48), and makes no mention of enclosures in the description of the view from the " Hogmogoge Hills " (p. 49), but she speaks of " good enclosure " between Cambridge and Huntingdon.

Though Cambridgeshire was on the whole so late in undergoing enclosure, the conversion of arable into tillage had so far proceeded that about one-fifth of the county was included in the Inquisition of 1517, and it was found that in this part 1,422 acres had been enclosed and converted into parks or pasture (Leadam, " Domesday of Inclosures ").

HUNTINGDON.

George Maxwell, the Board of Agriculture reporter, says that Huntingdon contains one hundred and six towns and hamlets, of which forty-one were then (1793) wholly enclosed, and of the remaining sixty-five a very considerable part was enclosed. He computes that about a half of the " high land part " of the county, which would, of course, include all old arable land, was still unenclosed (" Agriculture of Huntingdon," p. 16).

Fifty-eight parishes were enclosed by Acts subsequently to the date of his report, and one parish (Lutton) remained open to the date of tithe commutation. This leaves six out of the sixty-five open or partially enclosed parishes of his report, in which enclosure was completed by the middle of the nineteenth century without any Act.

Of the forty-one parishes wholly enclosed before 1793, twenty were enclosed by Acts of Parliament, leaving twenty-one parishes which might have been enclosed contemporaneously without Acts, or to be assigned to the time previous to the beginning of Parliamentary enclosure.

Some of this enclosure is certainly to be assigned to an early date. Celia Fiennes, as we have seen, found more enclosure as she came to Huntingdon from Cambridge. Leland also found enclosure in the smaller county.

" From Cambridge to Elteste village al by champeyne

counterey 8 miles.   St. Neotes 4 miles.   From St. Neotes to Stoughton Village by sum enclosid ground a 3 Miles, it is in Huntendunshir.   From Stoughton to Meichdown Village a 4 Miles be much Pasture and Corne ground . . . there be goodly Gardens, Orchards, Ponds, and a Parke thereby."

THE EASTERN COUNTIES.

The story of the enclosure of Essex and Suffolk is almost completely told by the map.   Each is sharply divided into a larger part very anciently enclosed, without Acts of Parliament, and a smaller part close to the boundaries of Hertford, Cambridge, and Norfolk, which was enclosed at a late date by Acts of Parliament.   Essex has but one Act belonging to the eighteenth century, and that is dated as late as 1795. Suffolk has nine Acts belonging to the eighteenth, and forty-four belonging to the nineteenth century.

The additional information available only serves to bring out more clearly the very striking contrast between the regions of ancient and recent enclosure.

On the one hand we find that the Parliamentary enclosure of the extreme west and north-west portion of Essex is only part of the recent enclosure of that part.

The Enclosure Acts cover twenty-nine parishes, and an area of 22,000 acres, about 760 acres per parish.   Vancouver, who reported on Essex, as well as Cambridge, tells us, " The arable land in about forty parishes lies very much in open common fields, and which in point of quantity is found to average 1,200 acres per parish."[1]   He gives a list of open field parishes ; Thraxted and Streethall, which have not since been enclosed by Act, are included ; and each of those had some common field at the time of tithe commutation.

On the other hand, he tells us that the neighbourhood of Great Dunmow, which is quite close to the region of nineteenth century enclosure, had been enclosed from time immemorial.[2]

---

[1] "Agriculture of Essex," p. 185.   [2] *Ibid.*, p. 195.

The well-known passage in the " Discourse of the Common-weal," " Countries wheare most Inclosures be, are most wealthie, as essex, kent, devenshire, and such," sufficiently establishes the ancient enclosure of the greater part of Essex.   And though the evidence is not very full, it is, I think, sufficient to show that the enclosure of the corresponding part of Suffolk had a similar history.   Celia Fiennes says that the journey from Ipswich to Woodbridge is " 7 miles mostly Lanes, Enclosed countrys " ; and from Woodbridge to Saxmundham " The wayes are pretty deep, mostly Lanes, very little Commons " (p. 107).

John Norden (1602) also makes mention of Suffolk methods of hedging.

The question then arises with regard to this region of ancient enclosure in Essex and Suffolk, whether it ever passed through the typical English common field system.   To this question we are able to give an unhesitating answer.

In Suffolk, far away from any other Parliamentary enclosure, in the south-east corner of the county are the parishes of Orford and Iken.   The enclosure at Orford was in 1881.   There were but forty-six acres to enclose, and these lay in strips alternately belonging to the lord of the manor and to the Corporation of Orford.   The existence of corporate property in this small spot of land preserved it from enclosure to such a late date.

The case of Iken appears to have been somewhat similar.   It was enclosed in 1804.   There was only the small area of 100 acres to enclose, comprising "certain open and common fields, meadows, commonable lands, and waste grounds."   The Marquis of Hertford was lord of the manor, and six individuals by name, and " divers others " are said to be the other proprietors of land.   There is a special clause authorising the parish authorities, if they will, to accept rents from the Marquis of Hertford in lieu of allotments, so there must have been corporate property in the commonable lands, and this no doubt accounted for the survival of this small area of common field.

But the clearest evidence is from the town of Colchester.   The borough is of great extent, and includes the four agricultural parishes of Greenstead, Bere Church, or West Donyland,

Lexden and Mile End.   In these four parishes, says Vancouver, "one-third of the arable land lies in half-yearly common fields" (p. 40).   The Corporation of Colchester is to this day a very large owner of arable land ; how it was enclosed, and how the Corporation, as distinct from the free-men, secured the property after the passing of the Municipal Corporations Act of 1835, I do not know.   The important point is conveyed in the word "half-yearly."   The arable fields of Colchester were genuine common fields, subject to rights of common of pasture after harvest.

I think there can be little doubt that though much of Essex and Suffolk might have been ancient woodland, and have been enclosed directly from that condition, the primitive village community of Essex was approximately of the same type as that of central England.

NORFOLK.

Adequate material does not exist for a statistical survey of the enclosure of Norfolk, because of the disappointing habit which the promoters of Enclosure Acts for this county fell into about the year 1793,[1] and persisted in later, of not making any statement with regard to the area covered by the Act. The best statement that we can make is that 297 parishes out of 682 were enclosed by Act of Parliament.[2]

We have already dealt with some peculiar features of Norfolk agriculture revealed by preambles of Enclosure Acts.   The chief other fact which is striking in its enclosure history is that the county is divided by the chalk ridge, which passes through the centre of the county, from north to south, and which reaches the coast at Cromer, into two parts of approximately equal area. The patches of colour which indicate enclosure by Act of Parliament are scattered indifferently over the whole map of the county ; but the significance of the colour varies.   East Norfolk

---

[1] Before 1793 thirty-one parishes were enclosed by twenty-two Acts, the area covered by nineteen of which is stated, amounting altogether to 50,187 acres. The total area so enclosed was probably not less than 54,000 acres.

[2] There were also eighty Enclosure Acts for the enclosure of common waste or pasture merely.   In these also the area is stated for a small minority only.

has all the aspect of a country of very early enclosure. The fields are small, the hedges are big and high, like Devonshire hedges, the roads are narrow and winding. The aspect recalls Kent's previously quoted words. "There is a considerable deal of common field land in Norfolk, though a much smaller proportion than in many other counties; for notwithstanding common rights for great cattle exist in all of them, and even sheepwalk privileges in many, yet the natural industry of the people is such, that whenever a person can get 5 or 6 acres together, he plants a white-thorn edge round it, and sets an oak at every rod distance, which is consented to by a kind of general courtesy from one neighbour to another" ("Agriculture of Norfolk," 1st Edition, p. 22). The Parliamentary enclosure which took place in a parish where the neighbours had been showing this courtesy to one another consisted mainly in the extinction of common rights over enclosed land.

The making of hedges had proceeded to such an extent in East Norfolk by the end of the seventeenth century, that an anonymous author who brought out an annotated edition of Tusser's "Five hundred points of Husbandry," and "Champion and Severall," under the title "Tusser Redivivus," in the year 1710, explains the term "woodland" (a term which Tusser really used as a synonym for "several" or enclosed land) to mean East Norfolk, saying that this district was so much enclosed in small fields with fine trees in the hedges, that it was known as "the Woodlands."

At this time the western half of the county was still almost entirely open. Arthur Young wrote in 1771, "From forty to sixty years ago, all the Northern and Western and a part of the Eastern tracts of the county were sheepwalks, let so low as from 6d. to 1s. 6d. and 2s. an acre. Much of it was in this condition only thirty years ago. The great improvements have been made by reason of the following circumstances :

(1) By enclosing without the assistance of Parliament.

(2) By a spirited use of marle and clay.

(3) By the introduction of an excellent course of crops.

(4) The cultivation of hand hoed turnips.

(5) Clover and ray grass.

(6) Long leases.

(7) By the county being divided chiefly into large farms.

" Parliamentary inclosures are scarcely ever so complete and general as " (non-Parliamentary enclosure) " in Norfolk " (" Eastern Tour," Vol. II., p. 150).

William Marshall supplies a confirmatory note. " Norfolk, it is probable (speaking generally of the county), has not borne grain, in abundance, much above a century. During the passed century " (the eighteenth) " a principal part of it was *fresh land*, a newly discovered country in regard to grain crops " (" Review of the Reports to the Board of Agriculture for the Eastern Department," p. 314).

Enclosure in the western half of Norfolk and along the central chalk ridge in the eighteenth and nineteenth centuries, whether common field arable were included or not, meant the reverse of what it had meant in the first half of the sixteenth century—the conversion of land from sheeprun to arable land and to highly cultivated land. Kent, in a second edition of his report of Norfolk, published in 1796, estimated that two-thirds of the whole area of the county was then arable; and of the arable land three-quarters was enclosed, one-quarter in common field. In other words, one-half of the area of the county was enclosed arable, one-sixth common field arable. The remainder he describes as follows :

Meadows, parks, and upland pasture...	126,692 acres.
Unimproved commons	80,000 ,,
Marsh lands...	63,346 ,,
Warrens and sheepwalks	63,346 ,,

with small areas for woods, plantations, roads, lakes, rivers, and swamps. Whatever ancient common field arable had been enclosed before the beginning of the eighteenth century and converted into pasture, was apparently re-converted into arable before the end.

THE SOUTHERN MIDLANDS.

MIDDLESEX.

I have found very little information with regard to the enclosure of Middlesex beyond that obtained from the Enclosure Acts. It is remarkable that these should cover so large a part (19·7 per cent.) of the area of the county.

Of twenty-six Acts, covering 35,757 acres, twenty-three, covering 30,000 acres, belong to the period after 1793. The Board of Agriculture reporters, Thomas Baird and Peter Foot, tell us respectively (1) that there were about 50,000 acres under tillage in 1793 (" Agriculture of Middlesex," p. 7), and (2) " The Common Fields in the county of Middlesex, which are at present in a good course of husbandry, form a large proportion as to the number of acres when compared to the cultivated enclosures " (*Ibid.* p. 72).

That the common fields were " in a good course of husbandry " very probably means that the exercise of common rights had been largely restricted, and it is not improbable that while some of the ancient common fields of Middlesex became converted into small dairy farms, others became market gardens by means of a very moderate amount of interchanging of properties and holdings.

HERTFORDSHIRE.

The county of Hertford is rather remarkable for the extent of open field land (common rights have so far decayed that one can hardly call it common field) persisting to the present day. Notes have already been given on Hitchin, Bygrave, Clothall, and Wallington. There were further no less than seventeen enclosures under the Act of 1845, a number only surpassed by Oxfordshire, and in a number of other parishes small remnants of common fields are indicated by the tithe maps.

But on the whole Hertfordshire was a county of early enclosure. When the Board of Agriculture survey was made only four parishes and a part of Hitchin had undergone

Parliamentary enclosure ; but the reporter says, " There are several small common fields in this county, but these are mostly by agreement among the owners and occupiers cultivated nearly in the same way as in the enclosed state " (D. Walker, " Agriculture of Hertfordshire," p. 49).

Walter Blyth in 1649 included " Hartford " with " Essex, Kent, Surrey, Sussex," etc., as enclosed counties (" The English Improver," p. 49).

" An insurrection in hertfordshire for the comens at Northall and Cheshunt," was, according to Hales, the first beginning of the enclosure riots and rebellions in the reign of Edward VI.

It is somewhat remarkable that Hertford was in the seventeenth and eighteenth centuries so much more enclosed than the surrounding counties, than Middlesex as well as than Bedford and Cambridge, and even more enclosed than the part of Essex immediately adjoining.

Leland gives no account of the condition of the county with regard to enclosure ; but as no earlier author than Blyth speaks of Hertford as an enclosed county, I am inclined to believe that its enclosure mainly took place in the sixteenth and in the first half of the seventeenth century. It is to be noticed that Hertford was excluded from the operation of the last (39 Elizabeth, c. 2) of the Depopulation Acts, requiring that all old arable land should continue under tillage and be cultivated according to the local custom.

BUCKINGHAM.

Buckingham is, on the whole, a county of late enclosure. A large proportion (34·2 per cent.) of the area was enclosed by Acts of Parliament ; two-thirds of this enclosure belonging to the eighteenth and one-third to the nineteenth century.

The reporters to the Board of Agriculture, William James and Jacob Malcolm, supply a list of the parishes containing common fields in 1794, with an approximate statement of the area. The majority of these parishes have, of course, undergone Parliamentary enclosure since. By comparing their list with that of

the Enclosure Acts and with the summary of the tithe documents, we find that the following seventeen parishes were enclosed
without Acts between 1794 and the date of tithe commutation:—

Astwood	Little Hampden	Medmenham
Buckland	Hedgerley	Great Missenden
Dinton	Horsendon	Little Missenden
Drayton Beauchamp	Great Horwood	Newton Longueville
Halton	Ickford	Quainton
Great Hampden	Marsh Gibbon	

The following five still had remains of common field at the
time of tithe commutation, though the area was considerably
reduced in each case :—

—	Common Field Acreage.	
	In 1794.	According to Tithe Map.
	Acres.	Acres.
Burnham and Lower Boveney ...	1000	525
Chesham	300	66
Dorney	600	277
Eton	300	181
Chipping Wycombe	200	100

As so much gradual non-Parliamentary enclosure took place
during the nineteenth century, it is to be supposed that the
same process was also going on right through the eighteenth
century.

Buckingham is traversed by the Chiltern Hills, and so is
divided into two distinct regions. About half the county lies
north-west of the Chilterns, on a sub-cretaceous formation, like
Bedfordshire, with fertile soil, and villages thickly scattered.
The remainder consists of the chalky downs and the later
formations, like most of Hertfordshire and Middlesex.

The enclosure of the south-east portion was earlier than that
of the north-west part. Arthur Young in 1771 was much struck

by the extent of the open fields in the latter part. The vale of Aylesbury,[1] he says, was good clay, and open field ("Eastern Tour," p. 18). From Aylesbury to Buckingham "nearly the whole country is open field, the soil among the richest I ever saw, black putrid clay" (p. 19). "As for the landlords, what in the name of wonder is the reason of their not enclosing! All this vale would make as fine meadows as any in the world" (p. 23). However, about Hockston (Hoggeston) he saw many new enclosures (p. 24). Hoggeston itself was never enclosed by Act, but several neighbouring villages had been enclosed by Acts passed previously to 1771.

Celia Fiennes passed through the same part of Buckinghamshire about eighty years before. From Stony Stratford to Great Horwood, she says, "this country is fruitfull, full of woods, Enclosures, and rich Ground. The little towns stand pretty thicke. You have many in view" (p. 97). This does not imply anything more than very partial enclosure; for Celia Fiennes, accustomed to the complete absence of hedges of her own part of Wiltshire, always notices enclosure rather than the absence of enclosure. That many little towns should be in sight of one passing through a flat country implies that it is open, except close to the villages.

Leland, in 1536, came from Bedfordshire along the boundary between Herts and Bucks and into the extreme south of Buckinghamshire, and found that enclosures had already begun. He describes the whole county in one luminous sentence, "Looke as the countrye of the Vale of Alesbury for the most part is clean barren of wood, and is champaine, soe is all the Chilterne well woodid and full of Enclosures" (fol. 192 a).

It seems quite clear, then, that the enclosure movement of the south-east of Berkshire was ancient; that it moved up the long slope of the Chilterns from the Thames and Middlesex, but stopped at the open chalk downs which marked the summit of the range; and that the movement which affected the enclosure of the Vale of Aylesbury and all north-western Buckinghamshire

---

[1] An Act for the enclosure of the common field land of Aylesbury itself was passed in the same year.

was part of the general enclosure movement of the Midlands, spreading southwards from Leicester and Northampton, as we have seen it spread eastwards.

Oxford.

Oxfordshire may be termed a sister county to Buckinghamshire; but by far the greater part of the county lies north-west of the Chiltern Hills, which occupy the south east extremity. We find, as we should expect, that the history of the enclosure of Oxfordshire resembles that of Bedfordshire and of North-West Buckinghamshire; 45·6 per cent. of the area of Oxfordshire underwent Parliamentary enclosure compared with 46·0 per cent. of Bedfordshire and 34·2 per cent. of Bucks; in Oxford about 62 per cent. of the total Parliamentary enclosure belonged to the eighteenth century, in Bedford 54 per cent., in Buckinghamshire 66 per cent. Oxford, however, is remarkable for the extent of the enclosure (eighteen Acts enclosing 23,578 acres) under the General Enclosure Act of 1845.

Richard Davis, the Board of Agriculture reporter, while he gives a very full statement of the methods of cultivating the common fields of the county, makes no statement with regard to their extent.

As in Buckinghamshire, partial enclosure, particularly in the immediate neighbourhood of the villages, had taken place before the eighteenth century. Celia Fiennes found " Oxford Environ'd round with woods and Enclosure. vet not so neare as to annoy the town which stands pleasant and Compact," and from the Malvern Hills she says " Oxford, Gloucestershire, &c. appears in plaines, enclosures, woods and rivers and many great hills " (p. 33). By " plaines " stretches of common fields are to be understood.

Leland found no enclosure in Oxfordshire in any part he visited.

THE NORTH OF ENGLAND.

Lincoln.

Lincoln and the East Riding of Yorkshire have a similar enclosure history. Each was largely enclosed by Acts of

Parliament; in each nearly four-fifths of the Parliamentary enclosure was effected in the eighteenth century; in each enclosure was not marked either by a general conversion of arable into pasture, as in Leicestershire, or by a general conversion of pasture into arable, as in Norfolk; in both a considerable proportion of the common-field land before enclosure was worked on the two-field system. As much as 40·1 per cent. of the East Riding of Yorkshire is covered by the Acts for enclosing common-field parishes, and 29·3 per cent. of Lincolnshire; but for the latter county there are also Acts for enclosing great extents of commonable marshes; and including these and other Acts for enclosing commons and wastes, about 35 per cent. of Lincolnshire has undergone Parliamentary enclosure.

A good deal of non-Parliamentary enclosure took place during the nineteenth century. Thomas Stone, the Board of Agriculture reporter, estimates that there were in 1793, 200,000 acres of commons, wastes, and unimbanked salt marshes, and 268,000 acres of common fields. He over-estimates the total area of the county so much, that to rectify his figures we have to deduct 10 per cent.—this leaves 421,000 acres of common fields and other commonable lands. There have been enclosed by Parliamentary action since 207,659 acres by Acts for enclosing common-field parishes, and about 74,000 acres by Acts for enclosing other commonable lands; if we suppose there are 12,000 acres of common fields and commons surviving, this accounts for 293,659 acres, and leaves about 127,000 acres unaccounted for—i.e., enclosed by non-Parliamentary process during the nineteenth century.

If the same proportion between the scope of the two methods be supposed to have held good during the earlier part of the period of Parliamentary enclosure, it would follow that at the beginning of that period (1730) Lincolnshire was about half enclosed and half open.

From the references to Lincolnshire by our tourists, one would expect to find a less degree of enclosure. Arthur Young, in 1768, that is, after fifty-three Enclosure Acts for Lincolnshire had been passed, found the country from Stamford

to Grimsthorpe mostly open ("Northern Tour," p. 77), from
Grimsthorpe to Colsterworth chiefly open, Colsterworth to
Grantham, enclosed on the right hand, open on the left (p. 84),
and from Grantham to Newark all open (p. 94).   Celia Fiennes,
about 1695, following the same road, found no enclosures but a
"fine champion country." Leland gives the same testimony.

By comparing Celia Fiennes with Arthur Young, we have
evidence of enclosure proceeding in the south-west of Lincolnshire between 1695 and 1768, which is partly, but not entirely,
accounted for by Parliamentary enclosure.   The three descriptions give the impression that up to the beginning of Parliamentary enclosure Lincolnshire was much less than half
enclosed.   It is, however, not difficult to reconcile this with the
conclusion inferred from Thomas Stone's statement and the
Enclosure Acts; for none of the three travellers touched more than
the western part of the county.   No doubt the eastern part was
earlier enclosed.   This is, indeed, indicated by the distribution
of Parliamentary enclosure, as shown by the map.

The East Riding of Yorkshire.

We have no estimate of the extent of common-field land in
the East Riding from the Board of Agriculture reporter ; but
Arthur Young, in his "Northern Tour," describes the part
betwene Sheffield and Goole and the East Riding as about half
open and half enclosed (pp. 172—210).   He further says (p. 178)
that in the East Riding "Inclosures and turnpikes were carried on
with great spirit during the late war" (i.e., "The Seven Years'
War ").   Nine Acts were passed for the enclosure of eleven
parishes during that war ; but this can only have been a part of
the spirited proceedings.

As in the case of Bedfordshire, when we allow for marshes
along the Humber, and hill country on the Wolds, which never
passed through the common-field system, for the indubitable
non-Parliamentary enclosure proceeding side by side with Parliamentary enclosure, and particularly for the active enclosure
spoken of by Arthur Young in the middle of the eighteenth

century, there remains but little enclosure of common fields to be attributed to earlier centuries. Some such enclosure must be assigned to the sixteenth century. The Commission of 1517 inquired into nearly the whole riding and found 1560 acres of arable land enclosed, 1545 acres of which were laid down to grass (W. S. Leadam, " The Domesday of Inclosure ").

Leland also found some enclosure in the East Riding, which he traversed pretty completely. (*See* Appendix C.)

We have mention of a park and of enclosed land in four different places, though in each of the four only for about a mile of the route.

THE NORTH AND WEST RIDINGS.

The North and West Ridings of Yorkshire were much earlier enclosed than the East Riding. This is the natural consequence of the fact that in early times they possessed a much smaller proportion of arable land, and, as I have shown in a previous chapter, the more pasture predominates, the less the common-field arable is able to resist the tendency to enclosure. The difference between the proportions of the three ridings covered by Enclosure Acts, by which common fields were enclosed is striking: East Riding 40·1 per cent., West Riding 11·6, North Riding 6·3. But this understates the case, for I include all Acts whereby any arable common field at all is enclosed, and in the North and West Ridings many of these Acts are for the enclosure of a great stretch of moor and a mere remnant of common field, and these unduly swell the total. Examples are an Act in 1791 for the enclosure of 6000 acres of common, and 30 acres of " mesne inclosures," *i.e.*, of intermixed tilled land which is separated from the surrounding common pasture by a hedge ; an Act in 1801 for the enclosure of 150 acres of common field and common meadow, and 4000 acres of common pasture at Kettlewell and Conistree ; an Act in 1815 for the enclosure of a wretched remnant of nine acres of common field arable, and 6330 acres of common. The existence of such remnants of common field arable bears witness to the gradual enclosure which would have entirely extinguished them a little later, if

the opportunity of the enclosure of the commons had not been
seized to bring them also within the scope of the Acts.

William Marshall's account of the enclosure of the Vale of
Pickering has already been given. Arthur Young in 1768
describes the view from the road from Kirby Moorside to Cleve-
land as one of "extensive valleys cut into innumerable inclosures"
("Northern Tour," Vol. II., p. 93). Enclosure was the rule
all the way from Driffield northwards.

Celia Fiennes kept more to the West Riding. From Dar-
lington to Richmond, "I went through Lanes and Woods, an
Enclosed country" (p. 183). Richmond to Boroughbridge was
for 3 or 4 miles through narrow lanes, then for 5 or 6
through common (p. 184). From Knaresborough to Leeds
"it was much in Lanes and uphills and Downhills, some little
part was open common" (p. 184). From Leeds to Eland
"much in enclosures" (p. 185). About Eland "all the hills
full of inclosures" (*ibid.*). From Eland to Blackstone Edge, "these
parts have some resemblance to Darbyshire, only here are more
woody places and inclosures" (p. 186).

The earlier history of the enclosure of most of the West
Riding and North Riding is summed up in the passage from
Walter Blyth :—" Woodlands wont before inclosure to be
relieved by the Champion, and now become gallant corn
countries. . . . West of Warwick, North of Worcester, Staffordshire, Shropshire, Derbyshire, Yorkshire, and all the Countries
thereabouts" ("English Improver," p. 40). For while Celia
Fiennes found so much enclosure, Leland found chiefly moor
and forest, yet more enclosure than "Chaumpaine."

The great contrast between the description given by Celia
Fiennes and that given by Leland sufficiently confirms the
statement of Walter Blyth, which we may amplify as follows :—
Enclosure made little progress in Yorkshire before the middle
of the sixteenth century, but thenceforward it was pushed
steadily on mainly by the tilling and enclosing of common
wastes and pastures, and the clearing and cultivation of forests
in the North and West Riding, and the common-field arable
also underwent division and gradual enclosure. That the Vale

of Pickering in the North Riding and the district between Sheffield and Goole in the West Riding, being the parts where arable common fields most predominated, were the last of the cultivated districts to be enclosed; the Vale of Pickering being mainly enclosed by non-Parliamentary means in the first half of the eighteenth century; the South Yorkshire district being largely enclosed by Acts of Parliament in the second half of the eighteenth and the beginning of the nineteenth century.

Lastly attention must be drawn to the great number of Acts of Enclosure for Yorkshire enclosing common pasture or waste only.

NOTTINGHAMSHIRE.

Nottinghamshire may be said to consist of an ancient " champain " district, which has an enclosure history exactly similar to that of the neighbouring districts of Northamptonshire and Lincolnshire, and an ancient forest district.

The county as a whole has a percentage of Parliamentary enclosure, 32·5, which must be considered high when allowance is made for the fact that so much land must have been enclosed directly from the forest state without passing through the common-field system. The two surviving examples of common-field parishes, Laxton and Eakring, have been before described; Bole also was till recently unenclosed.

The Board of Agriculture reporter, Robert Lowe, attempted to give an account of the state of enclosure of the different parishes in 1793, but evidently found it beyond his powers to make the lists at all complete. But his list of unenclosed parishes enables us to give the following nine parishes as enclosed without Parliamentary intervention since 1793 :—

Askham	Saundby	South Wheatley
Kirklington	Treswell	Kneesall
Rampton	North Wheatley	Widnerpool

together with the hamlets of Ompton and Clipston.

And his list of recently-enclosed parishes enables us to give the following nine parishes as enclosed without Parliamentary sanction shortly before 1793 :—

Bingham	Shelton	Orston
Carcolston	Cotham	Sibthorpe
Selston	Kneeton	Thoroton

together with the hamlets of Aslacton, Newton, Oldwork, and Cropwell Butler.

All these had been enclosed, he says, within the previous twenty years.

The fact that the extent of non-Parliamentary enclosure in Notts., in the period from 1773 to 1793 is just equal, according to this, to that of the non-Parliamentary enclosure after 1793, is a slight clue to the probable extent of non-Parliamentary enclosure in the eighteenth century in other counties similarly circumstanced.

We should expect, then, to find the part of the county which was anciently tilled, practically entirely open, at the beginning of the eighteenth century. This is confirmed by the evidence, so far as it goes. Celia Fiennes says: "From Nottingham Castle I saw a prospect more than 20 mile about. The land is very rich and fruitfull, so the Green meadows with the fine corn ffields which seemes to bring forth in handfulls. They soe most of Barley and have great encrease, there is all sorts of Graine besides, and plaines and Rivers and Great woods and Little Towns all in view " (p. 56).

Leland was similarly struck with South Nottingham. Coming south from Rotherham he found "very woody Grounde," then "hethy," then "Corny and Paster," then "Ground very fruteful of Corne" (Vol. V., fol. 91, 92). But when he got past Nottingham the view made him burst into Latin. "After that I cam a little beyond Trent I saw all Champaine Grounde undecunque within sight, and very little wood but infinita frugum copia."

DERBY.

The enclosure history of Derbyshire closely resembles that of the West Riding of Yorkshire. A somewhat larger part

(16·5 per cent.) of it underwent enclosure by Acts for the enclosure of common-field arable in conjunction with other commonable land, and about 5 per cent. more by Acts for the enclosure of common pasture and waste. The common-field arable is frequently called "mesne inclosures" (sometimes "mesne field"), showing that the idea of a hedge was that it surrounded the corn crops to keep out beasts, not the pasture to keep them in. Celia Fiennes gives a general description of the county: "You see neither hedge nor tree but only low drye stone walls round some ground, Else its only hills and dales as thick as you Can Imagine" (p. 77). "All Darbyshire is but a world of peaked hills."

It will be remembered that it had by 1649, according to Blyth, become a gallant corn country through enclosure. Leland passed it by.

DURHAM.

The history of the enclosure of Durham is told by the Board of Agriculture reporter in a sentence: "In this county the lands, or common fields of townships, were for the most part inclosed soon after the Restoration. . . . The common fields are few in number and of small extent" (Joseph Granger, "Agriculture of Durham," p. 43).

All other evidence simply confirms this statement. The Enclosure Acts for enclosing common fields are but five in number, and the most extensive of them covers only 800 acres, of which part only is common field. (The Enclosure Acts of the other type are numerous in comparison and extensive in scope, one covering 10,000, one 20,000, one 25,000 and one 28,000 acres).

The statement, too, is confirmed by two contemporary authors, previously quoted, and by the records of Leland and Celia Fiennes. Celia Fiennes says that from Newcastle to Durham "the whole county looks like a fruitful woody place" (p. 178), and she compares it to the neighbourhood of Blackheath (p. 179), from which we must infer some open common, but all the cultivated land in a state of enclosure.

Leland traversed the whole county but found no enclosure. Nor does he describe any part of the county as " champaine" but merely as good corn, or grass, or moor, or mountain. It is, I think, safe to conclude that there were no extensive stretches of common-field arable within view; but also, one is inclined to infer that enclosure had not yet begun.

Further, there is an illuminating note from Arthur Young (1768): "Farms become large on entering Northumberland, after the small ones of Yorkshire and Durham" ("Northern Tour," Vol. III., p. 61).

It has to be borne in mind that the disorder on the Border checked the development of agriculture till the accession of James I., probably at least as far south as the North Riding of Yorkshire. With the gradual increase of population, and improvement of roads, cultivation spread over the wastes; first in Yorkshire, then in Durham, then in Northumberland. At first the agent was a peasant, carving a small farm for his own maintenance, later a landlord or farmer able to employ labourers and work a large farm.

That the enclosure of Northumberland took place later than that of Durham, and was the work of the eighteenth and nineteenth centuries, is on *a priori* grounds probable, and is further indicated by the fact that Celia Fiennes makes no mention of enclosure in her account of her ride from the Scottish border into Durham. A further reference to the enclosure of Northumberland will be made when we come to Cumberland.

THE SOUTH-EAST OF ENGLAND.

KENT.

Kent is certainly a county of very ancient enclosure. This is clearly indicated by the fact that not a single Act for the enclosure of common field has been passed by the whole county. It is also witnessed by a whole series of writers, from Boys, the Board of Agriculture reporter, who says, "There are no Common Fields in Kent,"[1] to the author of the "Discourse of

---

[1] "Agriculture of Kent" (1796), p. 44.

the Commonweal," "those counties which be most enclosed, as essex, kent, devenshire."

But in Kent it would appear that if some investigator as careful as Vancouver had at a somewhat earlier date reported on the agriculture of Kent, he would have found some remains of arable common fields in the far eastern corner of the county. William Lambarde, in the "Perambulation of Kent," 1570, says: "The soile is for the most part bountifull, consisting indifferently of arable, pasture, meadow and woodland. Howbeit of these wood occupieth the greatest portion even to this day except it be towards the east, which coast is more champaigne than the residue" (p. 3).

More than a hundred years later, Celia Fiennes says: "Canterbury to Dover was a good road and a sort of Champion Country" (p. 103). It was open, it was mainly arable land, but it differed in some respect from the Champain of the Midlands; and again, a hundred years later, William Marshall writes in 1798 of the Isle of Thanet: "The whole country lies open, excepting in the immediate environs of villages. . . . The present productions, if we cut off the marsh lands, may be said to be arable crops" ("Southern District," Vol. II., p. 6).

This was written, it will be noticed, just after Boys had written his statement that there were no common fields in Kent. We can reconcile the two statements if we suppose that by the disuse of rights of common, and by the consolidation of scattered properties and holdings by mutual exchanges, the characteristics of common field had been abolished, while in consequence of there never having arisen any tendency to convert the arable land into pasture, no necessity for the expensive labour of making hedges arose. But I have no evidence to show at what date the open arable land ceased to be common field.

The question arises whether the common-field system of the ordinary English type ever existed in this part of Kent; and here again there is no decisive evidence that I know of by which to answer the question. The fact that the similar question for Essex is answered in the affirmative by the Colchester common fields perhaps counts for something; and that the Surrey common fields come at Croydon close to the county boundary, for a little more.   At Eltham there is an old charity called the Fifteen Penny Lands; only a few acres remain in the form of land, the rest having been sold and the proceeds invested; but there still remains an acre described as " Land in East Field, Dockland's Shot." In 1578 a member of the Roper family, perhaps Margaret Roper, the daughter of Sir Thomas More, or her husband, bequeathed to Eltham " a parcel of ground containing by estimation four acres, in the common field, called East Field." [1]   Eltham was a royal manor, hence likely to preserve old customs to a later date than other manors, and the arrangement of ancient common fields, particularly towards Eltham Common, seems clearly traceable.   In Addington, an ecclesiastical manor, it seems easy to trace the signs of ancient common, commonable meadow, and common fields.

THE WEALD.

The whole of the Weald of Kent, Surrey, and Sussex appears never to have passed through the common-field system.   This is indicated in the first place by the fact that there have been no Enclosure Acts for enclosing common fields.   Secondly, we have what may be termed the expert evidence of William Marshall, the shrewdest of all the eighteenth-century agricultural writers, and the only one really interested in the origin and early history of the common-field system.   He says of the Maidstone district, " the entire district appears to have been inclosed from the forest or pasture state.   I observed not a trace of common-field lands " ("Southern District," Vol. I., p. 21). Of the Weald of Kent, " The whole is in a state of inclosure, and mostly divided by wide woodland belts, into well sized fields " (*Ibid.*, p. 345).   Of the Weald of Sussex, " . . . there being, I believe, no trace at present, of common fields having ever gained an establishment " (Vol. II., p. 100).   " The whole of the district (between Pulborough and Midhurst) under view

---

[1] Geo. Rathbone, " History of the Eltham Charities," p. 5.

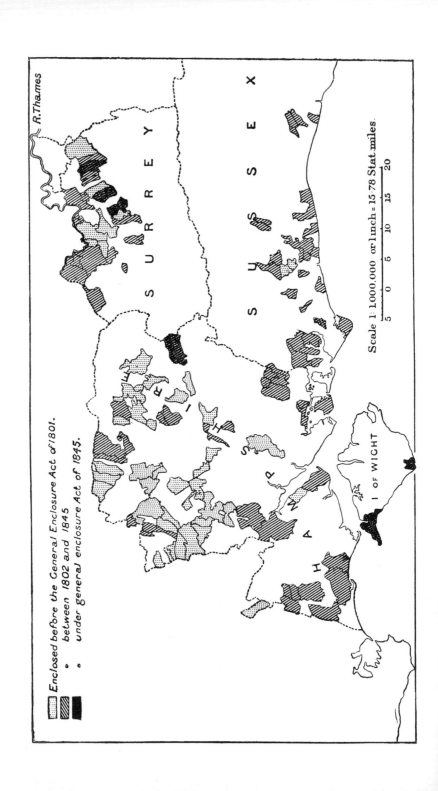

Enclosed before the General Enclosure Act of 1801.
"   between 1802 and 1845
"   under general enclosure Act of 1845.

R.Thames

S U R R E Y

S U S S E X

I of WIGHT

Scale 1: 1,000,000 or 1 inch = 15·78 Stat. miles.

5   0   5   10   15   20

is in a state of Inclosure ; except a few small heathlets and commons ; and except a small remnant of common field in the Maam soil." The Maam soil, he says, is a vein of land of peculiar nature at the foot of the chalk hills, to be identified, presumably, with the Gault formation.

In 1649, seeing that a considerable amount of common field survived in the part of Surrey north of the North Downs, until the time of Parliamentary enclosure, and some in Sussex south of the South Downs, and in spite of this, Blith speaks of Surrey and Sussex as enclosed counties, enclosure must at least have predominated in the Weald.

Celia Fiennes adds a confirmation.   Sussex, she says, is " much in blind, dark lanes" (p. 32).   This implies narrow roads, with well-grown hedges, that is, ancient enclosure.   For roads are everywhere broad in proportion as the industrial state at which enclosure takes place is advanced.   Again, from Calvery to Branklye, " the way is thro' lanes, being an Enclosed Country for the most part, as is much of Sussex which joyns to Kent " (p. 112).   And the view from Boxhill was that of " a fruitfull vale, full of inclosures and woods " (p. 32).

NORTH SURREY.

The part of Surrey which lies on the north slope of the North Downs, from the Kent boundary to the Bagshot sands, contained up till the time of Parliamentary enclosure a considerable proportion of common-field land, as may be seen by the appendix and the map.

James and Malcom, the reporters for Surrey, give a list of the chief common fields remaining in 1793 ("Agriculture of Surrey," p. 43), from which we find that besides Merrow, enclosed about 1870, East and West Clandon, Ashtead and Thorpe have been enclosed without Acts since. In each of these four cases enclosure took place before the date of tithe commutation.

But even this part of Surrey must be considered as on the whole an early enclosed district; as much so, in fact, as the corresponding slope of the Chiltern Hills, and the Hertfordshire Hills on the other side of the Thames.

THE SEA COAST OF SUSSEX.

The western part of the south slope of the Sussex Downs has a few examples of common fields surviving to a late date, but they are fewer in number and smaller in area than on the north slope of the Surrey Downs. William Marshall says: " In the Isle of *Selsey* I observed some common field land; also about Chichester, in the year 1791 " (Southern District, Vol. II., p. 230.) The accompanying map shows the parishes enclosed by Acts.

WESSEX.

Under the heading of Wessex I include the counties of Hampshire, Wiltshire, Berkshire and Dorset. There is a close resemblance between the enclosure history of each of these; while Gloucester is a connecting link between them and the Midland counties on the one hand, and the south-western on the other. It may be described as at present a country of very large farms, with a very large proportion of open down, the cultivated land itself remaining remarkably open, being divided in general into large rectangular fields by hedges which are frequently full of gaps. Rights of common here more than elsewhere have decayed, irrespective of actual enclosure; and using the word enclosure in its broad sense, it may be said that in Wessex the process of enclosure has least of all taken visible shape, either in the growing of hedges, or building of walls, or in the conversion of arable to pasture, or pasture to arable, or in the scattering of the habitations of the inhabitants over the whole parish; but that it has most profoundly affected the social life of the villages. The case of Grimstone, in which the nine "livings" for generations held by about a dozen different copyholders, was converted into a single farm, and by no means an exceptionally large one, is typical of the whole district. This aspect has been previously treated. What here has to be noticed is that these characteristics of Wessex enclosure make it more difficult to trace the progress, at least so far as the higher lands are concerned. If Celia Fiennes could revisit the neighbourhood of Amesbury and Stonehenge, she would probably again describe it as " all on the downs, a fine champion country." It is fortunate that we have the accounts of two such expert observers as Thomas Davis and William Marshall. They wrote practically at the same date, Marshall apparently in 1792, Davis in 1793 ; but as Marshall confines himself to the actual condition, while Davis deals with the past, he must here take precedence.

" THE WESTERN CHALK HILLS.

" *Basingstoke to Salisbury.*—The state of inclosure varies. To the eastward the country is mostly inclosed, much of it in large, square, regular inclosures. More westward, it is entirely open ; as are the tops of the higher hills throughout. Extensive views, with no other break, than what is given by corn or flocks, fallows or the sheep fold.

" *Environs of Salisbury.*—To the southward of the town there are some well-sized, square fields, with good live hedges (at least on three sides) apparently of forty or fifty years' growth ; yet, extraordinary as it is, many of these fields lie open to the roads ; the fences on the sides next the lanes lying in a state of neglect. And, to the north of the Avon, the country for many miles every way, lies open, unless about villages and hamlets, and along the narrow bottoms of the watered valleys. To the eastward of Salisbury an attempt has been made at inclosure ; the ruins of the hedges are still evident ; broken banks, with here and there a hawthorn. And similar instances are observable in other parts of the Downs.

" Are we to infer from hence, that chalk down lands are not proper to be kept in a state of inclosure ? Or that where sheep are kept in flocks, and few cattle are kept, fences are not requisite ? Or is the foliage of shrubs a natural and favourite food of sheep, and hence, in a country chiefly stocked with sheep, it is difficult to preserve a live hedge from destruction ?

"*Ludgershall to Basingstoke.*—The country is wholly in-closed : excepting a few plots to the right; mostly in large square fields, doubtless from a state of open down ; the hedges in general of a Middle Age; some instances of vacant inclosure.

"With respect to the present state of appropriation of this tract of country,[1] the mere traveller is liable to be deceived. From the more public roads, the whole appears to be in a state of divided property. But on a closer examination, much of it is found to be in a state of commonage. In the immediate environs of Salisbury, there are evident remains of a common field, lying in narrow strips, intermixed, in the south of England manner ; and not far from it, a common cow pasture and a common meadow. About Mere " (on the Somerset border of Wiltshire) " I observed the same appearances. In the Valley of Amesbury much of the land remains, I understand, under similar circumstances, though they do not so evidently appear in the arable lands, which by the aggregation of estates, or of farms, or by exchanges among landlords and their tenants, lie mostly in well-sized pieces. But the after-eatage,[2] whether of the stubbs or the meadows, is enjoyed in common. And the grass downs of the common field townships are in a state of common pasture the year round; being stinted by the arable lands " (" Southern District," p. 308, etc.).

One fact to be noticed is that Hampshire was earlier enclosed than Wiltshire ; which is in accordance with what one would have expected. Enclosure spread westwards into Hampshire from Surrey and Sussex.

Davis I have previously quoted. " The greater part of this county (Wiltshire) was formerly, and at no very remote period, in the hands of great proprietors. Almost every manor had its resident lord, who held part of the lands in demesne, and granted

---

[1] *I.e.*, the whole of the district he calls " the Western Chalk hills."

[2] " After-eatage." This is Marshall's variant of " average," showing his theory of the etymology of the word, a theory which might have been suggested to him by the quaint phrase common in Enclosure Acts: " The averages whereof are eaten and enjoyed by the proprietors according to a recognised stint."

out the rest by copy or lease to under tenants, usually for three lives renewable. A state of commonage, and particularly of open common fields, was peculiarly favourable to this tenure. Inclosures naturally tend to its extinction.

" The North-West of Wiltshire being much better adapted to inclosures and to sub-division of property than the South, was inclosed first ; while the South-East or Down district, has undergone few inclosures and still fewer sub-divisions " (" Agriculture of Wiltshire," p. 8).

We have previously seen that Cobbett, traversing that same South-East district of Wiltshire, found in 1825 the common field or " tenantry " system completely superseded by that of great farms. Parliamentary enclosure only partly effected the change, which appears to have been so complete in the space of a single generation, 1793—1825. The violent fluctuations in the price of grain during the great war, the wholesale ruin of farmers in 1815 and 1816, the abuse of the Poor Law peculiarly rampant in Wiltshire, by which the peasants who held such little holdings as we have observed in Fordington and Stratton and Grimstone, by lease or copy, were compelled to pay in their rates the wages of the labourers employed by the great farmers who were superseding them, and the decay of home industries to which Cobbett bears witness, all these were complementary parts of the social transition, each assisting all the others, and all together converting the tiller of the soil from the peasant with a medieval status, a responsible member of a self-governing village community, into a pauperised, half-starved labourer.

Though North-West Wiltshire was enclosed earlier than the South-East, Berkshire was enclosed later than Wiltshire as a whole. This is indicated by the scope and distribution of Enclosure Acts. Parliamentary enclosure covers 26·0 per cent. of Berkshire, 24·1 per cent of Wiltshire. Of the total 120,002 acres enclosed by Act in Berkshire, 42,631 acres was enclosed in the eighteenth century ; 77,371 acres in the nineteenth. In Wiltshire the proportions are reversed ; 126,060 acres were enclosed in the eighteenth century, 86,073 acres in the nineteenth.

The non-Parliamentary enclosure in the nineteenth century was peculiarly active in Berkshire. William Pearce, the Board of Agriculture surveyor, computed that in 1794 the common fields and downs occupied 220,000 acres; forests, wastes, and commons, 40,000 ; and the enclosed lands, including parks and woods, only 170,000 acres ("Agriculture of Berkshire," p. 13). He further assures us that at least half of the arable land was in common fields (p. 49). As rather less than 20 per cent. of the total area of the county was enclosed by Acts at a later date, it would follow that about 30 per cent. of its area was enclosed without Acts after 1793 ; and from my own inquiries I can quite believe this conclusion is accurate. Enclosure under the general Acts of 1836 and 1840 may have been specially extensive in Berkshire.

Dorset underwent enclosure at an earlier period. The percentage of Parliamentary enclosure is only 8·7, which is similar to that of Hampshire, 6.0 ; and there is no evidence of very extensive non-Parliamentary enclosure in the nineteenth century. Stevenson in 1812 reported, "There are but few uninclosed fields remaining" ("Agriculture of Dorest," p. 194) ; and the earlier reporter, Claridge, in 1794, said, "Very few parishes in this county have of late years been enclosed" ("Agriculture of Dorset," p. 46). In the intervening period only fourteen Acts enclosing sixteen parishes were passed ; Dorset must therefore have been mainly enclosed before the time of the American War ; enclosure having no doubt spread eastwards from Devonshire, which was a very old enclosed county.

Celia Fiennes adds little to our information, except that she says the Vale of the White Horse, in Berkshire, "extends a vast way, a rich jnclosed country" (p. 19), that there were "Good lands, meadows, woods and jnclosures in the Isle of Purbeck, (p. 6), and that the country round "Stonidge," like that round Newtontony, was "most champion and open, husbandry mostly corn and sheep" (p. 10). But there is a significant passage in John Norden, which shows that the characteristic Wiltshire and Dorsetshire common-field management in 1600 prevailed over all four counties. "In Dorset, Wiltshire, Hamshire, Barkeshire, and other places champion, the farmers do much inrich their land indeed with the sheepfold " (Book V., p. 232).

Leland, however, is full of information. He came into Berkshire at Wallingford, and rode thence to Abingdon and to Oxford. The first touch of description is " About this Sinodune beginneth the fruteful Vale of White Horse—this Vale is not plentifulle of woodde " (Vol. II., fol. 14). This must be compared with Celia Fiennes' description of the same Vale, " a rich jnclosed country." He next proceeded westwards along the southern side of the Thames. " From this place " (Hinxey hill, one mile from Oxford) the hilly ground was " meately woody for the space of a mile, and thens 10 miles al by Chaumpain, and sum Corne, but most pasture, to Farington." He crossed the river and entered Gloucestershire, but turning south entered Wiltshire, and found the eight miles from Cirencester to Malmesbury " about a Mile on Furse then al by Champayne Ground, fruteful of corne and Grasse, but very little wood " (fol. 26). To Chippenham " al the Ground on that side of the Ryver was Chaumpayne " (fol. 28) but towards Bradford " the countre beginneth to wax woddy " (fol. 30) ; and then he went west into Somerset, Devon and Cornwall. He came back into Dorset from Axmouth, and in the extreme western part of Dorset gives no distinct description of the state of enclosure—it is " meately good ground " or " corne, pasture and wood ; " but from Melbury to Frome was " vj miles stille by Champaine ground on an high rigge " (Vol. III., fol. 47). He came through Weymouth and Poole, and specified neither enclosure nor champain, till he reaches the north-west corner of the county ; but from Hoston to Cranbourne is " al by Champain Ground having nother Closure nor Wood," and all the way to Salisbury continues " al by Champayne " (fol. 56). Again, " all the way from Salisbury to Winchester is Champayne," but from Winchester to Southampton, while there is " mouch drye feren Ground," " the most part of the Ground betwixt is enclosid and reasonably woddyd " (fol. 74).

To Portsmouth enclosure predominated in the cultivated land. There is " much enclosid and Hethy Ground myxt with Ferne " (fol. 79), and " the Ground within the Isle of Portsmouth is partely enclosid " (fol. 82). Turning north there was some "playn Ground " before entering Bere forest, afterwards " enclosid Ground " to Bishops Waltham, and for three miles beyond; the remaining four to Winchester being " Champain " (fol. 83).

But particularly in Dorset, instead of describing the land as enclosed, or " Champain," he frequently uses such expressions as "meately well woddid " or " good Corne and sum Grasse," which it is difficult to interpret in terms of enclosure. The choice of such expressions probably implies (1) that there is not much actual enclosure by hedges, and (2) that there are no *extensive* arable common fields. Such descriptions would suit land passing directly from the condition of forest or moor into separate cultivation, but in which the cultivated patches were not as yet enclosed with hedges; or a district in which small arable common fields were surrounded by such later extensions of cultivation. But leaving Dorset in doubt, it is clear from Leland's notes that enclosure was well begun in the south of Hampshire, while the country to the north was all open.

In the above journey Leland skirted the central chalk district; later he passed directly through it, going from Oxford through Abingdon, Lambourn, Marlborough and Devizes to Trowbridge. He passed the forests of Savernake and Blake, but all the cultivated land is described as " champayne " (Vol. VII., Part 2, fol. 63-7).

To sum up, we find that in the south of Hampshire, the cultivated land was early enclosed, and also probably in the south and west of Dorset, that enclosure gradually spread from the middle of the sixteenth century into the rest of the four counties, the movement attacking the " champain " district on three sides, on the east from Surrey, on the south from the early enclosed district between Winchester and Southampton and Portsmouth, and in the west from Devon and Somerset; the progress of enclosure appears to have been practically confined to Dorset and Hampshire in the seventeenth century; to have had the north-west of Wiltshire for its chief scene in the greater part of the eighteenth century, and finally to have attacked south-east Wiltshire and Berkshire, the former in the first quarter, the latter throughout the first half, of the nineteenth century.

GLOUCESTER AND WORCESTER.

The whole of Gloucester, with the exception of the Forest of Dean and its neighbourhood in the west, has scattered over it parishes enclosed by Acts of Parliament ; and the enclosure so effected amounted to nearly a quarter (22·5 per cent.) of the whole area of the county.   The rich land in the Severn Valley was the latest enclosed district.   William Marshall tells us that in 1789 " perhaps half the vale is undivided property." ("Rural Economy of Gloucestershire," Vol. I., p. 16.)   As enclosure by Act of Parliament, and doubtless also without Acts, had been proceeding vigorously since 1726, it is probable that at the earlier date nearly the whole was in "a state of commonage."   Of the Cotswold Hills, Marshall says: "Thirty years ago (*i.e.*, in 1759) this district lay almost entirely in an open state, namely, in arable common fields, sheep-walk, and cow-down.   At present it may be said to be in a state of Inclosure, though some few townships yet remain open." (*Ibid.*, Vol. II., p. 9.)

I have already pointed out that in Gloucestershire enclosure without Acts was specially easy, in consequence of the custom of holding land.   The ancient custom of "copyhold by three lives renewable" had very generally been converted into "leasehold by three lives renewable," the difference being that the lord of the manor's option of accepting a new life became real instead of nominal.   It was easy for a landlord who wished to enclose to convert each such lease as it fell in to one for a short period of years ; and it was in this way, Marshall says, the enclosure of the Cotswold Hills was mainly effected.

The south-west of Gloucestershire, towards Somerset, to a considerable extent shared in the early enclosure of that county ; though for Somerset we have also to say that while the western half was, like Devonshire, very early enclosed, the eastern half to a certain extent shared in the comparatively late enclosure

Gloucestershire and the north-west of Wiltshire, as the map shows.

Worcester similarly shows the transition between South Warwickshire, the enclosure history of which has been dealt with, and the counties on the Welsh border. Pomeroy reported in 1794 to the Board of Agriculture : " The lands are in general inclosed ; there are, however, some considerable tracts in open fields." About 45,000 acres have since been enclosed by Acts for enclosing common fields *inter alia ;* which is perhaps as large an area as the phrase " considerable tracts " is intended to describe. Just one-sixth of the total area of the county is covered by the whole series of such Acts, mainly in the eastern half of the county. Leland tells us " most part of all Somersetshire is yn hegge rowys enclosid " with elms, and from his other notes we find that the north-west half of Worcestershire was enclosed by about 1540, and the southern extremity of Gloucestershire about half enclosed by that date. We further find, from evidence quoted above, that the rest of Worcestershire shared the enclosure experience of Warwick and Leicester, though probably at a somewhat earlier date, that is, undergoing enclosure mainly in the seventeenth and eighteenth centuries, though in the end the process dragged on and was only completed after the Act of 1845 was passed. We find the Cotswold Hills enclosed mainly between 1750 and 1790, the Severn Valley undergoing enclosure during this period, but only about half enclosed at the end of it, and enclosure continuing steadily to the very end of the nineteenth century, with Elmstone Hardwicke still remaining uninclosed, waiting for leases for lives to expire.

THE CELTIC FRINGE.

The part of the country which remains to be considered is that in which the problem is complicated by the question whether the primitive village community was of an English or Celtic type. The remaining counties may be grouped under the titles West Wales, Strathclyde and the Welsh border.

We have previously seen that fluidity in the tenure of the soil,

which is one characteristic of the Celtic run-rig as compared with
the Anglo-Saxon common field system, favours the separation of
properties and holdings at the time when co-aration ceases to be
practised; and, in consequence, to early enclosure without any
special efforts of the type of an Act of Parliament. But we have
also seen that a prevailingly pastoral country tends to have its
arable lands more easily and earlier enclosed than a prevailingly
arable country. There are therefore two explanations available
for the early enclosure of the whole western half of England
and Wales.

First, however, the broad facts with regard to the history of
enclosure must be made clear.

There are no Acts specifically for enclosing common arable
fields in Wales, nor any in which the phraseology of the preamble
clearly indicates the existence in Wales of land possessing all
three of the essential characteristics of English common field :
(1) intermixed ownership or occupation, (2) absence of adequate
hedges or other obstacles to the passage of men and animals
from one holding to another, (3) common rights exercisable over
the tilled land.

But there were[1] in Wales open tilled fields in which properties
and holdings were intermixed—that is, land possessing the first
two characteristics. Several Welsh Acts for enclosing commonable waste also enclose "intermixed lands," and one (1843,
c. 14) is for the enclosure in Llandudno and three neighbouring
villages, of "Divers Commons, commonable lands and waste
grounds, Heaths, open and Common and other Fields and Waste
lands, and other Common lands and Waste grounds, which lie
intermixed in small parcels, and are inconveniently situated for
the use and enjoyment of the several proprietors."

The following are the reports on the subject by the Board of
Agriculture reporters in 1793 and 1794 :—

"Open or Common Fields are rarely met with in South Wales.

---

[1] Many townships in North Wales still contain "quilleted" areas, i.e., enclosed
fields containing unenclosed strips of land belonging to a different owner or
owners from that of the rest of the field. Such scattered "quillets" are, as in
Berkshire, frequently glebe land.

It is a mode of cultivation only practised in a few instances, where ecclesiastical and private property are blended." (John Fox, " Agriculture of Glamorgan," p. 41.)

"The only tract like a common field is an extent of very productive barley land, reaching on the coast from Aberavon to Llanrhysted. This quarter is much intermixed, and chiefly in small holdings." (Thomas Lloyd, " Agriculture of Cardigan," p. 29.)

Carmarthen. " I do not know of any considerable extent of open common field in the county." (Charles Hassell, " Agriculture of Carmarthen," p. 21.)

Pembroke. " In the neighbourhood of St. David's considerable tracts of open field lands are still remaining which is chiefly owing to the possessions of the church being intermixed with private property." (Charles Hassell, "Agriculture of Pembroke," p. 20.)

Radnor. "Here are no Common Fields." (John Clark, " Agriculture of Radnor," p. 21.)

Flint. " There are no common fields, or fields in run-rig, in this county, except between Flint and St. Asaph, and it is in intention to divide and inclose them." (George Kay, " Agriculture of Flint," p. 4.)

Cærnarvon. " Run-rig. There are no lands of this description that I could hear of, but there is a good deal of mixed property that might be exchanged." (George Kay, " Agriculture of Cærnarvon.")

There was in existence a mere remnant of open intermixed, arable land, which one reporter evidently thinks ought to be described as run-rig, and not as common field. Though in many respects agricultural methods were of the most primitive type, yet enclosure was practically complete; in two out of the four counties in which open fields are stated to be surviving, the explanation of such an exceptional circumstance is given in the intermixture of church and lay property. This well corroborates the *a priori* argument that the Celtic type of village community easily yields to enclosure; and that a predominance of pasture over arable also facilitates early enclosure of what arable there is.

Mr. A. N. Palmer shows that the varying operation of the custom of gavelkind (equal inheritance by all sons) is also closely connected with the recent phenomena of the distribution of holdings. Everywhere the land which was ancient open arable fields is now, and has been for an unknown period dating at least as far back as 1620, divided by hedges into small enclosures, as in Devonshire; but in some districts these contain, or are known to have contained in comparatively recent times, intermixed quillets of other ownership. In these districts Mr. Palmer supposes the ancient " gafæl " or " gwely " (which may be roughly defined as a patriarchal family holding), was at the time when co-aration ceased, very much sub-divided. In other districts where the " gafæl " or " gwely " was little sub-divided, so that each occupier could support his own plough team, when co-aration ceased, holdings became entirely separated from one another. (" History of Ancient Tenures of Land in North Wales," pp. 35—37.)

We have now to fix with what accuracy we may the time of the enclosure of the western counties, and then to search for evidence in those counties of variations from the typical English village community.

DEVON, CORNWALL AND WEST SOMERSET.

These counties were very early enclosed. There is so much earlier evidence that it seems superfluous to quote Celia Fiennes, but there are some suggestive touches in her description.

" I entered into Devonshire 5 miles off from Wellington, just on a high ridge of hills which discovers a vast prospect on Each side full of Inclosures and lesser hills which is the description of most part of the West. You could see large tracts of grounds full of Enclosures, good grass and corn beset with quicksetts and hedgerows " (p. 206). In very similar words she describes the views on the roads from Exeter to Chudleigh, and from Chudleigh to Ashburton.

" Devonshire is Much like Somersetshire, fruitfull countrys for corn, graseing, much for inclosures that makes the wayes very narrow, so as in some places a coach and waggons cannot pass. They are forced to carry their corn and carriagis on horses backes with frames of woods like pannyers on either side of the horse, so load it high and tye it with cords.	This they do altogether the further westward they goe, for the wayes grow narrower and narrower up to the land's end " (p. 9).	As Celia Fiennes rode into the far west of Cornwall, hers is the evidence of an eye-witness.	She points to the explanation of the extreme narrowness for which Devonshire lanes are still noted—enclosure took place before the introduction of carts.

Devonshire is spoken of in the previously quoted passage in the " Discourse of the Commonweal," about 1550, as, with Essex and Kent, one of the most enclosed counties.	Leland, about the year 1537 passed through North Devon into Cornwall, as far as Wadebridge and Bodmin, and back through South Devon.	His statement that Somerset was much enclosed with hedgerows of elms, has already been quoted.	In Devon and Cornwall he found no "champaine," but frequently "meately good corne and grasse;" on the other hand, he frequently found enclosure.

After recording his arrival at Dunster, he says: "From Combane to the Sterte most part of the Shore is Hilly Ground, and nere the Shore is no Store of wood ; that that is ys al in Hegge rowes of Enclosures " (Vol. II., fol. 63).	There was enclosed ground between Bideford and Torrington (fol. 68) ; from Torrington to Launceston was either "hilly and much enclosid," or "hilly and much morisch" (fol. 69), and also from Launceston to Boscastle (fol. 72).

Entering South Devon, he remarks simply on the fertility of the soil, but remarks: "The hole Ground bytwixt Torrebay and Exmouth booth sumwhat to the shore and especially inward is wel inclosed " (Vol. III., fol. 31).

In the year of Leland's visit, probably either 1537 or 1538, the cultivated lands of Devon and Cornwall and Somerset were largely, but not entirely, enclosed.	In East Somerset alone did Leland find any land which he could describe as "champaine " ; we may infer therefore that though no doubt there was a good deal of open field arable, probably still cultivated by co-aration, it existed in the form of comparatively small areas round villages and hamlets; nowhere, in Leland's route, extending over a considerable tract of country.

Carew, in his book on Cornwall, dated 1600, gives an account of the enclosure of that county. Of the manorial tenants, he says: " They fal everywhere from Commons to Inclosure and partake not of some Eastern Tenants envious dispositions, who will sooner prejudice their owne present thrift, by continuing this *mingle mangle*, than advance the Lordes expectant benefit, after their terme expired " (p. 30).

This pregnant passage tells us—

(1) That the Enclosure of tilled land in Cornwall had been proceeding rapidly up to 1600 and was then nearly complete;

(2) That previous to enclosure the system of cultivation, whether it most resembled the English common field system or Scotch run-rig, had for one of its features the intermixture of holdings; and for another some elements of collective ownership or management entitling it to the name " Commons ";

(3) That Carew's conception of a manorial tenant is not that of a freeholder, nor of a copyholder, but that of a leaseholder, whose term expires, the lord of the manor reaping the fruit, on the expiration of the lease, of any improvements the tenant may have made. He further on explains that the system of leases for three lives was practically universal in Cornwall, not in the modern form in which any three lives may be named in the lease, but depending for its continuance on the lives of the lessee, his widow and his son. It is obvious that this condition of land tenure would be more favourable to early enclosure than copyhold.

Another passage in Carew bears witness to the practical completion of enclosure. Writing of the legal conditions under which the miners pursued their enterprise, he says: "Their workes, both streame and Load, lie either in severall or in waistrell," that is, either in enclosed land under separate exclusive ownership and occupation, or in waste. One cannot draw the inference that there was absolutely no open field land;

but merely that its extent was in comparison so small as to appear negligible in this connection to Carew.

Though it is not improbable that the enclosure of Cornwall took place at an earlier stage of agricultural evolution than that of Devonshire, it is somewhat improbable that it took place at an earlier date. It is a reasonable inference from the evidence that by the end of the sixteenth century the enclosure of Devon and Cornwall was practically complete. When it began is a different question.

The charter of John by which all Devonshire except Dartmoor and Exmoor was deforested, expressly forbids the making of hedges on those two forests. This is itself some evidence that enclosure of some sort, probably enclosure of waste, for the purpose of cultivation, was going on actively in the beginning of the thirteenth century.

Attention must here be drawn to an ancient custom in Devon and Cornwall surviving to the end of the eighteenth century. William Marshall gives an account of it, and shows its probable importance in determining the character of enclosure and of all the attendant circumstances in Devon and Cornwall.

" *West Devonshire.* This district has no traces of common fields. The cultivated lands are all enclosed, mostly in well sized enclosures; generally large in proportion to the sizes of farms. They have every appearance of having been formed from a state of common pasture; in which state, some considerable part of the District still remains; and what is observable, the better parts of these open commons have evidently been heretofore in a state of aration; lying in obvious ridges and furrows; with generally the remains of hedgebanks, corresponding with the ridges, and with faint traces of buildings.

" From these circumstances it is understood by some men of observation, that these lands have formerly been in a state of permanent inclosure, and have been thrown up again, to a state of commonage, through a decrease in the population of the country.

" But from observations made in different parts of Devonshire, these appearances, which are common, perhaps, to every part of the county, would rather seem to have arisen out of a custom, peculiar perhaps to this part of the island, and which still remains in use, of lords of manors having the privileges of letting portions of the common lands, lying within their respective precincts, to tenants, for the purpose of taking one or more crops of corn, and then suffering the land to revert to a state of grass and commonage.

" In the infancy of society, and while the country remained in the forest state, this was a most rational and eligible way of proceeding. The rough sides of the dells and dingles with which it abounds were most fit for the production of wood ; the flatter, better parts of the surface of the country were required for corn and pasturage ; and how could a more ready way of procuring both have been fallen upon than that of giving due portions of it to the industrious part of the inhabitants, to clear away the wood and adjust the surface, and after having reaped a few crops of corn to pay the expense of cultivation, to throw it up to grass, before it had become too much exhausted to prevent its becoming, in a few years, profitable sward ? In this manner the county would be supplied progressively as population increased, with corn and pasturage, and the forests be converted, by degrees, into common pasture.

" The wild or unreclaimed lands being at length gone over in this way, some other source of arable crops would be requisite. Indeed, before this could take place, the pasture grounds would be disproportionate to the corn lands ; and out of these circumstances, it is highly probable, arose the present In-closures." (" Rural Economy of the West of England," 1795, p. 31.)

The same custom was observed in Cornwall by G. B. Morgan, the Board of Agriculture Reporter. (" Agriculture of Cornwall," p. 46.)

I believe this custom is the explanation of the huge size of the hedges which is frequently observable in Devonshire. A mound about eight feet high, and six or seven feet through, surmounted by a quickset hedge, is not uncommon. When a plot of land which had once been enclosed from the waste for cultivation, and then thrown into common pasture, with its hedges cast down, had recovered its fertility, it would naturally again be selected for enclosure and cultivation ; the cast down rough stone wall, now overgrown with vegetation, would be made the foundation for a new hedge ; and the same process might be repeated several times before final enclosure.

Braunton Great Field.

I have said above that it is reasonable to infer from the evidence that enclosure was practically complete in Devon and Cornwall by the end of the sixteenth century. It is not, however, absolutely complete to the present day ; for Braunton Great Field remains uninclosed. Braunton is a little town of about two thousand inhabitants, situated between Ilfracombe and Barnstaple, near the sea coast. Braunton Field is said to have "as many acres as there are days in the year," each nominal acre being a strip of land of about an acre in area. Properties and holdings are very much intermixed, many of the holdings are very small and cultivated by their owners. Each " acre " is separated from the rest on each side by a balk of untilled land, growing grass, yarrow, hawkweed, etc., just a foot wide. They are locally known as " launchers," which one associates with the Dorset name " lawns " for the strips of ploughed land, and the name " landshare," in the Stratton Court rolls for the unploughed balks.

There is also always a path, or a broader balk, called an "edge," separating the different sets of acres, which elsewhere would be called " Shots " or " Furlongs," from one another.

No common rights exist at present, or have existed in living memory over either the unploughed balks, or the tillage lands themselves. But old villagers remember that long ago one half of the field was kept for wheat, and the other half for potatoes, clover, etc., in other words, that there use to be a common rule for the cultivation of the field and this common rule was similar to that prevailing in the Gloucestershire every year lands. At

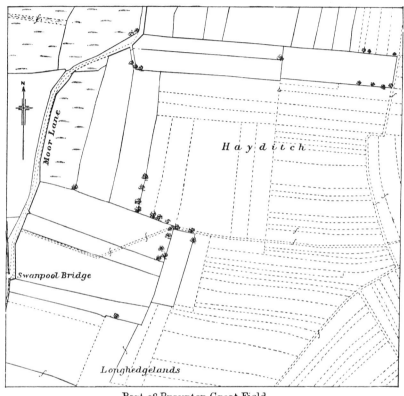

Part of Braunton Great Field.

Scale 3000

50   0   50   100 Yards.

The dotted lines represent bulks separating adjacent strips in the open field; the continuous lines represent hedges. It is easy to see how the enclosures on the edge of the field were made out of two or three strips thrown together.

present each occupant cultivates his strips just as he pleases. It is of course possible that this obsolete common rule is itself a survival from an older one, and that originally this field was cultivated on the two-field system so prevalent in Lincolnshire; half under wheat, half fallow, the fallow being commonable all the year, and the wheat after harvest. But on the other hand, the custom of getting a crop every year may have been the original one, and Braunton Great Field may be ancient " Every Year land " or " Infield."

Braunton Field is noteworthy in that it shows that however the primitive village community of West Wales may have differed from that of Wessex, it must have had certain characteristics in common with it, by which open arable fields of intermixed occupation were created in the neighbourhood of villages. Braunton cannot have been from the beginning an isolated example. The process of enclosure by the method Marshall describes went on around and outside these ancient tilled open fields.

Another interesting fact is revealed by the study of the twenty-five inch Ordnance map for Braunton. Braunton Field has been much reduced in area; one can easily see that the adjoining lands were once part of the open field, for the hedges in the lands are so placed as to form a continuation of the spider-web lines of the " launchers " within the field. The average size of the enclosed fields outside the Great Field is indeed a little greater than of the separate lands within it, but there is an imperceptible gradation, beginning with the smallest " lands " in the Great Field which are nearest the village, on through those more remote, the nearer enclosed fields, and then the more remote of them. Enclosure has been effected by simply enclosing the strips of arable land in the open field as they are. The fact that no common rights existed over the Field, supposing this always to have been the case, would have made such enclosure almost a matter of indifference to the other occupiers; and the motive, no doubt, would be the desire to lay the strip down in pasture. The whole field is known to the villagers as " the tillage land."

The Welsh Border.

The enclosure history of the counties along the Welsh border is somewhat similar to that of Devonshire. It took place early, partly in consequence of the predominance of pasture over arable, and partly under the influence of a custom of temporarily enclosing the waste and common pasture, similar to that in Devon and Cornwall.

The percentages of area of these counties enclosed by Acts for enclosure of common field arable are respectively:

						Per cent.
Cheshire	...	...	...	...	...	0·5
Hereford	...	...	...	...	...	3·6
Monmouth	...	...	...	...	...	0·4
Shropshire	...	...	...	...	...	0·3
Staffordshire	...	...	...	...	...	2·8

The Board of Agriculture reporter's statements on the common fields surviving in 1793 are that in Cheshire there was not so much as 1,000 acres (Wedge, "Agriculture of Cheshire," p. 9); in Staffordshire little more than 1,000 acres (Pitt, "Agriculture of Staffordshire," p. 85); that Shropshire " does not contain much common field land " (J. Bishton, "Agriculture of Shropshire," p. 8); but that in Hereford some of the best lands of the county are common fields (Clark, "Agriculture of Hereford," p. 69). Of Hereford, William Marshall gives a fuller account. " Herefordshire is an inclosed county. Some few remnants of common fields are seen in what is called the upper part of the county; but in general it appears to have been inclosed from the forest state; crooked fences and winding narrow lanes " (p. 224).

Celia Fiennes found from Nantwich to Chester "much Enclosures" (p. 147), but from Salford to Northwich, "I went a very pleasant roade, much in the downs, mostly campion ground, some few Enclosures "; Herefordshire, " a country of Gardens and Orchards, with apple and pear trees thick in the hedgerows" (p. 33); Staffordshire, "well wooded and full of Enclosures,

Good Rich Ground, extremely differing from Derbyshire" (p. 89). This was her first impression, confirmed later. "Harteshill is so high that from the top of it you see near 20 miles round, and shows all the county which in this part of Staffordshire is full of woods and jnclosures and good lands, except the Knackwood" (p. 137). From "Nedwoodforest" . . . . "you have a fine prospect of the country, enclosed good lands" (p. 139). Also beyond Stafford towards Cheshire was mostly enclosures (p. 144), and from Stafford to Wolverhampton the journey was through lanes (p. 194).

Walter Blyth includes Staffordshire and Shropshire as part of "the Woodlands, who before Enclosure, were wont to be relieved by the Fieldon, with corn of all sorts. And now grown as gallant Corne countries as be in England" ("The English Improver," 1649, p. 40).

Evidence of early enclosure is supplied by Leland. About White Castle, which I take to be Bishop's Castle, in south-west Shropshire, "the Countrys is Champion" (Vol. IV. fol. 176 b), but from Hereford to Leominster was enclosed ground (176 b and 177 a), thence towards Ludlow "by goodly corne Ground, part by enclosed" (178 b), Bridgenorth to Kidderminster "most by enclosed Ground" (182 b), to Bewdly was by "a fayre downe," but all the way thence to Milton (4 miles), Hertlebury (2 miles), Salopbrook (5 miles), Worcester (3 miles), Wick (6 miles) and Bromsgrove (4 miles), each stage is said to be by enclosed ground (fols. 183 b—186 a).

As for Monmouthshire, "The soyle of al Venteland" (Gwent, the country between the Wye and Usk) "is of dark reddish Yerth ful of slaty stones, and other greater of the same colour. The country is also sumwhat mountaynous and well replenished with Woodes, also fertile of Corne; but men there study more to Pastures, the which be wel inclosed" (Vol. V., fol. 5), and "Erchenfeld is full of Enclosures very (fruteful) of Corne and Wood" (fol. 9). Round Shrewsbury there is "ground plentiful of Corne, wood and pasture" (Vol. V., fol. 80), at Whitchurch "meately fruteful sandy ground" (fol. 81), and sandy ground on to Northwich (*ibid.*).

Nowhere else in these counties is either "enclosure" or "champaine" specified.

The evidence as to the existence of a custom of temporary enclosure of the waste, is supplied by Robert Plot's book on "Staffordshire," published in 1686 : "For the heathy land of this County, it is seldom enclosed ; but when they intend it for tillage, which is never for above five years neither, and then it is throwne open to the Commons again " (p. 343). " Their gouty, moorisch, peaty, cold black land, they husbande also much after the same manner as they doe the heathy lands in the Moore Lands " (p. 345).

Another passage brings into juxtaposition the more recent enclosures from forest or moor for the sake of tillage, and the ancient arable common fields. " Others again have placed the origin of mildewing in making small inclosures, corn not being so lyable to this evil in the common open fields " (p. 351).

It is reasonable to suppose that the custom found in Staffordshire and in Devon and Cornwall also prevailed in other counties, particularly in those along the Welsh border. It is some confirmation that Eden about a hundred years later found a similar custom still surviving in Sutton Coldfield, in Warwickshire, but near the Staffordshire boundary.

" The poor here, besides the right of commonage, have this peculiar privilege, that every house-keeper may take in one acre of common, and plough it four years : and the fifth year he must sow it with clover and lay it to the common again; after which he may take another acre, and work it in the like manner. By this method, about 400 acres of common are kept constantly in tillage" ("State of the Poor," Vol. III., p. 749, written probably in 1795).

The enclosure history of these five counties may be summed up in the statement that it probably proceeded very similarly to enclosure in Devonshire, but at a somewhat later date ; and that enclosure was later towards the north. Monmouth, we see, was "full of enclosures " before 1540; Shropshire "partly enclosed " with some " champion " ; but though Leland passed through Cheshire, he does not mention enclosures, and Celia

Fiennes found the North of Cheshire mostly open as late as about 1697. In Hereford and Staffordshire there was a large proportion of ancient arable land, and complete enclosure was consequently longer delayed, leaving an appreciable area to be enclosed by Acts of Parliament.

STRATHCLYDE.

Lancashire had no common field enclosed by Act of Parliament. It is possible that its partial autonomy as a Palatine County may account for this; but it must be noticed that the Acts of enclosure for Lancashire for enclosing commonable waste, are numerous right through the period of Enclosure Acts. Nor, though Lancashire was an early enclosed county, can we explain the absence of Enclosure Acts by the assumption that the enclosure of tilled land was completed by the beginning of the eighteenth century, for some common field persisted to the end of that century.

John Holt, the Board of Agriculture reporter, tells us: " There are but few open, or common fields, at this time remaining; the inconvenience attending which, while they were in that state, have caused great exertions to accomplish a division, in order that every individual might cultivate his own lands, according to his own method; and that the lots of a few acres, in many places divided into small portions, and again separated at different distances, might be brought together into one point " (" Agriculture of Lancashire," p. 49). It would appear from this that the open fields of Lancashire, like Braunton Great Field, though unenclosed, and intermixed, and subject to some common rule for cultivation, were not subject to common rights. Any owner, therefore, who by exchanges or by buying and selling, could get his lands together in a convenient plot, might enclose without trespassing on his neighbours' rights.

From Holt's statement we find that enclosure was nearly, but not quite, complete by 1793. It was certainly far advanced a hundred years earlier. Celia Fiennes rode from Prescot to Wigan, " seven long miles mostly through lanes " (p. 153);

from Gascoyne to Lancaster, "mostly all along lanes being an enclosed country" (p. 157). From Blackstone Edge the view was of "a fruitfull valley full of jnclosures" (p. 186). From Rochdale to Manchester, "the grounds were all enclosed with quicksetts" (p. 187).

Similarly Leland : " Manchester to Morle I passid by enclosid Grounde partely pasturable, partely fruteful of corn" (Vol. V., fol. 83). " The Ground bytwixt Morle and Preston enclosid for Pasture and Cornes. . . . Likewyse is the soile bytwixt Preston and Garstan ; but alway the moste parte of Enclosures be for Pasturages" (fol. 84).

Cumberland and Westmoreland were later enclosed than Lancashire ; and some few remnants of open arable field were dealt with by Acts. At Bolton, in Westmoreland, " certain open or common fields called Broad Ing Bartle and Star Ing " of 22 acres, at Soulby 90 acres of open field, and at Barton 130 acres, were enclosed by Acts mainly passed for the sake of enclosing waste ; and at Kirkby, in Kendal, " a common open field " of 105 acres was enclosed. There were five Acts in Cumberland enclosing open fields; but only two say precisely how much. At Torpenton, 20 acres of field and 700 acres of waste was enclosed ; at Greystoke, 240 acres of field and 3260 acres of waste.

But the enclosure of open-field arable was proceeding very steadily through the eighteenth century ; and a clear account of the process is furnished us by two keen observers.

Eden gives an account of the condition of the arable land in seven Cumberland parishes, written either in December, 1794, or January, 1795.

" *Gilcrux*. About 400 acres of common field have been enclosed within the last fifty years " (" State of the Poor," Vol. II., p. 76).

" *Hesket*. No more than 200 acres have been enclosed within the last fifty years. A large part appears to have had its hedges planted a little before that period" (*Ibid.*, p. 81).

" *Ainstable*. Area 5,120 acres of which 3,480 are common.[1]

---

[1] *I.e.*, common pasture or waste.

About 400 acres have been enclosed in the common fields within the last fifty years. . . . The average rent of land is about 18s. per acre; but it is observable that here and in most parts of Cumberland, an extensive common right[1] is attached to most arable land " (p. 46).

" *Croglin.* The average rent of open fields is 9s. 6d. the acre, of inclosures, 15s. or 16s. About 100 acres of common-field land have been enclosed within the last fifty years; but a great part of the arable land still remains in narrow, crooked *dales*, or *ranes*, as they are called " (p. 67).

" *Castle Carrock.* The greatest part of this parish remains in *dales*, or *doles* as they are called; which are strips of cultivated land belonging to different proprietors, separated from each other by ridges of grass land; about 100 acres may have been enclosed in the last fifty years " (p. 65).

" *Cumrew.* The land is cultivated in the old Cumberland manner; the grass ridges in the fields are from twenty to thirty feet wide; and some of them are 1000 feet in length. Grazing cattle often injure the crops " (p. 68).

" *Warwick.* Almost the whole of the cultivated land (1126 acres) has been enclosed within the last fifty years. It formerly, although divided, lay in long strips, or narrow *dales*, separated from each other by *ranes*, or narrow ridges of land, which are left unploughed. In this manner a great deal, and perhaps the whole, of the cultivated lands in Cumberland, was anciently disposed " (p. 92).

The other observer is the poet Wordsworth. In his book on the scenery of the lake district, he quotes from West's " Antiquities of Furness " to show that in the troubled times between the union of the Crowns of England and Scotland, holdings were let to groups of four tenants, each group dividing its tenement into four equal parts. " These divisions were not properly distinguished; the land remained mixed; each tenant had a share through all the arable and meadow land, and common of pasture over all the wastes. . . . The land being

---

[1] *I.e.*, over the neighbouring common pasture.

mixed and the several tenants united in equipping the plough,
the absence of the fourth man" (who was called out for military
service) "was no prejudice to the cultivation of his land, which
was committed to the care of three." In High Furness, " The
Abbots of Furness enfranchised these pastoral vassals, and permitted them to enclose quillets to their houses, for which they
paid encroachment rent."

Wordsworth then proceeds with the tale of enclosure : " The
enclosures, formed by the tenantry, are for a long time confined
to the homesteads, and the arable and meadow land of the fields
is possessed in common fields ; the several portions being
marked out by stones, bushes, or trees ; while portions, where
the custom has survived, to this day are called *dales*, from the
word deylen, to distribute ; but while the valley was thus lying
open, enclosures seem to have taken place upon the sides of the
mountains ; because the land there was not intermixed, and was
of little comparative value; and therefore small opposition
would be made to its being appropriated by those to whose
habitations it was contiguous.   Hence the singular appearance
which the sides of many of these mountains exhibit, intersected,
as they are, almost to the summit with stone walls. . . . There "
(in the meadows and lower grounds), "where the increasing
value of land, and the inconvenience suffered from intermixed
plots of ground in common field, had induced each inhabitant
to enclose his own, they were compelled to make fences of alders,
willows, and other trees . . . but these last partitions do not
seem to have been general till long past the pacification of the
Borders, by the union of the two crowns" (Fourth Edition, p. 23).

The date of the enclosure of the intermixed arable and
meadow land is thus fixed within certain broad limits.   It did
not begin till " long past the pacification of the Borders, by the
union of the two crowns." It took some time to effect the
pacification of the Borders, even after the accession of James I.
made it possible ; " long past " that event is a vague date, but
may very well bring us at least as late as the date when the
enclosure of the common fields of Durham is supposed to have
begun, " soon after the Restoration." It is certain, further,

from Eden's information, that enclosure was going on steadily right through the second half of the eighteenth century, but by no means complete in 1795. The high prices of the war period would have greatly stimulated the movement, for it is obvious that if rents were thereby doubled both for open and enclosed land, the gross profit of enclosing would also be doubled; the net gain probably more than doubled. When Wordsworth wrote, the open fields were apparently still fairly numerous, but they had become a mere survival.

The date of the enclosure of this district is, however, the least interesting of the inferences to be drawn.

We find that up to the union of the Crowns, cultivation was carried on by a system very closely resembling the "run-rig" of the Hebrides. Groups of four tenants combined together, and yoked their horses to a common plough, and equally divided the holding between them, each tenant having his equal share in all parts of the holding. We next find that on the decay of this co-aration, for a long period, varying in duration in different parishes, holdings remained intermixed, but it seems clear that as in the one surviving Devonshire open field, and probably as in Lancashire, common rights were not exercised over the arable fields; though it might happen that besides the "ranes," the grassy balks between the strips of arable land, there might be considerable stretches of grass amidst the arable field which was used for a common pasture. Lastly, we find that open, inter-mixed arable land and meadows, having this history, passes into a state of enclosure where increase of population, agricultural progress, and the increasing value of land make enclosure suffi-ciently profitable, by a gradual, piecemeal process, without the need for Act of Parliament, or reference to a Commission, or any combined resolution on the part of the lord and tenants of a manor.

It is because the process was late in Cumberland and West-moreland and because it happened to interest three authors, West, Wordsworth, and Eden, who were not agriculturists, that the record of it for these two counties is available. All the indications suggest that Northumberland and Durham underwent a similar evolution ; and all the preceding information with regard to the enclosure of Wales and much of the land imme- diately on the Welsh border, and of West Somerset, Devon and Cornwall, harmonises with the hypothesis that in those districts also the process was fundamentally the same, though with local differences, due to a very much earlier pacification.

CHAPTER XVIII.

THE scenery of England and Wales has been transformed by the enclosure of its lands, but the extent and results of the transformation vary. Here you have the landscape cut into little fields with great hedges, looking from an elevated point of view like a patchwork quilt; there the skimpy quickest hedges only slightly emphasise the natural sweeping lines of the hills: here you have narrow winding lanes; there broad, straight roads with margins of grass on either side: here you have compact villages in which almost all the habitations in the parish are clustered together; there farmhouses and cottages so scattered that were it not for the church, which seems to attract to its neighbourhood the inn and the smithy, there would be no recognisable village at all.

This diversity in the effect of enclosure on the face of the country is a symbol of the diversity of its effect upon the material, social, and moral conditions of the local peasantry, who, like the land itself, may be said to have undergone Enclosure.

Where, as in Devon and Cornwall, in Cumberland and Westmoreland, the division of intermixed arable and meadow land took place early and gradually, and in subordination to the reclamation of waste, that reclamation itself being carried on steadily and gradually, the result was the creation of numberless small holdings and properties. A career was offered to the enterprising and laborious, and enterprise and industry grew accordingly,—" Devonshire myghty and Strong," says Leland; and the great part taken by Devonshire in the national struggles in the reign of Elizabeth must be partly attributed to the reaction upon the character of the people of the conquest over the difficulties of bringing the rocky soil, woodland or moor, into cultivation : a conquest which made Devonshire husbandry famous for two generations, and "Devonshiring" a well-known term for a particular method of preparing waste land for cultivation.

Perhaps the greatest evil of Acts for the enclosure of waste in the past, was that they prevented such gradual reclamation and enclosure by peasant cultivators. At the present day the vital objection applies to enclosure of waste by any method that the area of such free open spaces is already sufficiently curtailed, that every remaining acre is becoming continually more precious, so that while public-spirited people fight for their preservation in remote places, in the neighbourhood of towns, citizens tax themselves to add to their area.

The enclosure of arable common fields, and of all the commonable lands of whole parishes within what I have called the Parliamentary Enclosure Belt, is of immeasurably greater historical importance. The ethics of such enclosure has been the subject of fierce debate for centuries ; now the process is practically complete, and it is possible to apraise its results.

We have observed that with regard to the immediate results, capable of being contemporaneously verified, there is no real controversy between the disputants; it is on the inferences to be drawn as to the more ultimate results on the nation as a whole, and in the judgment pronounced upon the desirability of such results, that the dispute turned. The more candid disputants on either side admit the vital points in their opponents' case : thus, for example, no opponent of enclosure denies that it tended to raise rents ; and, on the other hand, it was the greatest advocate of enclosure who declared that "By nineteen out of twenty Enclosure Acts the poor are injured."

The increase of rent was, of course, the motive of enclosure ; and though there were exceptional cases in which the results were very disappointing to the promoters, as a rule the increase of rent was very great. Arthur Young gives the full financial details of twenty-three Acts for the enclosure of open field parishes in Lincolnshire.[1] The total rents before enclosure amounted to

---

[1] "Agriculture of Lincoln," p. 83.

£15,504; on an average they were nearly doubled, the increase of rent obtained being £14,256, and the expenditure necessary to obtain this result was £48,217. Assuming that the money was borrowed at 6 per cent., there remained to the landowners a net profit of £11,363. These results were no doubt something above the average, but they were not exceptional. In Long Sutton the rent was raised from an average of 5s. per acre to between 30s. and 50s. per acre.[1]

The increase of rent was not a concern purely of the land-owning class. As the advocates of enclosure continually pointed out, the rent was a pretty accurate test of the net produce of the agriculture of the parish; it was roughly proportional to the amount of food grown but not consumed on the spot, and sent away to markets to feed urban consumers at a distance. It was upon this net produce, they pointed out, that the taxable resources of the country depended. It was argued that an addition to the population of the country which was all engaged in gaining its own subsistence from the soil, added neither to the number of soldiers who could be enlisted for war without paralysing industry, nor to the power of the State to equip and support an army. On the other hand, a change by which a whole village of peasants who consumed nearly all the food they produced, was swept away and replaced by one or two highly rented farms, producing a less quantity of food, but sending much more to market, did supply the State with additional resources for the maintenance of its forces.

Private interests stimulated the appreciation of these public advantages. Money had to be borrowed to meet the heavy initial expenses of enclosure, and the banking system grew with the enclosure movement of the eighteenth century. And hence a secondary gain to the State. Increased opportunities for the remunerative investment of capital increased the supply of loanable capital, and made possible the enormous State loans by which the Napoleonic war was carried on. Lawyers, land surveyors, Parliamentary agents and others,

---

[1] " Agriculture of Lincoln," p. 77.

reaped a copious harvest; and further, London in particular, and other towns in varying measure, grew in wealth by ministering to the increased "effective demands" of the enriched aristocracy.

But the opponents of enclosure were concerned with the gross rather than the net produce of land, and, as we have seen, it can be proved from the testimony of the advocates of enclosure and of impartial witnesses, that over a great part of the Midlands enclosure meant the conversion of arable to pasture, and local depopulation. The Board of Agriculture gives what may be considered an official estimate of the diminution of gross produce which would follow. An acre of common field arable might be expected to produce 2010 lbs. of bread in a three years course (that is, 670 lbs. of bread per annum), and 30 lbs. of meat per annum. The same area enclosed and converted to pasture would produce 176 lbs. of mutton, or 120 lbs of beef. If we split the difference between the production of beef and mutton, we have on the average 148 lbs. of meat produced. There is on enclosure a gain of 113 lbs. of meat against a loss of 570 lbs. of bread; supposing the food values of equal quantities of bread and meat to be equal, there is a loss of 557 lbs. out of a total produce of 705 lbs.

And yet, through a chain of causation which can now be clearly perceived, but which at the time was not evident, though locally there might be a loss of gross produce, there was a gain throughout the kingdom. The key to the position was the operation of the Poor Laws.

Enclosure of arable fields and open field parishes in the Parliamentary Enclosure Belt in many ways greatly affected the operation of the Poor Laws.

By increasing rents it made a given poor-rate yield more. Further, the increase of rent reconciled the enclosing landowners to an increase in the poor-rate; more especially when it fell, not on them, but on their neighbours. For, as we have seen, the effect of enclosure in some parishes in a given neighbourhood was often to drive the poor into the parishes which remained unenclosed; these bore the burden, while the others reaped the profits.

As we have seen, enclosure, even when arable was not converted to pasturage, tended to ruin small owners and to eliminate small farmers, so that these had to join the ranks of agricultural labourers. The number of potential paupers was thus increased.

Destitution and recklessness among the labouring classes also increased. The common rights and small holdings of a few acres in the common fields were, at best, as we have seen, exchanged for a sum of money for which no investment offered itself, which therefore soon disappeared. With these small holdings disappeared also the hope of gradually taking more and more additional strips of land in the fields and the fear of losing the little already gained.

Early marriage was particularly encouraged by the change from the open field condition to enclosure. Before enclosure, the conditions of labour made the common field farmers who employed labourers, desire young unmarried men and women who would live in the farmhouse ; such farm servants postponed marriage till they had accumulated some savings and could begin their married life with some resources—a cow, for example— over and above their labour. After enclosure, the enriched farming class preferred to pay board wages, and the young labourer with nothing to gain by waiting, with the assurance of Poor Law assistance if needed, naturally preferred to marry early.

Lastly, the disappearance of the yeoman class and of the connecting links between the largest farmers and the day labourers naturally tended to make the careful local adminis- tration of the Poor Law more difficult ; it even to a great extent destroyed the motive for economical administration. The open field parish retained some of the social vitality of a self-governing community ; men who had to concert together for the regulation of the fields, for the purchase of a parish bull, were more likely than the farmers of an enclosed parish to settle in concert questions of Poor Law relief in accordance with the interest of the parish as a whole.

This last point of connection between the enclosure and the Poor Law history of the country during the eighteenth century and

the first part of the nineteenth is, however, interesting in itself,
apart from the present argument. The point here laid stress
upon is that whatever hardships for labourers and others resulted
from the enclosure of arable fields, they did not starve, they did
not eat less bread ; they might be rendered miserable, but they
married earlier and reared large families, somewhere or other.
Poor Law relief ensured their offering an " effective demand "
for bread. This effective demand compelled the increase of
arable cultivation somewhere within the country; for foreign
supplies were practically unavailable. The enclosure of waste for
tillage and the enclosure of arable for pasture were economically
inter-dependent.

The gross agricultural produce of the country as a whole was
therefore increased by common field enclosure.

The effect upon urban industries was also great. The greater
the local depopulation in rural districts produced by enclosure,
the greater the supply of needy labourers of industrious habits
and robust physique drafted to the growing industrial towns.
Local depopulation was the usual result of Enclosure, as we
have seen, in the Midlands and in Wiltshire, and parts of
neighbouring counties. Where, as in Norfolk and parts of
Lincoln and Yorkshire, local depopulation did not ensue, there
was a vast increase in the agricultural produce sent to market,
and in consequence, in the manufactured commodities demanded.
Enclosure tended to assist urban industry therefore by an
increased labour supply, an increased market, and perhaps also,
an increased supply of capital.

Summing up, therefore, the economic results of the whole mass
of little village revolutions under examination, we find increased
population, increased production of all sorts of commodities,
increased national resources for purposes of taxation and foreign
war. The moral effects we find to have been increased misery
and recklessness, showing itself in increased pauperism and
drunkenness. An increase of the quantity of human life is attained
at the expense of a degradation in its quality.

APPENDIX A.

	Acts specifying Acreage Enclosed.		Acts not specifying Acreage Enclosed.		Total.		Acres Enclosed per annum.
	Acts.	Acreage as stated.	Acts.	Acreage estimated.	Acts.	Acres.	
1727—1760	49	65,203	7	9,315	56	74,518	2,192
1761—1792	292	411,952	47	66,307	339	478,259	14,946
1793—1801	153	230,249	29	43,642	182	273,891	30,432
1802—1815	469	615,970	95	123,773	564	739,743	52,839
1816--1845	202	164,994	42	34,306	244	199,300	6,643
Totals.	1,165	1,488,368	220	277,343	1,385	1,765,711	

From 1727 to 1760 the number of Acts of this class passed per annum was steadily increasing, the Seven Years' War (1756–1763) apparently acting as a stimulus. During this period the average acreage enclosed per Act was 1330·7 acres. The increase in the number of Acts continued up till 1792, and again at a greatly enhanced rate after the beginning of the great French war. From 1761–1792 the average acreage enclosed per Act was 1410·8 acres; from 1792–1801, 1504·9 acres. In 1801 a Clauses Act, termed " A General Enclosure Act" was passed to facilitate Parliamentary proceedings. This had the double effect of increasing the average number of Acts passed per annum from 20 to 43, but of reducing the average acreage per Act to 1313·4 acres. From 1816–1845 the average acreage per Act was 816·8 acres.

APPENDIX B.

—◆—

PRIVATE ACTS ENCLOSING COMMON FIELDS.

Abbreviations { A. F. Acres of common field arable.   P. Parish.
A. P. Acres of common pasture.   M.I. Mesne inclosures.
A. M. Acres of common meadow.   yl. Yardlands.
F.'s. Common fields.

* Indicates that the area enclosed is not stated in acres in the Act, but in yardlands, oxgangs, or other such units, or otherwise has been estimated from data supplied by the Act.

NOTE.—The spelling adopted is that used in the Act. In many cases it varies from that now in use.

BEDFORD.

Date.	Enclosure.	Area enclosed.	Date.	Enclosure.	Area enclosed.
1742	Sutton	2,200		Brought forward	33,048
1760	Apsley Guise		1796	Marston Moretaine	
1765	Felmersham		,,	Pertenhall	850
,,	Podington	2,400	,,	Ridgmont	950
1768	Tilsworth		1797	Bedford	400
1769	Pavenham		,,	Campton with Shefford	
,,	Sundon		,,	Chalgrove	1,780
1770	Souldrop, 350 A. F., 150 A. P.	500	,,	Dunton	2,200
1774	Potton		,,	Elstow	1,060
1775	Lidlington		,,	Harrold	3,300
1776	Odell		,,	Southill	2,600
1777	Tempsford	2,000	,,	Toddington and Carlton	2,800
1778	Little Berkford	1,500	1798	Sandy	
,,	Bolnhurst	953	1800	Over and Nether Dean	1,570
1780	Northill and Sandy		,,	Farndish	672
1783	Turvey		,,	Tilbrooke	1,380
1793	Milton Bryant	1,400	1801	Little Staughton	1,000
,,	Riseley	2,000	,,	Wrestlingworth	1,860
1794	Shelton	1,000			
1795	Bedford	1,450			55,470
,,	Crawley	1,400			
,,	Eaton Socon	4,650	1802	Cardington	3,000
,,	Henlow	2,000	,,	Everton cum Tetworth	420
,,	Milbrooke	900	,,	Kempston	2,600
1796	Blunham	2,695	,,	Shillington and Holwell	
,,	Houghton Regis	4,000	1803	Keysoe	1,700
,,	Maulden	2,000	,,	Milton Ernest	1,350
			,,	Oakley	1,450
	Carried forward	33,048		Carried forward	10,520

BEDFORD—*continued.*

Date.	Enclosure.	Area enclosed.
	Brought forward ...	10,520
1804	Arlsey	
,,	Astwick	600
1805	Thurleigh	1,460
,,	Carlton, Chillington and Steventon	
1806	Haughton Conquest ...	1,500
,,	Eversholt	130
,,	Flitwick	1,000
1807	Salford	500
1808	Clophill	
,,	Harlington	700
1809	Flitton cum Silsoe and Pulloxhill	
,,	Ravensden	1,000
,,	Barton in the Clay ...	
,,	Sharnbrook	
,,	Wilshamstead	
1810	Roxton	3,000
1811	Wymington	700
,,	Wilden	1,600
1812	Biddenham	
,,	Stagsden	
1814	Potton	
1820	Great Barford	
,,	Greenhurst, Upper and Lower, and Upper Stondon	
	Carried forward ...	22,710

Date.	Enclosure.	Area enclosed.
	Brought forward ...	22,710
1827	Langford	1,700
1832	Clifton	1,400
1834	Colmworth	1,600
1836	Wootton	
,,	Stepingley, 300 A. F. ...	400
1837	Cranfield	
		27,810

Enclosed under the General Enclosure Act, 1845.

Date of Act.	Date of Award.	Parish.	Area.
*	1851	Stotfold	2,030
1847	1852	Goldington ...	1,040
1855	1858	Streatley and Sharpenhoe ...	1,662
	1860	Eton Bray ...	1,860
	1891	Totternhoe ...	1,717
			8,309

	Acres.
Before 1802 ...	55,470
1802–1845 ...	27,810
After 1845 ...	8,309

BERKSHIRE.

Date.	Enclosure.	Area enclosed.
1724	Sunninghill, c. Bayworth, liberty of Sonning, 5 F.'s, 3 Commons ...	*1,190
1743	Aston Tirrold, 12 F.'s ...	
,,	Early, F. only	423
1746	Inkpen	
1758	Upton, 57 yl.	1,800
1761	Hinton, 60 yl. F. and 620 A. P.	*2,420
1764	Haversham	844
1770	Ashbury	
1771	East Garston	
,,	Hampstead Norreys, 750 A. F., 700 A. P. ...	1,450
1772	Great Faringdon, 52 yl. F., 100 A. M. ...	1,660
,,	Upper Letcombe and Childrey	
1776	Eastbury and Blagrove	
	Carried forward ...	9.787

Date.	Enclosure.	Area enclosed.
	Brought forward ...	9,787
1776	Ferry Hinksey	
1777	Farnborough	
,,	Uffington, Balking, Woolston, Kingston, Lisle, Fawler	
1778	Bockhampton	
1779	Elcot	338
,,	Speen	
1783	Stanford, 80 yl.	2,000
1785	Bray	320
1788	Little Faringdon (part of Langford)	
1793	Aston Upthorpe	
1794	Compton Beauchamp ...	
,,	Shilton	
1795	Walton and Boreshill ...	
1796	Longcott	
1799	Remenham	
	Carried forward ...	12,445

BERKSHIRE—*continued*.

Date.	Enclosure.	Area enclosed.
	Brought forward ...	12,445
1800	Sparsholt and Westcote	
1801	Little Coxwell	
,,	Denchworth	700
,,	Lyford	506
,,	Letcomb Regis and Bassett	
,,	Sutton Courtney and Sutton Wick	
,,	East Hendred	
		13,651
1802	Buckland	2,074
,,	West Challow	403
,,	Harwell	
,,	Kennington	
,,	Up Lamborne	
1803	Chipping Lamborne and Blagrave	
,,	East Hanney	
,,	Waltham St. Lawrence	700
,,	Wantage and Grove ...	2,400
1804	Charney	950
,,	Ufton	
1806	Kingston Bagpuize ...	655
1807	Shottesbrook and White Waltham	
,,	Hurst, 700 A. F., 600 A. P.	1,300
1808	Aston Upthorpe and Aston Tirrold ...	
,,	Ardington	
,,	Langford	
1809	Basildon	110
,,	Englefield, 327 A. F., 36 A. P. ...	363
,,	Milton	663
,,	Long Wittenham ...	
1810	Chieveley	600
,,	Enborne, Hamstead Marshall, Inkpen and Kintbury	1,400
1811	Chaddleworth	
,,	Hungerford	780
,,	Thatcham Borough, Henwick and Greenham...	825
,,	Brightwell	
,,	Beenham and Padworth	574
,,	Fyfield	1,100
,,	Sulhamstead and Meales	
,,	Tilehurst, 600 A. F., 600 A. P.	1,200
,,	Woohampton	1,995
	Carried forward ...	18,092

Date.	Enclosure.	Area enclosed.
	Brought forward ...	18,092
1811	Drayton	
1812	West Compton	2,000
,,	Ashall	1,500
,,	Great Shefford and West Shefford	520
1814	Chieveley	400
,,	Wytham	620
,,	Bray	
,,	Cumner and South Hincksey	3,000
,,	Streatley	
,,	Welford	1,400
,,	Wargrave and Wearfield	2,000
,,	Boxford	1,500
,,	Marcham	
,,	Sandhurst	3,400
1816	Sonning	2,500
1818	South Moreton ...	
1821	Easthamstead	2,250
1825	West Ilsley	1,270
,,	Marcham	700
1827	Ruscombe	
1828	Appleton	1,500
		42,652

Enclosed under the General Enclosure Act, 1845.

Date of Act.	Date of Award.	Parish.	Area.
*	1849	Newbury (E. & W. Fields)	212
*	,,	North Moreton ...	1,025
*	1851	Cholsey	2,190
*	1853	East Lockinge ...	970
1851	1856	Shinfield	312
1851	1858	St. Giles, Reading	242
1860	1868	Charlton in Wantage	1,280
1880	1883	Steventon... ...	1,373
			7,604

BERKSHIRE AND OXFORD.

1852	1855	Bampton and Shilton	2,730
*	1856	Purley, Sulham and Whitchurch ...	300
		Half Area, assigned to Berks.	1,515

		Acres.
Before 1802	...	13,651
1802–1845	...	42,652
After 1845	...	9,119

BUCKINGHAMSHIRE.

Date.	Enclosure.	Area enclosed.
1738	Ashenden, 900 A. F. ...	*1,300
1742	Wotton Underwood, 1,168 A. F., 500 A. P. ...	1,668
1744	Shipton (Winslow cum Shipton P.), F. only...	640
1762	Swanburne, 77 yl. ...	*2,695
,,	Shenley Brookend ...	960
1764	Westbury	3,000
1765	Westcote...	1,300
1766	Little Horwood... ...	960
,,	Winslow (Winslow cum Shipton P.)	1,400
1767	Olney	1,600
,,	Shalstone, 28 yl. F., 530 A. P.	1,370
1768	Loughton	
,,	Woughton-on-the-Green	
1769	Cublington, 25 yl. ...	875
,,	Grendon Underwood, 37 yl.	*1,295
1770	Simpson	
,,	Stoke Goldington ...	1,000
1771	Aylesbury, all F. ...	
,,	Great Brickhill	1,260
,,	Whitchurch	
1772	North Crawley	
,,	Soulbury and Hollington	
1773	Tingewick and Radcliffe cum Chackmore ...	
1774	Dunton	629
,,	Stoke Hammond ...	
,,	Twyford and Charndon	1,900
,,	Waddesdon, 49 yl. ...	*1,715
1776	Hartwell and Stone, all F.	1,740
1777	Ludgershall, 1 F., 53 yl.	1,800
,,	Wendover	
1778	Hardwicke	1,200
,,	Hitcham...	
,,	Hanslop	1,900
,,	North Marston	2,000
1779	Bierton and Hallcott ...	
,,	Taplow	
1781	Preston Bisset	1,000
1782	Calverton, and west side of Stony Stratford ...	
1788	Bradwell...	1,000
,,	Wavendon	2,000
1789	Bourton and Watchfield	
1790	Bowbrickhill and Fenny Stratford	2,000
1791	Little Woolston... ...	
1793	Castlethorpe	
	Carried forward ...	40,207

Date.	Enclosure.	Area enclosed.
	Brought forward ...	40,207
1794	Akeley cum Stockholt, 13 yl.	*455
,,	Newport Pagnell ...	900
,,	Wendover ...	2,000
1795	Aston Abbotts	650
,,	Padbury, 69 yl.	*2,415
,,	Steeple Claydon, 80½ yl.	*2,817
1796	Little Brickhill	600
,,	Grandborough	1,100
,,	Sherington	1,600
,,	Great Woolstone ...	300
1797	Adstock, 47 yl.	*1,645
,,	Drayton Parslow ...	
,,	Thornborough, 62 yl. ...	*2,170
,,	Wing	3,402
,,	Wingrave with Rowsham	2,400
,,	Stoke Mandeville ...	1,000
1798	Emberton	1,300
,,	Weston Turville, 1,000 A. F. and M.	1,000
1799	Horton	
,,	Singleborough	
,,	Walton	1,200
,,	Wraisbury	
1800	Iver, 817 A. F., 473 A. M., 1,172 A. P.	2,462
1801	Lavendon and Brayfield	
,,	Weedon	1,700
,,	Maidsmorton and Buckingham	
		71,323

Date.	Enclosure.	Area enclosed.
1802	Donnington	900
,,	Moulsoe	1,600
,,	Woburn	800
1803	Great Kimble, Little Kimble and Ellesborough	2,500
1805	Chearsley	917
1806	Saunderton	1,200
1807	Newport Pagnell ...	900
1808	Upton cum Chalvey ...	752
1809	Langley Marish... ...	
,,	Bledlow	4,000
,,	Marsworth	1,200
1810	Datchett...	
,,	Stoke Pogis	
,,	Bletchley	2,200
,,	Newnton Blossomville...	
	Carried forward ...	16,769

BUCKINGHAMSHIRE—*continued*.

Date.	Enclosure.	Area enclosed.
	Brought forward ...	16,769
1810	Slapton and Horton ...	
1811	Stewkley...	3,000
1813	Turweston ...	
1814	Aston Clinton	2,200
,,	Mursley	
1815	Amersham	890
1820	Little Marlow	450
,,	Princes Risborough ...	2,900
1821	Farnham Royal... ...	
,,	Ivinghoe...	
1822	Clifton Reynes	450
,,	Towersey	986
1824	Long Crendon	2,500
1830	Haddenham	2,945
,,	Monks Risborough ...	
		33,090

Enclosed under the General Enclosure Act, 1845.

Date of Act.	Date of Award.	Parish.	Area.
1850	1855	Penn	1,078
,,	,,	Hitchendon or Hughendon ...	488
1852	,,	Great Marlow ...	608
1853	1856	Pitstone	1,140
,,	1857	Cheddington and Ivinghoe ...	1,350
1856	1865	Edlesborough ...	2,350
			7,014

	Acres.
Before 1802 ...	71,323
1802–1845 ...	33,090
After 1845 ...	7,014

CAMBRIDGE.

Date.	Enclosure.	Area enclosed.
1770	Abington Pigotts ...	1,000
1775	Knapwell	1,100
1777	Weston Colville... ...	1,970
1796	Barrington	2,500
1797	Great Wilbraham (with old enclosures) ...	*2,300
,,	Little Wilbraham ...	1,600
1798	Harston, Hauxton, Little Shefford and Newton	
,,	Longstow (with old enclosures)	1,400
,,	Swaffham Bulbeck (with old enclosures) ...	4,000
1799	Carlton cum Willingham (with old enclosures)	1,500
,,	Grantchester and Coton	
,,	Pampisford	2,000
1800	Connington	1,500
,,	Elsworth	3,900
,,	Guilden Morden ...	2,500
,,	Milton	1,550
1801	Great Abingdon... ...	1,560
,,	Little Abingdon ...	1,350
,,	Balsham	4,000
,,	Bassingbourne	3,500
,,	Bottisham	4,000
,,	Histon and Impington...	
,,	Trumpington	2,000
		45,230

Date.	Enclosure.	Area enclosed.
1802	St. Giles, Cambridge ...	1,200
,,	Graveley...	1,500
,,	Horningsea (with old enclosures)	1,450
,,	Sawston	1,040
1803	Fen Ditton	1,400
1804	Manea in Ely	900
1805	Snalewell	
,,	Swaffham Prior... ...	
1806	Dullingham	
,,	Fulbourn	
,,	Cherry Hinton ...	
,,	Kirtling and Ashley cum Silverley	3,000
1807	Barnwell...	
,,	Landbeach	
,,	Steeple Morden ...	
1808	Girton	
,,	Harlton	1,100
1809	Bourn	
,,	Chatteris...	
,,	Dry Drayton	
,,	Fordham...	
,,	West Wratting	
,,	Whittlesford	2,000
1810	Hastingfield	
,,	Ickleton	
,,	Kinston	
	Carried forward ...	13,590

CAMBRIDGE—*continued.*

Date.	Enclosure.	Area enclosed	Date.	Enclosure.	Area enclosed.
	Brought forward ...	13,590		Brought forward ...	30,674
1810	Teversham		1839	Melbourn	
1811	Brinkley...		,,	Barton	
,,	Croxton	1,200	,,	Comberton	
,,	Great and Little Eversdon		,,	Rampton (with old enclosures)	1,100
,,	Lanstanton All Saints ...		1840	Whittlesea	
,,	Shepreth...	1,000	,,	Thriflow	
1812	Stapleford	1,400	,,	Wicken	
,,	Toft		1841	Cheveley...	
,,	West Whickham ...		,,	Gamlingay	
1813	Great Cransden... ...		1842	Coltenham	
,,	Langstanton St. Michael		1843	Haddenham	
,,	Meldreth, Melbourn and Whaddon		1845	Foulmire...	2,111
,,	Little Shelford	1,200			
,,	Wood Ditton				33,885
,,	Waterbeach				
,,	Kennet				
1814	Burwill				
,,	Stretchworth				
1815	Papworth Everard ...				
1819	Hinxton				
1822	Duxford	2,500			
1825	Doddington and Coveney	290			
1826	Foxton	1,586			
1828	Litlington	1,686			
1829	Wentworth	990			
1830	Caxton	1,500			
1833	Oakington				
1834	Great Shelford				
1835	Stretcham				
1836	Hardwick				
,,	Orwell				
1838	Sutton				
,,	Swavesey				
,,	Linton	3,732			
,,	Witcham...				
,,	Chesterton				
,,	Fen Drayton				
1839	Stow cum Quy				
	Carried forward ...	30,674			

Enclosed under the General Enclosure Act, 1845.

Date of Act.	Date of Award.	Parish.	Area.
*	1854	Isleham	1,370
1848	,,	Caldecot	747
1850	,,	Mepal	442
1851	,,	Newton	1,041
1847	1855	Wilburton... ...	780
1855	1857	Westwick in Oakington	217
1858	1863	S h u d y Camps, C a s t l e Camps and Bartlow ...	1,037
1864	1868	Ellisley	1,490
1883	1889	Hildersham ...	1,174
			8,298

		Acres.
Before 1802	...	45,230
1802–1845	...	33,885
After 1845	...	8,298

CHESHIRE.

Date.	Enclosure.	Area enclosed.	Date.	Enclosure.	Area enclosed.
1805	St. Mary on the Hill (certain quillets of intermixed lands) ...	126		Brought forward ...	126
			1814	Wendon and Arksden ...	3,200
	Carried forward ...	126			3,326

APPENDIX B.

CUMBERLAND.

Date.	Enclosure.	Area enclosed.	Date.	Enclosure.	Area enclosed.
1772	Great and Little Stanton, Newbiggin and Great Blencow		1813	Greystoke, 240 A. F. ...	3,500
			1814	Torpentrow, 20 A. F., 700 A. waste	720
1779	Irthington, 3,600 A. waste and divers open fields	4,000	1825	Dearham...	480
		4,000			4,700

	Acres.
Before 1802 ...	4,000
1802–1845 ...	4,700

DERBYSHIRE.

Date.	Enclosure.	Area enclosed.	Date.	Enclosure.	Area enclosed.
1727	Scarcliffe and Palterton, 500 A. F., 420 A.P....	970		Brought forward ...	15,118
1756	Weston cum Membris and Sawley		1783	Boilstone...	500
1760	Mackworth		1785	Holbrooke	500
1762	Aston-upon-Trent ...	1,500	1786	Weston upon Trent ...	1,500
„	Elvaston and Thulston		1787	Barrow upon Trent ...	1,000
1763	Draycott		„	Little Eaton	900
„	Scropton...		„	Melbourne and King's Norton	2,500
„	Tideswell	1,000	„	Sawley	750
1764	Ashford and Sheldon (Bakewell P.) ...		1786	Parwich	1,000
1765	Long Eaton, 131 oxgangs	1,600	„	Spondon	1,000
„	Hartshorn		1789	Marston upon Dove, Hatton, Horn and Hornhay	830
1766	Repton		„	Osmaston next Derby, 270 F.	*500
„	Willington	1,300	1790	Mickleover	800
1768	Littleover	1,200	1793	Taddington and Priestcliff	1,600
„	Normanton next Derby	700	1794	Ilkeston	760
1771	Fairfield, 860 A. P. ...	*1,000	1795	Barlborough, 250 A. F., 650 A. P.	900
„	Stapenhill and Winshill, 400 A. F., 160 A. P.	560	„	Eckington, 200 A. F. and M. I. 1,070 A. P. ...	1,270
„	Stretton, Hordington, Bondend and Braunston, 600 A. F., 610 A. P.	1,210	1797	Etwall	1,600
1772	Ockbrook	700	1798	Hartington	12,000
1773	Church Broughton, 160 A. F., 100 A. P. ...	360			45,028
1777	Killamarsh, 60 A. F., 350 A. P.	410			
„	Tibshelf, 42 A. F., 404 A. P.	446	1802	Alvaston and Boulton ...	1,200
1778	Bolsover and Clown ...		„	Chellaston	700
1780	Findern	500	1803	Brassington and Bradbourne...	4,000
„	Hilton, 400 A. F., 600 A. P. ... ·... ...	1,000	„	Great Hacklow, mesne fields	400
1782	Sandicare	662	1804	Little Hacklow, 400 A. P. and mesne fields ...	600
	Carried forward ...	15,118		Carried forward ...	6,900

DERBYSHIRE—*continued.*

Date.	Enclosure.	Area enclosed.
	Brought forward ...	6,900
1805	Chelmorton and Flagg	1,300
1806	Bakewell and Over Hadden	2,800
„	Hope, Bradwell and Thornhill	1,400
1807	Wheston and Tideswell, M. I.	4,000
1808	Hathersage	10,000
1809	Dronfield, M. I. ...	5,000
„	Elton and Winster ...	500
1810	Great and Little Langstone and Wardlow, M. I.	1,500
1811	Beeley	2,000
1813	Whitwell	950
1814	Breadsall	1,461
	Carried forward ...	37,811

Date.	Enclosure.	Area enclosed.
	Brought forward ...	37,811
1814	Brampton, M. I. ...	3,000
1815	Youlgreave, mesne or intermixt lands ...	1,160
1816	Homesfield	3,000
1817	Hollington	280
1818	Norbury, 100 A. P. ...	200
1820	Smisby	550
1821	Whittington	284
1824	Snelston	160
1834	Kirk Langley, 110 A. F., 120 A. P.	230
		46,675

	Acres.
Before 1802 ...	45,028
1802–1845 ...	46,675

DORSET.

Date.	Enclosure.	Area enclosed.
1733	Buckland Newton, 800 A. F., 800 A. P. ...	1,600
1736	West Stafford c. Froome Bellet	600
1761	Langton Herring ...	
1762	Portesham	1,200
1768	Winfrith Newburgh ...	2,254
1779	West Knighton	1,000
1785	Wimborne Minster ...	3,000
1789	Podington	
1794	Tolpuddle	
„	Preston and South Poyntz	
1796	Hanley	
1797	Hintel Murtel and Gussage All Saints ...	
„	Wyke Regis	
1798	Bradford Peverell ...	
1799	Charlton Marshall ...	2,200
1800	Winterborne Strickland	1,050
1801	Turnwood	800
		13,704
1803	Chickerill	
„	Spetisbury	1,000
1804	Beaminster, 290 A. F., 235 A. P.	525
	Carried forward ...	1,525

Date.	Enclosure.	Area enclosed
	Brought forward ...	1,525
1805	Broadmaine	990
1806	Hampreston	
1807	Corfe Mullen, 200 A. F., &c., 1,500 A. Heath ...	1,700
„	Cattistock	1,200
1808	Winterborne Waste ...	777
1809	Abbotsbury	1,500
„	Compton Vallance ...	
„	Gillingham and Motcombe	500
„	West Melbury	
„	Pimperne	
1809	Plush	359
„	Great Washbourne ...	
1810	Litton Cheney	780
„	Walditch, 187 A. F., 9 A. P.	196
1811	Shapwick	1,160
1812	Gussage St. Michael ...	1,100
1814	Tarrant Keinston, all F.	169
1815	Dawlish	400
1818	Loders	450
1819	Brodd Sydling and Up Sydling	
1820	Chilfrome	900
1824	Bincombe	1,300
„	Tarrant Hinton	2,000
	Carried forward ...	17,006

DORSET—*continued.*

Date.	Enclosure.	Area enclosed.
	Brought forward ...	17,006
1830	Charminster	700
1831	Maiden Newton ...	800
„	Piddle Hinton	1,600
1834	Upway	320
1836	Godmanstone	
		20,426

Enclosed under the General Enclosure Act, 1845.

Date of Act.	Date of Award.	Parish.	Area.
1851	1853	Compton Abbas ...	704
		Carried forward ...	704

Date of Act.	Date of Award.	Parish.	Area.
		Brought forward ...	704
*	1854	Askerswell ...	635
1855	1857	West Lulworth ...	634
1857	1860	Ashmore	635
1861	1863	Winterborne Steepleton ...	558
1866	1868	Warmwell ...	620
			3,786

	Acres.
Before 1802 ...	13,704
1802–1845 ...	20,426
After 1845 ...	3,786

DURHAM.

Date.	Enclosure.	Area enclosed.
1761	Norham, In fields, 437 A., moor 1,500 A. ...	1,937
1769	Wolsingham	200
1782	Bolam	800
1783	Barnard Castle	800
1794	Crawcrook	700
		4,437

Date.	Enclosure.	Area enclosed.
1814	Gateshead	200

	Acres.
Before 1802 ...	4,437
1802–1845 ...	200

ESSEX.

Date.	Enclosure.	Area enclosed.
1795	Great Parndon, 227 A. F., 124 A. P.	351
1801	Great Chesterford ...	1,200
„	Little Chesterford ...	600
„	Hadstock	1,400
„	Littlebury	3,000
		6,551
1807	Chrishall...	1,500
1811	Great and Little Chishill	2,500
1812	Saffron Walden... ...	
1814	Heydon	
1820	Farnham	240
1824	Wendon Tofts and Elmdon	1,950
1838	Berden, Manewden, Stansted Mountfichet ...	
		6,190

Enclosed under the General Enclosure Act, 1845.

Date of Act.	Date of Award.	Parish.	Area.
1846	1850	Walthamstow ...	198
*	1851	Henham ...	630
1847	„	Netteswell ...	204
*	„	Langley	360
*	1853	Haverhill	298
*	„	Wicken Bonhunt...	292
1855	1860	Roydon	285
1856	1861	Newport	815
1859	„	Clavering... ...	750
1866	1869	Widdington ...	820
			4,652

	Acres
Before 1802 ...	6,551
1802–1845 ...	6,190
After 1845 ...	4,652

GLOUCESTER.

Date.	Enclosure.	Area enclosed.
1726	Little Rissington	...
1727	Cherrington, 3 F.'s, 1,800 A.	2,200
1729	Wick Risington, 58 yl....	*2,000
1731	Prestbury	
„	Upper and Lower Slaughter, 87 yl.	*2,845
1739	Shipton, Moyle and Dovel, all F.	800
1744	Westonbirt, 2 F.'s ...	350
1753	Eastlechmartin, 53¼ yl....	*1,863
„	Quennington	3,000
1755	Hawling	881
1759	Little Barrington, 42 yl. F., 600 A. P.	*1,860
„	Preston upon Stower, 25¾ yl.	*900
1761	Snowshil, 500 A. F., 18 A. M., 1,100 A. P. ...	1,618
1763	Childswickham, 83 yl....	*2,905
1765	Donnington (Stow on the Wold P.)	
1766	Haselton	858
„	Hatherop, 966 A. F., 150 A. P.	1,116
„	Maugersbury	
1767	Bibury, 3,000 A. F., 300 A. P.	3,300
„	Willersey, 36 yl. ...	*1,260
1769	Ampney Holyrood and Ashbrook	2,080
„	Bleddington, 52 yl. ...	*1,820
„	Coln St. Aldwin's, 1,950 A. F., 100 A.P. ...	2,050
1770	Notgrove	1,200
1771	Aston Subedge, 31 yl. F., 150 A. P.	*1,235
„	Preston and Stratton ...	2,000
1772	Eastleach Tourville, 1,574 A. F., 877 A. P. ...	2,451
„	Kemerton, 36 yl. ...	*1,260
„	Quinton, 39¼ yl. ...	*1,372
1773	Bourton on the Water ...	
„	Beckford...	2,500
„	Longmarston, 43 yl. ...	1,505
1774	Oxenton	1,000
„	Staunton...	700
1775	Addlestrop	926
„	Claydon, all F.	1,081
„	Todenham, 32 yl. F. ...	*960
1776	Dorsington, 40 yl. ...	900
1777	Condicote, 26 yl. ...	*910
„	Duntisborne Abbots ...	
	Carried forward ...	53,706

Date.	Enclosure.	Area enclosed.
	Brought forward ...	53,706
1777	Shirburne and Windrush	
1778	Chapel Honeyburn, 32 yl.	*1,120
„	Frampton and Hayley...	1,500
„	Leckhampton and Cheltenham	
„	Naunton, 53 yl.... ...	*1,855
„	Siddington St. Peter and St. Mary	534
1779	Ablington	1,000
„	Buckland	2,000
„	Clifford Chambers ...	400
„	Mayseyhampton ...	1,600
1780	Salperton	1,354
„	Shennington, 1,500 A. F.	*1,800
1782	Eastrington	2,500
„	Winstow (Winstone) ...	770
1786	Oddington	1,000
1789	Lower Swell	
1792	Broadwell	
„	Rodmarton and Coates...	
„	Shipton, Whittington and Dowdeswell	
„	Turkdean	
1793	Aldsworth	
„	Marsmore	1,800
1794	Little Compton	
„	Corse	
„	Elmore Brockworth and North Cerney... ...	
„	Longborough	1,453
„	Old Sodbury and Little Sodbury	800
1795	Cold Aston	1,600
„	Hasfield	
„	Trinley	
1796	Awre	
„	Barnwood, Matson, Wotton	
1797	Ashelworth	
„	Coln St. Dennis... ...	
„	Horton	611
1798	Guiting Power	
1799	Berrington, Broad Campden and Westington...	
„	Kempsford and Dryffield	
1800	Welford	
„	Arlington	
1801	Cheltenham	
„	Down Ampney, Lutton, Eisey	1,242
„	Slimbridge, Cam and Coaley...	
		78,645

GLOUCESTER (*continued*).

Date.	Enclosure.	Area enclosed.
1802	Churcham	
1803	Chedworth and Compton Abdale...	6,200
„	Staverton with Bodding- ton	
„	Beverstone	2,200
1804	Sutton	1,120
„	Temple Guiting... ...	
„	Broyden	
1805	Tredington	
1806	Gotherington	
„	Norton	
1807	Downhatherley	
„	Pannington	
„	Stanley Pontlarge ...	
„	Alderton...	
1808	South Cerney	
„	Deerhurst and Lye ...	
„	Tewkesbury	
1809	Alvington	
„	Stanway	
1811	Fiddington	
1812	Aston upon Carrant and Pamington Home- downs	
„	Greet and Sudely (in Winchcomb parish)...	
„	Haresfield	
„	Longney	
„	Pebworth (with old enclosures)	2,000
„	Wormington	
1813	Ebrington and Hitcoat...	
„	Frampton upon Severn and Slimbridge ...	
„	Great Rissington ...	1,600
„	Withington	
1814	Hempstead, Barnwood and Upton St. Law- rence	*200
„	Sevenhampton	
„	Winchcomb	
1815	Miserden...	
1818	Hawkesbury	
„	Morton Vallance and Standish	
1819	Bitton 70 A. F., 190 A. P.	260
1821	Bourton on the Hill and Moreton in the Marsh	3,000
1829	Didmarton and Oldbury on the Hill	
	Carried forward ...	16,580

Date.	Enclosure.	Area enclosed.
	Brought forward ...	16,580
1830	Cheltenham	430
„	Stanley St. Leonards and Eastington	170
1832	Thornbury	514
1833	Elkstone	280
1834	Duntsbourne Rouse ...	496
1838	Quedgley	90
„	Wickwar, Cromhall and Tortworth 90 A. F., 600 A. P.	690
1839	Fretherne and Saul 380 A. F., 106 A. M. & P.	486
„	Berkeley	700
1841	Olveston	180
		20,616

Enclosed under the General Enclosure Act, 1845.

Date of Act.	Date of Award.	Parish.	Area.
*	1851	Tibberton ...	222
*	1852	Westbury on Severn	855
1851	1853	Marshfield ...	290
1850	1854	Weston Subedge ...	879
1855	1862	Dymock	208
1864	1867	Sandhurst, Norton and Wotton ...	506
1865	1869	Stinchcombe ...	205
1866	1871	Minsterworth ...	400
„	1876	Coaley	154
„	„	Cam	166
1895	1899	Upton St. Leonards	534
			4,419

	Acres.
Before 1802 ...	78,645
1802–1845 ...	20,616
After 1845 ...	4,419

HAMPSHIRE.

Date.	Enclosure.	Area enclosed.
1740	Andover	
1741	Chawton, 7 F.'s and the Common	
1743	Dunmer, 1260 A. F., 500 A. P.	1,760
1749	East Woodhay and Hollington, 1,000 A. F., 300 A. P.	1,300
1757	Barton Stacey, 1807 A. F., 678 A. P. ...	2,507
„	Earlstone	488
1759	Bishop's Waltham ...	205
1760	Folkesworth	510
„	Fletton	
1774	Abbott's Ann	1,259
1778	Gratley	
1780	Leckford Abbots ...	
1781	Highclere (or Burghclere)	
1783	Kingsomborn	1,890
„	Andevor	
1785	Upper Clatford	
1786	Basingstoke	
„	Upper Wallop, Harsbourn Pryors and Tuffton	
1788	Headbourn Worthy ...	1,400
1789	Broughton	2,700
„	Odiham, Northwarnborough, Hillside, Rye and Stapely	
1790	Dibden	
1792	Monk Sherburne ...	700
„	Shipton	
1794	Crawley and Bishop's Sutton...	
„	Houghton	
„	Quarley...	
„	Upton Gray	
1796	Basing and Mapplederwell	
„	Mitchelmarsh, Braishfield and Awbridge...	
„	Nether Wallop	
1797	Whitchurch	
1798	Welstead and Bentworth	400
„	Rockbourne and Wichbury	
1799	Easton	
		15,459

Date.	Enclosure.	Area enclosed.
1802	West Aston and Middleton	750
1803	Kilmiston	
1804	Romsey Extra	
1805	New Alresford, 326 A.F., 84 A. P.	410
1806	Monxton...	600
1807	Ringwood	
1808	Porchester	1,050
1810	Eling and Fawley ...	
1812	Charlton, Catherington, Clanfield, Blendworth and Idsworth ...	2,500
„	Ovington	
„	Wimmering, Widley Cosham, and Hilsea	800
„	Weyhill and Appleshaw	680
1813	Ecchinswell	500
1817	Harbridge	
„	Portsea	170
1820	Preston Candover and Nutley	1,800
1822	Ellingham and Ilsley ...	
1825	Christchurch and Milton	
1827	Tangley, 286 A. F., 10 A. P.	296
1829	Sherborne St. John ...	1,000
1842	Kingsclere	2,300
		12,856

Enclosed under the General Enclosure Act, 1845.

Date of Act.	Date of Award.	Parish.	Area.
*	1852	Chale	126
1849	1857	Binsted	990
1856	1859	Niton (Isle of Wight)	449
1861	1866	(Easton common fields) Freshwater	37
			1,512

		Acres.
Before 1802	...	15,459
1802–1845	...	12,856
After 1845	...	1,512

HEREFORD.

Date.	Enclosure.	Area enclosed.
1772	Wigmore, 600 A. F., 80 A. P.	680
1795	Marcle Wolton and Kinaston	1,000
1796	Tarrington	450
1799	Yarkhill, Weston Beggard, Dormington w. Bartestree, Stoke Edith with Westhide	1,380
,,	Leintwardine and Burrington	
1801	Frome, Much Cowarne and Evisbeach, 250 A. F., 160 A. M. ...	410
		3,920

Date.	Enclosure.	Area enclosed.
	Brought forward ...	2,900
1811	Eardisland	
,,	Kingston...	270
1813	Clehonger	
,,	Much Cowarn	
,,	Stretton, Grandsome and Bishops Frome ...	
,,	Eastnor, 180 A. P. ...	*220
,,	Ledbury, 50 A. F., 90 A. P....	140
1814	Norton Canon	
,,	Aymestrey and Kingsland	340
,,	Puttenham	
		3,870

Date.	Enclosure.	Area enclosed.
1802	Bodenham	2,000
1807	Byford	
,,	Marden, Sutton and Withington	
1809	Bredwardine and Dorston	
,,	Bishopston and Mancell Lacy	
,,	Mordiford	
,,	Shobden, Aynestry and Lingen	900
1810	Steepleton	
,,	Wigmore...	
1811	Allesmore	
	Carried forward ...	2,900

Enclosed under the General Enclosure Act, 1845.

Date of Act.	Date of Award.	Parish.	Area.
*	1854	Bosbury	105
*	1856	Ullingswick ...	260
1858	1862	(Lyde Fields) Pipe and Lyde ...	13
			378

		Acres.
Before 1802	...	3,920
1802–1845	...	3,870
After 1845	...	378

HERTFORD.

Date.	Enclosure.	Area enclosed.
1766	Hexton, 1,527 A. F. ...	*2,000
,,	Walsworth (Hitchin par.)	1,000
1768	Lilley and Offley ...	
1776	Ickleford...	
1795	Kelshall (with old enclosures)	2,233
1796	Norton	1,850
1797	King's Walden	500
,,	Tring	
,,	Weston	1,100
1798	Kensworth	1,200
1799	Cheshunt, 1,555 A. F., 1186 A. P.	2,741
	Carried forward ...	12,624

Date.	Enclosure.	Area enclosed.
	Brought forward ...	12,624
1799	St. John and All Saints, Hertford	
1801	Aldenham	500
,,	Barkaway and Reed ...	7,000
,,	Hertingfordbury ...	400
		20,524
1802	Hinxworth	1,264
1806	Cottered	
1807	Offley	
1809	Barley	1,700
	Carried forward ...	2,964

HERTFORD—*continued.*

Date.	Enclosure.	Area enclosed.
	Brought forward ...	2,964
1810	Codicate, Welwyn and Knebworth	
1811	Pirton	
,,	Wymondby and Ippolitts	
1812	Braughing	1,300
1813	Westmill...	400
1814	Great Hormead	900
1820	Bishop's Stortford ...	300
1826	Anstey	1,200
1830	Standon	1,400
		8,464

Enclosed under the General Enclosure Act, 1845.

Date of Act.	Date of Award.	Parish.	Area.
*	1850	Walkern	540
*	1852	Bengeo, Sacombe and Stapleford...	410
*	1853	Great and Little Munden ...	860
*	,,	Buckland	795
*	1854	Stevenage ...	556
		Carried forward ...	3,161

Date of Act.	Date of Award.	Parish.	Area.
		Brought forward ...	3,161
1852	1855	Watford Field ...	70
*	,,	Hoddesden ...	860
*	1856	Widford	320
1853	1858	Wormley	232
1858	,,	Aston, Bennington, and Little Munden ...	1,280
*	1859	Little Hadham ...	214
1857	1863	Ashwell	2,474
*	1864	Little Hormead and Layston... ...	450
1862	1867	Datchworth and Knebworth ...	161
1866	1869	Throcking... ...	108
1863	,,	Albury	305
1866	,,	Aspedon	376
		Layston and Widdial	764
			10,775

		Acres.
Before 1802	...	20,524
1802–1845	...	8,464
After 1845	...	10,775

HUNTINGDON.

Date.	Enclosure.	Area enclosed.
1727	Overton Longville and Botolph's Bridge ...	
1766	Laighton Bromeswold ...	1,515
1767	Yaxley	
1769	Stoneley	1,000
1770	St. Noets	300
1771	Hartford...	1,400
1772	Brampton	2,500
,,	King's Ripton	1,100
,,	Wolley	1,000
1773	Houghton cum Witton...	2,500
,,	Little Stukely	
1774	Ellington	1,500
,,	Easton	
,,	Graffham	
1775	Spaldwick with Upthorpe	
1779	Elton	3,000
1780	Barham	800
,,	Little Catworth... ...	
1786	Ravely	2,000
1794	Broughton	1,600
,,	Winwick...	1,660
	Carried forward ...	21,875

Date.	Enclosure.	Area enclosed.
	Brought forward ...	21,875
1795	Great Catworth... ...	2,000
,,	Wornditch	700
,,	Warboys...	4,300
1796	Woodhurst, Somersham, and Pidley with Fenton, 2,625 A. P. ...	*3,000
1797	Diddington	1,100
,,	Eynesbury	2,000
,,	Southoe	1,100
1799	Molesworth	1,000
1800	Bythorn	1,200
,,	Holywell and Needingworth	3,000
,,	Offord Cluny	1,100
1801	Covington	850
,,	Hemingford Grey and Abbotts	3,000
,,	Old Hurst	1,000
,,	St. Ives	1,400
,,	Stanground and Farcet...	1,522
		50,147

HUNTINGDON—*continued.*

Date.	Enclosure.	Area enclosed.
1802	Denton	1,000
,,	Fenstanton	2,200
1803	Godmanchester	4,600
1804	Brington (with old enclosures)	1,250
1804	Saltree	2,700
,,	Great Staughton ...	900
1805	Cherry Orton, Waterville and Alwalton... ...	
,,	Stilton	1,200
1806	Offord Darcy	1,000
1807	Stibbington cum Wandesford and Sibson ...	565
,,	Great Staughton and Graffham	2,000
1808	Swineshead	900
,,	Waresley and Gamlingay (with old enclosures)	2,000
1809	Glatton with Holme ...	1,300
,,	Woodstone	500
1811	Great Paxton and Toseland	2,100
1812	Little Paxton	720
,,	Upton	900
1813	Bluntisham w. Earith and Colne	3,000
,,	Buckdon...	1,900
	Carried forward ...	30,735

Date.	Enclosure.	Area enclosed.
	Brought forward ...	30,735
1813	Stukely	2,000
1819	Yelling, whole year lands	1,800
1830	Wistow	1,300
1836	Abbotsley	
1843	Great Gransden... ...	3,000
1844	Bury	299
,,	Ramsey	230
		39,364

Enclosed under the General Enclosure Act, 1845.

Date of Act.	Date of Award.	Parish.	Area.
*	1852	Keystone	520
1848	1853	Upwood and Ramsey	1,600
1864	1869	Great Gidding ...	1,735
			3,855

		Acres.
Before 1802	...	50,147
1802–1845	...	39,364
After 1845	...	3,855

LEICESTER.

Date.	Enclosure.	Area enclosed.
1730	Horninghole	916
1734	Little and Great Cleybrooke	430
1744	Langton	
1749	Norton juxta Twicross...	1,744
1752	Narborow, 30 yl. ...	*1,050
1755	Knighton, 48 yl. ...	*1,680
1757	Wimeswould ...	*1,440
1758	Great Glen, 32½yl. ...	1,000
1759	Breedon	1,336
,,	Belgrave, 34 yl.... ...	1,000
,,	Desford and Peckleton...	1,010
,,	Evington and Stoughton	1,000
,,	Hoton	1,100
,,	Loughborough, 6 F.'s and P.	
,,	Oadby, 71 yl.	1,800
	Carried forward ...	15,506

Date.	Enclosure.	Area enclosed.
	Brought forward ...	15,506
1759	Sileby	2,200
1760	Barrow upon Soar ...	2,250
,,	Frisby upon the Wreak..	1,500
,,	Hoby	1,000
,,	Hinckly	2,000
,,	Melton Mowbray ...	2,000
,,	Somerby...	1,400
,,	Seagrave	
1761	Ashfordby	1,800
,,	Ansty	1,100
,,	Abkettleby	900
,,	Rearsby	1,600
1762	Belgrave and Barkby ...	1,600
,,	Hungerton	900
,,	Quorndon	1,020
1764	Billesden	2,500
,,	Nether Broughton ...	900
	Carried forward ...	40,176

LEICESTER—*continued.*

Date.	Enclosure.	Area enclosed.
	Brought forward ...	40,176
1764	Husband's Bosworth, 96 yl.	4,000
,,	St. Margaret's, Leicester, 34 yl.	*1,190
,,	Sharnford, 48¾ yl. ...	1,400
,,	Stoney Stanton, 46¼ yl.	1,400
,,	Wartnaby	700
,,	Whetston, 49½ yl. ...	*1,733
,,	Great Wigstone... ...	
1765	Burton Overy	1,600
,,	Grimston	1,000
,,	Houghton-on-the-Hill ...	1,800
,,	North Kilworth, 80 yl....	1,800
,,	Scalford	2,000
1766	Braunston	1,500
,,	Blaby, 38¼ yl.	1,200
,,	Croxton	2,100
,,	Countesthorpe, 38 yl. ...	1,400
,,	Lubenham, 31 yl. ...	960
,,	Ratcliffe Culey	560
,,	Waltham in the Wolds...	2,000
1767	Aileston	1,200
,,	Cosby, 52½ yl.	*1,837
1768	Ashby de la Zouch ...	1,040
,,	Little Sheepey, 24 yl. ...	500
1769	Eaton, 97½ yl.	1,800
,,	Fleckney, 47¼ yl. ...	*1,654
,,	Markfield	380
,,	Shackston, 28 yl. ...	*980
,,	Thurlstone, 23½ yl. ...	750
1770	Bottesford, Eastthorpe and Normanton, 203¾ oxgangs	4,300
,,	Foxton	1,500
,,	Halloughton	3,000
,,	Norton, 25 yl.	665
,,	Ratby, all F.	850
,,	Ravenstone	250
,,	Saddington	1,500
1771	Appleby	1,000
,,	Kirkby Mallory... ...	780
,,	Keyham (Rothley P.) ...	900
,,	Kilby and Newton Harcourt, 78 yl.	2,000
,,	Sproxton, 49 yl. ...	2,000
,,	Saltby, 54 yl.	2,400
1772	Gumley	1,145
,,	Skeffington	1,200
,,	Stapleford	390
1773	Knaptoft, 48 yl.... ...	1,050
1774	Hucklescote and Donnington on the Heath	500
	Carried forward ...	104,190

Date.	Enclosure.	Area enclosed.
	Brought forward ..	104,190
1774	Ratcliffe upon Wreak, 26 yl.	800
1776	Bruntingthorpe, 44 yl....	1,200
,,	Great Bowden, 88 yl. ...	2,600
1777	Gilmorton, 44½ yl. ...	2,200
,,	Shepshead	2,000
,,	Syston and Barkly ...	1,600
,,	Wykeham and Candwell, 26½ yl....	750
1778	Earl Shilton	1,500
,,	Kimcoate and Knaptoft, 84 yl.	2,600
,,	Sapcote	1,300
,,	Long Whatton	800
,,	Castle Donington, 1400 A. F., 290 A. M., 610 A. P.	2,300
,,	Kegworth	2,000
1779	Barkby	1,800
,,	Croft	850
,,	Claxton or Long Clawson, 169 oxgangs ...	*3,380
,,	Knight Thorpe	450
,,	Leire, 31½ yl.	370
,,	Stanton under Barden...	600
,,	Kibworth and Smeeton Westerby, 148 yl. ...	3,900
1780	Stonesby...	1,100
,,	Swinford...	1,400
1781	Cropston...	360
,,	Mountsorrell, 300 A.F....	*450
,,	Rothley	1,200
1782	Orton on the Hill ...	1,000
1783	Tugby	1,150
1785	Osgathorpe	200
1786	Bitteswell	1,600
1788	Humberstone	1,400
,,	Mousley	1,100
1789	Grooby	500
,,	Hemmington	1,000
,,	Harston	*800
,,	Thrussington, 47 yl. ...	*1,645
1790	Harby	
,,	Lutterworth, 69 yl. ...	1,400
1791	East and West Langton, &c., 152 yl.	*5,320
1792	Redmile	
,,	Strathern	
,,	Walton in the Wolds, 52½ yl....	1,500
1793	Queneborough	2,200
,,	Slawston...	1,400
	Carried forward ...	163,915

LEICESTER—*continued*.

Date.	Enclosure.	Area enclosed.
	Brought forward ..	163,915
1794	Arnesby	1,200
,,	Barseby and South Croxton, 82 yl.	*2,870
,,	Diseworth	1,630
,,	Sutton Cheney	
,,	Thornton and Bagworth	920
1796	Dunton Bassett... ...	750
,,	Twyford	900
,,	Walcott	1,000
1797	Knipton	
1798	Swithland	350
,,	Thurcaston	745
1799	Nether Seal	*1,000
		175,280

Date.	Enclosure.	Area enclosed.
1802	Breedon on the Hill ...	1,200
1803	Sibson	740
,,	Thringstone and Pegg's Green	*100
	Carried forward ...	2,040

Date.	Enclosure.	Area enclosed.
	Brought forward ...	2,040
1804	Bringhurst, Great Easten and Drayton	3,400
,,	Leicester, 490 A.F., 116 A.M.	606
1806	Higham (to confirm Inclosure made in 1682)	
1809	Glenfield	700
1810	Great Sheepey	
,,	Newbold Verdon and Newbold Heath, little F.	900
1812	Belton	400
1823	Congerston	900
1825	Glooston and Cranoe ...	950
1842	Hedbourn	
		9,896

	Acres.
Before 1802 ...	175,280
1802–1845 ...	9,896

LINCOLN.

Date.	Enclosure.	Area enclosed.
1731	Biscathorpe ...	
1734	Woollesthorpe, 12 oxgangs	240
1736	Stallingborough, 2166 A. F., 776 M., 700 A. P.	3,642
1751	Dunsly (Dunsby) ...	*1,500
1752	Wytham on the Hill, one F....	1,370
1754	Normanton, 150 oxgangs	*3,000
1757	Baumber, or Banburgh	2,048
,,	Stragglethorpe, F. ...	287
1758	Hareby	451
1759	Coleby	
,,	Fillingham, 2,000 A. F., 800 A. P.	2,800
,,	Harmston, 1,734 A. F. & M., 794 A. P. ...	2,528
1762	Barrowby	2,000
,,	Wintringham	
1763	Glentham, 1800 A. F., 770 A. P.	2,570
,,	Pilham	525
,,	Wellingore	3,100
1764	Fotherby	1,269
	Carried forward ...	27,330

Date.	Enclosure.	Area enclosed.
	Brought forward ...	27,330
1764	Heckington	4,000
,,	Horbling...	2,600
,,	Haughton in the Marsh	1,500
,,	Stainton in the Hole (with old enclosures)	1,900
,,	Scarby	1,200
1765	Aukborough	2,000
,,	Branston, 2,000 A. F. ...	*2,500
,,	Kettlethorpe, 840 A. F., 835 A. P.	1,635
,,	N. and S. Cockerington	1,390
,,	Keelby and Stallingbrough	2,000
,,	Newton and Kettle-. thorpe, 970 A. F., 400 A. P.	1,370
,,	Rothwell...	2,700
,,	Tetford	
1766	Bourn	2,450
,,	Barnelby on the Wolds	
,,	Bickar	2,300
,,	Cosby	1,527
,,	Grimoldby	1,700
	Carried forward ...	60,102

LINCOLN—*continued.*

Date.	Enclosure.	Area enclosed.
	Brought forward ...	60,102
1766	Keddington	400
,,	Kettlethorp	645
,,	Scothorne and Sudbrooke	2,800
1767	East Barkwith	1,200
,,	Donnington	3,100
,,	Newton	1,000
,,	Scamblesby	2,100
,,	Wootton	3,000
1768	Billingborough and Birthorpe	2,700
,,	Morton	4,400
,,	Threckingham	500
,,	Toynton Supra	1,100
,,	Willoughton	2,600
1769	Atterby, Smitterby and Waddingham	3,000
,,	Barnolby le Beck ...	1,200
,,	Beckenham and Sutton	
,,	Claypole	
,,	North Hickham	
,,	Ingham	2,000
,,	Sudbrooke (Ancaster P.)	1,200
,,	South Willingham ...	1,800
,,	Waltham	2,250
1770	Benniworth	2,292
,,	Great Carlton	2,000
,,	Matton	1,180
,,	Navenby	2,800
,,	Scawby	2,500
,,	Waddington, 195 oxgangs	3,500
,,	Winterton, 2,000 A. F., 360 A. M., 1,000 A. P.	3,360
,,	Westborough cum Doddington	
,,	Welton (near Louth) ...	
1771	West Ashby	3,000
,,	Boothby Graffoe ...	1,600
,,	Bishop Norton	1,700
,,	South Reston	500
1772	Hammeringham ...	1,000
,,	West Halton	
,,	Moorby and Wilksby ...	1,000
,,	Great Paunton	*3,000
,,	Middle Raisin	4,000
,,	Stainby	1,380
,,	Low Toynton	373
,,	Welton	3,000
1773	Brinkhill	600
,,	Goxhill	7,000
,,	Hemingby	2,600
,,	Hackonby	2,000
	Carried forward ...	147,482

Date.	Enclosure.	Area enclosed.
	Brought forward ...	147,482
1773	Helpringham	3,000
,,	Haltham and Roughton	2,000
,,	Horsington	1,500
,,	East Keal	900
,,	Toynton All Saints and St. Peter	1,000
,,	Thorpe on the Hill ...	1,700
,,	Whitton	1,200
,,	West Willoughby, 34 oxgangs and large common	*1,000
1774	Ibstock	1,200
,,	Ludborough	
,,	Owmby	1,600
,,	Potterhamworth ...	3,000
,,	Spridlington	2,400
,,	Timberland	2,500
,,	Wilsford	2,400
,,	West Keal	1,000
,,	Wroot	700
1775	Fulletby	2,000
,,	Quadring, 70 A. F., &c., 2,400 A. fen	2,470
1776	Asterby and Goulesby ...	2,600
,,	Gunby and North Witham	1,650
,,	North and South Killingholme	5,000
,,	Nocton	4,500
,,	Raithby, nr. Spilsby ...	600
,,	Upton, 1430 A. F., 1150 A. P.	2,580
,,	Welby, 970 A. F. ...	*1,200
,,	Nettleham	3,000
1777	Brampton	1,060
,,	Candlesby	900
,,	Hatherne	1,300
,,	Kirnington	1,800
,,	Leadenham	3,000
,,	Metheringham	5,000
,,	South Winstead	1,700
,,	South Sturton	1,500
,,	Surfleet, 1,240 A. fen., 300 A. F., &c. ...	1,540
1778	Hackthorne	2,660
,,	Ruskington	3,000
,,	Thimbleby	1,200
1779	Amcotts	1,300
,,	Brattleby	1,050
,,	Huttoft, 1,200 A. F., 670 A. P.	1,870
,,	Market Raisin	725
	Carried forward ...	229,787

LINCOLN—*continued*.

Date.	Enclosure.	Area enclosed.
	Brought forward ..	229,787
1779	Willingham	1,500
1780	Ligburn ...	1,213
1785	Donnington upon Baine	1,600
1786	Canwick	2,240
1787	Dorrington	1,800
1788	Swaby and Belleau ...	1,500
,,	North and South Rauceby	5,450
1789	Denton	2,650
,,	Normanby next Spittal	1,700
1791	Nettleton	3,600
,,	Ludford	2,400
1792	Hemswell	2,220
,,	Tealby	2,600
,,	Uffington	2,600
,,	Wood Enderby	600
,,	Welton in the Marsh ...	
1793	Allington	900
,,	Barton upon Humber ...	5,770
,,	Covenham	1,600
,,	Dunston	1,220
,,	Greetham	1,000
,,	Kirton in Lindsey ...	4,600
1794	Althorpe	380
,,	Long Bennington and Foston	3,860
,,	Bottisford and Yadlethorpe	1,750
,,	Faldingworth	2,400
,,	South Kelsey	3,200
,,	Martin	550
,,	Skillington	1,950
,,	New Sleaford and Holdingham	2,000
,,	South Witham	1,646
1795	Grantham	1,688
,,	Hagworthingham ...	800
,,	Londonthorpe	680
,,	Osmournby, Newton and Scott Willoughby ...	1,600
,,	Owmby	580
,,	Ropsley and Little Hamby	4,000
,,	Scartho	1,200
,,	Swarby	1,000
1796	Caistor	390
,,	Hibaldstowe	3,800
,,	Luddington and Garthorpe	1,200
,,	Scredington	2,800
,,	North and South Stoke	1,200
,,	Tattershall, Thorpe and Kirkby super Bane ...	
	Carried forward ..	317,224

Date.	Enclosure.	Area enclosed.
	Brought forward ..	317,224
1797	Barrow	4,700
,,	Blankney and Scopwick	3,850
,,	Greatford	850
,,	Swayfield and Corby ...	
1798	Messingham and East Butterwick	5,000
,,	Mavis Enderby	800
1800	Barholm	930
,,	Braceborough	1,110
,,	Wrawly cum Brigg ...	2,450
1801	Belchford	2,300
,,	Little Bytham and Ormby	1,500
,,	West Deeping and Tallington	2,000
,,	South Ferriby	1,500
,,	East Halton	2,500
,,	Langtoft and Baston ...	2,100
,,	Sotby	1,000
,,	Scremby	550
,,	Ashby	1,830
,,	Louth	1,854
		354,048
1802	Kelby, Aiseby and Oseby	2,500
,,	Thurlby, 1,100 A. F., 1,100 A. fen	2,200
,,	Coningsby	1,750
,,	Saxelby	1,200
1803	Burton and West Halton	1,400
,,	Boultham	636
,,	Kirkby cum Osgodby ...	1,350
,,	Rippingale and Kirkby Underwood, 2,150 A. F., 2,032 A. fen ...	4,182
,,	West Rasen	1,240
,,	Salesby with Thoresthorpe	680
,,	Castle Bytham	2,500
,,	Horncastle	1,000
,,	Lincoln	1,500
,,	Stowe, Sturton and Bransly	2,000
1804	Carlby and Aunby ...	*1,220
,,	Fulbeck	1,300
,,	Great and Little Gonerby and Manthorpe ...	4,000
,,	Hogsthorpe and Mumby cum Chapel	2,590
,,	Skellingthorpe	2,000
1805	Anderby	730
	Carried forward ...	35,978

LINCOLN—*continued.*

Date.	Enclosure.	Area enclosed.
	Brought forward	... 35,978
1805	Colsterworth	3,500
,,	Mareham on the Hill ...	656
,,	Mauten	
,,	Swallow	2,550
1806	Easton	1,000
,,	East Kirkby	375
,,	Market Deeping and Deeping St. James ...	2,000
1807	Crosby	
,,	Ashby de la Laund ...	1,500
,,	Waith	
,,	Yarburgh	900
1808	Scotter	4,500
1809	Croxton	1,300
,,	Friskeney	
1810	Boston (with old enclosures)	1,338
,,	Fishtoft, 2,795 A. F., and old enclosure, 95 A. P.	2,890
,,	Sibsey	
,,	Withcall	2,700
,,	Leverton, 410 A. F. and M., 135 A. P.	545
,,	Leake	
1811	Ashby juxta Partney ...	500
,,	Cabourne	2,700
,,	Little Ponton (with old enclosures)	1,980
,,	Thrusthorpe and Hannah cum Hagnaby ...	540
1813	Crowle	
,,	Haburgh	2,500
,,	North Kelsey	3,000
,,	Witham on the Hill ...	2,400
1814	Thorseway	2,600
1815	Benington	
	Carried forward	... 77,952

Date.	Enclosure.	Area enclosed.
	Brought forward	... 77,952
1815	Grasby	500
,,	Manby	500
1817	Fulstrow	1,900
1818	Skirbeck	
,,	Welsthorpe	800
,,	Ulceby with FotheringTon	1,026
1819	Alvingham	1,300
,,	Cumberworth	580
,,	Firsby	
1824	Ulceby	3,500
1825	Appleby	950
1826	Farlesthorpe	390
1827	Great Grimsby	1,000
1842	Clee	
		90,398

Enclosed under the General Inclosure Act, 1845.

Date of Act.	Date of Award.	Parish.	Area.
1855	1858	North Cotes ...	520

LINCOLN AND RUTLAND.

1871	1875	Stamford and Tinwell, total area 1,621 A., in Lincoln	811
			1,331

	Acres.
Before 1802 ...	354,048
1802–1845 ...	90,398
After 1845 ...	1,331

MIDDLESEX.

Date.	Enclosure.	Area enclosed.
1774	Laleham	
1780	Ickenham	
1789	Stanwell	3,000
1795	Hillingdon and Cowley, 3 F's.	
1799	Teddington	883
1800	Edmonton	1,231
	Carried forward	... 5,114

Date.	Enclosure.	Area enclosed.
	Brought forward ...	5,114
1800	Hanworth, Feltham and Sunbury, 1,500 A. F., 1,700 A. P.	3,200
1801	Enfield	3,540
		11,854

APPENDIX B.

MIDDLESEX—*continued.*

Date.	Enclosure.	Area enclosed.		Date.	Enclosure.	Area enclosed.
1803	Harrow				Brought forward ...	11,431
1804	Ruislip			1819	Harlington	820
1805	Harmendsworth ...	1,100		1824	West Drayton	
1809	Echelford or Ashford ...	1,200		1825	Northolt	
„	Hayes	2,000				
1811	Hampton					12,251
1812	Hillingdon	1,400				
1813	Greenford	640			*Enclosed under the General Enclosure*	
„	Hanwell	350			*Act,* 1845.	
„	Great Stanmore, all F.	216				
„	East Bedfont	1,100				
„	Isleworth, Heston and					
	Twickenham	2,470				
1815	Willesden	560				
1818	Cranford	395				

Date of Act.	Date of Award.	Parish.	Area.
1848	1851	Littleton	625

	Acres.
Before 1802 ...	11,854
1802–1845 ...	12,251
After 1845 ...	625

Carried forward ... 11,431

MONMOUTH.

Date.	Enclosure.	Area enclosed.
1776	Ifton	780

Enclosed under the General Enclosure Act, 1845.

Date of Act.	Date of Award.	Parish.	Area.
1852	1854	Undy	128
„	„	Caldicot	243

Carried forward ... 471

Date of Act.	Date of Award.	Parish.	Area.
		Brought forward ...	471
1858	1859	Magor	142

513

	Acres.
Before 1802 ...	780
After 1845 ...	513

1,293

NORFOLK.

Date.	Enclosure.	Area enclosed.		Date.	Enclosure.	Area enclosed.
1755	Brancaster	2,350			Brought forward ...	16,420
„	Swanton, Morley and			1774	Beetley, Great Bittering	
	Worthing	1,400			and Grassenhall ...	1,130
1760	Litcham	600		„	Barton Bendish	4,370
1762	Snettisham (half year			„	Tottington, 1,710 A. F.,	
	inclosures)	5,000			1,300 A. P.	3,010
1766	Carlton Forehoe and			„	Weeting	4,450
	Kimberley			1777	Little Cressingham, 300	
1767	Sherborn	1,600			A. F., 467 A. P. ...	767
1769	Hilborowe, 2,600 In-			„	Carlton Rode	3,000
	fields and Outfields ...	3,020		1779	Dersingham	2,000
1772	Fineham	2,450		„	Grimston	4,000
„	Roudham			1780	Foulden	3,000

| Carried forward ... 16,420 | | | | Carried forward ... 42,147 |

NORFOLK—*continued.*

Date.	Enclosure.	Area enclosed.
	Brought forward ...	42,147
1780	Heatcham	4,000
,,	Salthouse and Kelling ...	1,490
,,	Tottenhill and West Briggs	1,400
1781	Great Ringstead ...	3,000
1785	Ashill, 900 A. F., 1,000 A. P.	1,900
1786	Tichwell	
1793	Marham	3,700
,,	Stiffkey and Morston ...	
1794	Little Dunham, 1,300 A. F., 400 A. P. ...	1,700
,,	Shouldham and Garboise Thorpe	5,570
,,	Thornham	
1795	Bintry and Twyford ...	
,,	Great Hockham ...	
,,	East Lexham and Great Dunham	
,,	Sedgeford	
1796	Northwold	
,,	Reymerstone, Letton, Cranworth and South Barrow	
,,	Sherington	
1797	Acle	
,,	Saham Toney	
1798	Hethersett	
1799	North Ellingham ...	
,,	Hovingham and Marsham, 297 A. F., 1,400 A. P.	1,697
,,	Keninghall	
,,	Ransworth	
,,	Shropham	
,,	Upton and Fishley ...	
1800	Cawston	
,,	Forsford, Horsham and Newton St. Faith's ...	
,,	Ovington	
,,	Ludham	
1801	Alburgh and Wortwell ...	
,,	Blofield and Hembling-ton	
,,	Boughton	
,,	Great and Little Cres-singham	
,,	East Harling	
,,	Happisburgh and Les-singham	
,,	Holme Hale and West Bradenham	3,900
	Carried forward ...	70,504

Date.	Enclosure.	Area enclosed.
	Brought forward ...	70,504
1801	Mattishall	1,100
,,	Thorpe Abbotts	
,,	Walton and Carbrooke ...	
,,	Burgh and Billockby ...	
,,	Downham Market, Wim-bocham and Bexwell ...	
,,	Hickling	
,,	Potter Higham	300
,,	South Walsham	
		71,904
1802	Ellingham, Broome, Kirby Cane and Geldestone	
,,	Filby	
,,	Gooderstone	3,000
,,	East Tuddenham ...	
,,	Catfield and Sutton ...	
,,	Runham	
1803	Aslacton	
,,	Whitwell and Hackford	225
1804	Brigham	
,,	Crimplesham	2,000
,,	Sporle and Palgrave ...	
,,	Thetford	
,,	Waborne	
1805	Brunstead	
,,	Briningham, Stody and Brinton	
,,	Great and Little Fran-sham and North Pick-enham	4,000
,,	West Newton	
,,	Palling	
,,	Scoulton	
,,	Winterton, East and West Somerton ...	
,,	Methwold	7,375
1806	Hackford	850
,,	Weasenham and Welling-ham	
,,	Griston	
,,	Moundford	1,000
,,	Little Snoring	
,,	Sparham and Billingford	
,,	Wymondham	
,,	Wormegay	
1807	Stalham	
,,	Martham	
	Carried forward ...	18,450

NORFOLK—*continued*.

Date.	Enclosure.	Area enclosed.	Date.	Enclosure.	Area enclosed.
	Brought forward ...	18,450		Brought forward ...	19,950
1807	Repps with Bastwick and Eccles near the Sea		1811	Scarning, Hoe, Worthing and Dillington ...	
„	Holt and Letheringsett		1812	Earsham, Ditchingham and Edenham ...	
„	Pentney		„	Honingham	160
1808	Cley next the Sea ...		„	Witton Bacton, Edingthorpe and Paston ...	
„	Claxton and Rockland...		„	Attleburgh	
„	Fulmodeston, Stibbard and Ryburgh... ...		„	Congham c. Brandon Parva or Little Brand	
„	Neatishead		„	Caston	
„	Twetshall		„	Deopham	
„	North Walsham and Felmingham		„	Hempstead	
„	Bawdswell and Ling ...		„	Horsey	
„	Bodham		„	Rockland	
„	Gaywood and Mintlyn...		„	Mysingset Stanfield and Horningtoft	
„	Wicklewood	1,500	„	Barford	
„	Walsingham and Houghton next Walsingham		1813	Croxton	
1809	Barton Turf		„	Morley	
„	Bunwell		„	Seething, Kirkstead, Mundham and Sisland	
„	North Creake		„	Tasburgh	
„	Forncett...		„	Wramplingham... ...	
„	Sherringham		„	Woodton...	90
„	Strumpshaw and Surlingham		„	Feltwell	
„	Swanton, Abbot, Lamas and Buxton		„	Geist	
„	Thurlton, Haddiscoe and Thorpe next Haddiscoe		„	Hardingham	
1810	Gayton		„	Rollesby	
„	Hemsby		„	Stow Bedon	
„	Hardley and Langley ...		1814	Suldey	200
„	Thuxton		„	Skeyton, Burgh next Aylesham and Tottington	
„	Great Plumstead and Postwick		„	Wendling	
„	Thorne		„	East Bradenham ...	
„	Yaxham, Westfield, Whinbergh and Garvestone		„	Foxley	
1811	Bathley		„	Hockwold cum Wilton...	
„	Drayton, Banburgh and Hellesden		„	Middleton	
„	Gressenthall and Great Bittering		1815	Hindringham	
„	Mattishall Bergh ...		„	Langham	
„	Great Snoring		„	Necton	
„	Welborne		„	South Runcton and Holme...	
„	Barnham Broome and Bickerstone		„	Smallburgh	
„	Fundenhall and Ashwelthorpe...		„	Stoke, Wretton, Wereham and Winnold ...	
			„	Thompson	
			1816	Larling	
			1817	Hempnall	
			1818	Great Melton	
	Carried forward ...	19,950		Carried forward ...	20,400

NORFOLK—*continued.*

Date.	Enclosure.	Area enclosed.
	Brought forward	20,400
1818	East Rudham, West Rainton and Helhoughton	
1820	Blo' Norton	
,,	Blakeney, Wiverton and Glandford	
,,	Holme next the Sea	
,,	Tibenham and Moulton	
1821	Little Barningham and Calthorpe	*60
1825	Hockering and Morton	400
,,	Weston	
1827	Thursford and Kettlestone	
1828	Belaugh, Scottow, Little Hautbois and Hoveton St. Peter	
1829	North Elmham	
,,	Gunthorpe	90
,,	Sculthorpe	
1836	West Runeton	
1837	Ashby and Hellington	
1839	West Beckham and Alby	
1840	Garboldisham, 226 A. F., 10 A. M., 680 A. P.	916
,,	Freethorpe, Limpenhoe and Reedham	100
	Carried forward	21,966

Date.	Enclosure.	Area enclosed.
	Brought forward	21,966
1841	Bodingham	
,,	Elsing	
1842	Ormesby and Scratby	
		21,966

Enclosed under the General Enclosure Act, 1845.

Date of Act.	Date of Award.	Parish.	Area.
*	1851	Feltwell	860
1849	1852	Brandiston, Haverland and Swannington	490
*	1854	Heacham	213
1857	1860	Cossey	810
1859	1863	Docking	4,640
1863	1869	Swaffham	5,160
			12,173

		Acres.
Before 1802		71,904
1802–1845		21,966
After 1845		12,173

NORTHAMPTON.

Date.	Enclosure.	Area enclosed.
1727	Grafton, 4 common fields 272 A., 1 common	318
1733	Chipping Warden, 63½ yl.	1,964
1743	Great Brington	4,000
1745	Faxton, 23½ yl.	1,170
1749	Wakerley and Wittering	
1750	Nether Hoyford, Stow with Nine Churches and Bingbrooke, 39 yl. F.	*1,365
1751	Farthingstone, 47½ yl.	*1,662
1752	Drayton, 42½ yl.	*1,487
1753	Hinton, 30 yl.	*1,050
1754	Welton, 72 yl.	*2,520
1755	Norton by Daventry, 25¾ yl.	*901
1756	Boughton and Pitford, 85½ yl.	*2,993
	Carried forward	19,430

Date.	Enclosure.	Area enclosed.
	Brought forward	19,430
1758	Upper and Lower Boddington	3,000
,,	Helmdon, 70 yl.	1,550
,,	Woodford, 30½ yl.	*1,067
1759	Ecton, 103 yl.	*3,605
,,	Slapton, 38 yl.	*1,330
1760	Blakesley, 64 yl.	2,000
,,	West Farndon, 20 yl.	*700
,,	Marston St. Lawrence, 48 yl.	*1,680
,,	Sulgrave, 71 yl.	*2,485
1761	Eydon, 28 yl.	*980
,,	Morton Pinkney, 42 yl. F., 1,200 A. P.	*2,460
,,	Wappenham, 52 yl.	*1,820
1762	Towcester Wood, Burcott and Caldecott	2,000
	Carried forward	44,107

292 APPENDIX B.

NORTHAMPTON—*continued.*

Date.	Enclosure.	Area enclosed.
	Brought forward ...	44,107
1763	Woodford ...	2,000
1764	Everdon, 43¾ yl. ...	1,930
,,	Guilsborough, Coton and Nortoft 20¾ yl. ...	1,337
,,	West Hadden, 48 yl. ...	*1,680
,,	Ledgers Ashby, 32¼ yl.	*1,146
,,	Newnham, 48½ yl. ...	1,580
,,	Warksworth, 55½ yl. ...	1,700
1765	Long Buckby ...	3,800
,,	Denford	1,450
,,	Hardingstone and Cotton, 79½ yl. ...	*2,783
,,	Spratton ...	2,200
,,	Syresham, 61 yl. ...	*2,135
,,	Twywell	1,000
,,	Wellingborough, 80 yl. F.	4,000
1766	Great Doddington, 56 yl.	*1,960
,,	Hinton in the Hedges, all F.	1,330
,,	Harleston, 28½ yl. ...	*1,000
,,	Kingsthorp ...	1,743
,,	Thenford or Fenford, 33 yl. ...	750
1767	Arthingworth	1,400
,,	Cosgrave, 1700 A. F., 130 A. P.	1,830
,,	Old or Would, 49 yl. ...	2,000
,,	Great Oxendon	1,300
1769	Knuston	
,,	Middleton Cheney, upper and lower, 41 yl. ...	*1,435
1770	Denton	700
1771	Earl's Barton ...	2,400
,,	Lowick	1,150
,,	Pattishall, Eastcote, Astcote and Darlescote	2,500
,,	Slipton	560
,,	Weedon or Weston, 58½ yl. F., 1600 A. P. ...	*3,647
,,	Watford and Murcott ...	1,250
1772	Astrop, 77 yl.	*2,695
,,	Aldwinckle	2,000
,,	Charlton, 59 yl.... ...	1,000
,,	Denshager	900
,,	Moulton	2,600
,,	Thorpe Achurch ...	1,500
1773	East Hadden	1,530
,,	Irchester, Wellingborough and Great Doddington	
	Carried forward ..	112,028

Date.	Enclosure.	Area enclosed.
	Brought forward ..	112,028
1774	Duddington	800
,,	Harringworth ...	1,600
,,	Hellidon	1,500
,,	Hollowell	425
,,	Staverton ...	2,400
,,	Warmington ...	3,000
1775	Braunston	2,300
,,	Cranford, 22½ yl. ...	*787
,,	Pottersbury and Cosgrave	
,,	Scaldwell	1,000
1776	Clipston and Newbold, 84 yl.	2,900
,,	Crick	3,000
,,	Dustin	1,500
,,	Desborough ...	1,890
,,	Walgrave	1,850
,,	Weedon Beck ...	1,700
,,	Yelvertoft	2,000
,,	Yardley Hastings ...	1,630
1777	Grafton Underwood ...	1,229
,,	Holcot	1,300
,,	Killesby, 36¼ yl.... ...	2,200
,,	Mears Ashby ...	1,400
,,	Thorpe Malsor ...	600
,,	Tansor	1,300
,,	Welford	1,800
,,	Whitton, Norton and Brockhall ...	1,060
,,	Nassington, Yarwell, Apethorpe and Woodnewton	3,800
1778	Bulwick	1,400
,,	Titchmarsh ...	3,000
,,	Great Billing, 48½ yl. ...	*1,697
,,	Braybrooke ...	1,500
,,	Barby	2,200
,,	Byfield and Westrup ...	2,500
,,	Floore	1,800
,,	Harpole	1,800
,,	Isham	1,400
,,	Maidford, 28 yl.... ...	700
,,	Northampton Fields ...	840
,,	Rushden	3,500
,,	Wooton, 50 yl. ...	1,800
1779	Bugbrooke ...	1,500
,,	Badby	1,500
,,	Little Bowden, 51 yl. ...	1,350
,,	Evenly	1,200
,,	Kislingbury, 80¼ yl. ...	1,708
,,	Milton, Malsor and Collingtree, 70¾ yl.	2,000
,,	Woodend	600
	Carried forward ..	190,994

NORTHAMPTON—*continued*.

Date.	Enclosure.	Area enclosed.
	Brought forward	.. 190,994
1780	Brixworth, 102¾ yl. ...	2,700
„	East Farndon, 45 yl. ...	1,400
„	Tiffield	1,100
„	Grendon	1,600
„	Thrapstone	1,060
1781	Little Harrowden, 48½ yl.	1,500
1782	Great and Little Crexton, 28¾ yl.	1,200
„	Piddington and Hackleton	1,500
1786	Broughton ...	
1788	Wollaston, 89 yl. ...	2,760
1790	Polebrooke	1,400
1792	Aynho, 45 yl.	*1,575
„	Great and Little Weldon	2,400
1793	Orston and Thorston ...	2,200
„	Wadenhoe	675
1794	Lamport and Hanging Houghton	539
1795	St. Martin Stamford Baron...	600
„	Ravensthorpe	1,400
1796	Ufford with Ashton and Bainton	2,700
„	Whitfield	
1797	Raunds	4,700
„	Whittlebury	670
1798	Bozeat	2,268
„	Wilbarston, 60 yl. ...	1,200
1799	Queen's Norton and Duncott	1,400
„	Grasthorpe	350
1800	Barnack with Pilsgate...	2,500
„	Islip	1,300
„	Newton Bromshold ...	820
1801	Chelston cum Caldecott	1,700
„	Wilby, 29 yl.	1,000
		237,211
1802	Daventry	1,600
„	Hargrave	1,350
„	Hannington	800
„	Weston by Welland and Sutton Bassett, 70 yl.	*2,450
1803	Great Addington ...	1,100
„	Braddon	700
„	Burton Latimer... ...	3,000
„	Werrington and Walton	2,450
1804	Kettering	2,300
„	King's Sutton	1,200
1805	Cranford St. John ...	897
	Carried forward ...	17,847

Date.	Enclosure.	Area enclosed.
	Brought forward ...	17,847
1805	Thingden or Finedon ...	3,000
1806	Ashley	1,200
1807	Oundle and Ashton ...	2,600
„	Croughton, 54 yl. ...	*1,890
„	Warkton, Little Oakley and Luddingham ...	2,418
„	Weekly and Geddington	2,160
1808	Blisworth	1,500
„	Irthlingborough ...	3,500
„	Orlingbury	1,300
1809	Longthorpe (with old enclosures)	1,240
„	Rothersthorpe	1,200
„	King's Cliffe	1,100
„	Maxey with Deepingate, Northborough, Glinton w. Peakirk Elton and Kelpstone	
1811	St. John Peterborough...	
1812	Cold Higham w. Grimscote and Potcote ...	1,150
„	Rothwell (with old enclosures)	3,200
1813	Calterstock cum Glapthorn	1,500
„	Marston Trussell (with old enclosures) ...	1,200
1814	Quinton	504
1815	Cottingham cum Middleton	1,750
1817	Easton on the Hill ...	3,000
1819	Aldrington	680
„	Paulerspury with Heathencote...	2,500
1820	Eye	800
„	Naseby	*2,000
1823	Abthorpe	280
1827	Little Houghton, Brafield in the Green and Cocknoe	2,500
1829	Brackley...	1,318
„	Corby	1,035
1830	Little Addington ...	1,160
1834	Stanwick	1,275
1838	Higham Ferrers... ...	
1839	Ringstead	
1840	Stoke Bruern and Shuttlehanger	
1841	Barnack w. Pilsgate and Southorpe	
„	Collyweston	
		66,807

APPENDIX B.

NORTHAMPTON—*continued.*

Enclosed under the General Enclosure Act, 1845.

Date of Act.	Date of Award.	Parish.	Area.
1864	1867	Lutton	754
1895	1898	Castor and Ailesworth	3,500
		Carried forward ...	4,254

Date of Act.	Date of Award.	Parish.	Area.
		Brought forward ...	4,254
1901	—	Sutton	450
			4,704

	Acres.
Before 1802 ...	237,211
1802–1845 ...	66,807
After 1845 ...	4,704

NORTHUMBERLAND.

Date.	Enclosure.	Area enclosed.
1740	Gunnerton, Ingrounds 1,300 A., Out 1,000 A.	2,300
1757	West Matfen, 1,250 A. F., 50 A. P.	1,300
1776	Corbridge	5,300
1784	Elrington	757
		9,657

Date.	Enclosure.	Area enclosed.
1804	Simonburn, 40 A.F. and M., 3,000 A. P. ...	3,040
	Carried forward ...	3,040

Date.	Enclosure.	Area enclosed.
	Brought forward ...	3,040
1809	Simonburn, 300 A. F., 5,000 A. P.	5,300
1812	Ovingham	2,951
1844	Haltwhistle Common, 1,360 A., also certain lands called Rig or Dale lands	1,400
		12,691

	Acres.
Before 1802 ...	9,657
1802–1845 ...	12,691

NOTTINGHAM.

Date.	Enclosure.	Area enclosed.
1759	Barton and Clifton ...	1,500
„	Everton, 1,300 A. P. ...	*2,000
„	Staunton...	
1760	Costock or Cortlingstoke	710
„	Broughton Sulney ...	2,000
„	Coddington	1,780
„	Clifton	
„	Hawksworth	
„	Hayton	1,260
„	Nusson, 900 A. F., 860 A. M., 2,000 A. P. ...	3,760
1765	Carlton upon Trent ...	
„	Lowdham	2,500
„	Wilford	1,100
1766	Balderton	
1767	Carlton in Lindrick ...	2,492
„	Farndon	
„	Lenton and Radford ...	1,000
„	Ruddington	2,700
1768	Burton Joyce and Bulcoate	1,600
	Carried forward ...	24,402

Date.	Enclosure.	Area enclosed.
	Brought forward ...	24,402
1768	Epperstone	1,000
„	Rempstone (Rampton)...	1,230
1769	Blidworth, 200 A. F., 3,300 A. P.	3,500
„	Hucknal Torkard ...	1,200
1770	Mattersey	2,300
„	Normanton upon Soar ...	1,100
1771	North Muskham Holme and Bathley	3,000
„	Misterton	500
„	Stapleford and Brancote	1,100
1772	Laneham...	
1773	Cromwell	
1774	Finningley	7,000
„	West Redford	900
„	Sutton St. Ann's, 50½ yl.	1,200
1775	Flintham	
„	Hickling, 2,100 A. F., 800 A. P.	2,900
„	Normanton and Southwell	
	Carried forward ...	51,332

NOTTINGHAM—*continued.*

Date.	Enclosure.	Area enclosed.
	Brought forward ...	51,332
1775	Scrooby	1,350
„	Sutton cum Lound ...	4,000
1776	Beckingham	2,000
„	Clareborough and Welham	1,180
„	Sutton Bonnington, 32½ yl.	800
„	Screveton, one F. ...	350
1777	Bleasby	
„	Farnsfield	
„	Halam and Edingley ...	
„	Winthorpe	5,000
1778	Kersall	800
1779	Calverton	
1780	Scarrington and Oslacton	
1787	Cropwell Butler and Cropwell Bishop ...	
„	Ratcliffe upon Trent ...	1,500
„	Trowell, 72 oxgangs, 680 A. F., 252 A. P. ...	1,012
1789	Arnould	2,500
„	Whatton	1,700
1790	North Collingham, 740 A. F., 674 A. M., 160 A. P.	1,574
„	Cotgrave	2,365
„	Clayworth	2,000
1792	Basford, 160 A. F. and M., 1,200 A. P.	1,360
„	Lambley, 60 A. F., 600 A. P.	660
„	Syerston	500
„	Gedling, Stoke, Bardolph and Carlton	*4,300
1793	Granby and Sutton ...	
„	Willoughby on the Wolds	1,700
1795	Caunton	823
„	North Leverton and Habblesthorpe ...	1,400
„	South Leverton	1,600
„	East Stoke and Elston...	2,500
„	Upton	1,384
„	Woodborough	1,000
1796	Gateford and Shireoaks	
„	Gringley on the Hill ...	3,000
„	Snenton (? Shelton) ...	800
„	Weston	1,230
1797	Bunny	1,000
1798	Keyworth	1,500
„	Great Leke	3,000
1799	Harworth ·	1,300
„	Tuxford	1,700
	Carried forward	.. 110,220

Date.	Enclosure.	Area enclosed.
	Brought forward	.. 110,220
1800	Normanton upon Trent	750
„	Ordsall, 200 A. F., 210 A. M. & P.	410
„	Wysall	1,100
„	Newark upon Trent ...	400
		112,880
1802	Blyth and Harworth ...	
„	Cropwell...	1,500
„	Runskill and Scrooby ...	1,300
„	Walkeringham	
1803	Dunham and Ragnal, 900 A. F., 200 A. M., 330 A. P.	1,430
„	Sutton upon Trent ...	1,800
„	Tollerton...	440
1804	Alverton	400
„	Gotham	1,800
1805	Plumptree	1,770
1806	Beeston	840
1807	Barnby	
„	Elton	900
1808	Gamston	520
„	West Markham	
„	Strelley and Bilborough	400
1809	Eaton	796
1810	East Markham	
1814	Headon cum Upton ...	
1818	Warsop, 344 A. F., 1,400 A. P., M. I.	*1,800
1819	East Drayton	700
1821	Nolesby, Kirton and Egmonton	
1822	Sturton and Littleborough, 455 A. P. ...	*900
1826	Norwell, M. I.	1,300
		18,596

Enclosed under the General Enclosure Act, 1845.

Date of Act.	Date of Award.	Parish.	Area.
*	1851	Girton (South Searle P.)	584
1849	1852	Oxton	1,140
1849	1854	Mansfield Woodhouse	1,545
			3,269

		Acres.
Before 1802	...	112,880
1802–1845	...	18,596
After 1845	...	3,269

OXFORD.

Date.	Enclosure.	Area enclosed.
1730	Mixbury	2,400
1757	Burchester	1,200
,,	Piddington, 22 yl. F., 400 A. P.	*1,060
1758	Northleigh, 52 yl. F., 600 P.	*2,160
1759	Neithrop and Wickham, 60¼ yl....	*2,109
1761	Ferringford, 32½ yl. ...	980
,,	Wardington, Williamscott and Coton, 108 yl.	3,000
1763	Merton, F. only... ...	740
1765	Horley and Horton, 104 yl.	2,000
,,	Somerton, 48½ yl. ...	1,800
,,	Shutford	900
1766	Adderbury, 156½ yl. ...	*5,477
,,	Bladon, 16 yl.	*560
,,	Steeple Aston, 41 yl. ...	1,435
,,	Great Tew, 79 yl. ...	*2,765
1767	Chesterton, 62 yl. ...	*2,170
,,	Kencott, 731 A. F., 232 A. P.	963
,,	Sandford, 63⅝ yl. ...	*2,227
1768	Shipton upon Charwell	1,100
1769	Chipping Norton and Salford, 185½ yl. ...	*6,572
,,	Wootton, 40 yl.... ...	*1,400
1770	Balckbourton, 41½ yl. ...	*1,452
,,	Westwell, 39 yl. F., 400 A. P.	1,300
1771	Swalcliffe	1,000
1772	Epwell, 27 yl.	1,400
,,	Handborough, 51 yl. ...	*1,785
,,	Heath, 39¼ yl.	800
1773	Burford	800
,,	Hook Norton and Southtop, 112½ yl.	5,000
,,	Broad Sibford or South Gower and Burdrup ...	2,000
,,	Stanton Harcourt ...	
1774	Copredy	1,550
1775	Burcott (Dorchester P.)... 32½ yl....	*1,137
,,	Broadwell and Filkins ...	
,,	Brize Norton	
,,	Great Rolewright, 70 yl.	*2,450
,,	Upper and Lower Tadmarten, 81 yl. (one field)	2,000
1776	Alkeston, 1 F., 38 yl. ...	1,000
,,	Blackthorn, 39¾ yl. ...	1,850
	Carried forward ...	68,542

Date.	Enclosure.	Area enclosed.
	Brought forward ...	68,542
1777	Great and Little Bourton, one F.	1,500
,,	Stanton St. John, 50 yl.	*1,750
1779	Bucknell...	800
,,	Dean	
,,	Idbury	1,072
1780	Stratton Audley and Caversfield, 37¼ yl. ...	2,200
1783	Hanwell	*2,000
1787	Coggs	
,,	Goring	
,,	Sarsden, Churchill, Lyneham, Merriscourt and Finescourt	4,140
1788	Little Faringdon ...	
1789	Sibford Ferris, 41 yl. ...	950
1791	Oddington	
1792	South Leigh	
1793	Little Barford	
,,	Burchester King's End	1,200
,,	Dunstew...	
,,	Milcomb, 1 F., 56½ yl. ...	1,695
,,	Stoke Lyne and Fewcott	
,,	Little Tew, all F., 40½ yl.	*1,215
1794	Burford	
,,	Southnewington ...	
1795	Westcot Barton and Middle Barton, 84 yl.	*2,940
,,	Wigginton, 37½ yl. ...	*1,312
1796	Alvescott...	
,,	Hampton Poyle... ...	
1797	Mollington, 40½ yl. ...	1,150
1798	Kelmscott	
1799	Bloxham...	
,,	Cassington and Worton	
,,	Ensham	1,000
,,	Wendlebury	1,160
,,	Whitchurch	
1801	Drayton...	270
,,	Lower Heyford and Calcot	1,700
,,	Headington	
,,	Stonesfield	
		96,596
1802	Baldwin Brightwell ...	977
,,	Swerford...	1,200
,,	Spelsbury	
	Carried forward ...	2,177

OXFORD—*continued.*

Date.	Enclosure.	Area enclosed.
	Brought forward ...	2,177
1803	Broughton	600
,,	Wroxton and Balscot ...	
1804	Islip	
,,	Shuttington	660
1805	Shirburn, 920 A. F., 261 A. P.	1,181
1807	Fritwell	1,900
,,	Deddington and Great Barford	
1808	Watlington	
1809	Wheatley, 60 A. P. ...	*100
1810	Launton	
,,	Culham	1,160
,,	Kidlington	
,,	Lewknow and Portcomb	
,,	Newington	636
1811	East and West Chadlington and Chilson ...	3,800
,,	Garsington	
,,	Kirtlington	
1812	Bampton...	
1813	Swinbrooke	800
1814	Ambrosden	
1817	Fulbrook...	1,500
,,	Iffley	800
1818	Noke	
1820	Great Haseley	500
1821	Taynton	1,800
,,	Witney	500
1823	Thame and Sydenham...	
1827	Beckley	
1829	St. Giles, Oxford ...	
1831	Woolvercot	550
1832	Aston Rowant	
,,	Caversham	600
1836	Baldon (Marsh and Toot)	
1838	Curbridge	1,500
1840	Great Milton	1,300
1841	Upper Heyford	
1842	Britwell	
1843	Grafton	
,,	Chalgrove	
		22,064

Enclosed under the General Enclosure Act, 1845.

Date of Act.	Date of Award.	Parish.	Area.
1846	1849	Milton (Shipton under Wychwood P.) ...	1,960
*	1849	Fencot and Murcot (Charlton upon Otmoor P.) ...	1,005
1849	1852	Pyrton	640
1850	1852	Shipton under Wychwood ...	1,710
1848	1853	Warborough ...	1,520
1849	1853	Standlake, Brighthampton and Hardwicke ...	2,860
1849	1853	Cowley	1,000
1850	1853	Southstoke cum Woodcote ...	1,765
1848	1854	Chinnor	1,000
,,	,,	Cottisford and Hethe	1,210
1854	1856	South Weston ...	470
*	1858	Charlton Field (Charlton upon Otmoor) ...	595
1855	1858	Horsepath... ...	900
1859	1861	Drayton	900
,,	,,	Dorchester ...	1,000
,,	1862	Ramsden	488
1852	1863	Bensington, Berwick Salome, and part of Ewelme	2,450
1860	1864	Cheekendon ...	590
			22,063

BERKSHIRE AND OXFORD.

See above. 2 Acts, for Oxford
1515 A. 1,515

23,578

	Acres.
Before 1802 ...	96,596
1802–1845 ...	22,064
After 1845 ...	23,578

RUTLAND.

Date.	Enclosure.	Area enclosed.
1756	Egleton or Edgeton, F...	844
,,	Tinwell	1,013
1758	Edith Weston, 32 yl. ...	1,200
	Carried forward ...	3,057

Date.	Enclosure.	Area enclosed.
	Brought forward ...	3,057
1759	Thistleton	1,380
1762	Whissondine	
	Carried forward ...	4,437

RUTLAND—*continued*.

Date.	Enclosure.	Area enclosed.
	Brought forward ...	4,437
1763	Greetham, 44 yl. ...	2,200
1768	Ketton, 2,200 A. F., 800 A. P.	3,000
1770	Uppingham (part of the common fields) ...	500
1772	Barleythorpe (Oakham P.), 23 yl.	1,000
„	Manton, 30 yl.	1,200
„	Wing, 40 yl.	*1,400
1773	Preston, 28 yl.	1,100
1793	Normanton	500
1794	Belton	900
„	Empingham	3,700
1795	Bridge Casterton ...	1,770
„	Bisbrooke and Seaton ...	
1796	Little Casterton... ...	700
1799	Lyddington with Caldecott and Uppingham	3,750
1800	Exton and Cottesmore	3,700
„	Ryhall with Belmesthorpe	2,500
1801	Braunston	1,500
		33,857

Date.	Enclosure.	Area enclosed.
1803	Market Orton	800
1820	Oakham	1,900
		2,700

Enclosed under the General Enclosure Act, 1845.

Date of Act.	Date of Award.	Parish.	Area.
1852	1854	Thorpe by Water (Seaton P.) ...	610
1855	1858	Seaton	1,305
1878	1881	Barrowden ...	1,925
„	„	North Luffenham	1,620
„	1882	South Luffenham	1,074
			6,534

LINCOLN AND RUTLAND.

See above. 1 Act, in Rutland | 810

		7,344

		Acres.
Before 1802	...	33,857
1802–1845	...	2,700
After 1845	...	7,344

SHROPSHIRE.

Date.	Enclosure.	Area enclosed.
1771	Donington	340
1772	Much Wenlock	630
1785	Kinnerley and Melverley	
1793	Idsall or Shiffnal ...	700
		1,670
1807	Knockin (in 3 parishes, 6 townships)	640
	Carried forward ...	640

Date.	Enclosure.	Area enclosed.
	Brought forward ...	640
1818	Bucknell and Clungunford	
1819	Stanton Lacy and Bromfield	500
		1,140

		Acres.
Before 1802	...	1,670
1802–1845	...	1,140

SOMERSET.

Date.	Enclosure.	Area enclosed.
1794	East Camell or Queen Camell	650
„	Tintinhull	
1795	Cheddar, 4,000 A. P., 400 A. F.	4,400
	Carried forward ...	5,050

Date.	Enclosure.	Area enclosed.
	Brought forward ...	5,050
1796	Woollavington, 460 A. F. 230 A. P.	690
1797	Aller, 280 A. F., 570 A. P.	950
	Carried forward ...	6,690

SOMERSET—*continued.*

Date.	Enclosure.	Area enclosed.
	Brought forward ...	6,690
1797	Higham and Huish Episcopi, 1,000 A. F., 840 A. P.	1,840
,,	Huish Episcopi, 1,100 A. F., 220 A. P. ...	1,320
,,	Moorlinch, 430 A. F., 175 A. P.	605
,,	Othery,550 A. F.,600 A.P.	1,150
,,	Somerton and Compton Dundon	
1798	Chilton	620
,,	Catcott, 350 A. F., 550 A. P.	900
,,	Caddington	2,000
,,	Middlezoy	1,100
1800	Huntspill, Cannington, Stockland Bristol and Stogursey	
		16,225
1802	Pitney, 600 A. F., 300 A. P.	900
1803	North Perrott	220
,,	Lilstock	210
1804	Kings	260
,,	Keinton Mandefield ...	
,,	Alford	250
1806	Martock	1,025
1809	Congresbury, Week St. Laurence and Puxton	820
,,	Long Sutton	
1810	Weston super Mare ...	993
	Carried forward ...	4,678

Date.	Enclosure.	Area enclosed.
	Brought forward ...	4,678
1811	Cheddar, Priddy and Rodney Stoke ...	1,100
1812	Charlton Horethorne ...	313
,,	Milborne Port	800
1813	Long Ashton, 690 A. P.	*1,000
,,	Uphill, 40 A. F., 340 A. P.	380
,,	Wraxall, Nailsea and Burton, 1,617 A. P. ...	*2,000
1814	Berkeley and Standerwick	300
,,	Moorlinch	350
,,	Portishead	
1818	Martock	278
1819	Martock in Muchelney, 596 A. F., 426 A. M., 2 A. P.	1,024
1826	Chilthorne Domer, 50 A. F., 130 A. P. ...	200
,,	West Lyndford	400
1830	Kingsbury Episcopi, 300 A. F., 400 A. P. ...	700
,,	Weston Zoyland and Middlezoy, all F. ...	500
1836	South Petherton, all F.	600
1837	Clapton	
		14,623

	Acres.
Before 1802 ...	16,225
1802–1845 ...	14,623

STAFFORD.

Date.	Enclosure.	Area enclosed.
1765	Elford	1,500
1770	Comberford and Wigginton	3,000
1773	Whitgreave	1,087
1783	Allstonefield, 160 A. F., 300 A. P.	460
1792	Great and Little Saredon and Great Wyrley ...	
1794	Abbotts Bromley, 100 A. F., 900 A. P. ...	1,000
1798	Stone, all F.	400
1799	Pattingham and Patshull	2,500
	Carried forward ...	9,947

Date.	Enclosure.	Area enclosed.
	Brought forward ...	9,947
1800	Stafford	470
,,	Castlechurch	120
1801	West Bromwich... ...	387
		10,924
1806	Knightley, Mill Mecce, Standon	400
1807	Basford	359
1808	Checkley...	500
	Carried forward ...	1,259

STAFFORD—*continued.*

Date.	Enclosure.	Area enclosed.	Date.	Enclosure.	Area enclosed.
	Brought forward ...	1,259		Brought forward ...	1,801
1809	High Offley	142	1816	Newcastle under Lyne,	
1811	Caverswall			Trentham, Woodstan-	
1812	Barton under Needle-			ton, Stoke upon Trent,	
	wood, Tatenhill, Yox-			600 A. F., 100 A. P. ...	700
	all, Hoarcross, Nether-		1834	Allstonefield	3,500
	town and Hampstead				
	Ridware				6,001
1813	Upper Elkstone... ...	400			
1814	P e n k r i d g e , Cannock,				Acres.
	Berkwick, Tiddesley...			Before 1802 ...	10,924
	Carried forward ...	1,801		1802–1845 ...	6,001

SUFFOLK

Date.	Enclosure.	Area enclosed.	Date.	Enclosure.	Area enclosed.
1736	Ixworth, 1 C. F., and			Brought forward ...	6,850
	other common land ...	1,300	1811	Great Waddingfield cum	
1772	Cavenham	1,100		Chilton and Great	
1776	Coney Weston	1,500		Cimard	
1794	Tuddenham	2,500	1812	Lidgate	
1796	Little Barton		„	Ousden	
1797	Barmingham		„	Great Wratting... ...	
1798	Stanton		1813	Chevington and Ched-	
1799	Honington			burgh	
„	Worlington		„	Great Horningsheath and	
1801	Risby and Fornham All			Westley	
	Saints		„	Icklingham	
			„	St. Mary in Newmarket	
		6,400	„	Rougham	
			„	Whepstead	*100
1802	Great Barton		1814	Bury St. Edmunds ...	
„	Fakenham	200	„	Durrington	458
1803	Ixworth and Thurston		„	Nettingham and Bungay	
	(F. in Thurston only,			Trinity	
	M. in Ixworth) ...		1815	Freckenham	
1804	Iken	100	„	Rickinghall Superior and	
1806	Troston			Inferior and Hinder-	
„	Great Thurlow	350		cley	
1807	Exning		1816	Dalham	966
„	Herringswell		1817	Erriswell	
„	Mildenhall		„	Fornham...	
„	Brandon, 2,820 A. war-		1818	Thelnetham	
	ren	*4,000	1826	Kentford	
1809	Bradwell, Belton and		1827	Nowton	350
	Fritton	1,000	1829	Bardwell, 430 A. P. ...	*500
„	Corton, Hopton and		1833	Lakenheath	1,132
	Gorleston	600	1838	Gazeley	
1811	Great Bradley	600	1839	Moulton	3,000
	Carried forward ...	6,850			13,356

SUFFOLK—*continued*.

Enclosed under the General Enclosure Act, 1845.

Date of Act.	Date of Award.	Parish.	Area.
*	1848	Stuston	42
1848	1853	Barrow	1,330
*	1854	Withersfield ...	508
		Carried forward ...	1880

Date of Act.	Date of Award.	Parish.	Area.
		Brought forward ...	1880
1854	1857	Haverhill, No. 2 ...	524
1878	1880	Orford	46
			2,450

	Acres.
Before 1802 ...	6,400
1802–1845 ...	13,356
After 1845 ...	2,450

SURREY.

Date.	Enclosure.	Area enclosed.
1779	Cobham	370
1797	Croydon, 750 A. F., 2,200 A. P.	2,950
1800	Byfleet and Weybridge	
„	Walton upon Thames ...	
1801	Ewell	1,200
„	Fetcham	620
		5,140

Date.	Enclosure.	Area enclosed.
1802	West Horsley, 400 A. F.	*800
1803	Sutton next Woking ...	412
1805	Pyrford and Chertsey ...	
1806	Cheame	1,760
1807	Thorpe	800
1808	Chertsey...	2,000
„	Kingston upon Thames and Imworth, 50 A. F.	1,350
1809	Sutton	
1812	Brockham and East Bletchworth ...	
„	Beddington with Bandon, 500 A. F.	*1,000
„	Windlesham, 156 A. F., 4,000 A. P.	4,156
	Carried forward ...	12,278

Date.	Enclosure.	Area enclosed.
	Brought forward ...	12,278
1814	Egham	
1815	East and West Moulsey	700
1818	Long Ditton	400
1821	Great Bookham... ...	700
1827	Peckham...	
		14,078

Enclosed under the General Enclosure Act, 1845.

Date of Act.	Date of Award.	Parish.	Area.
1850	1853	Carshalton and Waddington ...	1,200
1855	1856	Barnes	24
1859	1863	Leatherhead ...	858
1865	1869	Epsom	414
1902		(Not by Enclosure Act) Ham	300
			2,796

	Acres.
Before 1802 ...	5,140
1802–1845 ...	14,078
After 1845 ...	2,796

SUSSEX.

Date.	Enclosure.	Area enclosed.
1799	Houghton and South Stoke, 900 A. P. ...	*1,400
1803	Lancing	730
„	Rustington, all F. ...	360
1804	Goring	307
	Carried forward ...	1,397

Date.	Enclosure.	Area enclosed.
	Brought forward ...	1,397
1804	Tottington, all F. ...	163
1805	Broadwater	779
1809	Angmering	234
„	Chidham...	
„	Warningcamp	
	Carried forward ...	2,573

SUSSEX—*continued.*

Date.	Enclosure.	Area enclosed.
	Brought forward ...	2,573
1810	Amberley	2,000
„	Tellescomb, 454 A. F., 236 A. P.	690
1812	Poling, all F.	170
„	West Thorney	960
1813	Eartham	1,500
„	Warminghurst, Ashington, and Chaukton ...	
1818	Westbourne	800
1819	Chidham, Westbourne, and Warblington ...	320
„	Selsey, 535 A. F., 134 A. P.	689
1821	Bosham and Funtington, 300 A. F., 530 A. P....	830
„	Tangmere	200
1826	Felpham	400
1830	Kingston near Lewes and Ilford	2,405
1841	Bury	

13,537

Enclosed under the General Enclosure Act, 1845.

Date of Act.	Date of Award.	Parish.	Area.
*	1849	Oving	178
1868	1871	Hunston	78

248

	Acres.
Before 1802 ...	1,400
1802–1845 ...	13,537
After 1845 ...	248

WARWICK.

Date.	Enclosure.	Area enclosed.
1726	Bobenhull	1,000
1730	Lillington	
„	Welsbourne Hastings ...	
1731	Bishop's Tachbroke ...	688
„	Nuneaton and Attleborough, 76 yl. ...	*2,670
1732	Little Kinneton, 46½ yl.	*1617
1733	Barston	400
„	Westbourne Hastings and Newbold Pacy, 40 yl.	1,400
1739	Pailton, all F.	900
1740	Stichall	600
1741	Brinklow	1,700
1742	Aston Cantlow, 116½ yl.	4,067
1744	Wolfamcoat	1,690
1753	Kilmorton, 16¼ yl. ...	*569
1755	Churchover, 32 yl. ...	*1120
„	Great Harborow, 27 yl.	*945
„	Kenilworth	1,100
1756	Clifton upon Dunsmore, 20 yl.	*700
„	Radway, 36½ yl.... ...	*1,277
„	Sow	1,400
1757	Loxley, 18½ yl.	*647
„	Morton Morrell, 35 yl....	*1,225

Carried forward ... 25,715

Date.	Enclosure.	Area enclosed.
	Brought forward ...	25,715
1757	Priors Hardwick, 22 yl.	*770
„	Prior's Marston, 72 yl...	3,800
„	Wolfamcoat, 44 yl. ...	1,800
1758	Geydon, 42 yl.	*1,470
„	Wilncote, 4 F.'s... ...	
1759	Honington, 39 yl. ...	*1,365
„	Willoughby, 36 yl. ...	1,500
1760	Barford, 49½ yl.... ...	*1,733
„	Southam, 50 yl.... ...	2,200
1761	Exhall, 11 yl.	*365
„	Pailton, 28¾ yl.	*1,008
„	Ryton	
1762	Princethorpe, 14½ yl. F.	1,000
1764	Atherstone, 24 yl. ...	650
„	Chilvers Coton	1,100
1765	Bourton, 20 yl.	1,300
„	Granburrow, 24½ yl. ...	*997
„	Snitterfield, 17¾ yl. ...	*621
1766	Bidford, 23½ yl.... ...	*822
„	Haselor, 43 yl.	1,400
„	Ruyton (Bulkington P.), 10 yl.	700
1767	Cubbington, 31 yl. ...	*1,085
„	Wixford and Exhall, 69 yl.	*2,415

Carried forward ... 53,816

WARWICK—*continued.*

Date.	Enclosure.	Area enclosed.
	Brought forward ...	53,816
1768	Lemington Priors ...	990
1769	Willey, 13 yl.	*455
„	Bedworth, 16½ yl. ...	500
1770	Aulcester, 185 A. F., 450 A. P.	635
„	Bulkington	1,600
1771	Alveston, 56¾ yl. ...	*2,091
„	Butlers Marston, 32½ yl.	*1,137
„	Knightcot and Northend, 32¾ yl....	*1,147
„	Monk's Kirby, 18½ yl....	*647
„	Polesworth, 24 yl. ...	840
„	Stretton on the Foss, 45 yl. F., 200 A. P. ...	*1,550
1772	Little Kington, Combrooke and Brookhampton, 19½ yl. ...	*682
„	St. Nicholas	1,650
„	Shilton, 15⅝ yl.	*547
1773	Rugby, 42 yl.	1,500
1774	Foleshill ...	
„	Halford, 34 yl.	*1,190
„	Stratford upon Avon, 50 yl.	1,600
1775	Long Itchington and Bascote, 87 yl. ...	2,000
„	Lea Marston and Dunton	770
„	Wootton Wawen ...	1,900
1776	Barton and Martcleeve, 30 yl.	*1,050
„	Warmington, one F., 46 yl.	1,200
1777	Weston under Wetheley	
1778	Fenny Compton... ...	2,200
„	Napton upon the Hill, 96 yl.	3,000
„	Shuckburgh Fields, 26 yl.	880
1779	Aven Dassett	1,200
„	Brinton and Drayton, 59 yl.	1,700
„	Coleshill, 900 A. F., 1,000 A. P.	1,900
„	Harbury, 120 yl... ...	3,600
1781	Ilmington, 52 yl. ...	*1,820
1783	Burton Hastings	600
1784	Lower Brailes, 3,000 A. F., etc.	*3,500
1785	Meriden, 103 A. F., 286 A. P.	389
1786	Shottery, 38¾ yl. ...	1,600
1791	Stockton...	1,320
1793	Shottiswell, 51 yl. ...	1,200
1794	Lower Pillarton, 57½ yl.	*1,802
	Carried forward	.. 106,208

Date.	Enclosure.	Area enclosed.
	Brought forward	.. 106,208
1795	Upper Eatington and Fullready, 72 yl. ...	*2,520
„	Newton Regis and Clifton Campsville ...	600
„	Ratley	900
1796	Tysoe, 131 yl.	3,000
1797	Oxhill, 42 yl.	*1,470
1799	Sherborne	1050
1801	Aston, 171 A. F. & M., 1,000 A. P.	1,171
		116,919
1802	Birbury and Marton ...	1,750
„	Saltley and Washwood...	300
„	Whatcote	
1803	Kinwarton	420
1805	Cherrington	
„	Milverton	
„	Whichford, Ascott and Sowerton	2,600
„	Hampton in Arden ...	600
1806	Polesworth and Grendon	450
1807	Norton Lindsey... ...	600
1811	Long Compton	2,300
1812	Grafton	
1813	Solihull and Hampton in Arden	
1817	Leek, Wootton	1,000
„	Stuiley	
1818	Brickenhill, Little Packington and Diddington	
1824	Sutton Coldfield ...	
1825	Nether Whitacre ...	400
1826	Wolverton	470
1831	Claverdon	60
		10,950

Enclosed under the General Enclosure Act, 1845.

Date of Act.	Date of Award.	Parish.	Area.
1847	1851	Whitnash	1,090
1856	1860	Coventry	975
1867	1870	Crimscott and Whimpstone (Whitchurch P.)...	1,170
			3,235

		Acres.
Before 1802	...	116,919
1802-1845	...	10,950
After 1845	...	3,235

WESTMORELAND.

Date.	Enclosure.	Area enclosed.
1808	Bolton (certain open or common fields called Broad Ing Bartle and Star Ings, 22 A., waste 540 A.)	562
1810	Soulby, 90 A. F., 1,300 A. P.	1,390
	Carried forward ...	1,952

Date.	Enclosure.	Area enclosed.
	Brought forward ...	1,952
1811	Kirkby in Kendal, a common open field ...	105
1819	Barton, 130 A. F., 1,050 A. P.	1,180
		3,237

WILTSHIRE.

Date.	Enclosure.	Area enclosed.
1726	Compton Bassett, 1 F. ...	
1732	Staunton...	800
1741	Sherston Magna, all F.	1,000
1748	Badbury, 2 F.'s	
1749	Broad Blumsden ...	*700
1766	Heddington	
1767	Ashen Keynes, 70 A. F., 176 A. M., 490 A. P....	736
1770	Endford	1,010
1772	Kemble and Pool ...	1,500
1774	Milton	
„	Titcombe, 450 A. F., 395 A. P.	845
1775	Southcott, Kepnell Down, Workdown and Pewsey	
1776	Liddington and Medbourn, 639 A. F., 427 A. P.	1,066
1777	Ashton Keynes	
„	Earl Stoke	1,737
„	Market Lavington ...	
1778	Ramsbury, Whitton, Eastridge and Baydon	
„	Coates	
„	Highworth	
„	Ogbourn St. Andrews ...	
„	Patney	
1779	Chisledon, 1,230 A. F., 12 A. P.	1,242
„	Milston and Brigmerston	
„	Mildenhall	*800
„	Wanborough	
1780	Charlton...	
„	Warminster and Corsley	4,000
1781	Chicklade	
1782	Kingston Deverill ...	2,500
	Carried forward ...	17,936

Date.	Enclosure.	Area enclosed.
	Brought forward ...	17,936
1782	Stanton St. Quintin ...	
1783	Heytesbury	5,700
„	Netherampton, Odstock, etc.	
1785	Colerne Down, 1,305 A. F., 238 P.	1,543
„	Foffint, Swallow Clift, Ebesborne Wake, Broadchalk, Bowerchalk, Alvedeston, Bishopston and Fifield ...	
„	Berwick St. John ...	
1788	Netherhaven	3,300
1789	Berwick St. James and Fisherton Anger ...	1,650
„	Urchfont and Beechingstoke	
1790	Great and Little Bedwin, Preshute ...	
„	Deverill, Longbridge, Hussey and Monkton Deverill	
1792	Avebury	
„	Knooke	
„	Ogbourne St. George ...	
1793	Durnford	
„	Keevil, Idmaston, Fittleton and Chisenbury ...	
„	Roundway, Bedbow, Chiltoe and Bishop's Cannings	
1795	Poulton	
„	Stratton St. Margaret ...	
„	Winterborne Earls and Allington	
„	Wroughton	
1796	Wroughton and Uffcot	
	Carried forward	.. 30,129

WILTSHIRE—*continued.*

Date.	Enclosure.	Area enclosed.
	Brought forward ...	30,129
1797	Allcannings and Allington	
„	Great and Little Chiverill	
„	Easterton	
1798	Shrewton	
„	Sutton Veny ...	
„	Upton and Milton ...	820
1799	Oare	
„	Purton	
„	Stratford under the Castle and Milford ...	
1800	Cherton	
„	Shalbourne	
1801	Charlton...	
„	Manningford Bruce ...	
„	Wilsford	
		30,949
1802	Coombe Bisset	
„	West Grinstead and White Parish... ...	
„	Uphaven...	3,350
„	Wilsford	800
„	Westbury, 3,900 A. F., 1,200 A. P. ...	5,100
1803	Upton Scudamore ...	
1805	Aldbourn	
„	Exford, Fifield, Coombe, Longstreet and East Chisenbury ...	
„	Norton Bavant	
„	Somerford Keynes ...	500
1806	Great Somerford, 900 A. F., 48 P.	948
1807	Mere	5,000
1808	Bishopstrow and Warminster	
„	Codford St. Peter ...	600
1809	Bishopston	
„	Chilton Foliat	400
„	West Kington	950
„	Orcheston St. George and Elston, 400 A. F., 130 A. P.	530
„	Stockton...	1,500
„	Barford St. Martin, South Newton and Baverstock	2,425
	Carried forward ...	22,103

Date.	Enclosure.	Area enclosed.
	Brought forward ...	22,103
1810	Pitton and Farley ...	1,500
„	Winterbourn, Stoke, and Stapleford	
1811	Bidderstone and Slaughterford...	293
„	Tileshead	
1812	Martin	350
„	Nettleton	981
1813	Calne, Calstone, Wellington and Blackland ...	
„	Steeple Ashton	
„	Winterbourne Moncton	955
1814	Codford St. Peter ...	
„	Broadchalk and Chilmark	3,577
„	Cricklade	
„	Chirton	
„	Exford	
„	Overton	
„	Sutton Mandeville, 375 A. F., 170 A. P. ...	545
1815	Bishop's Cannings	
„	Chitterne	5,784
„	Upton Lovell	1,500
1816	Crudwell	
„	Downton and Britford...	
„	Everley	
„	Roade and Ashton ...	2,300
1818	Berwick St. Leonards ...	1,100
„	Damerham South ...	
„	Froxfield and Milton ...	
„	Laverstock	1,211
1819	Durrington and Figheldeane	
„	Malmesbury (St. Paul P.)	
„	Rodborne Cheney	
1820	Cherhill, Calne, Calstone, Wellington and Compton Bassett	
1821	Broad Hinton and Cliffe Pypard	*350
1822	Dinton	
1825	Wilton, Burcomb, Netherhampton, and Fugglestone	
1827	Ham	
1828	Boyton (with old enclosures)	2,300
1833	Steeple Langford ...	1,000
		45,849

WILTSHIRE— *continued.*

Enclosed under the General Enclosure Act, 1845.

Date of Act.	Date of Award.	Parish.	Area.
1848	1851	Winterborne Dauntsey ...	440
*	1853	Maddington ...	862
1852	„	Winterborne Gunner	551
„	1855	Maddington (Homanton Fields and Tenantry Down)	554
		Carried forward ...	2,407

Date of Act.	Date of Award.	Parish.	Area.
		Brought forward ...	2,407
1863	1866	Steeple Langford...	983
1865	1867	Donhead St. Mary	535
			3,925

		Acres.
Before 1802	...	30,949
1802–1845	...	45,849
After 1845	...	3,925

WORCESTER.

Date.	Enclosure.	Area enclosed.
1733	Aston Magna	
1736	Alderminster, 1 great C. F., 2 C. pastures, several meadows ...	
1762	Holy Cross in Pershore...	950
1763	Pirton	
1765	Bretferton	
„	Emload, 28 yl.	980
„	Linchwick and Norton...	
1771	Broadway, 90 yl. ...	*3,150
„	Feckenham	220
„	Hill Croome	
„	Naunton Beauchamp, 13½ yl....	*472
1772	Blockley	2,300
„	Throckmorton	1,600
„	Nafford and Birlingham	*1,000
1774	Bricklehampton, 34 yl...	*1,190
„	Defford, 600 A. F. ...	900
„	Kidderminster	1,000
„	Upton Snodsbury, 800 A. F.	*1,000
1775	Bengworth, 39 yl. ...	*1,365
„	Cleeve Prior, 27 yl. ...	*945
„	Cutsden	800
„	Pinvin, 14½ yl.	*507
„	Wolverley	1,500
1776	Charlton, 53¼ yl. ...	1,864
„	Great and Little Hampton, 46 yl.	*1,610
„	Leigh	20
1778	Rouslench	1,300
1779	Cropthorne, 62 yl. ...	*1,860
	Carried forward ...	26,533

Date.	Enclosure.	Area enclosed.
	Brought forward ...	26,533
1779	Himbleton	2,000
„	Grafton Flyford ...	864
1781	Kington	1,000
1782	Church Bench, 20 yl. ...	*700
1786	Harvington	*1,800
1788	Fladbury	1,700
1790	Dormstone	
1795	Bishampton, 67 yl. ...	*2,345
„	Chattisley	
„	Hanley Castle	
1801	Ripple	
		36,942
1802	Abbotts Morton ...	700
„	Broughton	446
1803	Little Cemberton ...	
1805	Rushock	
1806	Crowle	
„	Wick juxta Pershore with Wick Burnel and West Waryn ...	
1807	Queenhill	
„	Broughton Hachett ...	
„	Aldington	550
1808	Bredon	
1809	Iccomb	
1810	Eckington	
„	Pensham in Pershore ...	
„	Sedgeberrow	
„	Tibberton	
1811	Churchill	
	Carried forward ...	1,696

WORCESTER—*continued.*

Date.	Enclosure.	Area enclosed.
	Brought forward ...	1,696
1811	North, South, and Middle Middleton	
,,	Overbury	
,,	Stoke Talmage	420
1812	Badsey	
,,	Holdfast	
,,	Shipton upon Stower ...	
1813	Flyford Flavell	
,,	North Piddle	800
1814	Bredon	
,,	Inkberrow	2,200
,,	Strensham, 196 A. P. ...	*300
,,	Ombersley	
1818	Great Cemberton ...	
1819	Alvechurch	450
1825	Whiteladies Aston ...	
1832	Fladbury	
1833	Yardley	200
		6,066

Enclosed under the General Enclosure Act, 1845.

Date of Act.	Date of Award.	Parish.	Area.
1847	1850	Newbold on Stour	957
*	1852	Welland	55
	1854	Norton juxta Kempsey (East field)	70
1855	1860	Berrow	300
1856	1863	Upton on Severn and Ripple ...	880
1861	1865	Armscote (Tredington P.)	954
1864	1868	Blackwell (Tredington P.) ...	793
			4,009

	Acres.
Before 1802	... 36,942
1802–1845	... 6,066
After 1845	... 4,009

YORKSHIRE, WEST RIDING.

Date.	Enclosure.	Area enclosed.
1729	Thurnscoe	500
1757	Bishopthorpe, 200 A. F., 50 A. M., 400 A. P. ...	650
1759	Bolton upon Dearne ...	1,000
1760	Adwicke in the Street ...	1,000
,,	Calton	
1762	Rotherham, 750 A. M., 220 A. P.	*1,720
1765	Kirkhammerton, 400 A. F.	*600
,,	Kimberworth (Rotherham parish)	105
,,	Wadworth	2,000
1766	Marston, 950 A. F., 750 A. P.	1,700
1767	North Auston and Todwick	1,100
,,	Adlingfleet, Fockerby and Haldenby, 450 A. F., 700 P. ...	1,150
1768	Hook	1,000
1769	Laughton en Le Morthen, 1,100 A. F., 360 A. P.	1,460
,,	Sutton, 63 oxgangs ...	700
	Carried forward ...	14,685

Date.	Enclosure.	Area enclosed.
	Brought forward ...	14,685
1770	Sherburn, Lennerton, Burkstone Ash, Church Fenton, Little Fenton and Biggin	3,013
,,	Great Useburne, 480 A. F., 390 A. P. ...	870
1772	Ackworth	
,,	Clareton with Coneystrop and Allerton with Flaxby	480
,,	Follifoot, 165 A. F., 1,100 A. P.	1,265
,,	Snaith and Kellington, 1650 A. F., 922 A. P.	2,572
1773	Armthorpe	
,,	Arkendale, 377 A. F., 250 A. P.	627
,,	Drax, all F.	150
,,	Snaith and Cowick ...	1,160
,,	Skipton and Kildwick...	2,329
1774	Acombe and Holgate ...	2,000
,,	Rawmarsh, 450 A. F., 800 A. P.	1,250
	Carried forward ...	30,401

YORKSHIRE, WEST RIDING—*continued*.

Date.	Enclosure.	Area enclosed.
	Brought forward ...	30,401
1775	Rigton (Kirkby Overblow P.) 2,000 A. F., 30 A. M.	2,030
1776	Cawood and Wistow ...	2,000
1777	Barnsley, 280 A. F., 500 A. P.	780
,,	Cantley, Brampton, Bassacar and High Ellers	2,700
,,	Monkbretton, 70 A. F., 300 A. P.	370
,,	Thornton, 844 A. F., 307 A. P.	1,151
,,	Thorner, 370 A. F., 500 A. P.	870
1778	Dinnington, 610 A. F., 203 A. P.	813
1780	Kighley, 80 A. F., 5,000 A. P.	5,080
,,	Moseley and Kirk Bramwith, 220 A. F., 730 A. P.	950
1783	North Deighton... ...	546
1784	Hextrope with Balby and Long Sandall ...	1,600
1786	Moor Monkton, 390 A. F., 690 A. P.	1,080
,,	Methley, 500 A. F., 300 A. P.	800
,,	Little Smeaton and Stubbs Walden, 440 A. F., 718 P. ...	1,158
1787	Spofforth	500
,,	Cracoe, 77 A. F., 595 A. P.	662
1788	Featherstone, 230 A. F., 450 A. P.	680
,,	Knapton, 5 F.'s... ...	230
1789	Thorpe, 26 A. F., 700 A. P.	726
1790	Burton Leonard ...	273
1791	Sheffield, M. I. 30 A., 6,000 A. P.	6,030
,,	Tadcaster	
1792	Monk Fryston	650
,,	Tockwith	900
1793	Brotherton, 286 A. P. ...	300
,,	South Milford and Lumby	1,370
,,	Jakefield, Stanley, Wrenthorpe, Alvesthorpe and Thorns	2,300
	Carried forward ...	66,950

Date.	Enclosure.	Area enclosed.
	Brought forward ...	66,950
1794	Hoyland	
,,	Rufforth	770
1795	Checkheaton	210
1796	Berwick in Elmet ...	2,500
,,	Hambleton	
,,	Kimberworth, 220 A. F., 250 A. P.	470
,,	Mirfield, 60 A. F., 500 A. P.	560
1797	Bolton Percy	1,300
,,	Dalton, 300 A. F., 150 A. P.	450
,,	Hillam	
,,	Pontefract	
1798	Ulley, 220 A. F., 100 A. P.	320
1799	Brayton, Thorpe Willoughby, Burton and Gateforth ...	
,,	Hirst Courtney	
,,	Long Preston, 15 F.'s, 150 A., 400 A. P.	550
,,	Sandall Magna, Walton and Crigglestone ...	759
,,	Kirkheaton	400
1800	Carlton and Camblesforth	
,,	Denby with Clayton West, M. I.	
,,	Kearley cum Netherby	
,,	Martin with Graffton ...	400
,,	Womersley	
,,	High and Low Egbrough, Sherwood, Hatgreen and Tranmere ...	500
1801	Staveley	
,,	Skellow	600
,,	Little Useburn	
,,	Whixley	
,,	Little Weeton, 1,200 A. F., 300 A. P. ...	1,500
,,	Kettlewell and Conistree, 150 A. F. & M., 4,000 A. P.	4,150
		82,389
1802	Crofton	473
,,	Hoyland Swaine ...	
1803	Barmby upon Dunn, 600 A. F., 604 A. P. ...	1,204
	Carried forward ...	1,677

YORKSHIRE, WEST RIDING—*continued.*

Date.	Enclosure.	Area enclosed.
	Brought forward ...	1,677
1803	Hemsworth	800
,,	Clifford, 300 A. F., 460 A. P.	760
,,	Halifax (Elland cum Greetland) 116 A. F., 600 A. P.	716
,,	Kippax	890
,,	Shadwell, 80 A. F., 580 A. P.	660
1804	Normanton and Woodhouse, 330 A. F., 260 A. P.	590
1805	Thresfield and Skirethorns, and Burnsal ...	1,690
1806	Kirk Sandall, 100 A. F., 95 A. P.	195
,,	Skelton	
1807	Halifax	1,900
,,	Bishop Monckton, 670 A. F., 150 A. M., 300 A. P.	1,120
,,	South Kirby and South Elmsall	600
,,	Ossett (Dewsbury), 230 A. F., 350 A. P. ...	580
,,	Low Dunsforth	630
,,	Bramham, 680 A. F., 650 A. P.	1,330
1808	Aldbrough, 580 A. F., 396 A. M. & P.	976
,,	Kirk Smeaton	900
1809	Altofts, 290 A. F., 470 A. P.	760
,,	Cudworth, 54 A. F. and M. I. 190 A. P. ...	244
,,	Horbury, 260 A. F., 100 A. P.	360
,,	Purston Jackling, 100 A. F., 70 A. P. ...	170
,,	Rothwell with Royds and Oulton with Woodlesford	450
,,	Cadeby, 500 A. F. & M., 180 A. P.	680
1810	Badsworth, M. I. ...	
,,	Garforth, 520 A. F., 280 A. P.	800
,,	Gowthorpe (with old inclosures)	500
,,	Thorp Audlin	540
,,	Wath upon Dearne, M. I.	
	Carried forward ...	21,518

Date.	Enclosure.	Area enclosed.
	Brought forward ...	21,518
1810	Rossington, 1,313 A. F., 1,070 A. P.	1,383
1811	Askham Bryan	660
,,	Hatfield, Thorne and Fishlake (N.R.) ...	1,755
,,	Langside, 30 A. F., 4,000 A. waste	4,030
,,	Ecclesfield (very little F.)	14,000
1812	Darrington	
1813	Fairburn...	820
,,	Askham Richard ...	220
1814	Collingham, 200 A. F., 230 A. P.	430
,,	Wath upon Dearne and Rotherham, 180 A. F., 80 A. P.	260
,,	Campsall, Norton and Askern	2,860
,,	Frickley cum Clayton ...	440
,,	Wickersley, 340 A. F., 200 A. P.	540
1815	Brodsworth	
,,	Brampton and Swinton	1,370
,,	Burnsal, 9 A. F., 6,330 A. P.	6,339
1816	Arncliffe and Hawkeswick, 80 A. F. & M., 1,800 A. P.	1,880
,,	Arncliffe and Kettlewell	3,000
,,	Thorpe Arch and Walton	
1817	Monkfryston	290
1818	Snaith	1,000
1819	Barnbrough, 800 A. F., 273 A. P.	1,073
,,	Peniston, 50 A. F. & M. I., 370 A. P.	420
1827	Arksey	1,800
1828	Kirburton and Almonbury, 300 A. F., 18,000 A. P.	18,300
,,	Knaresborough and Farnham, 78 A. F., 466 A. P.	544
,,	Moor Monkton	600
,,	Whitgift...	1,000
1831	Ferry Fryston	830
1835	Ulleskelf...	711
1837	Rothwell, 300 A. F., 80 A. P.	380
		88,453

Enclosed under the General Enclosure Act, 1845.		

Date of Act.	Date of Award.	Parish.	Area.
*	1849	Clapham	592
1855	1858	Conisbrough ...	592
1854	„	Sutton (Campsall P.)	553
		Carried forward ...	1,737

Date of Act.	Date of Award.	Parish.	Area.
		Brought forward ...	1,737
1859	1861	Mexborough ...	365
			2,102

		Acres.
Before 1842	...	82,389
1802–1845	...	88,453
After 1845	...	2,102

YORKSHIRE, EAST RIDING.

Date.	Enclosure.	Area enclosed.
1731	Catwicke, 2 C. F.'s and open pastures, 88 oxgangs	*1,760
1740	Bewholm, 2 fields, etc. ...	*1,600
1741	Great and Little Driffield, 190 oxgangs	*3,800
1746	Kelfield, 400 A. F. ...	*600
1755	Nunburnholme	
„	Stillingfleet, 40 oxgangs	*800
1757	Fulford, 330 A. F., 450 A. P.	780
„	Pocklington, 6 F.'s M. and P.	
1758	Ottringham	*2,400
„	Skirpenbeck, 99 oxgangs	*1,980
1761	Burton Pidsea (Holderness)	1,800
1762	Sproatley (Holderness) 119 oxgangs	*2,380
„	Dringhoe, Upton and Brough (Holderness), 71 oxgangs	1,420
1763	Marfleet (Holderness), 24 oxgangs	*480
„	Sutton (Holderness), 740 A. F., 3,400 A. P. ...	4,140
1764	Aldborough (Holderness), 80½ oxgangs	*1,610
„	North Cave	1,400
„	Sudcoates (Drypool), 94 nobles, 1⅛ gates, 1 foot F.	
„	Skipsea, 88 oxgangs ...	*1,760
„	Skeffling (Holderness) ...	1,440
1765	Benton (Bempton next Flamborough), 80 oxgangs	*1,600
„	Brantingham and Thorpe, 900 A. F., 300 A. P. ...	1,200
	Carried forward ...	32,950

Date.	Enclosure.	Area enclosed.
	Brought forward ...	32,950
1765	Everingham, 740 A. F., 850 A. M. and P. ...	1,590
„	Ellerker, 75 oxgangs ...	1,800
„	Flamborough	3,000
„	Ulrome (or Ourram), (Holderness)	1,200
1766	Bessingby	1,080
„	Beeford	3,000
„	Brigham (Foston P.), 48½ oxgangs	*730
„	Cottingham	3,000
„	Naburn, 350 A. F., 349 A. P.	699
„	Pattrington (Holderness)	2,500
1767	South Burton (Burton Agnes)...	2,800
„	Huggate, 131 oxgangs ...	*2,620
1768	Bridlington	2,500
„	Burton Fleming, 168 oxgangs	3,000
„	Hotham, 120 A. F., 1,500 A. P.	2,700
„	Welwich in Holderness...	
„	Willington	2,300
1769	Atterwick in Holderness	1,200
„	Aclome	1,060
„	Bishop Wilton	3,800
„	Elvington	800
„	Hutton Cranswick ...	3,000
„	Lelley in Holderness, 22¾ oxgangs	800
„	Nafferton and Wansford, 3,000 A. F., 1,200 A. P.	4,200
„	Poppleton (W. R.) and Scagglethorpe (E. R.), 920 A. F., 900 A. P. ...	1,820
„	Sancton, 1,200 A. F., 80 A. M., 330 A. P. ...	1,610
	Carried forward ...	85,759

YORKSHIRE, EAST RIDING—*continued.*

Date.	Enclosure.	Area enclosed.
	Brought forward ...	85,759
1769	Thwing	4,000
,,	Wheldrake, 500 A. F., 180 A. M., 1,500 A. P...	2,180
,,	Youlthorpe	681
1770	Great Cowden (Holderness), 54½ oxgangs ...	1,100
,,	Easington (Holderness)..	1,300
,,	West Heslerton and Yeddingham, 80 oxgangs	1,600
,,	East Heslerton	1,200
,,	East Newton (Holderness)	600
1771	Butterwick, 2 F.'s ...	
,,	Kilham on the Wolds ...	7,000
,,	Lockington and Ayde, 1,800 A. F., 250 A. P...	2,050
,,	Lisset, 400 A. F., 600 A. P.	1,000
,,	Melton	1,000
,,	Long Reston and Arnold	1,600
1772	Sigglesthorne (Holderness), 65½ oxgangs ...	1,000
,,	Welton	1,500
,,	Would Newton	2,000
1773	East Cottonwith, 400 A. F., 560 A. F. ...	960
,,	Everthorpe, 42 oxgangs	500
,,	Harpham, 1,400 A. F., 600 A. P.	2,000
,,	Holme upon Spalding Moor, 1,472 A. F., 285 A. M.	7,000
,,	Market Weighton, 4,200 A. F., 2,500 A. M. ...	6,700
,,	Preston in Holderness, 129 oxgangs	4,500
,,	Sheckling cum Burstwick	850
1774	Bainton	2,700
,,	Garton	4,050
,,	Rudstone...	4,000
1775	Goodmanham, 3,000 A. F., 100 A. P. ...	3,100
1776	Bilton	770
,,	Foston	800
,,	Sutton upon Derwent ...	708
1777	Boynton	2,000
,,	Bugthorpe, 640 A. F., 310 A. P.	950
,,	Barmby upon the Moor...	2,800
,,	North and South Newbald	6,000
,,	Tunstall (Holderness) ...	800
	Carried forward ..	166,758

Date.	Enclosure.	Area enclosed.
	Brought forward ..	166,758
1777	Melbourne and Storthwaite, 300 A. F., 300 M., 1,800 P.	2,400
1778	North Dalton	1,700
1780	Thornton, 800 A. F. ...	1,000
1783	Roos in Holderness ...	1,521
1785	South Cave	2,500
,,	Kilnwick, 86 oxgangs, 650 A. F., 250 A. P. ...	900
1788	Filey	620
1789	Coniston in Holderness...	500
1792	North Grimston, 75 oxgangs	660
1793	Hollym and Withernsee	1,800
,,	Speeton	1,800
,,	Skidby	600
,,	Southam in Kirkburn ...	1,200
1794	Elloughton, Brough and Walby	2,600
,,	Lund	2,300
,,	Tibthorpe	3,000
,,	Warter	7,500
,,	Walkington	3,000
1795	Holme upon the Wolds...	1,450
1796	West Ella, Kirk Ella, and Ellerby	1,600
1797	Settrington	1,100
1800	Holmpton and Hollym cum Withernsea ...	900
,,	Hunmanby and Fordon	
1801	North Frodingham ...	2,500
,,	Hornsea	2,500
,,	Langtoft upon the Wolds	3,200
,,	Molscroft	700
,,	Ruston Parva	900
,,	Weaverthorp	8,300
,,	Willerby	1,500
		227,009
1802	Ellerton (Ellerton Priory)	1,040
,,	Folkton and East and West Flotmanby ...	1,800
,,	Keyningham (Holderness)	1,350
,,	Withernwick	1,500
,,	Sewerby and Marten ...	2,000
1803	Gaxton, Potter Brompton and Binnington ...	3,800
,,	Middleton, 2,000 A. F., 1,800 A. P.	3,800
,,	Wetwang and Fimber ...	2,820
	Carried forward ...	18,110

YORKSHIRE, EAST RIDING—*continued.*

Date.	Enclosure.	Area enclosed.
	Brought forward ...	18,110
1805	Ryhill and Camerton ...	1,300
„	Huttons Ambo	2,500
1806	Elsternwick	875
„	Owthorn	650
1809	North Duffield	
1810	West Cottingwith and Thorganby	
„	Fridaythorpe	2,000
1811	Paghill	402
„	Righton	1,600
„	Osgodby	500
1813	Eastrington	
1814	Hayton, 1,150 A. F., 450 A. P.	1,600
1816	Londesborough	
1818	Etton, 2,000 A. F., 600 A. M. and P.	2,600
1819	Barmston, 160 A. F., 130 A. P.	290
1820	Hemingbrough (South Duffield township) ...	
1822	South Dalton (with old enclosures)	1,800
1823	North Burton	1,920
	Carried forward ...	36,147

Date.	Enclosure.	Area enclosed.
	Brought forward ...	36,147
1823	Ferriby and Kirk Ella...	3,350
1830	Blacktoft, Eastrington and South Cave, all F.	430
1832	Bubwith	1,700
1833	Great Gwindale... ...	650
1843	Hemingbrough	
1844	Brandes Burton... ...	
		42,277

Enclosed under the General Enclosure Act, 1845.

Date of Act.	Date of Award.	Parish.	Area.
*	1849	Mappleton ...	1,060
*	1851	Cottam (Langtoft P.)	2,515
1878	1880	Riccall	1,297
1901		Skipworth ...	321
			5,193

	Acres.
Before 1802 ...	227,009
1802–1845 ...	42,277
After 1845 ...	5,193

YORKSHIRE, NORTH RIDING.

Date.	Enclosure.	Area enclosed.
1748	Faceby in Cleveland, 700 A. F., 900 A. P. ...	1,600
1755	Marsk and Redcar ...	1,400
„	Slingsby	
1756	Sutton upon the Forest, 1,300 A. F.	3,000
„	Warthill, 40 oxgangs ...	800
1758	Brompton and Sawden, 8 F.'s etc.	
1759	East Cotham, 400 A. F., 400 A. P.	800
1766	Stillington	1,400
1768	East Ayton	1,337
1769	Ebberston	1,200
„	Haxby	1,640
„	Sheriff Hutton and West Lilting, 833 A. F., 837 A. P.	1,670
1770	Upper Dunsforth and Braxton, 500 A. F., 100 A. P.	600
	Carried forward ...	15,447

Date.	Enclosure.	Area enclosed.
	Brought forward ...	15,447
1771	Scalby and Throxenby or Newby, 2,000 A. F.	4,000
1773	Wilton (Ellerburn P.)	700
1774	Swinton (Appleton P.)	700
1776	Amotherby	
„	Lyth	
„	Stonegrave, Westness and Nunnington ...	1,110
1777	Bulmer	
1784	Lockton	
1785	Wykham and Ruston ...	2,000
1787	Lastingham	
1788	Kirkbymoorside, Fadmoor and Gillamoor	
1789	Cold Kirkby	
1790	Hutton Bushnell, 700 A. F., 170 A. M., 1250 A. P.	2,120
„	Linton, 50 A. F., 480 A. P.	530
	Carried forward ...	26,607

YORKSHIRE, NORTH RIDING—*continued.*

Date.	Enclosure.	Area enclosed.
	Brought forward ...	26,607
1791	Norton in the Clay ...	800
1793	West Tanfield, 80 A. F., 500 A. P.	580
1794	Old Malton, 2 F.'s, one 416 A., other 14 A. ...	1,500
,,	Skelton, 75 oxgangs, F., 200 A. P.	1,100
1798	Sowerby...	1,100
1800	Tholthorpe and L. Flawith	1,570
		33,257

Date.	Enclosure.	Area enclosed.
1802	Flixton	2,600
,,	Richmond, 344 A. F., 1,340 A. P.	1,684
1803	Wilton, Laxenby, Lackenby and West Coatham	1,100
1806	Kirkdale and Hemsley...	950
1807	Alne	600
,,	Hunton, about 40 A. F.	720
1808	Easingwold	500
1809	Helperby	
,,	Skelton	
	Carried forward ...	8,154

Date.	Enclosure.	Area enclosed.
	Brought forward ...	8,154
1809	Allerston...	14,000
1810	Gilling in Richmondshire	300
,,	Tollerton...	
1811	Westerdale, all F. ...	190
,,	Lune, Holwick and Romaldkirk, 302 A. F.	6,840
1812	Newton upon Ouze and Shipton	911
1815	Melsonby	600
1833	Bedale	176
		3,171

Enclosed under the General Enclosure Act, 1845.

Date of Act.	Date of Award.	Parish.	Area.
*	1853	Hinderwell ...	894
1864	1870	Leake	140
			1,034

	Acres.
Before 1802 ...	33,257
1802–1845 ...	31,171
After 1845 ...	1,034

APPENDIX C.

LELAND'S ITINERARY.

NORTHAMPTON, LEICESTER AND RUTLANDSHIRES.

LELAND entered Northamptonshire from Huntingdonshire, coming through Kimbolton and the village of Leighton. We have in Vol. I., folio 3 :—

"From Leighton to Barnewel Village" (in Northamptonshire) "a vi miles by exceeding faire Corne and pasture ground."

"Thence to Oundle . . . the Medowes lying on every side on a great Leavel thereabouts."

"Oundale to Foderingeye, a 2 miles by mervelous fair Corne ground and Pasture, but little wodde."

"From Welingborow to Northampton 8 miles al be champaine Corne and Pasture Ground, but little wood or none, even as it is betwixt Oundale and Welingborow" (fol. 7).

"Wedon is a praty throughfare, sette on a playne ground" (fol. 11).

"Towcester is 7 miles from Wedon and as much from Northampton, al by playne Corne ground and pasture."

"Northampton to Kingesthorpe a mile, and a little farther, by Multon Parke enclosed with Stone . . . thens by Champayne Ground, bering good grasse and Corne, a ix mile to Ketering" (fol. 12).

"Thens to Welledon, an uplandish Towne, 4 miles, where the Soile is sumwhat furnished about with wood, and plentee beside of Corne and Grasse . . . And thens 2 mile by Corne, Pasture and Wood to Deene."

"From Dene to Rokingham, by summe Corne and Pasture but more Wood grounde a 3 miles" (fol. 13).

"There lyeth a greate valley under the Castle of Rokingham, very plentifull of Corne and Grasse . . . The Forest . . . about 20 mile yn length, and in bradthe 5 or 4 Miles in sum places in sum less. And withyn the precinctes of it is good Corne and Plentie of Woodde."

" Rokingham to Pippewelle, the late Abbay, abut a 3 Miles of by Wood and Pasture."

" Dene to Haringworth a 3 Miles be Corne, Grasse, and sum Woody Grounde " (fol. 14).

Then entering Leicestershire, he says :—

" The grounde bytwixt Dene and Staunton is plentiful of corne, and exceeding faire and large Medowis on both sides of the Weland. But from Rokingham to Staunton there was in sight little Wodde, as yn a Countrey al Chaumpain.   From Staunton to Leycester al by Champaine Grounde an 8 or 9 Miles " (fol. 15).

" Leyrcester to Brodegate by grounde welle Wooddid 3 miles . . . Brodegate to Groby a Mile and a half much by Woodden lande " (fol. 19).

" Brodegate to Leighborow about a v Miles. 1st foreste of Charley communely called the Wast, xx miles or more in Cumpace, having plenty of woode " (fol. 20).   The forest of Leyrcester, the other forest of the county, he says, is five miles in length.

" Brodegate to Bellegrave Village a 4 miles by Woddy and Pasture Grounde " . . . " Bellegrave to Ingresby a 4 Miles, partely by Corne, Pasture, and Woddy ground . . . Thens to Wiscombe a 4 Miles by Corne, Pasture and Wood . . . faire Orchardes and Gardenes " (fol. 22).

" *Marke that such parte of Leyrcestershire as is lying South and Est is Champaine, and hath little Wood. And such parte of Leircester-shire as lyith by West and North hath much woodde* " (fol. 24).

Next he passes through Rutlandshire into Northamptonshire again :—

" From Wiscombe partely through Woddy ground of the Forest of Leefield, and so in Ruthelandshir by Woddy first, and then all champain Ground, but exceeding rich Corne and Pasture, to Upping-ham . . . from Uppingham to Haringworth (Northamptonshire) 3 little miles, al by Champaine . . . Dene to Cliffe Parke 3 Miles ; it is partely waullid with stone, and partely palid.   From Dene to Coliweston a 5 or 6 Miles, partely by Champaine, partely by Woodde ground" (fol. 25).

" From Coly Weston to Grimesthorpe (in Lincolnshire) about an

8 or 9 most by playne Ground, good of Corne and Pasture, but little wood" (fol. 26).

His journey then took him northwards, but returning, he again passed through Leicestershire, Rutland and Northamptonshire, and notes :—

"Notingham to Bever (Belvoir) all by champaine ground, 12 miles" (fol. 113).

"Bever to Croxton, 2 miles" (fol. 115).

"Croxton to Castleford Bridge by champaine" (fol. 115).

"Castleford Bridge to Stamford 1 mile" (fol. 115).

"Stamford to Colyweston 2½ miles, champayn" (fol. 115).

"Colyweston to Dene, moste by Chaumpaine" (fol. 115).

"Dene to Foderingeye, most by wood, 6 miles" (fol. 116).

"Foderingey to Undale, 2 miles, champaine" (fol. 116).

"Thens a 9 mile to Layton in Huntingdonshire, Champaine" (fol. 116).

"To Higham Ferrers in Northamptonshire, 8 miles" (fol. 116).

"To Bedford, 14 miles, champaine" (fol. 116).

WARWICK.

"From Charlecote to Stratford a 3 Miles by Champaine, good corn and grasse" (166 b).

"I roade from Stratford by champaine Ground, fruitfull of Corne and Grasse a 5 miles . . . thence 2 miles by Champaine to Coughton. From Coughton to Aulcester 2 miles by enclosed Ground (167 b). I roade from Aulcester towards Evvesham a 2 Miles by woody and inclosed Ground, and then a mile by Ground lesse inclosed, but havinge more Corne then wood. Thence a 4 miles by cleane Champion" (168 b).

Having thus entered Gloucestershire, he came through Worcester and Lichfield, and so re-entered Warwickshire from the north, and found—"Colishull to Meriden 4 m. by enclosed ground having some corne, wood and pasture. 3 miles by like ground to Coventry" (190 a). To Southam was "4 m. good corne and pasture in Champion," thence to Banbury in Oxfordshire "10 m. by champaine, noe wood but exceedinge good Pasture and corne."

BUCKINGHAM.

From Dunstable to "Mergate," as we have seen, was "al by Chaumpaine a vj miles" (vol. 1, fol. 120). But "thens by Chiltern

Hilles and woods and baren woody and ferne ground vij miles to Barkhanstede" (in Herts, near the Buckingham boundary, fol. 121). "Thens I passid by Hilly, Woody, and much baren ground to Cheynes (in Bucks) a v miles" . . . v miles good Pasture and Corne, v miles mory Ground, and 3 m. by sum enclosid and Woddy ground to Windelsore. From Windelsore by a 3 miles most be wood and enclosid, and 2 m. in faire open and levelle medow . . . to Tamise . . . Half a mile to Stanes Bridge" (fol. 122).

On a later journey he came from Oxford, and entered Bucks at Thame "by some Hilly and after great Pasture Groundes, fruitfull of beanes a 10 m. to Querendon in the Vale of Alesbury. Thens 5 m. to Alesbury all champaine" (Vol. IV. 191 b). But from Hagmondesham (Amersham) to Uxbridge was "9 miles by goodly enclosid grounds."

OXFORDSHIRE.

He came from Reading and crossed the river to Caushem (Caversham). "Thens I rode a v miles and more all by great Woddes. And thens by Chaumpaine hilly ground a 4 m. to Ewelm" (Vol. II. fol. 5). "From Ewelm to Haseley a v m. by Chaumpaine Ground somewhat plentiful of corn, but most layid to Pasturage" (fol. 7). "From Haseley to Chisilhampton by plaine ground fruteful of corne and Grasse, but baren of wood as al that Angle of Oxfordshire is, 3 miles. Thens to Drayton Village. Thens a mile to Dorchester" (fol. 10). "To Walingford 1½ m. by mervelus fair Champain" (fol. 12). Here he again crossed the Thames into Berkshire; but later he entered the north west of the county, and found the district from Sutton to Banbury "all by champaine barren of wood" (Vol. IV., fol. 162 b), and the first 12 miles of the road from Banbury to Warwick "by Champaine Groundes, fruitful of Corne and Grasse" (163 a). Similarly from Southam (in Warwickshire) to Banbury was "10 m. by champaine, noe wood but exceedinge good Pasture and corne," and from Banbury to Bercester (Bicester) was 10 or 11 miles of "champaine."

LINCOLN.

"From Coly Weston to Grimesthorpe about an 8 Miles or 9, most by playn Ground, good of corne and pasture, but little wood" (Vol. I. fol. 26). "From Grimesthorpe to Corby about a 3 Miles by Champayne Ground. . . . Thens to Boutheby a 3 Miles, and

thereaboute is meately store of Wodde scaterid" (fol. 27). "From
Boutheby to Hayder al by Champaine ground, fertile of corne and
grasse, 4 Miles.　From Hayder to Sleford a vj Miles al by Champaine
grounde (fol. 29).　From Sleforde to Ancaster a 4 Miles by Chaum-
paine (fol. 30).　Ancaster to Temple Bruern al by Champaine of
Ancaster Heth a 4 Miles. . . . From Temple Bruern to Lincoln 10
Miles by Champaine" (fol. 32).　"Lincoln to Torkesey parte by
Marsh Ground, and part by other, but very little wood, a 7 Miles.
Torkesy to Marton Village about a mile by plaine sandy ground"
(fol. 35).

YORKSHIRE, EAST RIDING.

"From York to Kexby Bridge by Champaine v miles" (Vol. I.
fol. 49).　Thence he went to Leckenfield, a village a little to the north
of Beverley, "And al this way betwixt York and the Parke of Leken-
feld is meately fruteful of Corn and Grass, but it hath little wood"
(fol. 49).　He then went south to Hull and returned to Beverley:
"From Kingeston to Beverle a vj Miles, a v by low pasture and
Marsch Ground, and a Mile by enclosid and sumwhat woddy ground"
(fol. 57).　Starting from Beverley again towards Goole he has
"Beverle to Walkington Village a 2 Mile, one by enclosid, and
another by chaumpaine good corne land.　Walkington to North
Cave Village 5 Miles by fair champain corn ground.　Northcave to
Scalby a 3 Miles al by low Marsch and Medow Ground" (fol. 57).

"From Scalby to Hoveden (Howden) 4 M. scant one by enclosid
Pasture and 3 by Morische and Fenny ground" (fol. 58).　"From
Hoveden to Wresehill (Wressel) a 3 Miles al by low Medow and
Pastureground, whereof part is enclosed with Hegges" (fol. 59).
"From Wresehill . . . Ferry about a Mile, most by Medow Ground,
and so a xj Miles to York, whereof most parte was in sight Medow
and Morisch Ground, and but meane corne, but toward York the
soyle and corne were better" (fol. 69).

NORTH AND WEST RIDINGS.

He came on his first journey from Scrooby in Notts to Doncaster.
He observes, "Bawtre to Doncaster an vij Miles by a great Plaine
and Sandy ground caullid Blitherle" (Vol. I. fol. 37),　Round Doncaster is "Medow, Corn and sum wood," but from " Tikhill to
Cunesborow (Conisbrough) a 4 Miles by stony way and enclosid

ground " (fol. 39), and from " Dancaster to Heathfield (Hatfield) by champayn sandy ground a 5 Miles," and here comes Hatfield Chase, the scene of Vermuiden's labours later. He return to Doncaster and went north and found "The ground between Dancaster and Pontefract in sum places meately wooddid and enclosid ground " (fol. 42) ; from "pontefract to S. Oswaldes by much enclosid and meately woddy ground a 3 Miles or more " (fol. 44). From St. Oswalds to Sandon village (a mile from Wakefield), "a 3 Miles by enclosid Ground " (fol. 44). From Wakefield to Pontefract direct was "a vj miles parte by Enclosure, parte by Champaine " (fol. 46). Thence to Leeds, he found first three miles of enclosed ground, then five miles of low meadow, and " good high plaine corne ground " (fol. 46).

From Leeds to Tadcaster was apparently unenclosed, but from Tadcaster to York there was first 4 miles of enclosed ground, then four by "playn Champaine " (fol. 48). " From York to Stockton yn the Moore a 3 Miles by low Pasture and moreisch Ground. . . . Thens a 5 Miles by much lyke Ground . . . a little beyond that as about half a M. is Whitewelle Village. Thereabout the Fieldes for a Miles space were inclosid. . . . Thens a 2 M. by Fyrry. Thens to Malton a 3 Miles, and the ground is hilly there and daly and plentiful of Corne and Pasture (Vol. I. fol. 63). From Malton to Shirburne Village about an 8 miles by Champaine Ground. From Shirburne by Hilles to Semar. Thens a Mile by Meately plaine Ground, and so 2 Miles more in a vale enclosid with stepe Hilles on ech side to Scardeburg (fol. 66).

"Moste of the Ground from Scardeburg to Pykering was by Hille and Dale meate plentiful of Corn and Grasse but little wood in sight " (fol. 70). The vale of Pickering was open field land.

North-west of York itself was the great forest of Galtres, ten miles through (fol. 74). At Herperly Village beyond was "meately good corn ground, Pasture and Medow and sum Wooddes " (fol. 75).

Further south. " From Kirkeby Wisk to Northalverton a 4 Miles by Pasture and Corne Ground " (fol. 75).

Returning later from Durham we have from Greta Bridge to Richmond, "sum good corn and much More (fol. 95). Richmond to Middleham, al by mory Ground and little wood " but " Middleham to Gervalx Abbay a 2 Miles most by enclosed Pastures." His route lay through Ripon, West Tanfield, Boroughbridge, to Knaresborough ; he notes pasture, corn, wood and moor. Then comes the great forest of Knaresborough, 20 miles long and 8 broad. Then he went south through Pontefract and Doncaster, finding after Doncaster "3 Mile al by Champain ground" (fol. 105).

He came again into Yorkshire from Lancashire, and found by the Ouse near York "the ground was fair of Pasture, Corne and wood" (Vol. V. fol. 91), and from "Shirburne to Pontfract 6 m. soile in sight plaine, wel cornid, but little wood" (*ibid.*), and coming south, there is "woddy Grounds," and "soile riche of wood, Pasture, corne," but no mention of enclosure.

WESTERN COUNTIES.

Leland's observations are as follows. He saw, approaching Lechdale on crossing the Thames from Faringdon, " In ripa ulterori . . . greate Enclosures of stone walls" (Vol. II. fol. 22). He turned into Wiltshire, and came from Bradford into the neighbourhood of Bath and East Somerset. Burton to South Cadbury, and thence to Sherborne, just over the Dorset boundary, was "fair and fruteful Champain" (fol. 47), but by another route back from Sherborne to South Cadbury "the Pastures and Fieldes be much enclosid with Hegge Rowes of Elmes" (fol. 50), and a little later he says that "most part of al Somertsetshire is yn hegge rows enclosid" with elms (fol. 55).

Some details are given later. Southtown to Midsummer Norton was "hilly and enclosid," but Midsummer Norton to Wells "chaumpayne" (Vol. VIII. fol. 5), but thence south to Munney Delamere "hilly and enclosid" (fol. 7). Midsummer Norton to Mells (near Frome) was champayn (Vol. VIII. part 2, fol. 78 a). From Bath to Kelston (in Wilts) was champaine (fol. 67 b) and the triangular district between Bristol, Bath and Chipping Sodbury about half enclosed and half "champaine," and also the district on the other side of the Bristol Avon towards Frome in Somerset, the immediate neighbourhood of Frome being open (Vol. VII., part 2, fol. 68–77).

Aulcester (in Warwick), to Evesham was " 2 Miles by woody and inclosed ground, and then a mile by Ground lesse inclosed. . . . Thence 4 miles by cleane Champion " (Vol. IV. fol. 168b), and the " champion Ground " continued for 6 or 7 miles to Stanwey, on the Cheltenham road.

North-west Worcester seems to have been generally enclosed. We have Bridgenorth (in Shropshire) to Kidderminster "mostly enclosed ground" (Vol. IV. fol. 182 b). "Bewdley to Milton, Milton to Hertlebury, and hence to Worcester is all described as enclosed Ground (183 b and 184 a), and so also the country between Worcester and Bromsgrove (185 a and 186 b).

APPENDIX D.

GENERAL LEGISLATION AFFECTING ENCLOSURE.

(Previous to the General Enclosure Act of 1845.)

STATUTE OF MERTON (1235), c. 4.

Enabled lords of manors, on leaving sufficient pasture for their tenants on the waste, to enclose the residue ; but the lord must prove that the tenants have sufficient pasture, and means of ingress and egress.

STATUTE OF WESTMINSTER. (1285), c. 46.

Enabled lords of manors in which the waste was used as a common pasture by other manors, to enclose against their neighbours, when no specific grant of a right of common pasture had been made. It also provided against the creation of new common rights. " By occasion of a Windmill, Sheepcote, Dairy, enlarging of a court necessary, or Courtelage, from henceforth no man shall be grieved by Assize of Novel Disseisin for Common of Pasture." If after enclosure under this act the hedges are pulled down, the neighbouring townships may be distrained upon for damages.

ACTS FOR THE PROTECTION OF FORESTS.

21 EDWARD IV. (1482), c. 7.

In a forest subject to common rights after a wood has been felled the land may be enclosed for seven years to protect the young timber.

35 HENRY VIII. (1544), c. 17.

Where woods are subject to common rights, lords of manors may enclose one fourth of the wood for seven years, and fell the timber, leaving 12 young trees per acre standing. Meanwhile the lord of the manor surrenders his common rights upon the remaining three fourths. Kent, Surrey and Sussex were excluded from the operation of the act.

13 ELIZABETH (1571), c. 25.

This makes the preceding Act perpetual.

DEPOPULATION ACTS.

The preamble of the first of this series of Acts, though well known, is here quoted in part.

4 HENRY VII. (1489), c. 19.

"Our King and Sovereign Lord . . . remembreth that . . . great inconveniences do daily increase by desolation and pulling downe, and wilfull waste of houses and townes within this realme and laying to Pasture Lands, which customably have been used in tillage, whereby idlenesse, which is the ground and beginning of all mischiefes, daily doth encrease. For where in some townes two hundred persons were occupied and lived by their lawfull labours, now there are occupied two or three heardmen, and the residue fall into idlenesse, the husbandrie, which is one of the greatest commodities of this Realme is greatly decayed, Churches destroyed, the service of God withdrawn, the bodies there buried, not prayed for. . . ."

To check these evils all occupiers of 20 acres and upwards of land that had been tilled in the previous three years, are required to maintain tillage, under pain of forfeiting to the lord of the manor one half of the profits of such land.

6 HENRY VIII. (1515), c. 5.

This was a temporary Act, in principle identical with the one passed in the following session.

7 HENRY VIII. (1516), c. 1.

This Act applied only to parishes " whereof the more part was or were used and occupied to tillage and husbandry." In such places " If any person shall decay a Town, a Hamlet, or House of

Husbandry, or convert tillage into Pasture " and have not " within j. yeere next after such wylfull decaye reedefyed and made ageyn mete and convenyent for people to dwell and inhabyte the same, and have use, and therein to exercyse husbandry and tyllage " he forfeits one half of his land to the lord of the manor, until the offence is reformed. Land converted to pasture must again be tilled " after the maner and usage of the countrey where the seyd land lyeth."

This Act was followed by the Inquisition of 1517.

ACT FOR RESTRAINING SHEEP FARMING.

25 HENRY VIII. (1534), c. 13.

This is an Act to deal with the economic cause of depopulating enclosures.

" Sundry persons have of late daily studied how to gather into few hands great multitude of Farms and great Plenty of Cattle, and in especial Sheep, putting such land as they can get to Pasture, and not to tillage, whereby they have not only pulled down Churches and Towns and inhanced the old Rates . . . so that poor men are not able to meddle with it . . . it is thought that the great occasions that moveth and provoketh those greedy and covetous people . . . is only the great Profit that cometh of Sheep."

It is said that " some have 24,000, some 20,000, some 10,000, some 6,000, some 5,000 and some more, some less."

It is enacted that with certain exceptions no one may keep more than 2,000 sheep under a penalty of 3s. 4d. per sheep per annum. half of the fine going to the crown, half to the informer. No man, further, may take more than two farms, and these must not be in the same parish.

DEPOPULATION ACTS.

27 HENRY VIII. (1536), c. 22.

This Act recites 4 Henry VII., c. 19, the first of the Depopulation Acts; and states that it had been enforced only in lands held immediately of the King. Now " the King shall have the Moiety of the Profits of those lands already converted for Tillage to Pasture sithence three years before Ann. 4 H. 7 until the Owner hath builded up a convenient House to inhabit, and converted the same Pasture to Tillage again; and also take the Moiety of the issues of those lands hereafter to be converted, if the immediate Lord do it not within one year," until the owners have built a Tenement for every 50, 40 or 30 acres, and have reconverted the pasture to tillage. Again it is stipulated that the land shall be tilled "according to the nature of the soil and the course of Husbandry used in the country where any such lands do lie."

27 HENRY VIII. (1536), c. 28.

Persons to whom monastic lands had been granted by Henry VIII. are required to maintain yearly as much of the land in tillage and husbandry as had commonly been so used within the preceding 20 years, under a penalty of 6*l*. 13*s*. 4*d*. per month.

CONFIRMATION OF STATUTE OF MERTON.

3 & 4 EDWARD VI. (1550), c. 3.

This Act cites and confirms the Statutes of Merton and Westminster and facilitates the recovery of damages for breaking down the hedges erected to enclose wastes.

DEPOPULATION ACTS.

5 & 6 EDWARD VI. (1552), c. 5.

This Act requires that so much land be tilled yearly in any parish as had been tilled at any time since the accession of Henry VIII., under a penalty of 5*s*. per acre per annum.

Four Commissioners were to be appointed to enquire into the conversion of arable into pasture.

The Act did not apply to—

(1) Land that had been pasture for 40 years.

(2) Waste ground, common downs, fens, moors, marshes.

(3) Lawful warren.

(4) Woodland converted into pasture.

(5) Land in deer parks.

(6) Salt marshes and inundated land.

(7) Land enclosed by licence of the King or his predecessor.

2 & 3 Philip and Mary (1555-6), c. 2.

This cites and confirms the original Depopulation Act of 4 Henry VII. and makes it apply to all houses with 20 acres of land, whether the land is in tillage or not.

Commissioners to be appointed to enquire into all grounds converted into pasture since St. George's Day, in the 20th year of Henry VIII. to see to the re-edifying of houses, and the reconversion of pasture into tillage. The exceptions permitted are where lands have been enclosed by the King's licence, and by discretion of the Commissioners in cases where no public benefit, but individual hardship would ensue by the execution of the Act.

Rents increased on the conversion of tillage into pasture were to be abated ; re-edified houses were to be let with 20 acres of land or 10 acres if the owner has no more.

The penalty of laying land down into pasture was again fixed at 5s. per acre per annum, half to be paid to the Crown, half to the informer.

5 Elizabeth (1563), c. 2.

By this Act the more recent Depopulation Acts, 27 Henry VIII. c. 28, 5 & 6 Edward VI. c. 5, and 2 & 3 Philip and Mary, c. 2, were repealed as ineffectual ; but the earlier ones, 4 Henry VII. c. 19, 7 Henry VIII. c. 22 and 27 Henry VIII. c. 22, ordered to be put into execution.

It was also enacted that " such lands or so much in quantity in any place as hath been put in Tillage and eared in any one year and so kept four years sithence the feast of St. George the Martyr, anno 20 Henry VIII. shall be eared and kept in Tillage, according to the Nature of the Soil and Custom of the Country by the Occupier thereof."

The penalty was raised to 10s. per acre per annum, and it could be recovered by the next heir in reversion if he sued for it within a year, if not, by the Remainderman, or in default by the lord of the manor, and if not so recovered, by the Crown.

This Act remained in force for thirty years, but was discontinued by 35 Elizabeth (1593), c. 5.

ACT FOR THE PROTECTION OF COTTAGERS' HOLDINGS AND RIGHTS OF COMMON.

31 ELIZABETH (1589), c. 7.

This Act prohibited the letting of cottages to agricultural labourers with less than four acres of land under a penalty of 40s. per cottage per month, or the occupation of one cottage by more than one family, under a penalty of 10s. per cottage per month. The amount of land attached to cottages let to countrymen following other occupations was also regulated. These holdings were evidently intended to be acres in the arable fields, carrying with them the proportional common rights of pasturage, &c. This Act was repealed in 1775.

DEPOPULATION ACTS.

39 ELIZABETH (1597), c. 1.

In the preamble of this Act it is stated that in late years more than in times past, sundry towns, parishes and houses of husbandry have been destroyed and become desolate. All previous Acts for the re-edification of houses are repealed, and it is enacted that when houses of husbandry have been decayed for more than seven years, half the number must be rebuilt, and 40 acres of land allotted to them; unless the property had been sold meanwhile; in that case the purchaser need only rebuild one quarter of the decayed houses.

Where houses had decayed within the previous seven years, they are to be rebuilt; and if previously they had less than 40 acres of land, they must now at least have 20 acres; if previously they had 40 acres or more, they must now have at least 40 acres.

The penalty for not rebuilding the farmhouse, was £10 per house per annum; for not assigning the prescribed quantity of land, 10s. per acre per annum. One third of the penalty went to the Queen, one third to the parish, one third to the informer.

It is also enacted that it shall be lawful for any lord of the manor to make exchanges of lands, whether arable, pasture or meadow, with his tenants, and for the tenants, with the consent of the lord, to make exchanges with one another, for the sake of more convenient occupation and husbandry. In other words the re-arrangement of the intermixed holdings in common arable fields and common meadows is expressly sanctioned.

39 ELIZABETH (1597), C. 2.

The preamble states that from the 7th year of Henry VII's reign to the 35th year of the current reign there had always been in force some Act for the maintenance of tillage, but in the latter year all such laws were discontinued; and that in consequence in the period 1593–1597 "there have growen many more Depopulacions by turning Tillage into Pasture than at any time for the like number of years heretofore."

It is enacted that lands converted from tillage to pasture shall be re-converted within three years, and that lands now in tillage shall remain so, under a penalty of 20s. per acre per annum. The Act applies to the counties of Bedford, Berkshire, Buckingham, Cambridge, Derby, Dorset, Durham, Gloucester, Hampshire, Hereford, Huntingdon, Leicester, Lincoln, Northampton, Northumberland, Nottingham, Oxford, Rutland, Somerset, Warwick, Wiltshire, Worcester, Yorkshire, with the Isle of Wight, and Pembroke in South Wales.

It did not apply to Cheshire, Cornwall, Cumberland, Devon, Essex, Hertford, Kent, Lancashire, Middlesex, Monmouth, Norfolk, Shropshire, Stafford, Suffolk, Surrey, Sussex and Westmoreland.

This Act remained on the Statute Book for 266 years. The earlier Depopulation Acts were repealed by 21 James I., c. 28, but this Act remained theoretically part of the law of the land until repealed by the Statute Law Revision Act of 1863. This was the last of the Depopulation Acts.

AN ENCLOSURE ACT.

4 JAMES I. C. 11.

This is really a local Enclosure Act. The people of the parishes of Merden, Bodenham, Wellington, Sutton St. Michael, Sutton St. Nicholas, Murton-upon-Lug, and Pipe in Hereford, had all their lands, whether meadow, pasture or arable, open and intermixed, and commonable "after Sickle and Sithe." They themselves were accustomed to house their sheep and cattle throughout the year, and the people of neighbouring villages took advantage of this custom to turn in cattle after harvest. The enclosure of one third of the land in each parish is authorised by the Act.

ACTS FOR IMPROVING THE CULTIVATION OF COMMON FIELDS.

13 GEORGE IV. (1773), c. 81.

This Act has been considered in the text.

41 GEORGE III. (1801), c. 20.

This was a temporary Act to encourage ths cultivation of potatose in common arable fields. The famine prices of 1800—1 caused a good deal of curious special legislation. Any occupier of land in common fields is authorised to plant potatoes, and to guard them from cattle grazing in the fields, on giving compensation for the loss of the common right to the other occupiers.

ACTS FOR FACILITATING ENCLOSURE.

41 GEORGE III. (1801), c. 109.

This is the General Enclosure Act promoted by the Board of Agriculture of 1793—1819. It is entitled "An Act for consolidating in one Act certain provisions usually inserted in Acts of inclosure, and for facilitating the mode of proving the several facts usually required in the passing of such Acts."

1 & 2 GEORGE IV. (1821), c. 23.

This amends the previous Act, so as to better regulate the cultivation of parishes during the progress of enclosure by Act.

1 & 2 WILLIAM IV. (1831), c. 42.

By this the churchwardens and overseers of a parish may enclose, up to 50 acres of waste, with the consent of the lord of the manor and the majority of the owners of common rights, for the relief of the poor rates, or let the land so enclosed to poor and industrious persons. By another Act in the same session (c. 57) the principle is applied to Crown lands.

4 & 5 WILLIAM IV. (1834), c. 30.

An Act to facilitate the exchange of intermixed lands in common fields, by removing difficulties caused by some owners being minors, insane, &c.

6 & 7 WILLIAM IV. (1836), c. 115.

This is an important Act " for facilitating the enclosure of open and arable fields in England and Wales." Two-thirds in number and value of common arable fields may appoint commissioners for carrying out enclosure, as if enclosure had been authorised by a special Act. The awards were to be deposited in the parish churches.

If seven-eighths of the proprietors were agreed, enclosure could be carried out without the appointment of commissioners.

This Act is not to authorise the enclosure of common fields within 10 miles of the centre of London, within 1 mile from the centre of a town of 5,000 inhabitants, 1½ miles from one of 15,000 inhabitants, 2 miles from one of 30,000 inhabitants, 2½ miles from one of 70,000 inhabitants, or 3 miles from one of 100,000 inhabitants.

3 & 4 VICT. (1840), c. 31.

This was an Act amending the last, by extending its scope to lammas meadows; and providing that persons who were dissatisfied with awards under the preceding Act forfeited their right of appeal if they took possession of the lands allotted to them.

APPENDIX E.

—◆—

A NORFOLK OPEN FIELD PARISH.

THE parish of Runton, adjoining Cromer, is unenclosed, and throws some light on Norfolk common field custom, and on the curious law with regard to "liberties of fold courses." There are in the parish two villages, East and West Runton. Most of the land in the parish is either common, or open field arable land. Of the open field arable, about 600 acres are "half year land" and between four and five hundred acres "whole year land." Both the whole year land and the half year land is intermixed, both in ownership and occupation, but the extent of intermixture has been steadily and continuously reduced. There is a tendency for adjoining strips of land to be let to one and the same farmer, and he is allowed to plough down the balks, in Runton called *lawns* or *loons*, which separate them. There are no common rights over the whole year land. There is an area of whole year land of 200 acres or more around each village, which is where one would expect to find it ; and very curiously, a detached area of about 20 acres half way between the villages. There is no well marked boundary separating whole year from half year lands.

The half year lands are commonable from Michaelmas to Lady Day old style, that is from October 11th to April 11th. There is no prescribed rule of cultivation, but the customary course is :—first year, wheat ; second, turnips ; third, barley sown with clover, the land under this crop being " new ley land " after the barley is reaped ; and in the fourth year the land remains under clover and is called " old ley land " or " ollay land."

The peculiar feature, characteristic of Norfolk common field agriculture, is that the owner of the Abbey Farm *in the next parish*, has the right to pasture sheep on the half year lands of Runton ; in the words of the old Act, he has the "liberty of fold courses " of Runton. Further, the Runton common right owners make up a flock called "The Collet Flock," and it is understood that wherever the Abbey flock goes, the Collet Flock can go too.

But the two flocks are kept distinct, grazing separately, each with its own shepherd.

INDEX.